GODS AND MONSTERS

GODS AND MONSTERS

THIRTY YEARS OF WRITING ON FILM AND CULTURE

PETER BISKIND

BLOOMSBURY

First published in Great Britain in 2005

Collection copyright © 2004 Peter Biskind

All essays used by permission of the author

The moral right of the author has been asserted

Bloomsbury Publishing Plc, 36 Soho Square, London W1D 3QY

A CIP catalogue record for this book is
available from the British Library

ISBN 0 7475 8094 4
ISBN-13 9780747580942

10 9 8 7 6 5 4 3

Printed in Great Britain by Clays Ltd, St Ives plc

All papers used by Bloomsbury are natural, recyclable
products made from wood grown in well-managed forests.
The manufacturing processes conform to the
environmental regulations of the country of origin

www.bloomsbury.com/peterbiskind

For Dick Sylbert, who wasn't finished

CONTENTS

DEEP FOCUS

INTRODUCTION

My name is Peter Biskind, and I am a recovering celebrity journalist. Which is to say, I started my career during the anti–Vietnam
War movement of the sixties as a political activist with a general
interest in culture and a particular interest in films, and more or less
ended it—or at least a lengthy phase of it—in the late nineties, writing about movie stars for *Premiere* magazine.

Movies and politics came easily to me. When I was growing up on
New York City's Upper West Side, I used to watch Charlie Chaplin
films during the long and inhospitable cold war freeze known as
McCarthyism, in the apartment of Tom Brandon, who owned a
small film distribution company specializing in Soviet and other
films of politically dubious provenance. Because Chaplin—who at
one time had been the global equivalent of Jim Carrey, Will Ferrell,
and Adam Sandler all rolled into one—had been effectively blacklisted and ruled persona non grata by the State Department (as a
noncitizen, his reentry visa was rescinded), to watch his films was
both a forbidden pleasure and a modest act of disobedience.

I developed a regular filmgoing habit during the early sixties at
Swarthmore College, the years that we now know were what Phillip
Lopate called the "heroic age of moviegoing," when every month
promised a new Bergman or Fellini, and I cadged rides from
Swarthmore into Philadelphia to see *L'Avventura* for the third and
fourth time. Later, my passion for movies saw me through an unpro-
ductive and seemingly interminable stint in the graduate English
department at Yale, where I spent my time reading Pauline Kael
instead of Harold Bloom and watching everything from Kenneth
Anger to Russ Meyer, instead of going to classes. Later, when I

started teaching myself, I much preferred to introduce my students to the mysteries of Antonioni's *Blowup* than to the joys of the nineteenth-century English novel, which was what I was being paid to do. I was teaching at the University of California, Santa Barbara, when the sixties really hit, like a hammer blow. For two or three years I did little but march and protest. I remember sitting on the runway of Santa Barbara airport with 500-odd other demonstrators in protest against Nixon's incursion into Cambodia, or maybe it was the shootings at Kent State. The "actions" tend to blur. When I did find myself in a classroom, it was to give my freshman English students three hundred *A*'s.

Meanwhile, Jean-Luc Godard and the French *nouvelle vague* had replaced Antonioni, the poet of postwar ennui who, despite his efforts to become *engagé* (*Zabriskie Point*), seemed increasingly irrelevant to the passions of the day. Godard's casual, shoot-and-run style and his to-hell-with-it disregard for Hollywood conventions made it seem like anyone could grab a camera and go out into the streets, especially since Newsreel, the movement's film arm, had done just that. I traded some colored beads and a couple of joints for a Bolex and, when I wasn't marching, I was teaching myself how to make documentary films. The best (made with Steve Hornick and Jake Manning) was called *Don't Bank on Amerika*, about the student protests at UCSB and the predictable overreaction by the authorities, which took the form of out-of-control police, the National Guard, tear gas, curfews, mass arrests, etc., etc., all those things that made the sixties so much fun. *Don't Bank* was truly guerrilla filmmaking, financed by passing the hat at demos. We sneaked into the filmmaking facilities at UCLA in the middle of the night to transfer sound and do our primitive mixes.

But when the draft was abolished in the early seventies, and the antiwar movement wound down, it became harder and harder to raise money for the political documentaries I wanted to make, and I drifted into writing, which was a whole lot easier and cheaper. You could sit down at the typewriter and pound out a piece without having to raise the $25,000 or $50,000 needed to make a film.

I began with analytical exegeses (once a graduate student, always a graduate student) of films that I liked, published in small journals like *Film Heritage, Film Quarterly,* Canada's *Take One,* and Britain's *Sight and Sound,* as well as political film magazines like *Cineaste,* and *Jump Cut,* which was published on paper so cheap it practically turned to dust in your hands while you were reading it, like one of those ancient manuscripts in *Raiders of the Lost Ark.* Some of those pieces are included in this volume, and the reader will see that I looked at films politically, with an eye to the ideology they were overtly or covertly conveying against the social context in which they were made. An example from *Jump Cut,* was a reading of *Thunderbolt and Lightfoot* (an early Michael Cimino exercise), that dredged up a barely submerged level of homoeroticism. One thing led to another, and I found myself, if not on the cover of *Rolling Stone,* at least among its pages, briefly, writing about Emile de Antonio's Weather Underground documentary (included here), and then I went on to *Seven Days.* This was not the Adam Moss *Seven Days* that followed a few years later, but the Dave Dellinger *Seven Days,* an attempt—ill-fated and perhaps foolish, as it turned out—to launch a four-color, slick, lefty *Time* or *Newsweek.* While I was there I met some people whom I greatly admired and who became lifelong friends, like Dellinger, a beacon of courage and common sense in an often insane movement; Barbara Ehrenreich, brilliant and funny, with a cutting wit; and my wife-to-be, Elizabeth Hess, who later reviewed art for the *Village Voice* and today writes about animals and their issues.

When *Seven Days* finally expired, I caught a break: I was hired to be the editor-in-chief of *American Film,* published by the American Film Institute in Washington, D.C. *American Film* was a glossy, four-color monthly devoted, like its parent, AFI, to the celebration of movies as an art form. The closest thing to it in the U.S. at the time was its poor cousin, the monochromatic *Film Comment. American Film* had been founded in 1975 and had flourished under the hand of its original editor, Hollis Alpert. I myself had never deigned to read it; to me, it was only a few steps away from a fan magazine, with all the zip and edge of an awards ceremony program, a semiofficial publication of the industry. That said, it had the biggest circulation among film magazines in the English-speaking world. And *American Film* had one thing going for it: fanzine or not, it had been born in the middle of the seventies, the year of *Jaws* and *One Flew Over the Cuckoo's Nest*. The year before, *Godfather II* had beaten out *Chinatown* for an Oscar, and the year after, Martin Scorsese released *Taxi Driver*. In other words, it pecked through its eggshell in the middle of the last great decade of Hollywood filmmaking. *American Film* may have done no more than add its voice to a chorus of hosannas, but there was no question that most of the films and filmmakers it celebrated—Scorsese, Francis Ford Coppola, Warren Beatty, Robert Altman, William Friedkin, Robert Towne—had earned it. By the time I came along, in 1981, this era was over, although it took some time to realize it.

I moved to Washington from New York only a few weeks after Ronald Reagan had been shot by John Hinckley, Jr., who claimed to have been inspired by Travis Bickle. Washington was so foreign to me I felt like I'd walked through the looking glass, traveling to work on the bus, I could clear a couple of seats for myself by pulling out a copy of *The Nation*. *American Film*'s offices were in the Watergate, the site of the notorious break-in at the offices of the DNC, just across the street from the Howard Johnson's where it had been planned. Entering the lobby of the hotel-cum-office building, I would encounter clusters of Chilean military officers—this, during the heyday of Pinochet. With their outsized uniforms, gilt-encrusted epaulets, mismatched blue trousers with red stripes running down the legs, they looked like members of, say, the Alabama State marching band who had wandered away from their bus tour. But it was hard to shrug off the thought that were I unlucky enough to have been a Chilean national, I would have had my fingernails extracted by these clowns.

The AFI board constituted a who's who of the industry—Charlton Heston was the chairman—and many of the studio and network heads, important producers, and super-agents, had seats at the big table. I learned shortly that the Institute lived and died by its goodwill. I had started a column at the back of the book called "Trailers," comprised of bite-sized previews of upcoming movies which, because of our long lead time, we were not lucky enough to have actually seen. Accordingly, the blurbs generally stuck close to the facts and were bland in tone. Every once in a while, in an effort to shake them up, I introduced a snarky note, and once wrote, apropos a film called *Quest for Fire,* that it "sounded like an upscale *Caveman.*" This incensed someone connected with the movie, who instantly pulled it from an AFI benefit, and landed me in very hot water. I was hauled before a committee of Institute panjandrums, and was told in no uncertain terms that I was not to ridicule studio movies. From then on I was careful to edit out of our stories anything that might give offense. Gossip of any sort was taboo, of course, and the private lives of the players we profiled were strictly off-limits. So narrow were the parameters of the permissible in which I operated, that I was once taken to task for not cropping out of a party photo a glass of booze in the hand of an Institute guest.

A year or so into my tenure at *American Film,* I came out with my first book, *Seeing Is Believing: How Hollywood Taught Us to Stop Worrying and Love the Fifties,* edited by my good friend Sara Bershtel and published by Pantheon. The film landscape, I felt, had been overgrazed by the herd of eager young film scholars coming out of university film programs—Hitchcock had been picked over almost as thoroughly as Shakespeare—whereas my particular bent was virgin territory, relatively speaking. I had read widely in the literature of the academic and public intellectuals of the 1950s— Lionel Trilling, David Riesman, Daniel Bell, et al.—in an attempt to show how the Hollywood movies of that era that were apparently politically naïve—that is, sci-fi, horror movies, westerns, weepies, thrillers, etc.—with no apparent political charge whatsoever, not only carried the various ideologies of the period, but were, in effect, engaged in political combat with one another. I slipped a piece of it into *American Film,* where it was published under the title "War of the Worlds," and is included in this collection.

The AFI was ill-suited to publish a film magazine, and Washington was a terrible place to do it; selling ads and building circulation were next to impossible. Eventually, the Institute more or less outsourced *American Film* to an even less suitable publisher, a medical foundation, and moved it to New York, where it continued to limp along. And, as the eighties progressed, it was becoming harder and harder to write about the movies as an art form. Most of the great New Hollywood directors had autodestructed. A high-minded magazine about an art form that for all intents and purposes had ceased to exist made less and less sense. After five years, in 1986, I jumped from a leaky vessel (the magazine folded a few years later) to *Premiere,* which was just starting up, a veritable cruise ship, fueled by Rupert Murdoch and Hachette's money, and based on its French prototype, yet with wholly original American content. (For a while, every issue included cool movie trading-card inserts.)

The biggest difference between *Premiere* and *American Film* was that *Premiere* was a real magazine, that is, published by an honest-to-god commercial company that knew how to sell ads, understood circulation campaigns, and had the clout to get good newsstand placement. Unlike *American Film, Premiere* took care never to take favors from the studios (we always paid our own way when we sent writers to sets), and was free to do real reporting on the entertainment industry, something that the trades never did—nor, for the most part, the big dailies like *The New York Times* and the *Los Angeles Times.* Occasionally, if a production were particularly bizarre, like *Godfather III,* or something egregious occurred, as it did on the set of *Twilight Zone—the Movie,* a story would appear in the pages of a general interest magazine like *Vanity Fair, Esquire,* or *New York.* (Later, I was able to do a profile of Terrence McKenna for *Vanity Fair* that I would never have been able to do for *Premiere.*) Still, in those days, *Premiere* did enough reporting so that every now and then the publisher's worst nightmare would actually occur—a studio would withdraw its advertising.

Still, like other single-topic magazines that exist in a symbiotic relationship with the industry they cover—*Rolling Stone, Car and Driver*, and so on—*Premiere* had to be careful not to foul its own nest. Like *American Film,* we treated films and filmmakers with kid gloves. We took readers behind the scenes and showed them how films are made. When we profiled actors, we focused on the craft. But it was operating in the same post-seventies environment as *American Film,* and confronted the same problem: mainstream movies were for the most part so undistinguished, they couldn't repay the gravitas we brought to them. We covered *Godfather III* as if it were the original, and when it turned out to be no more than a pale imitation, we looked, and felt, foolish. With a few exceptions, covering movies of the late eighties and nineties, we were reduced to describing the new clothes of a succession of emperors. (Independent films—the nineties' answers to the seventies—were just starting to make a dent, but the magazine was so Hollywood-focused it initially ignored them.) I'll never forget the meetings for the annual Academy Awards issue, during which the staff, all Ivy League alumnae with a cumulative I.Q. up there with the graduating class of any top-notch medical school, spent countless hours analyzing the race and handicapping the field as if they were hot on the trail of the cure for cancer.

Despite the virtual collapse of the movies to which *Premiere* devoted itself, the industry that churned out these widgets was flourishing, and I discovered it was much more interesting to report on that than the films themselves. Moreover, I liked doing it, liked the digging, liked getting people to tell me what they didn't want to tell me. So far as the cultural criticism I had been practicing went, most people didn't get it. I was always being accused of reading too much into films—the "sometimes a movie is just a movie" argument. Or attacked for treating films like sociological artifacts. (Significantly, it was the Right, not the Left, that took the culture wars seriously.) I felt like I was just spinning wheels. Reporting, on the other hand, dealt with facts, not ideas or opinions, which were a dime a dozen. And it made waves, particularly since not many people were doing it.

While *Premiere* was taking the high road, *People* magazine had legitimized gossip, and collaterally, the tabloids. When I got to *Premiere*, I read the *New York Times,* the *Los Angeles Times,* and the trades every morning, but now the *Star* and *National Enquirer* were shoved under my nose as well, and then, a few years later, copies of the gossip columns—Liz Smith, Page Six of the *New York Post*, Rush and Molloy of the *Daily News,* etc.—all of which became increasingly necessary to read and reference as celebrity journalism, now firmly ensconced on television (*Entertainment Tonight* was contemporaneous with *Premiere*), swallowed everything in sight.

I read them grudgingly, because as an end in itself, gossip is boring, and in the columns is used often as a weapon to settle scores. But eventually I became a believer, of sorts. People are interested in people, what makes them tick, why they do what they do. Gossip, not in the sense of rumor—true or false—but people acting badly when they think no one's looking, was important, especially in reporting on the industry, where the players believed they had license to kill. I realized that it is impossible to draw a firm line between the public and the private, because so much of the former is driven by ego, by pettiness, by vanity and venality, a truth brought home again and again by the best books on the film business from the eighties and nineties—David McCullough's *Indecent Exposure,* Steven Bach's *Final Cut,* William Goldman's *Adventures in the Screen Trade,* and Julia Phillips's *You'll Never Eat Lunch in This Town Again,* all of which are rich in personal detail.

Then came *Entertainment Weekly,* which changed the rules of the game. *EW* solved *Premiere*'s problem by being more newsy and more gossipy. It didn't care about film art, or inflate its subject with windy claims. As a weekly, instead of a monthly, *EW*'s lead time was dramatically shorter than ours, while its stories were briefer and pithier. Whereas we had indulged ourselves with six-, seven-, occasionally eight- or even ten-thousand-word articles, theirs rarely exceeded six hundred words, and were often less. Under pressure from *EW,* ours were pared down dramatically, but we still couldn't break news, and thereby gave up our only asset: in-depth reporting. It was the worst of both worlds. The magazine downsized, as if it had been shrunk in the washer. Circulation flatlined at around 500,000. No longer an exciting startup, *Premiere* had become a dowdy senior in the blink of an eye. Moreover, every magazine on the rack now had movie star covers. *Premiere* changed hands, again and again, eventually ending up half-owned by Hachette, and half by Ron Perelman. Susan Lyne, the founding editor (and no fool), left for greener pastures. She was barely out the door when the suits began tinkering with editorial. The interference fast became too blatant to swallow and the top editors left en masse. It was a dramatic affirmation of editorial independence, but ultimately useless and soon forgotten. David Pecker, Hachette's chief honcho, publicly wondered what all the fuss was about. After all, the purpose of editorial was to sell ads, wasn't it? (Pecker subsequently left Hachette to head up American Media, which publishes both the *Enquirer* and *Star.*)

It was high time for me to leave *Premiere*. I had never considered myself a celebrity journalist, but there was no denying that I was writing almost exclusively about celebrities, and as for whether it was really "journalism," that was questionable. We were never obliged to fetch when the studios whistled, nor, even as the demand for celebrity covers grew and the boutique publicity firms flexed their muscles, were any limitations imposed on what we could and could not write about—until, that is, the Perelman/Pecker fiasco that terminated so many careers at *Premiere*. Rather, it is more accurate to say that we were drowning in celebrity ooze. I had always assumed that celebrity culture would eventually collapse under its own weight, that celebrity fatigue would set in with our readers. After all, how many times can you put Tom Cruise on the cover? How many stories can you write about Tom Cruise? But it never happened. Tom Cruise covers always sold best, that was all there was to it. It was hard for me to avoid the conclusion that I was in the wrong business. Sure, there is very good writing in magazines, but rarely about the movies, and certainly not in magazines solely devoted to the movies like *Premiere,* whose fawning and simpering, by this time, had nearly exceeded *American Film*'s before it.

As luck would have it, I had been working, well below *Premiere*'s radar, on another book, a history of Hollywood in the seventies that would eventually be called *Easy Riders, Raging Bulls*. I discovered that writing a book gave me the freedom that had disappeared from—if it had ever existed—a lot of magazine journalism. I didn't need, metaphorically speaking, to put Tom Cruise on the front of the dust jacket, and therefore didn't need to suck up to publicists. I could write what I wanted. Obviously, there were pressures, and more so with my next book, *Down and Dirty Pictures,* but to its credit, my publisher, Simon & Schuster, and its multinational parent, Viacom, stood fast.

Movies are famously an art form *and* a business, and in *Easy Riders, Raging Bulls* I tried to do justice to both, to combine my early academic interest in film as art with what I had learned about the industry writing for *Premiere*. But film is also, like most things human, the site of a tug of war between the personal and the political. In the sixties, we had a saying, or more aptly a slogan—"the personal is the political"—which expressed our fervent belief that everything was political, even the personal, which seemed least so. This slogan often provided the excuse for obliterating the personal in the name of politics, but after the sixties receded into the mists of time, the personal—in the glittering guise of the cult of celebrity—took its revenge, and then some, especially in cultural discourse, casting politics into shadow. Both *Easy Riders, Raging Bulls* and *Down and Dirty Pictures* try, with admittedly uneven success, to rebalance the scales.

The entertainment industry is at once the number-one delivery vehicle for the cult of celebrity and its prime beneficiary. It has always been good at changing the subject, has always tried hard to depoliticize itself: "Have a message? Call Western Union" has always been its mantra. By exclusively purveying people, it has obscured issues. But it's time to admit that that attempt has failed. With entertainment America's biggest export, and with media ownership in fewer and fewer hands, corporate agendas rule, not to mention the requirements of the explicitly ideologically driven behemoths like News Corp. and Clear Channel. Politics never goes away; we never see the "end of history," despite wishful claims to the contrary. Hollywood may not want to admit it, but politics are very much with us, obvious to everyone else, from Moqtada al-Sadr to Murdoch.

Peter Biskind
August 2004

BETWEEN THE FRAMES

THE POLITICS OF POWER IN ON THE WATERFRONT

The Kazan revival has begun. Initiated in 1972 by the British journal *Movie*,[1] expedited in 1973 by Jim Kitses writing in *Cinema*,[2] and further assisted by the recent publication of a book-length interview edited by Michel Ciment of *Positif*,[3] it promises a long overdue reassessment of an unjustly neglected director. Whatever one's attitude toward either Kazan's political behavior in the fifties, or to the politics embedded in his films, it can no longer be denied that he is an important figure. He directed a half dozen major films of the fifties, and the Actors Studio, which he founded, left an indelible stamp on American screen acting. Marlon Brando, Lee Remick, James Dean, Julie Harris, Montgomery Clift. Shelley Winters, Paul Newman, Kim Hunter, Lee J. Cobb, Karl Malden, Rod Steiger, and many, many others cannot be understood apart from its influence.

Focussing on Kazan's work makes it no longer possible to evade the central question of film and ideology that *auteurists* and the more sophisticated *auteurists*-structuralists have thus far largely obscured or ignored. This is so because Kazan, more than most directors of the fifties, was overly concerned with political themes, while at the same time his own life was crucially affected by his appearance before the House Un-American Activities Committee as a "friendly witness" in 1952. It was just this proximity to the storm center of American culture in the fifties that made his reputation so vulnerable to changes in the political climate. Kazan, in a sense, has been doubly unlucky. After selling out his friends on the left and enthusiastically joining the fifties crusade against communism, he was cast out of the mainstream of American film history by *auteur* critics who, like himself, were cultural fellow-travelers of the post-war corporate consensus but who, even more than he, turned against the aesthetics of socialist realism. They disliked the residue of the thirties social seriousness still evident in his work. Even left wing *auteurists* who have not hesitated to paint right-wing action directors like Fuller, Siegel, and Aldrich in various shades of red have drawn back from Kazan.[4]

Despite the fact that Kazan's work as a whole is now being regarded with greater interest it is his later, more "personal" films like *America, America* and *The Arrangement*, made outside his longtime collaboration with major writers, that are gaining ground over the films of the high fifties like *On the Waterfront*. In other words, the reassessment is proceeding along typically *auteurist* lines, putting a premium on the expression of personality.

The new stress on the later films (not unlike previous *auteurist* rescue operations on Ford's westerns and late Renoir) depends on a confusion between personal and private, itself a product of the fifties attempt to cauterize ideology and valorize private life. The notion that *The Arrangement* is a more personal film than *On the Waterfront* is certainly an odd one. It would be hard to think of a film that more suggests an autobiographical reading than *On the Waterfront* which, after all, concerns informing, an issue which in reality marked Kazan's own life profoundly. Distinguishing early and late Kazan in this way can only proceed from a position like *auteurism* which seeks to expel politics from the area of legitimate artistic discourse with the aid of threadbare romantic notions of the artist, genius, personal vision, and so on.

Kazan, of course, was engaged in precisely the same effort. *On the Waterfront* is one of the earliest and most effective attempts to suppress politics with morality and private values that the fifties produced. It takes an important first step in detaching the self from a larger social context so that the idea of self can be redefined in narrower, safer terms. *Splendor in the Grass, America, America,*

3

and *The Arrangement* merely develop the notion of personality initially presented in *On the Waterfront*.

The congruence between the ideological projects of Kazan and *auteurism,* both firmly rooted in the necessities of the fifties consensus, suggest another reason for the critical antipathy towards Kazan. It is not that Kazan was too much a product of the thirties for fifties *auteurists,* too unlike them in political stance and emotional tone, but rather the opposite. He was too much *like* them. Kazan's were *les mains sales* which executed the deeds at which their eyes dared not look. His films performed the ideological dirty work of the fifties and thus had to be rejected in favor of the films of a director like Nicholas Ray, where the same process is not so embarrassingly obvious. But Kazan and Ray are two sides of the same coin. Kazan screwed others, and is therefore bad; Ray screwed himself, and is therefore good. His films have an overlay of romantic pessimism which allows liberals to weep away their bad conscience.

In the seventies, Kazan has received the benefit of an altered cultural climate. He has profited by a new catholicity on the part of *auteur* critics whose major battles seem won and who are now casting about to find new tenants for the Pantheon, and by the interest of European left and American New Left critics who find in Kazan's cold war anti-Stalinism a confirmation of their own antipathy towards the old left.

Times do change, and each generation sees the film classics with its own eyes. Wounds heal, memory falters, present needs require of the past different lessons from those drawn by our predecessors. One would not wish to deny Kazan the consolations of history. Yet the social situations within which films are made continue to live, in turn, within them. Films like *Viva Zapata!* and *On the Waterfront* bear the marks, the *inscription,* as the French would say, of their historical context. They cannot be fully understood outside the passionate political controversies of which they were part. This essay is an attempt to make this inscription clear. It is intended as a contribution to the reassessment of Kazan and beyond that, a contribution to the larger question of how Hollywood films respond to the requirements of the ideological context in which they are situated. Implicit in its approach is a critique of *auteurism*. While it cannot be denied that Kazan is an *auteur,* at the same time, like any other director, he must be seen as mediating conflicting cultural and aesthetic demands. Examining the cultural soil from which films grow does not impoverish them, as conservative critics often charge, but rather enriches them by restoring to them their original nourishment.

On the Waterfront falls in the middle of the seismic shift from the thirties to the fifties. By the time it was begun, in 1954, Kazan had long since abandoned the passionate commitment of the thirties. On the other hand, he had not yet attained the Fordian distance revealed in later films like *Baby Doll* (1956), *Wild River* (1960), and *Splendor in the Grass* (1961). *On the Waterfront* harnesses the methods of the thirties to the ideology of the fifties. It is political allegory cast in the form of a morality play. This requires a particularly skillful form of aesthetic footwork, since its success requires that the political allegory be simultaneously admitted and refused. To deny the allegorical level runs the risk that the message of the film will go unrecorded. To acknowledge the allegorical level runs the risk that the ideological project of the film will be unmasked. Films like *On the Waterfront* walk a tightrope between revelation and concealment, between clarity and mystification.

In *Viva Zapata!* (1952), the first part of Kazan's anticommunist trilogy, he had shown that the exercise of individual power is either perverse or tragic. Zapata had to renounce state power to avoid being corrupted by it, but even so he found that the requirements of leadership poisoned his relations with his wife, indirectly led to his brother's death, and forced him to execute a trusted lieutenant. The exercise of power, in other words, entails the violation of the intimate personal bonds which we hold most dear. Although the commonplace that power corrupts is a staple of Hollywood political wisdom, finding classic expression in the comedies of Frank Capra, in the fifties, and especially in the hands of Kazan, it became a weapon in the cold war struggle against the left in general, and Stalinism in particular. According to sociologists like Daniel Bell, it was the millennial, ideological movements, the Nazis and the Soviets, who exercised power; democrats did not. Liberal democracy was regarded as an ideal form of government because everybody and nobody exercises power. In America, remarks one of Zapata's band, "the government governs, but with the consent of the people. The people have a voice." In *On the Waterfront*, two years later, we see how power manifests itself in a democracy.

Where *Viva Zapata!* has aged quickly, *On the Waterfront* remains, after two decades, a tremendously powerful film, one of the best films of the fifties. In many ways, it was a child of the HUAC investigations, a blow struck in the ideological and artistic battle between those who talked and those who didn't. Many of its personnel, including Kazan, Budd Schulberg who wrote the script, Lee J. Cobb who played John Friendly, and Leif Erickson who played one of the Waterfront Crime Commission investigators, had gone before HUAC, confessed their past sins, and implicated close friends and associates. One of Kazan's closest friends (whom he did not name) was Arthur Miller with whom he had worked on *All My Sons* and *Death of a Salesman*. In 1953, Miller's play *The Crucible*, a thinly veiled attack on the witch hunt, opened on Broadway. In it, Miller has his central character go to his death rather than inform against his friends. Asked for names, he replies: "I speak my own sins; I cannot judge another. I have no tongue for it . . . I have three children—how may I teach them to walk like men in the world, and I sold my friends."[5]

On the Waterfront is Kazan's answer. It presents a situation in which informing on criminal associates is the only honorable course of action for a just man. The injunction against informing on friends and colleagues is axiomatic in most socieites where the state does not exercise overwhelming moral authority, but the film's dialogue repeatedly defines squealing not as an absolute but a relative matter. It depends on where you stand. Father Barry (Karl Malden) expresses this nicely: "What's ratting on them, is telling the truth for you." On the other hand, Charlie-the-Gent ("a butcher in a camel's hair coat") becomes the spokesman for the discredited principle of loyalty: "Stooling is when you rat on your friends."

By ratting on John Friendly and his boys, Terry Malloy (Marlon Brando) helps the Crime Commission destroy a corrupt union, wins the lady, Edie Doyle (Eva Marie Saint), and redeems himself in his own eyes and in those of the honest rank and file. He is the informer as hero.[6] Thus American society may not be perfect, its institutions may be fallible, but they contain the mechanisms for their own regeneration. Although corrupt unions run the docks, the regulatory and investigatory (HUAC included?) agencies of government—the open hearings covered by the free press, the benign investigators—are more than a match for the forces of darkness. Justice prevails. As the opening title says: "It has always been in the American tradition not to hide our shortcomings, but on the contrary, to spotlight them and to correct them. The incidents portrayed in this picture were true of a particular area of the waterfront. They exemplify the way self-appointed tyrants can be fought and defeated by right-thinking men in a vital democracy."

This optimism regarding the democratic process is not so much a betrayal of the thirties, but a fulfillment of certain attitudes towards the state implicit in thirties radicalism. Both the New Deal with its stress on activist big government, and the Communist Party with its admiration for the Soviet Union, contributed to a generally positive attitude towards state power on the part of the left. A 1938 film, *Racket Busters,* scripted by Robert Rossen who himself later informed before *HUAC*, applauds state coercion of reluctant witnesses. A Popular Front film like *Native Land* also portrays the state as an effective instrument of the people. If the state was indeed as benevolent as these films would have it, it is perhaps not so surprising that the state could later, under different circumstances, command the loyalty of its citizens against its enemies. The ex-Communist friendly witnesses of the fifties were still Stalinists at heart, only Truman and Eisenhower had become their Stalin. The USA had replaced the USSR.

The submerged analogy between the criminally corrupt waterfront unions and the "crime" of membership in the Communist Party reflected a belief dear to the hearts of cold war liberals—that the CPUSA was a criminal conspiracy falling outside the traditional guarantees of civil liberties. As Sidney Hook put it, "heresy, yes, conspiracy, no." The inadequacy of this model, obvious at the time and certainly obvious now, does not need extended discussion. Suffice to say, the equation between overt acts of violence and "crimes" of belief that is used to justify informing against Communists and fellow travelers, doesn't hold up. As Murray Kempton pointed out in 1963,

"Our laws deal with what a man has done, not what he might have done given the chance."[7]

Nor is the film's portrayal of union corruption very convincing. Although it is quite faithful to the texture of eastcoast waterfront life, it falsifies the overall picture. Just as Kazan conveniently overlooks the larger social and political implications of the class structure of Mexico in *Viva Zapata!*, attributing the dependent position of the dispossessed peasants solely to the venal generals and politicians, so here he is careful to circumscribe the tumor of corruption so that it may be neatly excised without undue injury or embarrassment to the body politic.[8] Despite one rhetorical gesture towards generality (a single shot shows "Mr. Upstairs" watching the Crime Commission hearings on television), Kazan emphasizes the limited and exceptional nature of his subject. He even goes so far as to have one of his dockers exclaim: "The waterfront . . . ain't part of America."

If, as Daniel Bell, Seymour Martin Lipset, and their followers maintained, the problems of the fifties were those of "piecemeal technology," amenable to technological solutions applied by an elite of experts, connections between the particular and the general which might suggest structural contradictions in society had to be suppressed. The notion that racketeering might be endemic rather than incidental, that it was a natural expression of a capitalist system that concentrates power and money in the hands of a few and employed graft to lubricate and stabilize the system, was unthinkable. Corruption was exclusively regarded as a moral evil, a sin perpetrated by bad men (the theological frame of reference is enforced by the prominent place occupied by the priest Father Barry), rather than a form of mutually beneficial and politically expedient collusion between unions, management, and the Tammany Hall machine. Joseph P. Ryan, the International Longshoreman's Association (ILA) boss who could have served as a model for John Friendly, held notorious annual dinners, attendance at which was obligatory for every politician in the city, the mayor and police commissioner included.[10] Management purchased "protection" from the crooked union, freedom from strikes and disruptions over pay and workplace grievances: "Industrial racketeering . . . performs the function of stabilizing a chaotic market and establishing an order and structure in the industry."[11] Yet *On the Waterfront* portrays the shipper, a major beneficiary of this arrangement, as neutral, as a bystander above the factional fight within the union. He doesn't care who runs the docks, so long as he gets his ships loaded and unloaded.

We can now turn to the critical question of the film's conception of power. What immediately becomes clear is that the film doesn't seem to deal with power at all. The arena of conflict in *On the Waterfront* which is, after all, a film about labor and unions, is not class but self. It is not without but within. It is Terry Malloy's interior struggle, his struggle to come to moral awareness and to act on his new perception of right and wrong.

The agent of Terry's awakening is the waterfront priest, Father Barry. Father Barry intervenes decisively at crucial moments to change the course of events: he precipitates the struggle against the mob, he persuades Terry Malloy to confess to Edie Doyle that he helped set up her brother Joey to be pushed off a roof, he prevents Terry from using his gun to avenge the death of his brother at the hands of John Friendly, he urges Terry to testify before the Crime Commission, and he prevents the dockers from aiding the badly injured Malloy so that he can make his heroic walk leading the men back to work in defiance of the mob. Kazan apparently approves of this kind of moral agency, since all these interventions turn out for the best, but they could have easily been catastrophic. What emerges is an alarming picture of a ruthless crusader who manipulates others like chess pieces in the name of a higher good for which no price is too high, no sacrifice too great.

That manipulation is not too strong a word for Father Barry's behavior is clear from the authority with which he employs his carrot-and-stick strategy to guide Terry through the intricate moral maze that Kazan has constructed for him. Although his interventions in the course of the action are frequently direct and forceful (at one point he knocks Terry down in order to prevent him from going gunning for Friendly), just as frequently this coercion is coyly denied or disguised. On the several occasions when Terry asks Father Barry or Edie (an ancillary manipulator) what course of action he should adopt, they insist that it is up to him, to his conscience, that they cannot tell him what to do. Invariably, this disavowal is contradicted by a moral imperative which immediately follows: do this or do that, as in this exchange in which Father Barry forcefully but obliquely urges Terry to reveal his part in Joey's death to Edie:

> FATHER BARRY: What are you gonna do about it? . . . about telling her, the Commission, the subpoena? . . .
> TERRY: I don't know . . .
> FATHER BARRY: Listen, if I were you I would walk right— nevermind. I'm not asking you to do anything . . . It's your own conscience that's gotta do the askin'—Edie's . . . coming here. . . . Come on, why don't you tell her.

Father Barry's method of persuasion is successful. Terry indeed perceives his choices as issuing from his own "conscience," his own deepest desires, when in fact they are elicited by a powerful, albeit disguised, form of psychological and moral pressure. It appears, in fact, that Charlie-the-Gent is correct when he tells John Friendly later that "This girl and the Father—they got the hooks in the kid so deep he don't know which end is up anymore."

Father Barry is doing no more than applying manipulative methods of social control which have deep roots in the American past, in the Progressive movement in general and in the philosophy of John Dewey in particular. Dewey's stress on social control and collectivism had a radical ring in the thirties, when it was intended as a counterweight to the chaotic conditions created by what seemed like an uncontrolled, irrational capitalist economy, but by the fifties Dewey's methods had become useful tools for constructing the new consensus. Christopher Lasch, in *The Agony of the American Left,* identifies the role of this manipulative liberal ideology in easing social conflict: "Even when it originated in humanitarian impulses, progressive ideas led not to a philosophy of liberation but to a blueprint for control. The task of the social reformer came to be seen as that of 'enlisting the person's own participating disposition in getting the result desired, and thereby developing within him an intrinsic and persisting direction in the right way.'" (Quoted from John Dewey, *Democracy and Education,* N.Y., 1961, 26–7.)[12]

In choosing to use persuasion rather than coercion, Barry is doing no more than acting in accord with the democratic ethos as defined, for example, by Arthur Schlesinger, Jr. in 1949: "The thrust of the democratic faith is away from fanaticism; it is towards compromise, persuasion, and consent in politics . . ."[13] Force was not used because it was not needed. As Schlesinger pointed out in the course of arguing against some of the harsher measures of the witch-hunt: "If we can defeat Communism as a political force within the framework of civil liberties, why abandon that framework?" Using the Church as a disguised instrument of social control, as Kazan does, was characteristic of the disingenuous approach of one strain of fifties liberalism towards problems of power. Reactionaries like Leo McCarey were a good deal more forthright. A film like *My Son John* clearly identifies the FBI as the locus of moral authority and power. The priest, in comparison, is a severely diminished figure.[14]

What is the significance of a ruthless and powerful but apparently moral figure like Father Barry when Kazan had shown us in *Viva Zapata!* that power corrupts? Although the power-to-the-people moral of *Viva Zapata!* would lead us to expect that in a democracy, where power is shared among the demos (in America, "the people have a voice"), such a figure should be either evil or unnecessary. But in *On the Waterfront* the people are incapable of exercising power. They are a passive herd who invariably fail to act when put to the test. At best they can follow the leader, or exercise their power in a negative refusal to act: "How 'bout Terry? He don't work, we don't work." The conclusion which inescapably emerges from the contradiction between the two films is that when Kazan wishes to show the self-regenerative capacities of liberal capitalist society, through mass political action, effective yet circumscribed, leaders are OK. But when he is faced with a real social upheaval, as he is in *Viva Zapata!,* which threatens to exceed the bounds of decorous reform, he enforces a self-serving moral that leadership will always become corrupt.

Rather than the egalitarian society we might have expected after *Viva Zapata!, On the Waterfront,* like many other films of the fifties, offers an elitist model of society in which power is the prerogative of experts in the law and its enforcement (police, judges, lawyers) in alliance with social engineers (priests, psychiatrists, social workers) and family (usually the hero's wife or girlfriend) to perform an essential task of social control. Acting in concert, the official and unofficial agents of society curb the hero's cynical self-interested asocial behavior by awakening in him, at the very most, a higher moral awareness (as in *On the Waterfront*) or, at the very least, a recognition that his own self-interest coincides with the larger purposes of the state (as in the films of Samuel Fuller). The control exercised by these figures is indirect rather than direct, manipulative rather than coercive. The hero perceives his commitment to family and a steady job, and his consequent acknowledgment of the legitimacy of the established order is a voluntary choice. Social directives are internalized. But Terry is in no sense free; he has merely exchanged one type of bondage for another. Authoritarian coercion exercised by the mob (he had to take a fall in a fixed fight) gives way to authoritarian manipulation exercised by the society.

12

Even though Terry rises bravely on his own two feet at the end, having successfully beaten Friendly in hand-to-hand combat, inspiring the men to defy the mob, his stance is an uncertain one; we have the feeling that Terry is still at the mercy of forces he cannot understand, forces much more subtle and dangerous than the ones he has overcome—an alliance of Wilsonian moral ferocity, Progressive institutions, the family, and management. As the film closes, and the great iron door of the shed crashes shut, we feel that Malloy is not so much liberated as trapped by the shadowy figure of the shipping boss who is the ultimate beneficiary of the action, and who has (almost) the last word: "All right, let's get to work." Once power abused (again, as in *Viva Zapata!*, concentrated in the hands of one man) has been eliminated, the ships can be loaded, and the happy collaboration between capital and labor that cemented the fifties consensus can prevail.

Kazan's view of reform is as elitist as his conception of democracy. Both social reform and individual salvation are top-down affairs, conducted by experts, the Crime Commission in the one case, and the priest in the other. The initiative in both instances comes from the experts, from above. This becomes clear if we look at a similar situation in Fuller's *Underworld USA,* a much more populist film: in the alliance between the Special Prosecutor and Tolly Devlin against the syndicate, the initiative comes from Tolly, from below.

Experts were seen by many political commentators in the fifties as the logical agents for social change. As Arthur Schlesinger wrote: "The experience of a century has shown that neither the capitalists nor the workers are so tough and purposeful as Marx anticipated: that their mutual bewilderment and inertia leave the way open for some other group to serve as the instrument of change; that when the politician-manager-intellectual type is intelligent and decisive, he can usually get society to move fast enough to escape breaking up under the weight of its own contradictions."[15]

A liberal science fiction film like Robert Wise's *The Day the Earth Stood Still* (1951) envisioned scientists and intellectuals alone as receptive to the message of peace on earth delivered by the interplanetary emissary Klaatu. The average man on the street was fearful, suspicious, or narrowly self-interested, like Patricia Neal's boyfriend, an insurance salesman. Confidently basing their analysis on a "post"-Marxist perspective which relegated class conflict to the dustbin of history, liberals like Kazan and Schlesinger could imagine evolutionary social change engineered by neutral managers without class affiliation on behalf of a state apparatus which was itself above class.

Although it is true that Kazan is ambivalent toward intellectuals his "bad ones" are ineffectual; they cannot get the job done.

Even though the main thrust of *On the Waterfront* is toward the socialization of Terry, it is necessary to pay close attention to the way this operation is carried out. It occurs through an apparently contradictory process of individuation. Terry is divested of old-world ethnic ties to immediate family ("they're asking me to put the finger on my own brother"), to the extended family of the union local ("Uncle" Johnny Friendly "used to take me to the ball games when I was a kid"), and to neighborhood. He is systematically detached from the social tissue that forms his natural habitat, and gathered into a larger notion of community-as-nation, associated with ahistorical absolutes like "democracy," "truth," "right and wrong," and anchored in the upwardly mobile nuclear family which provides its institutional base. For his blood brother Charlie he substitutes the claims of the Christian brotherhood of Father Barry ("you've got some other brothers") and the democratic brotherhood of America ("the people have a right to know.").

This transition is facilitated in several ways. First, it is rendered as a process of growth. Terry's testimony before the Crime Commission is an indication of self-knowledge ("I was ratting on myself all them years, and I didn't even know it") and the assumption of adulthood. The measure of his maturity is his decision to inform, to transcend local loyalties for larger and presumably higher ones. Loyalty to friends is regarded as an adolescent virtue, the province of his protege Tommy of the Golden Warriors who spurns him after he testifies. Although Tommy's reaction is experienced as a painful repudiation, it is somewhat undermined by being given a Freudian dimension. The sullen and hostile attitude he displays toward Edie earlier in the film suggests adolescent jealousy of the as yet latent adult relationship between Edie and Terry. Second, the mob, although in one sense Terry's family, is in another sense a false family. After all, it is an all-male group like the Golden Warriors, and it frequently acts to destroy family ties. It is responsible for Joey Doyle's death (Joey is defined in the film principally as Edie's brother); the core of Terry's accusation against his brother Charlie is that Charlie let his loyalty to Friendly take priority over his natural blood ties to his own brother. (Charlie later redeems himself by reasserting familial bonds in defiance of the mob.) Since the mob is exposed as a false family, it is not too difficult to convince Terry that they do not deserve his allegiance. Third, Terry's private goals, like his boxing career that the mob had frustrated, are legitimized. And, finally, all these strands are gathered up in the nuclear family represented by Edie. It offers maturity and responsibility, adult sexuality, upward mobility (Edie has been educated in a suburb, Tarrytown, and her father has labored so that she will enjoy the advantages of which he was deprived), and satisfaction of "private" goals. If his boxing career is over, he can at least experience the pleasures of romantic love, the peculiar province and strength of the nuclear family in a society where emotional gratification cannot be found outside the home. In terms of social control, society has successfully identified the "responsible" leadership (the family) within the community, and forged an alliance with it in order to destroy autonomous (and thus subversive) groups out-side its control.

Submerged in the valorization of romantic love, family, and "feminine" virtues is a new definition of what it meant to be a man in fifties America. The old-style immigrant morality of John Friendly, and the character structure that accompanied it, were obsolete. The ethnic ghettoes were being dispersed by assimilation and upward mobility; the protective reflexes based on fierce indi-vidual and ethnic loyalties were no longer necessary. New access to economic opportunity and suburban lifestyles, along with consti-tutional guarantees like due process and habeas corpus, afforded first-generation Americans all the protection formerly provided by ethnic protective associations, ethnic enclaves within unions, and tight, close-knit neighborhoods. Changed social circumstances required a new, softer, more pliable and trusting version of the male role. And if Terry had to move towards Edie, Edie had to move toward him, away from old-fashioned European notions of woman's role pressed upon her by her father, toward a superfi-cially more equal and activist stance. It is a comment on the dis-tance between the fifties and the seventies that the immigrant ethos which is discarded in *On the Waterfront* as "un-American" is sen-timentalized by a more radical film like *Godfather I,* with Brando now playing what could easily be the aging John Friendly.

In the fifties, the process by which Terry is detached from his old loyalties and incorporated into an abstract community was called "massification" by social critics when it occurred in totalitarian societies. It signified the emergence of "mass" man. Groups which mediated between the individual and the state, which might have competed with the state for the loyalty of the individual, were destroyed. By means of mass culture (TV, the press, and the movies), schooling, and work, all of which reproduced prescriptive hierarchical relationships, the state directly impinged upon the individual. The only institution which remained intact was the nuclear family. Although it was the locus of a less authoritarian set of habits than those instilled by school and factory, it was expected to generate goals of personal gratification through consumerism and emotional relationships which in turn were to motivate and guarantee the dichotomy between public life and private life.

It is worth noting that in the course of Terry's pilgrimage, he and Edie, who is initially a spokeswoman for the right-at-any-cost position of Father Barry, change places. As soon as she falls in love with Terry, she urges him to flee, to avoid the confrontation with Friendly that Father Barry demands, and for which he is ready to sacrifice Terry, Edie, and everyone else. It's just not worth it, she feels. Although the film fails to give credence to her point of view, she comes to represent a perspective from which to challenge Barry's manipulative morality. Within the limited terms that the film presents, it is not worth it. In the absence of a more profound insight into the politics of corruption, Malloy is being asked to sacrifice himself for nothing. As Pauline Kael pointed out at the time, John Dwyer, one of the real-life prototypes of Terry Malloy, defied the ILA but lost the support of AFL officials who abandoned him in the crunch. His attempts to challenge the ILA ended in failure; in fact the ILA gained even tighter control of the waterfront through a union shop. "For a happy ending," Kael wryly quoted *Time,* "dockers could go to the movies."

Although, as we have seen, Kazan falsifies the larger picture in the interests of his own political position, it is important to come to terms with the reasons the film works as well as it does. Part of the answer to this question lies in the kind of world Kazan presents. Nicholas Ray, close to Kazan in many respects, offers a Rousseauist vision; his heroes are sentimentalized innocents, noble savages inhabiting a benevolent natural world. They are presumably destroyed by the corrupt institutions of the civilized society, but since Ray's films are without a dimension of significant social criticism, they fail to dramatize this process. His films consequently lack a sense of real conflict, and issue, all too often, in saccharine happy endings in which previously antagonistic characters kiss and make up. Kazan's world, on the other hand, is entirely different. The state of nature is not innocent, but a Hobbesian jungle. As Terry tells Edie: "You know this city's full of hawks . . . they hang around on top of the big hotels and they spot a pigeon in the park—right down on them." This predatory morality informs the ethics of the mob and makes strong claims on Terry as well. "Down here, it's every man for himself. Do you wanna hear my philosophy of life? Do it to him before he does it to you," Terry tells Edie. Opposed to this philosophy in which the strong (hawks) consume the weak (the pigeons) is Edie's morality ("Isn't everyone part of everybody else?") and Father Barry's Christianity which promises that the meek shall inherit the earth. The battleground on which these two conceptions of man's fate contend is American democracy, and when Terry decides to become a stool pigeon, he fuses the spiritual and secular realms. Terry's protege Tommy calls attention to this as he throws a dead pigeon at Terry's feet: "A pigeon for a pigeon." In Christian terms, Terry voluntarily assumes the role of the meek (the dove); in secular terms, he assumes the role of the stool pigeon (the informer), and the one transfigures the other. The political informer as Christian saint.

Terry is well on his way to crucifixion before he testifies. He puts his hand through a plate-glass window (stigmata), and later when his friends avoid him after his testimony, he experiences the abandonment of Christ on the Cross. More important for the theme of power is the subsequent beating Terry undergoes at the hands of John Friendly and company. If power in the hands of one man is always abused, as Kazan emphasized in *Viva Zapata!* and reminded us again in *On the Waterfront* (Friendly), it has to be disguised (Father Barry) or, as manifest in a character like Terry Malloy, a potentially more explosive figure than Barry, must be domesticated. Marlon Brando was the ideal vehicle for the theme of power in the fifties. As the quintessential expression of the brooding, inarticulate, violent lumpen or laborer, his menacing strength with its lower class overtones had to be transformed into negative power, the capacity to endure the aggressions inflicted upon him by others. Thus the beating or humiliation became an essential part of the Brando character, occurring not only in *Viva Zapata!* and *On the Waterfront,* but in such diverse films as *The Wild One, One-Eyed Jacks, The Chase,* and *The Appaloosa.* The significance of Terry's final walk down the pier to the shed is that his power has been chastened, transfigured and spiritualized into the endurance of the martyr.

In a democracy, then, power is not confronted with power, but with Christian virtue. Liberal institutions (the Crime Commission) hand in hand with the Christian soldier (Terry) will insure the reign of the meek. Like Leo McCarey and other anti-Communist directors of the period, Kazan not only made the implicit claim that those who named names before HUAC were Christian saints, but that fifties America was the secular City of God on earth. A booming consumer economy offered ample proof that the God who had abandoned twentieth-century Europe to physical and spiritual destruction had come to roost in America. Father Barry's assertion that "Christ is down here, on the waterfront" is not a metaphorical or rhetorical device, but literal truth, expressing a world view peculiar to the fifties. I know nothing about Kazan's religious convictions, but *On the Waterfront* suggests that he shared with most Americans a belief in a providence that had saved America from the ravages of war, had given her the atomic bomb, and had delivered into her reluctant hands the responsibility for world leadership. This belief in the special destiny of America was responsible in part for the suppression of transcendence (or "negation," in Marcuse's sense) in films of the fifties, either the ridiculing of utopianism as childish or unrealistic, or the attempt to show that Utopian aspirations could be realized within American institutions. Thus the incarnation of the Christian (and transcendent) dove in the secular (and political) role of the stool pigeon.

Not only does the physical world incarnate spirit, but it is transformed and redeemed by spirit. The extraordinary scene between Charlie and Terry in the back of the car is an example of this process. Its effectiveness in part derives from the tension between the confined space and the potentially explosive nature of the interchange between the two men. A shallow and constricting physical space is converted into a deep spiritual space through a series of recognitions which clarify and transform their relationship, finally freeing Terry from the lies and bad faith that had clouded his relationship with his brother and himself. In the same way, physical falling is transformed into spiritual resurrection. Joey must fall from the roof so that Terry may rise; Father Barry must descend into the hold of the ship where Dugan lies dead before he can rise with the body, hoisted aloft in the sling.

Although the physical world is violent and menacing, like the fiercely percussive sound track that deafens Edie as she listens to Terry's confession, it is the presence of spirit that facilitates the creation of a moral geography which makes the physical world an expression, almost an allegory of spirit. The moral isolation of the neighborhood is enforced by an iron picket fence which separates it from the river and the New York skyline beyond. Terry's confession to Edie appropriately takes place outside the fence. This exposed ground becomes an index of the extent to which his relationship with Edie draws Terry away from safe rationalizations and familiar relationships towards the shadowy world on the other side of the river. The fog which perpetually shrouds the park in front of the church must be seen as an emblem of Terry's confusion, while the camera movements and shot compositions insistently reinforce the vertical orientation of the film, itself the physical analogue to the verbal play on falling and rising, going down and coming up, and an iteration in physical terms of the theological framework of fall and resurrection. One example of this is the scene of Dugan's death, where the characters are inversely arranged on a vertical axis according to their moral positions, an arrangement which at the same time directly reflects their secular power. Friendly at the top, Father Barry at the bottom, and Terry in between. By the end of the film, this layering has been reversed, and we take leave of a Friendly (who has just emerged from a precipitous descent into the water) diminished by an overhead crane shot.

Despite the redemptive immanence of spirit in the physical world, Kazan's vision, unlike Nicholas Ray's, includes real conflict. Terry's cynicism about the promises of democracy expresses a real contradiction within postwar America, one that eventually generated the opposite of fifties consensus: the radicalism of the sixties. Despite Kazan's efforts to the contrary, the line from Brando's Terry Malloy and Emiliano Zapata to the sixties is a direct one, indicated by the sympathy with which young New Leftists viewed Kazan's anti-Communism. That *On the Waterfront* finally produced its mirror image in *Godfather I* suggests that American popular culture is indeed dialectical in nature, contrary to the views of critics like Noel Burch who practice a mechanistic and undialectical Marxism which barely disguises their essential formalism.[16]

The seriousness of the contradiction Terry reflects is suggested by the fact that his socialization and redemption require real effort; the most sophisticated resources of Church and State must be brought to bear upon him. And this is not only because Kazan's vision includes a world of darkness, but because he gives this negation free expression. Despite the final harmonization of conflicting interests, the dissident voices are not hushed. Edie's anguished cries of protest are heard above Father Barry's efforts to propel Terry on his final walk. She is still opposed to his manipulation even this close to the end of the film. Likewise, the scene of the dead pigeons is extremely effective, and its power is not entirely dispelled by its Christ-abandoned overtones. There is real loss in this world, and its complexity is reflected in the richness of characterization and acting. Even John Friendly is sympathetic, as Cobb's villains usually are, through the tremendous impact of his screen presence. He usually overwhelms everyone else in his films; if he doesn't here, it is a tribute to the brilliance of Brando's performance, probably the finest of his career. Finally, the film succeeds because of the immensely powerful grip on the American psyche exercised by the myth of individual action and redemption which lies at its heart. Especially as embodied by Brando, this myth allows us to express the fantasy of antisocial rebellion at the same time that it allows us to submerge it in an even more compelling vision of social inclusion, wholeness, and renewal.

One is tempted by a Satanist reading of *On the Waterfront,* always the last resort of the hard-pressed Marxist critic faced with the excellence of reactionary art. Pauline Kael (no Marxist) has argued that "it is not Terry as a candidate for redemption who excites [the audience], but Terry the tough . . . Terry is credible until he becomes a social hero."[17] Much as I would like to agree with her, I can't. Terry is credible to the end. However deluded, he has paid his dues; he has earned his victory. By the time he staggers to the shed, we no longer care whether Kazan has falsified the power relations in fifties America or not. There is a fitness, a completeness to the film which defies criticism.[18] Meretricious as Kazan's politics are, they are deeply felt and in some sense true to the experience of significant groups of people in the early fifties.[19]

Finally, some conclusions. Kazan twists and turns to avoid confronting the implications of American power and power in America.

He presents a picture of an ideal democratic society in which power, as such, does not exist. It is only the enemy which exercises (and abuses) power, the John Friendlies of the world. Nevertheless, since power is in fact exercised by agents with whom Kazan is sympathetic, it must be disguised in order to maintain the fiction of its absence. Power struggles in the public sphere are displaced into moral struggles in the private sphere. Manipulation replaces coercion, and power, to the extent that it cannot be denied, is transformed into the negative power of the martyr.

This is the portrait of America that the film intends to present. But the picture of America that actually emerges from the film is quite different. Power, rather than being dispersed throughout the whole society, is concentrated in the hands of an elite of experts, both official and unofficial, who wield it with a ruthless singleness of purpose for their own ends. These ends include the socialization, if possible, of dissident individuals and groups or, if necessary, their destruction. Socialization is achieved by redefining individual allegiances and goals so that they conform to those sanctioned by society.

The two antagonistic portraits of America (egalitarian and elitist) offered by *On the Waterfront* are not entirely contradictory. A view of society as run by technical elites is one way of achieving the masking of power required by the egalitarian fiction. The state is viewed as a politically neutral organization of administrators standing above the petty quarrels of competing interest groups, a servant of the people.

The reasons for the felt necessity to disguise and deny the realities of power in America are not entirely clear, but they do invite speculation. Attitudes towards power distinguished and divided the various political factions during the postwar period. The older, liberal anti-Communists who came of age in the thirties felt uneasy about power. They associated it with the abuses of Stalinism. The new breed of cold-war liberals who came of age in the forties, on whom the experience of exercise of just power in World War II had a profound effect, felt it necessary to come to terms with power. Arthur Schlesinger, Jr., in his attempt to carve out a "vital center," a hard-headed "democratic left," denounced totalitarian communists on the one hand, and scolded soft-hearted progressives on the other for their common failure to employ power effectively. The

21

Stalinists used their power not for the general good, but to create a monolithic totalitarian state which served the interests of a new class of bureaucrats and state managers. Progressives, on the other hand, were afraid of power. Politics for them became merely the self-indulgence of private neuroses and guilts. The denizens of Schlesinger's vital center, on the other hand, were able to make a realistic appraisal of the potentials and limits of power. Unlike the progressives, they were not afraid to use it. Unlike the Stalinists, their power was "accountable" or "responsible" power, limited by the restraints inherent in the democractic system. For Schlesinger, as for most liberal intellectuals of the postwar period, the defining characteristic of a democracy such as America was that it was "pluralistic," that is, power was shared by a large number of different interest groups who competed on a more or less equal basis for a part of the pie. Social critics like C. Wright Mills who questioned this model, who suggested that power in America was concentrated in the hands of a ruling elite, were dismissed as cranks, communists, or both.

Kazan was considerably less frank than Schlesinger in his attitude towards power. Of an earlier generation than Schlesinger, a generation which had itself tasted the mixed fruits of CP politics, he revealed some of the special bitterness and engaged in much of the special pleading that characterized ex-Communists who collaborated in the cold-war witch-hunt. Schlesinger, after all, was somewhat nearer to the actual seat of power than was Kazan (by the time he wrote *The Vital Center* he had worked on the Marshall Plan as a special assistant to Averell Harriman); he was as much concerned with refurbishing liberalism for the purpose of providing a cloak of respectability for the new American hegemony, as he was with scarifying the USSR and the Stalinist left. While Kazan was satisfied to discredit the whole idea of political power and deny the existence of power in America, Schlesinger had, at the same time, to relegitimize power so that it could be used without scruple in the interests of American foreign policy. Kazan fought on one front, Schlesinger fought on two.

The reluctance to acknowledge or specify centers of power at a time of vast American military and economic strength may also be taken as an indication of guilt or bad conscience, a refusal to accept responsibility for the uses to which American power had already been put, not only at home in the witch-hunt, but in Hiroshima and Nagasaki. As Michael Wood has pointed out, many American films of the fifties, like *The Gunfighter* (1950), express a wish to relinquish power. Nevertheless, it would be another decade or so before these contradictions would surface. In the meantime, Kazan's longshoremen learned their lessons well. Ten years later, they would be loading weapons for Vietnam and their sons would be going off to fight.

Notes

1. *Movie,* 19, Winter 1961/72.

2. "Ellia Kazan: A Structural Analysis," Jim Kitses, *Cinema* (USA), vol. 7, #3, 25–36.

3. *Kazan on Kazan,* ed., Michel Ciment, New York, 1974.

4. There is certainly precedent in Marxist criticism for championing an artist who on the face of it seems to be reactionary. Engels defended Balzac (see his letter to Margaret Harkness) and other critics, most notably Lukacs, have followed suit. Yet in the case of Hollywood directors of the fifties, this claim seems to me highly dubious.

5. *The Crucible.* Arthur Miller (New York, 1971). It is interesting to note that Kazan could have worked with Miller on *On the Waterfront.* The idea, according to Miller, was originally his; he had done a considerable amount of work on a script before Schulberg came on the film. Schulberg's ultimate authorship of the shooting script represents, if nothing else, a symbolic shift to the right. Cf. "The Year It Came Apart," Arthur Miller, *New York Magazine,* Dec. 30, 1974/Jan. 6, 1975. Miller's account also throws light on the relationship between overt and covert anti-Communist films. *On the Waterfront* could have been made as an overtly anti-Communist film dealing with Party, not mob control of unions. In fact, it was only under these conditions that Harry Cohn would agree to produce the film. Kazan chose to remain faithful to his original conception and produce it independently. The film is still anti-Communist, but much more effective because it displaces and partially conceals its anti-Communism. Liberal anti-Communists like Dorothy Jones clearly saw the advantages of subtlety. She criticized Hollywood's anti-Communist productions for doing more harm than good in their vulgar lack of sophistication. (Cf. her "Communism and the Movies," in *Report on Blacklisting,* Fund for the Republic, 1956.) Liberal critics often point to the poor box-office showings of anti-Communist films of the fifties to argue against the idea that Hollywood films are ideological. Hollywood's infrequent forays into politics, they say, have been disastrous. In fact, the evidence merely shows that Americans are allergic to overt propaganda. Covert propaganda, like *On the Waterfront,* does very well.

23

6. For a different perspective towards informing, note the treatment accorded stool pigeons in Jules Dassin's prison film *Brute Force,* just a few years earlier.

7. *America Comes of Middle Age* (New York, 1963).

8. Compare Kazan's sanguine treatment of corruption-as-tumor to Lang's pessimistic view in *The Big Heat* of corruption as a gradually spreading stain which eventually blackens almost the entire society.

9. In *The End of Ideology* (New York, 1961) Bell argued that New York waterfront racketeering not only took the shape it did as a result of the antiquated physical condition of the docks, but was in fact caused, in large measure, by the fact that the port facilities were inadequate to handle modern trucks. Dockside congestion gave rise to the occupation of "loading" (goods had to be picked up off the docks and loaded onto trucks) which came to be a major source of graft. The solution, in other words, was wider streets.

10. The intimate relationship between the mob, big labor, city officials, and business can be glimpsed from the following facts. "Since the port is a municipal enterprise, a businessman had to negotiate pier leases from the city, get various licenses, and learn his way around the Office of Marine and Aviation . . . in 1947, during the (Mayor) O'Dwyer regime, an ex-bootlegger who sought to rent a pier was told to see Clarence Neal, a power in Tammany Hall, and to engage his services for $100,000. As a result of these disclosures, Mr. O'Dwyer's Commissioner of Marine and Aviation and his two chief deputies retired . . . From 1928 to 1938, Joe Ryan was chairman of the AFL Central Trades and Labor Council, and in that post spoke for 'labor' in the political campaigns . . . Another hidden source of ILA influence was the . . . friendship between Joe Ryan and a prominent New York businessman . . . William J. McCormack. He was . . . executive vice-president of the powerful U.S. Trucking Corporation, whose board chairman was Alfred E. Smith . . . His Morania Oil Company supplies fuel oil to the city. His largest enterprise, Penn Stevedore Company, unloads all the freight brought into the city by the Pennsylvania Railroad . . . Jarka, a stevedoring concern, had paid $89,582 in 'petty cash' to steamship company officials over a five year period to earn 'goodwill'; $20,000 had gone to Walter Wells, the president of Isthmian Lines (owned by U.S. Steel) . . ." (Bell, *op. cit.*, p. 176).

11. Bell, *op. cit.*, p. 176.

12. *The Agony of the American Left* (New York, 1969) pp. 9, 10.

13. All quotes here from *The Vital Center,* (London, 1970), pp. 245, 210, 218.

14. By way of contrast, compare the role of the priest in Hitchcock's *I Confess* (1952) with that in *My Son John* and *On the Waterfront.* As Leo Braudy has pointed out, the moral authority of the priest (Montgomery Clift) runs counter to the demands of the state voiced by the police inspector—played, curiously enough, by Karl Malden. Although the film eventually reconciles the claims of conscience with the demands of society, an authentic conservative like Hitchcock still comes off as a libertarian in the fifties, while a liberal like Kazan comes off as a totalitarian.

15. Schlesinger, *op. cit.*, 155.

16. Cf. especially "Propositions," Noel Burch and Jorge Dana, *Afterimage, #5,* Spring 1974.

17. *I Lost It at the Movies,* (New York, 1966), p. 47.

18. Nevertheless, the ending has always been puzzling. Lindsay Anderson, writing a famous and controversial piece in 1955 in *Sight and Sound* (vol. 24, #3, 127-30), said: "It is a conclusion that can only be taken in two ways: as hopeless, savagely ironic; or as fundamentally contemptuous, pretending to idealism, but in reality without either grace, or joy, or love." Anderson called the film "fascist" because it implies the necessity of strong leadership over the rank and file who are portrayed as children. This is certainly an important element in the film, but to call it fascist obscures more than it reveals. The ideology of the film is precisely *not* fascist, if by that term we mean authoritarian; rather, it can best be described by Marcuse's notion of manipulative repressive tolerance. Raymond Durgnat in *Films and Feelings* (Cambridge, 1971), p. 74, disagrees with Anderson, citing Bell's article as a rebuttal, but without particularizing. I would say, if anything, Bell contradicts Kazan. On the one hand, he stresses much more rank-and-file militancy than Kazan portrays. The frequent and vigorous wildcat strikes of the late forties hardly bear out Kazan's picture of docile, sheeplike dockers. On the other hand, Bell speculates that there was not as much resistance to the ILA as these walkouts seemed to indicate (as suggested by the results of two NLRB elections won by the ILA), and that they were largely provoked by rival mobs on the outside seeking a piece of the action. If this is true, it contradicts Kazan's picture of reform issuing from an apocalyptic confrontation of good and evil. Kazan himself has some odd comments on the ending in the Ciment interview, while Kael simply considers the end ("the shipowner, an oddly ambiguous abstraction") not "thought out." I think this is closest to the truth.

19. One place the film does ring false is its portrait of the Crime Commission. Kazan is at pains to underscore the scrupulous solicitude with which witnesses were treated by the Crime Commission: "You have every right not to talk if that's what you choose to do"; "You can bring a lawyer if you wish; you're privileged under the Constitution to protect yourself against questions which might implicate you in any crime." This kind of special pleading is particularly offensive and hypocritical in view of the actual treatment accorded witnesses during this period; it is hardly the place of an informer like Kazan to recommend the virtue of prosecutors to defendants who were not so cooperative as he and risked careers in the interest of principle.

I am indebted to Leo Braudy, Al LaValley, William Rothman, and Michael Wood for valuable suggestions which I have incorporated in this article.

WAR OF
THE WORLDS

Ever since Georges Méliès sent his rocket to the moon at the turn of the century, science fiction films have been familiar sights on American screens, but it wasn't until the fifties that they arrived in force. *Destination Moon* and *Rocket Ship X-M,* both released in 1950, inaugurated a flurry of films that before the decade ended would produce a veritable invasion of little green men, flying saucers, born-again dinosaurs, predatory plants, diabolical juveniles, and enormous insects.

Ideologically speaking, fifties sci-fi fell into two camps: centrist and radical. Centrist films often presented America in the grip of an emergency, attacked by giant ants in *Them!* or invaded by aliens in *Earth vs. the Flying Saucers.* These films did so because they were in the business of dramatizing consensus, the general, shared agreement on the basic premises that animated society. Emergencies made it crystal clear that if we wanted to survive to see another day, we had better pull together to overcome our local, petty differences in the common interest.

Relations among Americans were based on compromise, negotiation, and mutual respect. Centrists knew that consensus was more stable if dissenters were inside the magic circle of agreement, sharing the pie with Ozzie and Harriet, rather than outside, throwing stones against the picture window. They preferred, if possible, to include their enemies, not cast them into outer darkness. But the scope of the consensus was nothing if not narrow, and centrists did not hesitate to label those who refused to play the game "extremists." In centrist sci-fi, extremists were often presented as aliens.

Who were the alien extremists? It has long been evident, from the moment the first blob oozed its way across the screen, that the little green men from Mars stood in the popular imagination for the clever red men from Moscow. But extremists were not only Russians; they were everyone, left and right, who wandered from consensus.

Intellectuals like Daniel Bell, Talcott Parsons, Lionel Trilling, David Riesman, and Arthur Schlesinger, Jr., identified the center with the highest achievements of humanity, with the totality of man-made objects, the aggregate of human production, with no less than civilization itself—in short, with culture. Centrists invariably imagined society in man-made terms: It was a business, a building, a game, a machine—but rarely nature. Bell spoke of the "*fabric* of government" and Parsons of the "institutional *machinery* of society." Machines even had God's blessing. "A machine is an assembling of parts according to the law of God. When you love a machine and get to know it, you will be aware that it has a rhythm," wrote Norman Vincent Peale. "It is God's rhythm."

Centrist sci-fi adopted an Us-Them framework, whereby that which threatened consensus was simply derogated as the "Other." The Other, that which was not culture, was generally nature—not merely trees, animals, and bugs, but all that was not human, so that the conflict between centrists and extremists, consensus and the Other, Us and Them was often presented as a conflict between culture and nature. Since culture was good, nature was generally bad and threatened to disrupt or destroy culture.

In centrist sci-fi, then, the Other was imagined as nature run wild. In *Them!*, it was ants; in *The Beginning of the End,* it was grasshoppers; in *Tarantula*, it was a spider. In the same category were films like *The Creature from the Black Lagoon,* set in the jungle or other remote, wild places.

Since centrist films imagined society as a machine and looked fondly on science and technology, computers and robots—in contrast to

27

nature—were rarely dangerous. In *Forbidden Planet* and *Tobor the Great*, they were servants or tools, not masters or enemies; in *Unknown World*, a trip to the middle of the earth was facilitated by a giant mechanical mole.

Otherizing properties, ideas, life-styles, or groups that threatened the center was not only a way of discrediting specific alternatives to the "as is," but a way of discrediting the very idea of alternatives to the orthodox manner of living and being. If alternatives to mainstream institutions were dystopian, there was no place to go but home—that is, back to the center.

The whole genre of forties and fifties fallen-away, ex-Communist literature, from Arthur Koestler's *Darkness at Noon* to his *God That Failed*, was anti-utopian in character. Works with similar themes—like George Orwell's *Animal Farm* (made into a feature-length cartoon in 1955), his *1984* (adapted for the screen in 1956), and Aldous Huxley's *Brave New World*—were virtually canonized in the fifties.

The attack on utopias and utopians, dreams and dreamers, was a constant refrain in centrist literature. Utopians were our old friends the extremists, and utopianism was worked over so thoroughly that "utopian" and "millennial" became epithets of scorn, in contrast to adjectives like "realistic," "mature," and "sensible," with which centrists flattered one another. Alan F. Westin derided the "dangerously millennial proposals" of the Left and Right; Talcott Parsons ridiculed the "utopianism" of Republican isolationists.

Thus, in science fiction, if utopias began well, they ended badly, were apt to degenerate from the best of all worlds to the worst. Fifties sci-fi was full of futuristic civilizations that had fallen on hard times. In *Forbidden Planet*, for example, the Krell were the race that knew too much. In *This Island Earth*, the advanced civilization was Metaluna, and its gleaming array of gadgets by no means ensured it peace and prosperity; on the contrary, Metaluna was locked in a battle to the death with Zahgon, its archenemy, and had to turn to scientists from Earth for help. To judge by these films, Earth must have been the choicest morsel of real estate in the galaxy, the sweet center of the Milky Way, because it was repeatedly invaded by advanced civilizations that had fouled up in one way or another—exhausted their resources, overpopulated their cities, nuked one another, and so on. To be an advanced civilization was to look for trouble in these films, not because they were ambivalent about technology, but because they simply didn't like utopias.

Earth was the place where the hills were always greener, and there was good reason. Centrist sci-fi employed a double standard. On the one hand, the films attacked utopianism when it cropped up outside the center; on the other, they argued that Earth, by which they meant the U.S.A., circa 1955, was utopian enough for anyone. It was there, after all, that the contradictions that destroyed advanced civilizations were reconciled. Centrists believed, quite simply, that their country had the endorsement of the Almighty, the Divine Seal of Approval. A booming consumer economy offered ample proof that the God who had abandoned twentieth-century Europe to physical and spiritual destruction was alive and well in America. "God has set us an awesome mission: nothing less than the leadership of the free world," said Adlai Stevenson during the 1952 presidential campaign.

If America was the City of God on Earth, this meant that God, Christ, and values of any kind were immanent, that they were immediate, palpable, familiar, accessible in the activities of everyday life, not remote, distant, unreachable, transcendent. Utopia was to be found in our backyards; salvation lay in humdrum routine.

Although centrists agreed with one another on the goals of consensus and presented a common front against extremism, they quarreled among themselves about means, about how best to organize and impose consensus. This disagreement was reflected in centrist sci-fi, which can further be divided into corporate liberal films and conservative films. Both featured a coalition of scientists and soldiers, but differed on who had the upper hand.

Scientists and soldiers had first been thrown together in a big way during World War II, on the Manhattan Project, and the romance that blossomed then reached its climax at Hiroshima. In the fifties, when their infant A-bomb grew like a beanstalk into a strong and sturdy H-bomb, scientists became alarmed and fell to fighting with soldiers (and among themselves) over their child's future. Scientists like Albert Einstein and Robert Oppenheimer began to wish they had strangled him in the cradle; soldiers (and scientists like Edward Teller), however, wanted to pack him off to military academy, not reform school. Most scientists had been content to rest on their A-bomb laurels, but the soldiers wanted a bigger bang for their bucks, and pressed ahead with the H-bomb.

The disagreement over the choice of weapons had wider ideological implications. Scientists (and corporate liberals in general) didn't like force, because in their view society was consensual. Citizens did the right thing because they wanted to, or were persuaded to want to, not because they had to, or were forced to have to. For corporate liberals, moreover, reality was so complex that only scientists or experts were able to decipher it. "The problems of national security," wrote Daniel Bell, in a characteristic statement, "like those of the national economy, have become so staggeringly complex that they can no longer be settled by common sense or past experience."

In corporate liberal films, then, brawn deferred to brains, and scientists told soldiers what to do. The prestige of science was so high by the beginning of the fifties that the mad scientists of thirties and forties films—like Dr. Thorkel (Albert Dekker), who had shrunk his colleagues to the size of chickens in *Dr. Cyclops*—were all working for Bell Labs. They were no longer mad, but, on the contrary, rather pleased with the way things had turned out.

When the cops discover patches of sugar strewed all over the desert in *Them!*, it "doesn't make sense." Reality is too complex for traditional police procedure to unravel the mystery, and this is clearly a job for "myrmecologist" Edmund Gwenn. A far cry from Dr. Thorkel, avuncular Dr. Gwenn wouldn't hurt a fly, and he has no trouble reading reality. He quickly recognizes that giant ants are the problem, and his scientific expertise puts him at the center of world-shaking events. He meets with the president, lectures top public officials, and is able to command the full resources of the state. An Air Force general is reduced to the role of Gwenn's chauffeur, and when FBI agent James Arness complains he can't understand Gwenn's scientific lingo, the film makes us feel that he ought to take Biology 1 at night school.

Since *Them!* is a national-emergency film that dramatizes consensus, it endorses the intervention of the state and favors national over local interests. The alien threat emanates from the heartland and moves against a big city—Lost Angeles. Help, on the other hand, comes from Washington: Gwenn works for the U.S. Department of Agriculture. Corporate liberals generally favored Big Government, and corporate liberal sci-fi expressed confidence that the government, with its bombs and missiles, was equal to any emergency.

The corollary to the stress on consensus and Big Government was the disciplining of individualism. In corporate liberal sci-fi, individualists—the first one out of an air lock on a strange planet, the first one to investigate a peculiar cavernous pit, like the unhappy scientist in *Attack of the Crab Monsters*—were rewarded with death.

Likewise, the corollary to favoring experts and scientists with a hierarchical model of society, where those at the top were better—smarter, more moral, principled, and courageous—than those at the bottom. In *Them!* the Average Janes and Joes who are neither scientists nor soldiers are almost as bad as the ants. They spend most of their time fleeing for their lives, obstructing the best efforts of the government to save them from themselves. The war against the ants has to be waged behind closed doors. Reporters, conduits to the people, threaten official secrecy. Like their readers they have to be kept in the dark. "Do you think all this hush-hush is necessary?" someone asks Dr. Gwenn. "I certainly do," he replies. "I don't think there's a police force in the world that could handle the panic of the people if they found out what the situation is."

Conservative films, on the other hand, were more inclined to let the soldiers have their way. In *The Thing,* when Air Force captain Kenneth Tobey arrives at a remote Arctic outpost to investigate odd "disturbances" reported by a team of scientists, he discovers that he's in alien territory. "Dr. Cornthwaite is in charge here," one of the scientists tells him, referring to the Nobel Prize winner who heads the expedition, and it quickly becomes clear that Tobey's function is to assert the authority of the soldiers over the scientists. *The Thing* is about, among other things, a struggle over turf. It asks the question, which ideology—the conservative ideology of the military or the corporate liberal ideology of science—is best?

Fifties conservatives were considerably more suspicious of science than their corporate liberal allies. In 1943, for example, Richard

31

Weaver, the author of the influential book *The Southern Tradition,*
called science a "false messiah." Scientists in conservative films were
likely to be brothers beneath the beard of Dr. Jekyll—that is, the mad
scientists who had disappeared form the labs of corporate liberal
films were alive and well in conservative films.

In *The Thing,* the tension between science and the military that
is latent in *Them!* is not only more pronounced, but it is resolved
in favor of the military. Although FBI agent Arness complains in
Them! that he can't understand Gwenn, he is something of a clod
anyway, and it is probably his own fault. But when Captain Tobey
in *The Thing* asks a question and gets only mumbo-jumbo in
return, it's another matter. "You lost me," he says, and this time
it's *their* fault, a symptom of scientific arrogance. Gwenn's admiration for the "wonderful and intricate engineering" of the ant's
nest is reasonable, not unseemly or unpatriotic. But Dr.
Cornthwaite's scientific curiosity is given a sinister twist. He devel-
ops an altogether unhealthy interest in the alien. Whereas Gwenn
merely restrains the military because he wants to find out if the
queen is dead, Cornthwaite betrays it, defects to the Other side. He
helps the Thing reproduce itself, finds a nice warm spot in the
greenhouse for it to lay its spores, and sabotages Tobey's efforts to
kill it. Cornthwaite is an Oppenheimer, soft on aliens, a thing sym-
pathizer, and his behavior justifies the soldiers' mistrust of science.

Eventually Cornthwaite is confined to his quarters; when he tells
Tobey, "You have no authority here," one of the soldiers pokes a
revolver in his face and the scientist learns that power grows out
of the barrel of a gun. Conservative sci-fi, in other words, preferred
soldiers to scientists, force to persuasion.

But science was by no means rejected wholesale. There were
good scientists as well as bad, Tellers as well as Oppenheimers,
and the difference between them was that the good scientists sided
with the Tobeys, not the Cornthwaites. But, at the end of *The
Thing,* when the story of the struggle against the creature is
announced to the world, Cornthwaite is singled out for special
tribute. Soldiers and scientists, conservatives and corporate liberals,
may have fought among themselves, but their quarrel was all in
the family, and when the chips were down, they closed ranks in
defense of consensus.

Not all conservative films chastised science with the military; in some, religion played the role the military played in *The Thing*. These were the films in which the Faustian mad scientist was warned by a woman or a minister not to mess with God's work. In Kurt Neumann's *The Fly*, the fifties' infatuation with science once again transformed what would earlier have been a mad scientist into a sympathetic victim, but even here, when he exclaims, "I can transport matter!" his wife replies, aghast, "It's like playing God!" In these films, the cross was mightier than the test tube.

Fifties conservatives tended to favor local over national interests, the individual over the organization, and they displayed considerable skepticism toward large groups of all kinds—including the army—which they regarded as excessively bureaucratic. In *The Thing*, the conflict between soldiers and scientists is complemented by another between the individual and the organization. In this case Captain Tobey and the Air Force. Tobey begins the film as the perfect organization man. He can't blow his nose without clearing it first with headquarters in Alaska, which in turn refers back to Washington. But when Tobey goes by the book, it's a recipe for disaster, and red tape finally immobilizes him altogether. Although the Thing has been making Bloody Marys out of the boys at the base, Tobey is instructed to "avoid harming the alien at all costs." Eventually, he is forced to disobey orders, take matters into his own hands, pit his judgment against that of the organization, which is out of touch with reality. But he can't go too far; his rebellion is limited, confined to the framework of the organization. He remains the good soldier to the end.

Because *The Thing* is critical of bureaucracy and sympathetic toward individual initiative, it is more populist and less top-down than *Them!*. Although people in *Them!* obstruct authority, authority in *The Thing* frustrates people. Within the community of soldiers and scientists at the base, relationships are more egalitarian than they are in *Them!* Decisions are not made behind closed doors, and the Thing is not destroyed by the power of the federal government, not incinerated by soldiers wielding flamethrowers—like the ants in *Them!*—but rather it is destroyed by means of a do-it-yourself electric chair slapped together on the spot out of spit and chewing gum.

33

• • •

Radical sci-fi upended the conventions of centrist sci-fi, turned them inside out, held them up to a mirror. If centrist films dramatized consensus, radical films dramatized conflict, polarization, the antagonism between the self and society. If centrist films dramatized the views of insiders, radical films dramatized the views of outsiders. It was of course possible to attack the center from the right or left, so that radical sci-fi in the fifties broke down into right-wing films and left-wing films.

There was no question that giant ants were crawling all over Los Angeles in *Them!* or that a homicidal carrot was stalking the Arctic base in *The Thing*. Everyone could see it. Right-wing sci-fi, on the contrary, dramatized the struggle of the kook—the end-of-the-worlder—to force the community to acknowledge the validity of the self's private vision, even if it violated the norms of credibility that governed the expectations of experts and professionals. The focus of these films was the strenuous efforts of those who knew to alert those who didn't that there was trouble afoot—a blob in the basement or green slime in the attic. When Average Joe saw a flying saucer land in his bean field, nobody believed him. An abyss opened up between him and society. Far worse than invasion, these films anxiously imagined the loss of community, the estrangement of the one who knew from those that didn't, Us from Them—this time Us being the extremists, and Them the center.

Take Don Siegel's *Invasion of the Body Snatchers*. Kevin McCarthy, a small-town doctor, is besieged by patients telling him that their friends and neighbors aren't what they seem to be; they're imposters. At first, McCarthy advises them to see a psychiatrist. "The Trouble's inside you," he tells one patient. But gradually, as the whole town, including the psychiatrist and the police, are taken over by pods, McCarthy begins to change his tune.

In one scene, he and a pal argue with the psychiatrist about whether the pods exist. The cops burst in. "I have a good mind to throw you both in jail," says one of the cops, pointing at McCarthy and pal. But the psychiatrist intervenes: "These people are patients, badly in need of psychiatric help." The cops and docs (in this film analogous to the soldiers and scientists of *Them!* and

The Thing) argue about whether McCarthy and pal are felons or patients, but we know they're all wrong. In *Body Snatchers* the docs are sick and the cops are criminals. Society itself is the enemy; taken over by aliens, it becomes alien. When McCarthy finds an oversize pod in the greenhouse, he finally realizes that his patients have been right all along, that he must have faith in his own perceptions of the world, and not let experts and professionals mediate between himself and reality, or persuade him that he's wrong, crazy, or criminal.

Since the enemy in right-wing sci-fi was the society, the center, it should not be too surprising that the form in which this enemy was imagined was not nature but culture, specifically technology. If people betrayed technology in centrist films like *Forbidden Planet,* where disaster was caused by "human error," in right-wing films technology betrayed people; disaster was caused by "mechanical error." For the Right, "robot" and "mechanical" were epithets of scorn, and the center, perceived as dehumanized and technocratic, was represented in sci-fi by a whole army of robots, androids, and mechanical pod people that trudged across the screens of the fifties with their characteristic jerky motions. Whereas in centrist films robots like Robby of *Forbidden Planet* were friendly, they were dangerous in right- (and some left-) wing films, like *The Twonky, Target Earth, Gog,* and *Kronos.*

Susan Sontag first called attention to this fear of robots, which she contrasted with the older fear of the animal. "The dark secret behind human nature used to be the upsurge of the animal—as in King Kong. The threat to man, his availability to dehumanization, lay in his own animality," she wrote. "Now the danger is understood as residing in man's ability to be turned into a machine." But Sontag was only partly right. Although it is true that in the fifties the imagination of disaster took a mechanical turn, this new metaphor for dehumanization did not supersede the older one of animality. Rather, it coexisted alongside it. The alien as primitive, animal, natural was a centrist fantasy, just as the alien as mechanical and technological was a right-wing fantasy. In fact, since right-wing films used the past to flog the present, the primitive was often looked on with nostalgia. It was not barbarous, but rather a simpler, purer time. *Invasion of the Body Snatchers* is suffused with nostalgia for the past, for the old-fashioned, pre-technological GP, rather than the newfangled shrink with his glib theories.

Body Snatchers offers us a vision of the perversion of small-town life without the saving crosscutting to Washington that characterizes *Them!* In fact, Washington presents no help at all. McCarthy calls the FBI, but the operator tells him there's no answer. In right-wing films, the federal government—the state—either cannot be reached or is ineffectual. Its primitive weapons are useless against the aliens' superior powers. Therefore, individuals have to take the law into their own hands. After McCarthy finally realizes that the pods pose a threat, he spends the rest of the film trying to persuade others that he's telling the truth, but they don't believe him. When they finally do, community is restored, but on *his* terms, not theirs. They have been converted to his paranoid vision and, more, they have been mobilized for action. These films pushed the populist sentiments evident in conservative films like *The Thing* to vigilantism, do-it-yourself justice. The alien was destroyed by the resourceful citizens of Smallville without the benefit of federal aid.

36

In centrist films like *Them!* and *The Thing,* no one expresses a yen for utopias, except perhaps for Cornthwaite, and he is a villain. Alternative forms of life are simply monsters, and alternative societies, like the matriarchy of ants, are dystopias. But this doesn't matter, because utopian aspirations are attainable within the institutions of the center. In *Them!,* the FBI agent will marry Gwenn's daughter, just as in *The Thing,* Tobey will marry his girlfriend. But in the right-wing *Body Snatchers*, McCarthy and the heroine have been married—and divorced, which is to say, both have discovered that their aspirations cannot be realized within society.

For the radical Right, utopian aspirations did not find themselves realized in everyday life; they were transcendent, not immanent. Eric Voegelin, in a book called *The New Science of Politics* (1952), decried the liberal tendency to "immanentize" Christianity, to reduce its otherworldly perspective to an "intra-mundane range of action," while at the same time striving for the "redivinization of society." These films found their utopia in the new community, the transformed society based on their own principles. This utopia favored the heart over the head. Nature within was not a monster from the id, as it was in *Forbidden Planet,* but "natural" human warmth, normal emotion. "I don't want a world without love or faith or beauty," wails McCarthy's sweetheart, and later when she tries to pass for a podperson, tries to merge with the crowd, she gives herself away by expressing her feelings, screaming when a dog is run over.

Left-wing films shared the outsider perspective of right-wing films, but they differed from them (and from centrist films as well) in a significant respect. They did not fear aliens. In these films, the alien was neutral, benevolent, superior, or victimized. In Robert Wise's *The Day the Earth Stood Still,* space emissary Michael Rennie is shot dead twice, but miraculously resurrects himself in time to warn us to shape up or else our planet will be burned to a cinder. And in Jack Arnold's *The Space Children,* the alien is a good-natured disembodied brain that floats to Earth on the end of a rainbow to frustrate America's launch of a "doomsday missile."

37

Whereas the heroes of right-wing films in the fifties were Paul Reveres who tried to stir up people to take things into their own hands, these very same figures in left-wing films were villains—hysterical vigilantes, dangerous paranoids, and the "people" (as in corporate liberal films) were no better than a mob. Instead of mobilizing people against the alien threat, these films pacified them. What was justifiable alarm to the Right was hysteria to the Left. In the context of the Red Scare, these were anti-witchhunt films.

The right-wing whistle blower in *The Day the Earth Stood Still* is Hugh Marlowe, an insurance salesman who turns Michael Rennie over to the authorities. But in this film he's not treated like a hero; rather, he's a petty, jealous man. The proper behavior is displayed by Patricia Neal, who in effect defects to the Other side.

Like right-wing sci-fi, left-wing sci-fi polarized the center into a conflict between the individual and the community. The heroes of these films, who saw the spaceship land or shook hands with little green men, were also estranged form society, but whereas right-wing heroes were just Average Joes, left-wing heroes were more likely to have been estranged in the first place. They were Einsteins and Oppenheimers, the "eggheads" who thought for themselves.

PETER BISKIND

The special knowledge of the alien they came to possess merely rat-
ified their preexisting alienation. Therefore, they were not interested
in recasting the community in their own image. Unlike the Right,
the Left was pessimistic about the possibility of transforming the
community into a utopia—a pessimism that reflected its bitter, disillusioned anti-populism.

To the Left, as well as the Right, Christianity and utopian aspirations were transcendent, not immanent. They did not inhabit the
center but, on the contrary, existed without, in future worlds, or
within, beating in the breasts of their disaffected heroes. At the end
of *The Day the Earth Stood Still,* Michael Rennie just up and
leaves, goes back to the galaxy whence he came. He does not
marry Patricia Neal, get a job at Brookings, and settle down in
Chevy Chase.

TIGHTASS AND COCKSUCKER

SEXUAL POLITICS IN
THUNDERBOLT AND LIGHTFOOT

Michael Cimino's new Clint Eastwood vehicle, *Thunderbolt and Lightfoot,* has been given short shrift by reviewers but, like *Walking Tall* and several other recent films that have been scorned by big city critics, it has been doing well in neighborhood theaters and drive-ins. *Thunderbolt and Lightfoot* is a hybrid of several currently popular formulas: male friendship, paranoid chase, and big heist. It draws heavily on such films as *Vanishing Point, Scarecrow, Cops and Robbers, Midnight Cowboy, Slither, The Sting, Butch Cassidy and the Sundance Kid, The Outfit, The Last Detail,* and *Dirty Mary and Crazy Larry,* but is distinguished from its predecessors largely by the audacity with which it plays with the barely submerged homosexual element in the male friendship formula, and by its frank and undisguised contempt for heterosexuality. I saw the film in a medium-sized industrial city in upstate New York, and it was clear from the enthusiastic response of a predominantly working class audience that Cimino's efforts (he is responsible for the script as well as the direction) touched a responsive chord. The film seems to occupy and exploit an area where homosexual and working class attitudes towards women overlap.

Clint Eastwood plays Thunderbolt, an itinerant bank robber on the run from former members of his gang who are convinced he betrayed them to the cops. He is picked up by Lightfoot (Jeff Bridges) in one of those "customized" Detroit cars covered with spidery blue lines, and the two of them lead their pursuers, Red Leary (George Kennedy) and Goody (Geoffrey Lewis), on a merry chase, until the latter can be persuaded that Thunderbolt never did squeal on them after all. Following a lukewarm reconciliation, all four uneasily join forces to repeat the spectacular heist which gave Thunderbolt his name: the theft of one-half million dollars from Montana Armored with the aid of a U.S. Army artillery piece which launches armor-piercing shells through inches of heat-tempered steel. The theft is successful, but the thieves fall out among themselves. Leary beats up on Lightfoot, makes off with the loot, and is subsequently killed. Thunderbolt and Lightfoot not only escape, but stumble on an ancient one-room schoolhouse where the loot from the first Montana Armored robbery had been hidden behind a blackboard. They recover the money and fulfill Lightfoot's fondest wish—to pay cash down for a spanking new white Cadillac convertible—but while they are driving off into the sunset, Lightfoot dies of the beating he received from Leary. Thunderbolt must go on alone.

Whereas the boy meets boy formula is usually a peripheral element in what are primarily action films, in *Thunderbolt and Lightfoot* the male romance moves to the fore, while the action becomes a thinly-disguised metaphor for the sexual tensions between the two principle characters. The flavor of their relationship is established immediately by Lightfoot's overtures of friendship which descend quickly to innuendo. He observes that they shouldn't be seen together so much, since people will begin to talk: "Where there's smoke, there's fire." Lest we worry about Lightfoot's heterosexuality, however, the next scene shows him securing two girls for himself and Thunderbolt. Thunderbolt is reluctant and uncomfortable, but allows himself to be seduced. A close-up of his face while he is being worked over (making love is not quite the word for it) reveals a variety of emotions from embarrassment to boredom—anything but pleasure. God forbid the Eastwood character should obtain pleasure from another, especially a woman. As usual, he is sufficient unto himself. Both girls are treated badly, exploited for locker-room laughs. Only one woman in the film, a hippie motorcyclist, is able to withstand the overwhelming power of machismo; her independence is applauded, perhaps because the film is more angry at heterosexuality than at women per se.

All the heterosexual couples in the film are humiliated. Thunderbolt and Leary burst in on a comical middle-aged couple (Montana Armored's manager and his wife) in their suburban bedroom, and then on the couple's daughter who is energetically making love with a young man. Later we get a brief shot of this latter couple, naked and vulnerable, bound to each other with rope in an ugly parody of the sexual act. When Thunderbolt and Lightfoot stumble on the schoolhouse at the end, they surprise a Jewish couple who are sight-seeing. The couple's reaction to the macho vibes of Thunderbolt and Lightfoot is terror. The husband, in a comical display of urban fecklessness, unburdens himself of his Instamatic and other paraphernalia before fleeing to his station wagon.

Not only are heterosexual couples the object of ridicule, but heterosexual passion is portrayed as grotesque. Leary is mocked for his dirty-old-man view of women, while a porcine telegraph operator slavers over *Playboy* pin-ups and spends much of his time masturbating in the john. Frustrated heterosexual desires, then, are demeaning and obsessional, while unconsummated homosexual passion is sentimentalized as both ennobling and liberating.

The humiliation of women and heterosexual couples is contrasted to the affection and tenderness exchanged by Thunderbolt and Lightfoot to the male pin-up stance the film adopts toward Eastwood. He is constantly preening himself—removing his shirt, flexing his muscles, taking off his belt—while the camera prowls around him, looking for the most flattering angle, the most seductive pose.

The homosexual fable becomes more explicit when Lightfoot dresses in drag in order to incapacitate the telegraph operator so that he won't turn in alarm when the bank is busted. In a bizarre sexual allegory which one hesitates to disturb, Lightfoot zaps the man with a blackjack he pulls out of his underpants otherwise stuffed with gauze and tape for use in gagging the victim. We get a generous glimpse of Lightfoot's ass under his dress, covered with a body stocking, as he exits through a window.

Meanwhile, Thunderbolt and Leary are performing the heist. The two sequences are complementary, and their relationship is under-scored by crosscutting between them. This occasion is the only time in the film in which Thunderbolt and Lightfoot are separated, and the separation seems to allow them safely and symbolically to indulge in their homosexual role fantasies without danger of real consumma-tion. Lightfoot's feminine attire complements Thunderbolt's phallic cannon. Even the use of stockings underlines the symbolic relation-ship: Lightfoot wears women's stockings over the lower half of his body; Thunderbolt and Leary wear stockings over their heads.

Thunderbolt and Lightfoot (still in drag) are reunited in their car at a drive-in after the robbery; to avoid suspicion Lightfoot snug-gles up to Thunderbolt in a parody of a heterosexual couple. This is the highpoint of homosexual play—and as such, must be sup-pressed if the theme is not to become explicit. From here on in, it is downhill. The police find their trail, and Leary punishes Lightfoot by beating him senseless. This act itself is one of jealous rage; Leary and Thunderbolt had been friends since the Korean War. The beating gradually paralyzes Lightfoot's leg (castration!), complementing Thunderbolt's damaged leg (we get a glimpse of his brace in the beginning). Once castrated, Lightfoot can only die. After another symbolic exchange of cigars, he expires, his face con-torted in an ugly grin as he says he feels like a hero. But, and here the film adopts a tone of elegiac masculine sentimentality, the price has been too high. Lightfoot must die because society will not per-mit the consummation the film strains to achieve. Lightfoot's long-ing had become too explicit for him to be allowed to survive. Leary, the most sexually repressed and adolescent of the four male characters, goaded by Lightfoot's sexual precocity and his own semi-acknowledged jealousy, acts out society's prohibition by beat-ing Lightfoot to death. The violence of Leary's own death, torn to pieces by dogs, is an indication of the film's sympathies.

The relation between Leary, Thunderbolt, and Lightfoot is in one sense a commentary on the changing male image in films of the '50's, '60's, and '70's. Leary, the oldest, having had his most vital experience in the Korean War, embodies the repressed sexuality of the '50's, a decade of domesticity and sexual underdevelopment. Thunderbolt, some ten years younger, is the self-contained loner of

42

the '60's, identified with the Eastwood persona of the Leone cycle and the Siegel films. Lightfoot is the sexually ambiguous youth of the '70's, heir to the '60's breakdown of sex roles. He is as dangerous to the system of sex taboos as he is to the system of law and order. He threatens the '50's male image by mocking its bad faith, and tries to seduce the '60's loner into an idyllic male community. This proves to be impossible.

The lament for an impossible and fugitive homosexual love is merged with a tearful tribute to lost innocence and youth. The three older men live in the shadow of the past—of meaningful actions (the Korean War, the first Montana Armored job) which occurred years ago. Thunderbolt tells Lightfoot he appeared ten years too late. The second Montana Armored robbery is a pale copy of the first one; two of the original gang members have been killed—the mastermind and the electronics expert—and the survivors are barely adequate to the task. The association of the loot from the first robbery with the old schoolhouse where it was hidden (the schoolhouse is now an historical monument, and its original sight the scene of a large modern school—"Progress," comments Thunderbolt) accentuates the sense of loss. For a moment it looks as if the past can be recovered, but this proves a false hope. Lightfoot is already dying.

43

Who or what is responsible for this failure is not entirely clear. Leary is the proximate cause, but he in turn embodies a complex of cultural attitudes towards sex that must find their ultimate source in post-war American society. Society and its institutions do not figure heavily in the film except as caricature heavies. The most revealing sequence involves the quartet's attempts to find work to finance the heist. Aside from Thunderbolt, who works as a welder, the jobs they secure are intended to appear ludicrous. Goody works as a Good Humor man and is subjected to humiliations at the hands of small and impertinent children. The absence of all but the most submerged social criticism is itself suggestive; we just take it for granted that four men of different ages and indefinite class should exist in a criminal relationship to society. The only way men can be men, free from demeaning work and domestic suffocation, is on the road and outside the law in an idyllic male community, itself fragile and short-lived.

The most likely candidates for the Enemy are women who become the scapegoats for male frustration and dissatisfaction. True, it is Leary who kills Lightfoot, but he is merely the instrument of heterosexual oppression. Thunderbolt's complaint while passively enduring the sexual attentions of a woman early in the film can stand as an epitaph for all Cimino's men: "You're killing me."

PAT GARRETT
AND BILLY THE KID

It has been clear for some time to all but the most dogged of cultists that Sam Peckinpah's reputation, based on the undeniable merits of *Ride the High Country, Major Dundee,* and *The Wild Bunch,* but inflated beyond all recognition by his *auteurist* admirers, had to be scaled down in the light of his last four films. From *Ballad of Cable Hague* to *The Getaway,* from bad to worse, Peckinpah's talent seemed to have faltered, to have wandered from the material that engaged it most centrally, into a marsh of mushy masculine sentimentality. *Pat Garrett and Billy the Kid* changes all that. It is a brilliant and perverse film. Part of its brilliance lies in its very perversity: its lack of plot; its collection of aimless, static scenes; its mumbled, whimsical, raunchy dialogue; its refusal to be coherent or concise. The remainder lies in the world of loss and limitation it evokes.

The landscape of *Pat Garrett and Billy the Kid* is familiar. It is one of male friendship and conflict, of casual and sudden violence, of slow motion shoot-outs, of children cavorting on the hangman's scaffold. Most familiar is the story itself, the story of the West growing old, of the passing of the western hero, a story that Peckinpah has told many times. It boils down to an exchange between Garrett and Billy. Garrett says, "The West is growing old, and I want to grow old with it." Billy replies, "Times change, not me."

Pat Garrett and Billy the Kid, once the best of friends, are now riding separate trails. Garrett, the new sheriff, has been instructed by Chisum and the other big cattle ranchers to run Billy out of the territory of New Mexico. The bulk of the film is devoted to Garrett's desultory search for Billy and Billy's equally lethargic efforts to remain one jump ahead of him. Billy finally decides to change with the times, to move on to Mexico and then perhaps to California. On his way south, he comes across his friend Paco being brutally whipped by one of Chisum's men, while his wife is being raped by another. This chance encounter prompts him to retrace his steps, to go north to Fort Sumner where he will make a stand against Garrett and the interests Garrett works for.

The structure of each of Peckinpah's westerns is defined by two men, brothers or close friends, whose differing responses to the closing of the frontier lead to a conflict which gives form to the moral dimensions of the films. In *Ride the High Country* it is Steve Judd and Gil Westrum; in *Major Dundee* it is Dundee and Tyreen; in *Junior Banner* it is Junior and his brother Curly; in *The Wild Bunch* it is Pike Bishop and Deke Thornton; in *Pat Garrett and Billy the Kid* it is Pat and Billy.

Pat Garrett is a pragmatist who bows to the inevitability of change and uses the tools that are his—his speed with a gun, his familiarity with the ways of outlaws—to gain employment and to survive, while his former friends, relics of a passing era, are rendered obsolete by the big ranchers who moved in behind them. If he is redeemed, he is redeemed by his awareness of his own equivocal situation. He knows that his employers represent nothing more admirable than power; they want the territory pacified so that they can exploit it for their own profit. Further, he knows that by destroying Billy, he is destroying himself. His quest takes him through the landscape of his own personal history, past towns and faces as familiar to him as his own. In the course of his wanderings he is responsible for the death of many an old friend, like Black Harris, with whom he had first ridden into the territory fifteen years earlier. The price of survival is high. Garrett's pragmatism enables him to survive, but only as a cripple, a person whose shattered self-image is mirrored in the glass broken by his own bullets as he guns down Billy.

In *The Wild Bunch,* the conclusion of a similar pattern frees Deke Thornton, the Pat Garrett figure, from the circle of revenge and opportunism. Uneasily employed by the railroad interests to get rid of the Bunch, Thornton follows them to Mexico, but comes upon them after they have already been killed in the wild orgy of bloodletting that concludes the film. He inherits Bishop's gun, the spiritual talisman of the Bunch's virtues and, liberated from his police role, he rides off to new adventures with Sykes, the only survivor. The difference between the conclusion of *The Wild Bunch* and the conclusion of *Pat Garrett and Billy the Kid* is an index of the sense of pessimism and resignation that informs the latter. Pat Garrett is not redeemed but destroyed by the successful conclusion of his appointed task.

Billy the Kid, on the other hand, in rejecting Garrett's course, becomes the embodiment of values that are now obsolete. Not a hero in the old tradition of Gary Cooper and John Wayne, men of firm purpose animated by a high moral code, he is, as played by Kris Kristofferson, a softer character, plump rather than lean, of some moral ambiguity. Although he is a casual killer, the amoral, sadistic side of him is muted. He doesn't kill more than he has to. He shoots mostly in self-defense and on those occasions when he shoots first, there is a special reason: he shoots a fanatical deputy who torments him; he shoots his captor when the man foolishly dares Billy to shoot him in the back. He is cast in the traditional role of the knight-errant. He aids people in distress; he wreaks havoc on their tormentors. The primary value to which he subscribes, and which distinguishes him from Pat Garrett, is loyalty to friends.

With regard to the story-line, then, this film differs only in detail and circumstance from Peckinpah's other westerns. What gives *Pat Garrett and Billy the Kid* its peculiar flavor is the elegiac tone of the film, the lamentation for a lost world, for a fugitive innocence and beauty. The characters are dominated by the past, by memory and recollection. We have stumbled in on the last act of a melancholy drama that is largely over. Everything of importance has already occurred. We view only the inevitable denouement operating through passive characters who walk through their parts as if asleep. They are in the grip of an ineluctable necessity which they

47

make only half-hearted efforts to elude. The characters, like the man deputized by Garrett in the barber shop, are at the mercy of fate, of predetermined roles, of formulaic codes of behavior that have ceased to have any real claim on them, but which nevertheless refuse to relinquish them. This deputy is a reluctant participant, initially involved by accident because he was at the wrong place at the wrong time. Later, again by accident, he meets up with Billy. Each tries to figure out a way to avoid the inevitable ritual confrontation in which the deputy will be killed, but they cannot. They walk through the duel, each cheating, not so much from dishonesty as from exhaustion, despair, a refusal to play the game, and an inability to escape it. They have both seen too many westerns.

This overwhelming sense of external fate distinguishes *Pat Garrett and Billy the Kid* from Peckinpah's other films, which portray men as freely willing agents, fully responsible for their actions. Peckinpah's characters are complex beings, frequently overwhelmed by the savage self-destructive impulse that inhabit the self. In *Pat Garrett and Billy the Kid*, on the other hand, the autonomy of the characters is diminished, is subordinated to larger movement over which they seem to have little control. Interest shifts from interior conflicts or even from conflicts between characters, to the relation of the characters to the vast historical and economic changes that are transforming the land.

This shift, however, is incomplete. There are vestiges of Peckinpah's earlier conception of character still present and James Coburn's Pat Garrett seems to be a victim of this confusion. At first glance, Coburn seems miscast. The role appears to call for a performance like Robert Ryan's Deke Thornton, someone whose face reveals the ravages of time and inner conflict. In Coburn's silver-haired inexpressive Garrett, we have a taciturn and remote Sunset Strip cowboy who attempts to express the spiritual struggle of a man who hunts down his best friend by casting blank, enigmatic gazes into space. Coburn mechanically expresses Garrett's deeply ambivalent attitude towards his role in his relationship with his foil, Poe, a vicious agent of the financial interests lurking off camera, who tags along after Garrett and is brutally beaten by him when he tries to cut off the trigger-finger of the dead outlaw. But while Coburn is a poor Robert Ryan, his impassive performance does convey the pervasive sense of necessity that defines the world of the film.

Billy the Kid is its victim. In contrast to Garrett, he is open and smiling, a figure of innocence. He returns to Fort Sumner to make a last stand, in the fashion of the traditional western, but instead falls into bed with a beautiful Mexican girl (Rita Coolidge), seeming to consecrate his value with love. This scene is richly ambiguous. Coburn is never more remote and inaccessible than when he is seated quietly on a swing outside Billy's window, listening to the sounds of love-making. Whether he is sunk in recollection of their shared past; whether he, in his sorrow, is allowing Billy one moment of fulfillment before his death; or, in a more sinister fashion, is voyeuristically participating in a sexual and emotional passion he is incapable of, except, perhaps, for Billy himself, we don't know. He waits until Billy arises to find something cold to drink, gets up, and looks in on the woman before going after Billy. Billy makes it easy for him, managing to back his way right into Garrett's waiting gun. The pathos and vulnerability expressed in this scene are extraordinary and go a long way toward transforming Billy-the-outlaw into the embodiment of a fragile spirit of innocence and beauty. Billy accepts his death. He neither runs from it nor goes down in a hail of bullets, in a defiant self-destructive gesture, like the Wild Bunch. He is a sacrificial victim, half-naked when shot, unmarked by the bullets, a martyr to history. At the same time, he must be punished for his tender heterosexual relationship which violates the masculine code of the West. Billy-the-son is scourged by Garrett-the-father ("You were like a father to that boy, Pat") who upholds the rigid ethic of Calvinist sexual repression which divides women into whores and angels.

Although Billy and Peckinpah acquiesce to the new order that is being imposed upon the West, neither of them has much regard for it. Rule by law, civil society's great gift to the unruly frontier, is exposed as a sham. The law is arbitrary and illegitimate. It exists merely to protect the property rights of the big landowners and cattle ranchers as they carve up the open range into private fiefdoms. Chisum's assertion of his own property rights is emphasized repeatedly, as his gang of hired gunmen twice attack Billy's friends for "trespassing." Even Garrett recognizes that moral issues are irrelevant to his enforcement of the law. He tells Poe that he refuses to pass judgment on Billy. Earlier, Governor Lew Wallace, speaking to Garrett and a cabal of capitalist flunkies worthy of Eisenstein, makes this explicit when he asserts that the law is needed to protect the extensive financial investments in the new territory. The uses of the law to enforce class interests is further underlined in the prologue and epilogue, excised from the film by the studio, in which Garrett himself is assassinated nineteen years later by the same people who had hired him to kill Billy. Garrett had proved too independent; his investigations had come too close to exposing the shady dealings of the economic interests who impose the law on people less fortunate than themselves. "The law's a funny thing," says Billy, as he recalls the days when he rode for Chisum, and Garrett was the outlaw.

The exposure of the abstract principle of law and order, ostensibly standing above the conflict of private interests, but in fact subservient to the most powerful of these interests, is reinforced by the cruel and abusive ravings of the fanatical deputy, Ollinger, who becomes a parody of Peckinpah's early embodiments of strict moral principle, Judd and Knudson of *Ride the High Country*. Abstract standards of behavior are suspect. They either cloak self-interest or become, divorced from feeling, transparent expressions of the worst qualities of human nature. True morality, on the other hand, is visceral and concrete. It grows from intimate relations with fellow men, from shared experiences of loyalty in battle, of whoring and drinking and carousing together. As Pike Bishop says: "When you side [with] a man you stay with him . . . if you can't do that you're worse than some animal."

Garrett betrays this spirit; Billy upholds it. Yet Billy plays out his hand alone. He is continuously surrounded by remnants of his old gang, ready to pick up their guns again, like the old days, but he never calls on them. In this paralyzed, unrealized sense of community lies the final tragedy of the film. Their options closed off, they are helpless and pathetic, living only to be picked off one by one by the hired guns of the ranchers. When Billy turns his back on Mexico, he loses the possibilities of community and revolutionary collective action that Mexico represents in Peckinpah's world. But at the same time, he chooses fully to be himself, to be who he is, Billy the Kid. He turns back, goes north, and dies. Peckinpah's heroes, at once the agents and victims of the "civilizing" process, the rationalization of western society, rebel against its consequences but enjoy no historical alternatives. They must resist or surrender. Either way, they are doomed. If Billy survives, he survives only as legend, in the eyes and hearts of the fascinated spectators who watch with frozen, fixed gazes as the grim drama is played out before them.

Like *Major Dundee, Pat Garrett and Billy the Kid* has been angrily repudiated by Peckinpah. It was ravaged by his studio, MGM, which cut fifteen minutes from the film, including, according to Peckinpah, material that more fully explained the motivation of the characters: a prologue and epilogue in which Pat Garrett is himself killed; the entire character of Chisum, played by Barry Sullivan; and other material. He also attributes to MGM the overuse of Bob Dylan's music track (not one of his best compositions) which intrudes every time a speaker pauses for breath. The motive behind this musical blitz is presumably the desire for a best-selling album to serve as a teaser for the film on the top-ten charts.

With less reason, the film has also been scorned by the newspaper critics, probably because it does not conform to the received idea of the traditional western. Much of the film's gnomic quality can perhaps be attributed to the script writer, Rudy Wurlitzer, who was responsible for a similar effect in McBride's *Glen and Randa*. Like *Glen and Randa,* it is composed of a series of discrete episodes, more or less entire in themselves, remarkable for their mute beauty and pathos. I am thinking particularly of the death of Sheriff Cullen Baker (Slim Pickens); of the wandering recollections of old Pete who, oblivious to the absence of his auditors, rambles on to himself; of the aborted duel between Garrett and the unidentified man on the boat floating slowly up the river. *Pat Garrett and Billy the Kid* also marks the Hollywood debut of Bob Dylan who plays a knife-wielding pal of Billy's. He is the vehicle for much of the strain of whimsy that runs through the film. Despite the handicaps of an unfortunate resemblence to the Mad Hatter and some awful dialogue, he manages to convey the sense of slightly demented innocence that it is his lot to portray.

We will probably never know what Peckinpah's final cut would have looked like. Paradoxically, it may be the absence of some of the material cut by the studio, namely, the material that more fully establishes the motives of the characters, that is responsible for the melancholy sense of fate and resignation the film conveys. In any case, *Pat Garrett and Billy the Kid* is an extraordinary achievement and reestablishes Peckinpah's claim on our interest.

MACHISMO AND HOLLYWOOD'S WORKING CLASS

Peter Biskind and Barbara Ehrenreich

Whenever we cast our eyes up to the silver screen, wherever we look—at figures riding tall in the saddle, crouched in foxholes, careening down mountain roads in fast cars, or even cowering in the kitchen—we see men. One urgent and consistent theme that stretches through Hollywood films from Rudolph Valentino to Al Pacino has been masculinity. In the movies, masculinity is presented as an agonizing, unresolved *problem*. Will Sean Connery ever settle down? What would it have meant for James Dean to grow up? The problem that Hollywood addresses is not too different from that which Freud laid out in *Civilization and Its Discontents*: can man, that is, the male gender, find happiness in a world of nine-to-five jobs, the Little League, and aluminum siding sales?

In the real world, the seventies were a particularly trying decade for men and, not surprisingly, it is the trials of upper-middle-class men that are most poignantly recounted in best-sellers (*The World According to Garp*) and TV sitcoms. Safe, tame domesticity faded as a social ideal, and its traditional antithesis—untamed machismo—

came back from Vietnam with a castration complex. At the same time a reborn feminist movement undercut the moral authority of male paternalism. And that far-reaching social upheaval known to liberals as the "life-styles revolution," and to conservatives as "the breakdown of the family," left men as well as women adrift in a shifting landscape of "relationships." Woody Allen, more than anyone, articulated the sense of victimization men felt in the grip of the mid-seventies masculinity crisis: looking plaintive as Diane Keaton reads *The Second Sex* in bed (*Annie Hall*) or trying to "rescue" his son from Meryl Streep, his lesbian ex-wife (*Manhattan*). Dustin Hoffman and Richard Gere in *Kramer vs. Kramer* and *American Gigolo* tried to beat women at some of their own games: nurturance in the one and prostitution in the other.

In the late 1970s, the movies introduced a new, and politically intriguing, perspective on the male condition. After decades of cowboys, detectives, spies, and earnest young scientists, the cameras turned—long enough to establish a genre—on working-class men, in particular the white, ethnic variety. Previously encountered in the postwar period mainly as enlisted men in World War II films, working-class males now zoomed to individual prominence as the heroes of *Saturday Night Fever, Blue Collar, Bloodbrothers, Rocky I* and *II, Paradise Alley, FIST,* and a handful of others. Left critics have by and large viewed this new genre as Hollywood's latest experiment in social realism, judging the films on the basis of their accuracy in portraying working-class life. Here, we will not take them quite so literally. On the whole (and with some exceptions) these films are not about the working class any more than westerns are about the West. They use the working class as little more than a backdrop for Hollywood's latest exploration of the "man question." If they do reveal anything about class in America, it is not the working class, but the middle class. These films are, in a sense, middle-class male anxiety dreams in which class is no more than a metaphor for conflicting masculine possibilities. Violence and machismo, along with male bonding and obsessive determination, are allocated to the working class. Maturity and self-mastery are allocated to the middle class. The masculine dialectic between machismo and maturity is externalized; class struggle is internalized.

Flashback

THE FILMS OF the fifties were generally confident in their projection of a stable, moderate social order. Male mayhem was corralled into the play world of cowboy pictures. Grownup (and out of cowboys and Indians) men found themselves in the heterosexual middle-class married couple; any other social affinity was extremist or deviant. Films as disparate as *Marty, Blackboard Jungle, On the Waterfront,* and *Seven Brides for Seven Brothers* portrayed men in groups as either immature or criminal. In films like Ford's *My Darling Clementine,* Zinnemann's *High Noon,* Mann's *Tin Star,* and Hawks's *Rio Bravo,* the villains were the male clan, brothers without women. Male groups, whether united by class, family ties, or mere derring-do, were doomed to death or marriage.

Outside the movies, domesticity was also held up as the model for male adjustment. In an economy based on plenty, not scarcity (where, as David Riesman put it, the glad hand replaced the invisible hand), people flocked to shopping centers, not savings banks, and heterosexual "togetherness" was the hallmark of maturity. Men made their last stand in the hardware store, not the bar. The dominant ideology of the center, pluralism, viewed politics as the give-and-take among a multiplicity of interest groups competing on a more or less equal basis for a part of the pie. For this process to work, men (women were not even in the game) had to be willing to compromise. "The thrust of the democratic faith is away from fanaticism; it is towards persuasion and consent in politics, towards tolerance and diversity in society," wrote Arthur Schlesinger, Jr., in 1949. Pluralism, therefore, required a psychology, a character structure. Men were supposed to be "other-directed," not "inner-directed," "organization men," not individualists; they were supposed to be flexible, softer, more willing to give in and make the compromises that would keep the pluralist machine running smoothly. According to the conventional ideology of gender identity, the sex that embodied these traits was, of course, female. Pluralist men were thus "feminized" men, whereas old-style "masculine" men—heroic, rigid, moralistic—were derogated as "extremist" or "totalitarian." The hard-boiled male roles of the thirties and forties, and the actors who played them, became psychopaths in the late forties and fifties. Cagney played the gangster as psycho in *White Heat*. Wayne played the cowboy as an obsessive neurotic in Ford's *The Searchers*. Bogart played an unbalanced, violence-prone writer in Nicholas Ray's *In a Lonely Place*. Cooper played a neurotic capitalist in *Bright Leaf*. Meanwhile, in films as different from one another as *Red River, Rebel Without a Cause, On the Waterfront, Giant,* and *Creature from the Black Lagoon,* men were shown learning to be sensitive. A whole generation of male actors, like Montgomery Clift, Tony Perkins, James Dean, and Paul Newman, embodied pluralist psychology.

But there was a contradiction in the fifties construction of masculinity. Conservatives had never bought the feminized male in the first place, and even liberals like Schlesinger realized that the kind of character structure appropriate at home, for family barbecues and two-martini lunches, was not appropriate abroad. When it came to dealing with the Russians, compromise was foolhardy, flexibility fatal. As the mid-fifties Eisenhower thaw gave way to the tensions of the Berlin Wall and the Cuban Missile Crisis, the domesticated male began to be seen as one of America's greatest strategic weaknesses. The Korean War showed that American boys were too soft to stand up to enemy brainwashing; Sputnik showed that they were too dumb to compete with Soviet whiz kids. When U-2 pilot Francis Gary Powers ended up on Russian television instead of dead from cyanide, too chicken to have been a martyr for the CIA and the Free World, it was the last straw. In the late fifties and early sixties, American culture took a right turn away from permissiveness in child raising and "softness" in males. Films, so long preoccupied with the problem of how to tame men, took up the problem of the too-tame man. In 1960, Hitchcock put Tony Perkins, fresh from a bout of mental illness in *Fear Strikes Out* and one of the leading sensitive male actors, in *Psycho*. When Perkins killed white-collar thief Janet Leigh, he showed that women who rip off men go down the drain, and men who take women as role models go off their rockers.

The "man question" had been reopened. Films of the sixties took it up with a vengeance—so much so that, by the early seventies, actress Talia Shire complained in the *New York Times* that

Hollywood no longer had roles for women. But in the sixties, the old masculine dialectic (feminized domesticity versus male anarchy) was drastically rewritten. For one thing, domesticity, the bedrock of the cultural consensus of the fifties, was losing its postwar, post-Depression allure. Men in the fifties had joked about being "trapped" (presumably by their wives); now the same wives were getting jobs, going to night school, and reading *The Feminine Mystique*. There was no one left at home to do the trapping; Faye Dunaway had replaced Doris Day, the dishes were piling up in the kitchen, and weeds were growing in the front yard. Where there before had been only marriage, there were now "life-styles" featuring a bewildering multiplicity of relationships, all shored up by the seemingly inexhaustible affluence of the sixties. Babies were postponed, and the manufacturers of hula hoops and lawnmowers began to lose out to the purveyors of stereo components and sports cars. *Playboy* chased the *Saturday Evening Post* off the newsstands, and a youthful, glamorous president once again gave old-fashioned male intransigence a good name. Jack Kennedy could face down Khrushchev with a single glance, while ordinary mortals cowered in their backyard bomb shelters.

In the sixties, Hollywood's strongest appeal to the public id was the spectacle of exuberant, light-hearted male violence. As the center polarized into right and left under the pressure of the Vietnam War, the liberal conventions of fair play that had always governed male combat on the screen fell into disuse. In the sixties James Bond and male-bonding films, such as *Dr. No* and *The Wild Bunch*, the heroes no longer saved themselves for one final, decisive moment of truth at the end (although there was that too); they came out shooting and continued shooting until the last frame. Marlon Brando, in *On the Waterfront*, *The Wild One*, and *One-Eyed Jacks*, earned the right to violence only after a terrible but purifying beating; for Sean Connery and Clint Eastwood, mayhem was routine. And, breaking another taboo of fifties centrist films, positive images of men in groups and couples could now be found; women could hardly be found at all. The male bonds that united Borgnine and Holden in *The Wild Bunch*, or Newman and Redford in *Butch Cassidy and the Sundance Kid* and again in *The Sting*, could never be undone by matrimony, only by death.

The Seventies: A Touch of Class

WE ARE GETTING ahead of our story. By the mid-seventies, the sixties had already been rewritten as a time of "excess." Vietnam and
Watergate settled into mass consciousness as two "mistakes" of
roughly the same magnitude, parallel cases of federal hubris.
Carter ascended to the presidency in 1976 with the announced
political project of *healing:* reuniting the generations, restoring the
family, rebuilding trust in government, recreating the center, and
relegitimating the old pluralist ideology. Meanwhile, the economy
stagnated.* The ebbing of affluence reinforced the rising back-to-
basics mentality as Americans groped for a new cultural consensus.

Films by and large took a liberal approach to the problem of
reconstructing some sort of cultural unity. If the family could not
be restored, as Carter had somewhat rashly promised, then at least
we could learn to live with the various emerging life-styles.
Refreshingly, in the films of the late seventies, people could be single parents, never married, or occasionally, though at some risk,
gay; they could even, sometimes, be women. Feminism undercut
the age-old equation of masculinity and adventure. Women, too,
could act up, walk out (even though they were punished for it, as
in *Kramer vs. Kramer*), or even (like the woman in the TV perfume
commercial) drive off into the sunset—alone. But the rise of
women (in *Julia, Alice Doesn't Live Here Anymore, An Unmarried
Woman*) by no means drove "real men" from the screen. Instead,
they reappeared in a new setting—the white ethnic working class—
a world so far removed from Hollywood, so hopelessly parochial
by the standards of Malibu or Beverly Hills, that it became on film
a new realm of fantasy and glamor.

Before it could star in the movies, the working class had first to
be "discovered." In the fifties and sixties, studios had, perhaps

---

*Ironically, throughout the fifties, when leftists were daily predicting that the ter-
minal crash of capitalism was just around the corner, the economy refused to
oblige. But when leftists in the sixties and seventies finally explained why "postin-
dustrial," "postscarcity," "one-dimensional" society refused to roll over and die,
suddenly it began to decline. The energy crisis, stagflation, and the decline of the
dollar were upon us, making "postscarcity" analysis as obsolescent as last year's
car used to be, and forcing leftists to scramble for a post-postscarcity model of the
fall of the West.

wisely, concluded that the blue-collar world was not a setting for a profitable movie. No one could be expected to go out to a theater and pay money to see interiors that were drabber and more claustrophobic than the ones they had left at home. Technicolor and Vista-Vision would be wasted on faded upholstery and peeling wallpaper; who wanted to see an assembly line in 3-D or hear it in Sensurround? But for all its cinematic disadvantages, by the late seventies the blue-collar world had replaced the Old West as the mythical homeland of masculinity. Fifties pluralists acknowledged no class divisions; the working class, if it existed, only provided raw material for "upward mobility"; it was a stepping stone on the way up to the all-inclusive middle class. Then, in the early sixties, middle-class America discovered Michael Harrington's "other America," and by the mid-sixties, the poor—at least the black poor—had become a political force to reckon with. The liberal middle-class imagination divided society into "the white middle class" on the one hand and "poor people," seen as overwhelmingly black, on the other.

It wasn't until the "backlash" against the black and antiwar movements in the late sixties and early seventies that a new, previously unsuspected group emerged: people who were not black and yet were palpably not middle class either. (The black working class never gained cultural visibility, we suspect because of the continuing association of blackness with poverty and the "working class" with antiblack backlash.) This new group, the "working class," as it was soon labeled, entered middle-class consciousness in the form of hard hats: men who were well enough paid to be middle class but inexplicably liked Nixon and resented hippies, blacks, and student antiwar demonstrators.

Sociologists, anthropologists, psychologists, and student leftists hastened to make amends to this neglected group. The Department of Labor commissioned studies of "blue-collar alienation"; foundations that had funded civil rights activities began to promote the development of urban white working-class organizations; urban anthropologists turned away from "the culture of poverty" to explore exotic white ethnic enclaves. It was as if, in the early seventies, a kind of fossil culture was being excavated—people who had been curiously bypassed by the sexual revolution and the human potential movement, and had somehow managed to preserve their quaintly distinctive way of life.*

For a majority of the viewing public, this development was long overdue. Most people do not, after all, live in the well-furnished world of fifties and sixties sitcoms. So long as they had some hope of getting there, the media focus on the middle to upper middle class was pleasantly diverting, a promise of things to come. But the economic crisis of 1973–1974 dashed expectations of unlimited upward mobility—even sociologists couldn't find jobs. Visions of affluence became a reminder of mortgaged dreams, while the working-class world—or its media representations—became for the first time a commercially viable setting.

Still, the working-class world might not have become a subject for major Hollywood films if its "discovery" had not coincided with the middle-class "masculinity crisis" of the seventies. On the home front, there was the inexorable spread of battlefield stretching from the kitchen, through the den, to the bedroom. On the job front, the economic downturn was limiting middle-class opportunities. Careers offering relative autonomy from corporate domination—in academia, many of the service professions, the public sector—began to decline relative to careers requiring direct subordination to corporate priorities. The young man who might, in the sixties, have studied history or philosophy now swallowed his curiosity and took up accounting. In the fifties, sociologists had bewailed the "man in the gray flannel suit," the middle-class male swallowed up by the corporate behemoth; in the seventies, their sons were glad to find a white-collar job at all. They chase after their lost autonomy, away from work or home, on the edges of highways, in Adidas sneakers.

---

*Only two of the "working class" films of the late seventies address head-on the tensions at the interface of the middle class and the blue-collar working class. In *Blue Collar*, the auto workers fight the smooth-talking middle-class union bureaucrats rather than the bosses (the script preferred by most left critics) or just one another (the anticommunist script of the fifties). In *Breaking Away*, working-class youths battle pampered college boys, for reasons that are made to appear compelling and reasonable. We are amazed in the end not only that the sons of workers win against overwhelming odds, but also that the combat has been allowed to take place at all. A taboo has been broken.

It was in this context that the working-class male emerged, briefly, as a culture hero. In the films of the late seventies, the (previously invisible) working class becomes a screen on which to project "old-fashioned" male virtues that are no longer socially acceptable or professionally useful within the middle class—physical courage and endurance, stubborn determination, deep loyalty among men. The working-class films of the seventies draw their glamor from nostalgic images of male strength, male beauty, and nonsexual male passion.

The Godfather and Its Godchildren

THE GODFATHER CLEARED the way for the late seventies genre of ethnic working-class films. *The Godfather* was, of course, about gangsters, not workers, but it introduced the social setting that would become familiar in *Mean Streets, Rocky I* and *II, Paradise Alley, Saturday Night Fever,* and the others: the working-class world as refracted through middle-class imagination. This world is intensely parochial, ethnically defined, and inward-looking. The great dramatic value of this new cinematic world lay in what it had to offer in redefining the masculine experience. The sixties genre of reckless-buddy films had burned out. Defiant machismo, cut loose from community or convention, was ultimately self-destructive; its exemplars ended up dead (like Butch Cassidy and the Sundance Kid) or lonely (like Little Fauss and Big Halsey). *The Godfather* retained the male bonding of the buddy films, but placed it in a *family* setting. It was a bridge between the old buddies and the new ethnic families, showing that masculinity and the family were not mutually exclusive.

The Godfather revives the ancient possibility of *patriarchy*: the family restored, the community recreated. It is still a man's world, not because women are excluded this time, but because men are secure enough to rule. It is a world where authority is vested in strong men, and young men must test their strength. But at the same time, *The Godfather* introduces Hollywood's fundamental ambivalence toward the patriarchal/ethnic setting and the masculine possibilities it represents. On the one hand, ethnic life was romanticized and celebrated over and against society at large. The ethnic enclave, the neighborhood, was the locus of community, and was used as the ground from which to criticize society. On the other hand, as the Corleone saga unfolds, the violent inwardness of the old-world community destroys its distinctive values, so that the larger society ultimately critiques the ethnic community. These changes are played out in the fortunes of the Corleone men.

Don Corleone (Marlon Brando) represents the bright side of patriarchy. He is commanding, but also nurturant, at home with drastic violence and at peace with his wife and kids. After decades of domesticated "dads," here at last is a *father* in the biblical sense. A few flashbacks to the ancestral home in Sicily remind us that we are only a generation and a steamship ticket away from a true patriarchal, agrarian society. Underneath their pinstripe suits and shoulder holsters, the Corleones are good-hearted peasants, and the wedding scene that opens *Godfather I* is suffused with rustic *gemeinschaft*. But none of this can last. Don Corleone is too befuddled by principle to keep up with modern business practices (he refuses to diversify into heroin). His eldest son, Sonny (James Caan), is too macho, emotional, "Italian," to manage the mob, or even survive. His second son, Fredo (John Cazale), is too weak and "feminine" to fill his shoes. His youngest, Dartmouth-educated son Michael (Al Pacino) is a whiz at business and does succeed his father, but he can't keep the family together. He represents authority without love, power unchecked by feudal restraints, and he ends up as desolate as any sixties loner, having killed his brother and banished his wife. When he slams the door in Diane Keaton's face at the end of *Godfather I*, we know this patriarchy has gone too far. In Don Corleone's three sons, patriarchy has deteriorated into three alternative male styles, and none of them will do. Here was the crisis in masculinity with a vengeance.

The heroes of the films we will look at in more detail occupy the same ethnic community, the same network of kin and male bonding connections first glamorized in *The Godfather*. Like the Corleones, most of them are Italian—an ethnic choice that (thanks to the prevailing stereotypes) not only evokes patriarchy but also seems to give artistic license to a level of emotional intensity that would be unlikely, if not unseemly, among, say, Finns or Norwegians. Locating the working class in an intensely ethnic scene reflects the persistent middle-class view that anyone still trapped in the working class must have just gotten off the boat. The working class is a residual category, a cul-de-sac for those who couldn't climb up and out.

Politically, these films fall into three categories: liberal, conservative, and ambivalent. The ambivalent films, such as *Breaking Away,* romanticize the neighborhood, or in this case the town, but give it up anyway to go on to something better. The liberal films, such as *Saturday Night Fever, Bloodbrothers,* and *The Wanderers,* embody a frank middle-class attack on working-class life, a "modern" attack on ethnic enclaves, and a "feminist" attack on machismo. Although they contain a strain of romanticism and nostalgia, the ethnic world of the neighborhood is seen as narrow and parochial compared to the liberal and humane values of the world-out-there. The extended family is either ridiculed or patronized as a hotbed of social pathology. Domesticated women are bad, while career-oriented, upwardly mobile, "liberated" women are good. Working-class men are basically pigs, and must learn to become more sensitive.

Conservative films romanticize the ethnic working-class community and the traditional masculine values it nurtures. Far from attacking the family, the neighborhood, the working class, and machismo as narrow, parochial, and stultifying, films like *Rocky I* and *II, Paradise Alley, Moment by Moment,* and *The Deer Hunter* cherish them and use romanticized images of them as a standpoint from which to assail society for being decadent and corrupt. They value traditionalism and attack "modern," melting-pot values, often in frankly racist and sexist terms.

In the following pages, we will discuss two liberal films, *Bloodbrothers* and *Saturday Night Fever,* and two conservative films, *Rocky I* and *Rocky II,* that offer contrasting attitudes toward class and ethnicity and suggest alternative approaches to the crisis of masculinity.

Bloodbrothers: Family Feud

IN ROBERT MULLIGAN'S *Bloodbrothers* (1979), the masculine alternatives are laid out with stark clarity: Stony De Coco (Richard Gere) can either be a "man," like his father, Tommy (Tony LoBianco), and his uncle (Paul Servino), or he can—in the film's terms—"grow up." In practical terms, Stony has to decide between following in his father's footsteps as a construction worker or defying his father to work as a children's recreation assistant in a hospital. It's a choice between two worlds. On the one side are the union and the family— patriarchal, parochial, but able to command the loyalty of blood: "The blood that runs in your veins—that's De Coco blood. You're ours!" Tommy De Coco bellows at his son. And the attractions of the blue-collar world are real: the barroom camaraderie, the joy of a job well done, the loving ties between the older men. When Stony goes to work with his father for the first time, the hard-hitting score reaches a crescendo as the camera pans dizzily upward at the shell of the half-constructed building. There is no particular dramatic point to this sudden surge of adrenalin (after all, people go to work every day)— the drumbeats celebrate masculinity itself, father and son united in a world of men.

On the other side is the unfamiliar middle-class world of social service, which allows a more nurturing, softer side of Stony's personality to emerge. Anticipating Dustin Hoffman's Kramer (of *Kramer vs. Kramer*), Stony finds that he likes nothing better than being with kids, hard as that is to explain to dad. "A recreation assistant? That's woman's work," Tommy scornfully tells his son. As in *Breaking Away*, the conflict between father and son centers on what is acceptable male behavior. Dave's (Dennis Christopher) father in *Breaking Away* shudders at his son's affinity for opera and draws the line when Dave (in imitation of Italian bicycle racers) shaves his legs. In both films, traditional masculinity—for all its allure—is constrictive. Feminization opens up a broader world.

In *Bloodbrothers*, as in other films of this genre, this message is articulated by a young supporting actress. Stony's girlfriend, Annette (Marilu Henner), was a social flop in high school because she "put out," but what was regarded as promiscuity a few years ago is now regarded as sexual liberation and defiance of hypocrisy. She makes Stony treat her like a human being, not a sex object, and tells him that she likes him because "you know there's something more out there besides playing cool, macho and getting laid. You could even go to college, get a degree." Against the ties of family and class she pits self-interest. "Worry about your own ass," she tells Stony, " 'cause your dad's is way outta reach."

A similar female figure passes through *The Wanderers*. She is herself middle class, inexplicably slumming among the film's ethnic youth gangs. At the end of the film, the hero is forced into an engagement with a neighborhood girl, but he bolts from his own party when he catches a glimpse of his true love walking outside. He follows her for two blocks and suddenly he's out of the Bronx and into Greenwich Village. She vanishes into a dimly lit club where a Dylan clone is singing "The Times They Are A-Changing." But not our hero, who knows he will never fit into his lost love's faintly androgynous, bohemian world. It's back to the trattoria under the wing of his Hawaiian-shirted, mafioso father-in-law.

But *Bloodbrothers*'s Stony *will* make it out. For him it's not the attraction of the middle-class world (represented by the hospital) that tips the balance, but the horrors of the ethnic enclave, particularly dad's macho madness. The world that was romanticized in *The Godfather* is condemned in *Bloodbrothers*. Underneath the expansive male solidarity of the barroom and construction site lies the family-as-nightmare. Stony's mother is a hysteric who has managed to induce anorexia nervosa in his frail younger brother. If the mother-son dining scenes are hard to take, the wife-beating scene is the last straw. Stony's father beats his wife senseless for a suspected infidelity. With this, Stony begins to see his family (and class) from the perspective of the doctor who has befriended him at the hospital: the people he has grown up with are little more than emergency-room regulars, professional outpatients. This was also the judgment of *A Woman Under the Influence* (1974) and *The Wanderers*: the working class may be a refuge for uninhibited masculinity but, viewed "objectively" by a professional (doctor or filmmaker), it's sick. Stony grabs his little brother and runs for it, taking a cab to the "feminized" middle class.

65

Saturday Night Fever: Breaking Away

SATURDAY NIGHT FEVER passes the same judgment, but with fewer second thoughts. *Bloodbrothers* gave at least equal time to the strengths of the male-bonded, ethnic working-class world it portrayed; *Saturday Night Fever* is almost uninterrupted critique. Tony Manero (John Travolta) lives out a nocturnal male-fantasy life in Bay Ridge, a white, mostly Italian community trapped between the glamor of Manhattan and the just out-of-reach prosperity of the suburbs beyond. At home, there's not even a towering patriarch to give zest to family life; Tony's parents are dreary, bickering, beaten-down souls. Work—as a clerk in a paint store—is even duller. All the music and color in the film are reserved for Tony's leisure life as the local disco king. Out on the dance floor, with the big beat and the pulsing lights, he struts out a stunning pantomime of male transcendence. Surrounded by his male buddies, followed by adoring girls, and buoyed up by the BeeGees, Tony Manero is *somebody*.

But Saturday night fever is followed by Monday morning blues. Almost conscientiously, the film shows us the ugly, "real" side of life in Bay Ridge. When Tony's not working or dancing, he's gang-fighting Puerto Ricans or gang-banging the girls on the block. In *Saturday Night Fever*'s version of working-class teen life, sex roles are tediously traditional: boys will be boys and girls will go down—or get lost. The only exception is Stephanie Mangano (Karen Gorney), a Bay Ridge girl who's had a whiff of "culture." She takes ballet lessons, reads books, and wants a career in the big city. Like Annette in *Bloodbrothers,* Stephanie articulates the film's critique of the dead-end, working-class setting. From her point of view, Tony may be good enough to work out with on the disco floor, but he has no more lasting appeal than a cold pizza.

Gradually Tony comes to share Stephanie's judgment of Bay Ridge. First he has to find out that his special world of disco is corrupt. The moment of truth comes when Tony realizes that the dance contest he and Stephanie have won was fixed by the club's Italian owners because they didn't want the prize to go to a Puerto Rican couple. The purity of Tony's disco world—where all that seemed to matter was grace and skill—has been infected with the neighborhood's ethnic parochialism. Indignantly, he crosses the club's color line and hands the trophy over to the couple who, regardless of race-color-or-creed, were the best dancers. The next jolt is not so easy to handle, even symbolically. Tensions among

Tony's gang erupt into drunken high-jinks on the Verrazano Narrows Bridge. When a friend falls to his death, Tony finally realizes that life in Bay Ridge—his nothing job, sitcom family, and dumb friends—is a dead end. Even disco dancers have feet of clay.

But Tony has one more lesson to learn. In the tradition of Bay Ridge courtship, he tries to rape Stephanie in the backseat of a car. To Tony's surprise, she is not grateful, but furious, and vanishes back to Manhattan. Bleary-eyed and repentant, he crosses the Brooklyn Bridge to find her and apologize. Thanks to Stephanie, his first glimpse of a "liberated" woman, he now understands that what was boyish in Bay Ridge is boorish in the borough of Manhattan. When Stephanie forgives him and lets him know that they will be friends, not lovers, he meekly accepts a role that would have been unthinkable only weeks earlier. Machismo was fun, but it's passé. If Tony is going to get anywhere, he'll have to drop the stud role and develop a more sensitive, "feminine" personality.

But for Tony, as for Stony De Coco, it's hard to see which way is up. We left Stony with the possibility of a low-paid social service job *if* he gets a college degree. *Saturday Night Fever* takes its hero to Manhattan but then doesn't know what to do with him. The film rehearses the melody of success, but, in the economy of 1978, it sounds flat. Since Tony can't do anything except dance and sell paint, it's hard to know how he'll make a living in the big city—short of a lucky opening at Arthur Murray's. But by not solving Tony's practical problem, the film gives its own kind of answer. Social mobility is redefined as personal growth, material success as self-actualization and human development. Tony must triumph over himself (at least over the unruly male parts of himself), because he cannot triumph over the world. Werner Erhard replaces Horatio Alger.

In both *Saturday Night Fever* and *Bloodbrothers*, the spokespeople for upward mobility and feminized masculinity are women, Annette and Stephanie. They are single women on the make, the kind who are punished for their independence by death in a conservative film like *Looking for Mr. Goodbar*. But they still play woman's perennial role in American folklore, as the tamer of men. In the films of the 1950s, domesticated women showed alienated or defiant men the way to adjustment. In these films of the 1970s, the "liberated" woman takes on the same task, chiding the men for their boyish machismo and prodding them to accede to the "realities" middle-class men have already accepted.

Rocky I and II: The Same Old Song

If Tony Manero has to get "softer," Rocky Balboa has the opposite project; as the score tells us, he's "getting stronger." Where *Bloodbrothers* and *Saturday Night Fever* repudiate the working-class, ethnic world, *Rocky I and II* romanticize it. Rocky himself, a thirty-year-old, over-the-hill fighter, is a noble savage, a natural man—Truffaut's Wild Child plopped down in south Philadelphia. Images of nature abound. Rocky keeps two turtles, whimsically named Cuff and Link, and a goldfish, and in *Rocky II* he buys a dog. He meets his wife in a pet store and proposes to her in a zoo. Even the fact that Rocky's employer (in *Rocky I*) is a gangster and Rocky's job is collecting bad debts doesn't taint the idyll one bit. The gangster is a benign, Runyonesque character, and Rocky doesn't have it in him to break any legs. In fact, Rocky's problem is that he's too sweet. If he wants to get anywhere in the cruel, cynical world beyond the neighborhood, he'll have to toughen up, get into shape, and learn what it means to be a man.

Rocky's neighborhood is used to judge society in the same way that the Ukrainian Catholic world of western Pennsylvania, with its vitality, quaint customs, and strong loyalties, is used to judge society in *The Deer Hunter* and Travolta's world is used to judge Lily Tomlin's world in *Moment by Moment*.* Tomlin's world is dominated by I. Magnin snobs who think Travolta is a delivery

---

Moment by Moment could be a conservative sequel to *Saturday Night Fever*. Six months after the first film ends, Stephanie has fallen in love with an up-and-coming ACLU lawyer or an East Side gynecologist, and Travolta, unable to dance fast enough to make ends meet in Manhattan, has split to California where food stamps grow on every tree. There he becomes a beach bum and parlays the sensitivity training he picked up from Stephanie and his working-class background into an exotic attraction for bored, upper-middle-class divorcées. The slum he comes from is not the dead end it was in *Saturday Night Fever,* but a romantic world of drug dealing and petty crime. It is not Travolta who is corrupt, but Tomlin. Although she has enough credit cards to stretch from Malibu to Montecito, her life is bankrupt.

boy; the world into which the boys in *The Deer Hunter* are thrust is dominated by Vietnamese portrayed as savages; the world Rocky enters is dominated by blacks.

The heavyweight champion of the world is Apollo Creed, a black man. Where Rocky is all innocence, Creed is all cynicism and greed. (Not all ethnic groups are equal.) Their first match is a bicentennial-year publicity stunt concocted by Creed, who likes the idea of dressing up like Uncle Sam and messing up an unknown who calls himself the "Italian Stallion." It's the white underdog against the black champ: as Michael Gallantz argued in *Jump Cut*, it is, or was, Bakke backlash time. In an early scene in *Rocky I*, Rocky finds that his locker at the gym has been given to a black fighter. "I wanna know how come I been put outta my locker," Rocky says angrily. "Because the Dipper needed it," Mickey the manager replies. "He's a contender. Know what you are? A tomato." The film's implicit statement, that blacks have gone too far, that they've unmanned decent, ordinary white guys like Rocky, is at least part of the reason for its box office success. For white audiences, racism gives the *Rockys* an illicit thrill.*

69

What it means to be a man in *Rocky II* is first to establish some authority at home. Unlike the protomanagerial Stephanie in *Saturday Night Fever*, Adrian has no ambitions of her own. She's not a habituée of singles bars; she's not trying to make it to the Mainline and get away from bums like Rocky. She's so shy and overwhelmed when Rocky first drops by the pet store to buy turtle food that she can hardly speak. After a few dates, her glasses disappear, the dark circles under the eyes evaporate, and her sallow complexion gives way to a rosy glow. Rocky is her first and only love, and although they make a premarital bed-stop, it leads

---

*In *Rocky II*, a black man lays Rocky off from his job in a meatpacking plant. He's not a bad guy, but white paranoia dictates that, in both *Rockys*, blacks have power over whites. With the exception of *Blue Collar*, blacks are strikingly absent from all these films, they just don't exist. Racism is most overt in *The Deer Hunter*, where Vietnamese play the role that Turks play in *Midnight Express*, or, to a lesser degree, Puerto Ricans in *Saturday Night Fever*. The only recent film with a black hero that makes a point of his blackness (as opposed, say, to Yaphet Koto in *Alien*) is *Dawn of the Dead*, a liberal film in which the hero helps defend the melting pot from the hungry diners at the other end of the table.

directly to marriage and a baby. But pregnancy brings a fleeting assertiveness. They're out of money and she wants to go back to work at the pet store. Rocky doesn't want any wife of his working, so he puts his foot down, but she does it anyway. Worse, she decides in *Rocky II* that she won't let Rocky fight Creed in a rematch. "It's all I know!" Rocky protests. "I never asked you to stop being a woman. Please don't ask me to stop being a man." During Adrian's nearly fatal childbirth, the doctor tells Rocky that the complications are probably due to Adrian's job. Rocky was right. After the due intervention of her brother and the Almighty, she changes her mind and decides to let Rocky fight. Rocky wins both bouts, but it's clear that the real battle is the one between the sexes.

In his training, too, it becomes clear that his real opponent is not Creed, but himself. Early on in *Rocky I,* Mickey (Burgess Meredith) tells Rocky that he had the makings of a champ but just didn't try hard enough. Unlike, say, *On the Waterfront,* where the mob prevents Brando's Terry Malloy from becoming a contender, here it's Rocky's own fault. He has a morale problem (and by implication, white men in general have let themselves go to seed, trading in their heritage for a mess of mortgages and Saturday night six-packs, while leaner, hungrier blacks crept into positions of power). In Rocky's struggle with himself, success is measured by the number of laps and push-ups he can do. The sporting action in *Rocky I* is not so much boxing as running, not Rocky versus Creed, but Rocky versus Rocky panting through the streets of Philadelphia. The real high point of *Rocky I* occurs not in the ring but when Rocky bounds up the grand steps of the Philadelphia Museum of Art, faces the city sprawled out before him, and triumphantly throws up his arms to the sky. The climax at the museum comes across as a working-class victory; the high-culture types may step on his toes, but he walks all over their steps. Ironically, though, Rocky's triumph is still cast in middle-class terms—he's not so much a boxer as a jogger.

The *Rockys* are success stories, showing that anyone can make it if he runs far enough. The vision of success they present is radically scaled down to meet the reduced aspirations of the 1970s. In the prosperous late forties and fifties, films just *assumed* that their heroes would succeed. The problem in films like *The Sweet Smell of Success* and *Will Success Spoil Rock Hunter?* was whether the heroes really wanted to succeed. In the great forties fight films *Body and Soul* and *Champion,* the heroes won as a matter of course. The catch was that on the way up they lost their humanity. But in the *Rockys,* success is so problematic that there's no room left to nitpick about morality. After all, it takes Rocky two films to beat Apollo Creed, and when he does, his victory is one of endurance and attrition rather than dazzling skill. There's no dramatic KO in the last round; instead, both fighters fall to the canvas exhausted. Rocky is the winner because only he is able to drag himself to his feet. Success, in Rocky's world as in *The Deer Hunter,* is not so much winning as surviving.

Masculinity and Class

THERE ARE TWO, already well-worn, critical approaches to these films (and others of the genre). One is to look at them as attempts at social realism. Then the question is one of accuracy or, more precisely, correspondence: to what extent does the working class presented in these films correspond to that of the critic's experience—or imagination? what groups have been left out? what is likely or unlikely to have really happened? The goal of this line of criticism is to find, or apprehend, the "real" working class, and thus to outdo Hollywood at its presumed project of *representation*.

A second approach is to look at them as attempts at social control, messages beamed from Hollywood's corporate owners to, presumably, the working class. For this approach, the movies themselves are barely necessary; the screenplay is an adequate text. "Read" in this way, the films offer nothing more surprising than the ambient clichés: self-mastery is preferable to or necessary for success in the world; happiness can only be achieved through personal "growth"; and so forth. But these messages reveal nothing new about bourgeois strategy for social control. In a culture already permeated by evangelical pop psychology, the textual messages of the films are barely audible above the background noise.

We have tried to take another approach, concentrating on the central metaphor that runs through these films. It is in most cases really a double metaphor, first linking traditional ideals of masculinity with the blue-collar working class, then identifying that class with a parochial, ethnic subculture. By calling this equation a metaphor, we deliberately wave away questions of "accuracy" (are working-class men really more macho, more parochial, et cetera?). But we do so with no apologies, for what the metaphor has to reveal is not about the class presumably portrayed in the films, but about the portrayers themselves—and the social group, neither working class nor ruling class, that they belong to. To look at the *metaphor* is to look through the screen, past the compelling images of blue-collar men, into the mind of the *middle-class* male.

In a metaphor, each term modifies the other and is transformed by the mutual association. Consider first what happens to the idea of class. The metaphor linking class to certain styles of masculine exhibitionism and ethnicized tastes obviously takes us a long way from the almost mythic conceptions of Marxism: the working class as the agent of revolution, class struggle as the motor force of history, and so on. If any term is diminished by the metaphor these films present us with, it is this one. Class differences do not reflect conflict and exploitation, only different sets of possibilities the characters can opt for or against, as individuals. The differences are "interesting," even—by virtue of being so long suppressed—faintly shocking, but they are no cause for indignation. Some people stand on assembly lines, others sit behind executive desks; some like Perrier, some like Bud. In the ultimate middle-class judgment of the seventies, the concept of class is politically void: class is *life-style*.

But as quickly as class is depoliticized, it is sexualized, and if any term is enhanced by the metaphor, it is masculinity. When masculinity is located in the working class of these films, it takes on new properties—a touch of violence, glimpses of brawn, an aura of primitivism. If class is trivialized, masculinity achieves mythic proportions. The films' *texts* may hand down negative judgments on the versions of maleness they present, but the camera rests lovingly on naked biceps, strained and sweating male faces, macho tantrums. It is not the apologetic Tony Manero of the final scene who captures our imagination, but the wonderfully vain Tony of the dance floor. Whatever emotive power resided in the notion of the working class as a whole (strength, or perhaps the threat of violence) has now been concentrated, in this middle-class metaphor, into the individual male. Even when the film's prescription is sensitivity and gentleness, the spectacle is raw, "old-fashioned" masculinity.

What makes men—or this particular male possibility—so spectacular? We have already talked about the displacement of "unacceptable" male impulses—homoerotic, misogynistic, violent—to the collective fantasy world of the screen. But the pull of the "tough guy" is not simply sexual (in whatever sense these various impulses could be considered sexual). If the middle-class male imagination returns again and again, with anxiety and fascination, to images of men who are neither domesticated nor "sensitized," it is not only because they offer a pleasant break from repression. The seductive power of masculine imagery—for women as well as men—lies in its evocation of *defiance*: the underdog who beats incredible odds, the sullen adolescent who kicks beer cans (and clingy girls) out of his path, the tough guy who doesn't take shit from anyone. It is, in almost all the film versions, a defiance that falls far short of resistance—it is a politics of gesture and tone of voice. In real life women may be the rebels (including such unlikely subjects for Hollywood as elderly black women), but women lack the conventional mannerisms of defiance. They are attractive when they simper, not when they swagger.

To return to the metaphor presented by the "working-class" films: if class has been depoliticized, masculinity has, in an odd sense, been politicized. Defiant masculinity is the only subversive force left on this cinematic landscape. Linked to the working class, it gains a special cachet. In a curious inversion of reality, the working-class male seems to possess the autonomy the middle class feels it has lost. He gives "only" his body to the corporate endeavor, not (unlike the adman, executive, or even filmmaker) his mind and talent. And he leaves work for a world that is not yet penetrated and defined by the market—the neighborhood bar, the extended family, the women supposedly still innocent of feminist ambition. The "working-class" genre of films gives us the seventies' most powerful cultural image of defiance—the young working-class male, jacket slung over his shoulder, cigarette drooping from one corner of his mouth, arrogantly beautiful.

73

But the final term in the metaphor—ethnicity—qualifies even this limited image of defiance. White ethnic identity, no matter how relentlessly romanticized, has a vestigial quality. These are people who, from the camera's cosmopolitan vantage point, have not *yet* been fully assimilated, not *yet* left the urban neighborhoods for the mass anonymity of the suburbs or high-rise apartments downtown. Hollywood's defiant working-class male occupies a world whose time has gone by. It is the historical past, before the factories had run away and the parish churches had given up on Sunday morning attendance. And it is, at a subconscious level, the personal past: the world of early childhood, with its narrow boundaries, intense frustrations, towering male figures. If Hollywood was drawn to its glamorized working-class male out of a kind of secret admiration, it draws back with a sigh of nostalgia. In the end, middle-class smugness triumphs over male anxiety: the working-class male, so alluring in his small gestures of defiance, is ultimately an anachronism. Some boys, the films tell us, just never grow up.

BLUE COLLAR BLUES

PROLETARIAN CINEMA
FROM HOLLYWOOD

Three years ago, during a strike of screenwriters, Paul Schrader was brought up on charges by the Writers Guild for calling the strike "hooey," and vilifying his colleagues as "a bunch of uneducated artists who like to think of themselves as proletariat." Recently, in New York, he was overheard ridiculing the idea of boycotting the Shah of Iran's caviar party thrown in honor of the New York Film Festival. The last film he scripted, *Taxi Driver,* would have brought a blush to the cheek of Joseph Goebbels for its unabashed infatuation with psychotic violence.

Blue Collar was ripped off from a black screenwriter named Sydney A. Glass, who foolishly came to Schrader with his idea. According to *Cineaste* magazine, Schrader subsequently paid Glass off with $15,000, a screen credit, and 1 1/2 percent of the film to stay on his own side of the street. Glass did, and Schrader went on to make the best film about work and workers since the '30s.

Schrader's militantly anti-left, apolitical stance makes him an unlikely choice to do a film like this, and apparently no one was more surprised than Schrader himself. He told *Cineaste* that he "didn't set out to make a Marxist film," but while he was working on the script, he "realized it had come to a very specific Marxist conclusion.

It seemed the only way to end it." Well, beggars can't be choosers, so we had better not look this gift horse in the mouth.

Richard Pryor, Yaphet Kotto, and Harvey Keitel play three close friends, auto workers who are mortgaged to the hilt and only one jump ahead of the credit company. They're pinned to jobs they hate by the deadweight of the good life—split-level houses, color TVs—that presses down on them like the yellow smog that hangs heavily over the city of Detroit. They're prisoners of the assembly line; "plant is just short for plantation," as Pryor puts it.

The shop steward, a union man who's supposed to represent the rank and file, is a smooth politician on the way up. Pryor, Kotto, and Keitel expect to be screwed by the company, but the union officials' single-minded dedication to lining their own pockets is a constant affront. The three friends hate the union more than management, and for a few quick bucks, they knock over the union safe. But crime doesn't pay, except maybe for Pryor. He's promoted to shop steward in exchange for squealing on his pals. Kotto's killed in an "industrial accident" arranged by the union, and Keitel is driven into the arms of the FBI by union thugs.

Blue Collar ends with Pryor and Keitel at each other's throats frozen in postures of violence. It is a violence that, for once, is not the point, but the means to a point. Schrader intervenes with Brechtian boldness, stopping the action to underline a moral which, because it is the logical outcome of plot and character, has the beauty of irrefutable syllogism. We hear Kotto's voice, a commentary on this tableau, repeating something he said earlier in the film: "Everything they do, the way they pit the lifers against the new boys, the old against the young, the black against the whites, is meant to keep us in our place." That is didactic cinema at its best.

One reason that Schrader's touch of Brecht works so well is that *Blue Collar* is a political cliff-hanger until the very end. We don't know where it's going to come down, and Schrader harnesses his ambivalence to make the last shot a knockout. Pryor, who gives a funny and bitterly savage performance, plays the most "political" character. He wants to make changes in the union so things will be better. When he's given the chance, he sells out, and it looks like Schrader's telling us that militants are phonies; they're just using politics for their own ends. Yet Kotto, who does look out for himself and thinks Pryor is naive ("Politics don't change shit. It's money."), gets himself killed.

Keitel is a Polish John Garfield, just a regular joe trying to get by. He has neither Pryor's quickness nor Kotto's street smarts and physical presence. He's got integrity, but he's scared. When he finally sings to the FBI (the FBI, for some reason, is after the corrupt union local), it looks for a moment like we're back in the '50s watching Elia Kazan squeeze a confession out of Marlon Brando in *On the Waterfront*. It seems that Schrader is telling us that we've got to trust Uncle Sam to protect our interests.

Schrader is a bit confused, so he's telling us a little of everything. He doesn't like the unions, but he doesn't think they can be changed, especially by the rank and file who are so dumb they rob their own local's safe and then botch the job. But somehow, the film has eluded Schrader's own political limitations. It is an Aesopian fable, a case study in carrot-and-stick political pacification. Pryor, Keitel, and Kotto are pawns of the system, which divides and conquers. The irreconcilable elements (Kotto) are destroyed, while the "reasonable" elements (Pryor) are bought off and the weak ones (Keitel) are fatally compromised.

It is true that the film is guilty of sexual stereotyping (Kotto is a black stud and in one obligatory orgy scene he turns some fancy tricks) and sexism (the women are no more than ciphers), and it is also true that life on the line is much worse than it appears here. Checker Cabs, where the film was shot, produces about fifty cars a day, whereas the Big Three automakers produce more like fifty cars an hour. Nevertheless, most Hollywood films stare with a fixed gaze at the upper-middle class. *Blue Collar* doesn't, and for this we can be thankful.

Nobody wins in *Blue Collar*; it's a cynical, but not a pessimistic film, because it holds out the possibility that blacks and whites together can prevail. It's a teaching film, and like all films with a lesson, it is predicated on the assumption that people can learn. Schrader may have thought his characters were jerks, but they don't come off that way. Pryor, Kotto, and Keitel are so good, the script so electric, the images of racial accommodation so strong, that we can't help but feel that the friendship among these three men holds within it the seeds of rebellion. *Blue Collar*'s losers aren't victims because they're smart, tough, resilient, and above all, truthful. The audience cheered when I saw the film because they recognized themselves on the screen and liked what they saw. They liked the energy, the slashing, foulmouthed wit, and the promise, however muted, that things can be better.

HOLOCAUST FEVER

NBC's 9 1/2 hour mini-series, *Holocaust,* was an inspired marriage of convenience between commerce and conscience. It was at once a public service, educating a generation which knows little of the Nazis' crimes against the Jews, and at the same time a brilliant stroke of merchandising, intended to arrest the network's failing fortunes by hitching them to the destruction of European Jewry. It was NBC's answer to ABC's *Roots;* it was a *succes d'estime* that, by the nature of its subject, virtually foreclosed criticism. Now that the dust has settled and NBC has stopped patting itself on the back, let's see what we were sold.

The Selling of the Holocaust

THE HOLOCAUST HAS been a very good business indeed. NBC's version has spun off a number of products, including a sound track recording and a novelization, written by Gerald Green and published by Bantam. It went through nine printings in three weeks, sold 1,750,000 copies, and is well on its way towards becoming the Jewish *Jaws,* as one industry observer, with questionable taste, described the phenomenon. *Holocaust* is now number three on the best seller list, has been chosen as an alternate selection by the Doubleday Book Club and the Literary Guild and is being syndicated by the Newspaper Enterprise Association.

Bantam Books, which stands to make a pretty penny off the sales, is owned by a German firm, the Bertelsmann Publishing Group, which in turn is controlled by one Reinhard Mohn and family. Herr Mohn, according to the *New York Times*, was a lieutenant in the Afrika Korps and spent a good part of World War II interned as a prisoner of war in a detention camp near Concordia, Kansas. Another chunk of Bantam belongs to the Agnelli Group of Italy. Italy was, you may recall, the second of what used to be known in simpler times as the Axis countries. If you watched *Holocaust* on your Japanese Sony TV, the circle is complete. First the Axis annihilated as many Jews as they could; then they sell the story back to those who are left.

The show was cleverly sandwiched between Vanessa Redgrave's fortuitous (for NBC) remarks at the Academy Award ceremonies and the beginning of Passover; it also managed to touch two other bases, Hitler's birthday and the thirty-fifth anniversary of the Warsaw Ghetto Uprising.

NBC stood to make at least $5,000,000 off the series by selling 130 thirty-second spots for $45,000 each, "a tidy profit for the network," observed *Variety*, "no matter what the ratings turn out to be." An NBC spokesperson, when asked about profits, declared loftily, "We never discuss money."

NBC, intoxicated with its own virtues, has been doing its best to conceal the commercial side of this venture behind a smokescreen of moral uplift, portraying itself as a lone beacon of righteousness in a fog of ignorance and bigotry. When a handful of The-Holocaust-Was-A-Hoax cranks picketed NBC studios in New York, NBC News gave them VIP coverage and bravely announced that "The Program has been universally praised by religious leaders and NBC is proud to present it." (Last month's 15,000-person Bakke demonstration in Washington apparently never happened, as far as NBC is concerned.) It it easy, of course, to expose the brutality of others in faraway places many years ago, but it might have been easier to buy the network's line if it had spoken out just as strongly against the violation of human rights in various American client states or, God forbid, right here at home.

NBC's snowjob was eagerly abetted by the press in an avalanche of advance flackery. The *New York Post,* shamelessly pandering to its large Jewish audience, led the pack. For *Post* columnist Harriet Van Horne, the series was a test of American moral fiber. "How Americans respond to this $5 million drama will tell the world much about our soundness of spirit and goodness of heart," she burbled. "*Holocaust* comes at the crest of a rising wave of anti-Semitism in this country." This may or may not be true. The Anti-Defamation League, which notices these things, recently estimated that there are no more than 1,200 Nazis in this country and called them "politically impotent." Many traditionally right wing groups are becoming increasingly pro-Israel, like the fourteen evangelical ministers who took out full-page ads in support of Israel last November, or Billy Hargis of the Christian Crusade and Carl McIntyre of the 20th Century Reformation Hour, both of whom spoke fondly of Israel after the Six Day War. The same week *Holocaust* was aired, a group of well-known hawks, including Admiral E.R. Zumwalt, Jr., John P. Roche and Major General George J. Keegan, Jr., placed a full-page ad in the *New York Times* calling Israel a "matchless strategic asset." Quite a coincidence.

No sooner had TV critic Van Horne implied that anyone who preferred to watch *Laverne and Shirley* was spiritually bankrupt and probably a closet anti-Semite than Tom Shales, also in the *Post,* wrote that the future of television, no less, depended on the success of *Holocaust.* "We are at a crossroads," he announced grandly. "This is a pivotal moment for television. The ratings of *Holocaust* could affect programming decisions for years to come. . . . If it fails in the ratings, that would be the death knell for serious subject matter on television. And that would be tragic." Indeed.

In the face of moral blackmail like this, it was virtually impossible to take issue with the show. Watching *Holocaust* was like being held hostage by the Jewish Defense League, a prisoner of its chauvinist, Old Testament ideology.

PETER BISKIND

The War of the Stick People

WHEN *HOLOCAUST* WAS attacked, it was on the grounds that it was a soap opera. Elie Wiesel, a survivor of the Holocaust, called it "untrue, offensive, cheap . . . an insult to those who perished. . . . It transforms an ontological event into soap opera." But director Marvin Chomsky knows he's making soap operas and he's proud of it. "Soap opera has turned on human misery ever since I was a kid," he told the *Post,* "and it remains popular." (Chomsky, who was also responsible for six out of twelve hours of *Roots,* is fast becoming the Stanley Kramer of TV. Kramer is best remembered for well-intentioned, badly-executed films on Big Issues like *Guess Who's Coming to Dinner* and *Judgment at Nuremburg.* Film critic Stanley Kauffmann once compared Kramer to an Eskimo mother who pre-chews her childrens' food for easier digestion.)

Well, what's wrong with soap operas? Aren't they a genuine form of popular culture? They wouldn't be so popular if they didn't hit a responsive chord, right?

The problem with soap operas is that they reduce complex issues to black and white stereotypes and then manipulate audiences toward the desired responses. Like much traditional narrative, they carry concealed messages. By squeezing the unspeakable Nazi atrocities against the Jews into a soap opera format ("Can a boy from a nice Jewish family find happiness in the face of genocide?"), Chomsky not only betrays the "authenticity" of the experience, as Wiesel puts it, he also tailors "the lessons of the past" to the requirements of contemporary conservative Zionist politics.

What are the politics of *Holocaust*? Although the idea of a Jewish homeland is kept discreetly in the background, its absence is the "meaning" of the film. The Holocaust becomes the prehistory of Israel. At the same time that Israel is made to seem the logical result of the Holocaust, the *Holocaust* validates and legitimizes almost anything the Israelis choose to do.

The heroic figures in the film are all Zionists; they are the ones willing to fight, the ones with the dream of the Jewish homeland in their hearts. In one scene, the Zionist hero tells the craven Jewish Council of the Warsaw Ghetto: "If you are too cowardly to give the orders to fight, the Zionists will." But many Zionists were far from willing to fight. They were preoccupied with negotiating with the Nazis to buy the freedom of the European Jews. Among those who were ready to fight, there were many who were not Zionists at all. According to Lucy Dawidowicz' classic study, *The War Against the Jews,* the resistance was conducted by an alliance of young Zionists (many of whom were socialists), non-Zionist Labor Bundists, and Jewish socialists and communists who did not envision a Jewish homeland but thought of themselves as Poles or Germans. Choosing to caricature and depoliticize the complex relations between the various resistance groups by giving the Zionists a monopoly on resistance makes resistance and Zionism synonymous.

The first lesson the film teaches is that Jews cannot depend on anyone but themselves. Over and over again they are betrayed not only by the Germans but also by Lithuanians, Ukrainians, Poles and so on. The obvious contemporary corollary of this is that Israel must depend solely on its own strength of arms, not on treaties guaranteed by other (unreliable) nations.

The second lesson is that Jews must learn to pick up the gun. Not only is the willingness to fight necessary for survival, it will also be necessary in the future, to secure the Jewish state. One character tells another: Palestine, "the land the Zionists want . . . is in a desert, surrounded by Arabs. You think you're going to get that without a fight, without killing and being killed?"

Moreover, learning to fight is fun, a rite of manhood and the key to genuine racial identity. In one scene, the brother of the patriarch, Josef Weiss, whose family's fortunes the film traces, fires on the Germans from the window of a building in the Warsaw ghetto. While spraying the streets with bullets, he cries happily: "For the first time in my life I feel the blood of King David in me." This scene does more than ask us to cheer the long-overdue death of a few German soldiers: it is no less than an attempt to transform Jews from a race of victims to a race of warriors.

The same transformation occurs on the individual level as well. Rudi, Josef Weiss's youngest son, survives the Holocaust and is last seen smuggling a bunch of Jewish kids through the British blockade to Palestine. Karl, Weiss's oldest son, perishes in Auschwitz. Rudi is a fighter and, as played by boyishly handsome Joseph Bottoms, is indistinguishable from any all-American Joe College. Karl, on the other hand, as played by James Woods, is the sensitive, guilt-ridden, neurotic Jewish artist. He dies not only because he is killed by the Nazis, but because be is associated with traditional Jewish traits that the Jewish right wing finds embarrassing. Rudi lives, not only because he is a fighter, but because in effect *he's not Jewish;* he's divested himself of those same traits. To put it starkly, the strong survive and the weak die. *Holocaust* quietly endorses or internalizes a kind of Social Darwinism not too different from the Nazi racial theories it overtly attacks.

There are reasons other than political why *Holocaust* is somewhat less than a triumph. The performances are poor to bad. One of the leads, Michael Moriarity, who plays Erik Dorf, the John Dean of the SS, is a disaster. He delivers his lines in a strangulated squeak, suggesting that the collar of his SS tunic is perhaps too tight. The other Nazis, with the single exception of ravaged David Warner as Heydrich, the "Blond Beast," are the familiar Hollywood stereotypes, cynical, cowardly or diabolical, by turns.

The Jews, the Weiss family and their friends, are uniformly noble. Nazis and Jews alike are forced to mouth the same wooden lines. (Samples: "Who cares, we have each other"; "You're the prettiest girl in all Germany"; "I need someone to hold, someone to talk to.") Scenes of indescribable horror—naked people being machine-gunned into ditches, gassed, beaten—are punctuated regularly by commercials selling "Snoopy Sniffer's" Lysol Deodorant Cleanser, Efferdent stubborn blueberry stains between your teeth in minutes"), Free Spirit Fanny Briefs and so on. To see the grim history of the Jews reduced to the stock situations of a pulp novel by the heavy hands of director Chomsky and writer Gerald Green and then spoon-fed to a starving audience by the good graces of NBC and their stable of sponsors is indeed a depressing spectacle.

It may be true, as Elie Wiesel says, that fiction cannot do justice to the Holocaust, that we must rely on documentaries like Alain Resnais' *Night and Fog* to tell the tale that cannot be told, but we can't judge from Chomsky's version, because it isn't fiction, it's junk. On balance, it is probably better that it was aired than not. As was said about *Roots* and *King,* it will serve as a springboard for further study, but why do we always have to choose between the lesser of two evils, between knowing nothing or learning something in a debased and fraudulent fashion?

"COME BACK TO THE MILL, NICK HONEY"

THE DEER HUNTER MISSES THE TARGET

Michael Cimino's new film *The Deer Hunter* is the Vietnam film everyone has been waiting for—finally, a film that "gets beyond" the propaganda of right-wing films like *The Green Berets* and left-wing films like *Coming Home*. As Tweedledee and Tweedledum put it, "this is the first movie about Vietnam to free itself from all political cant" (*Time*); this "is the first film to look at Vietnam not politically, but . . ." (*Newsweek*). Trying to depoliticize a phenomenon as deeply rooted in American history and character as the Vietnam war would be a thankless task, like squaring the circle, but if anyone could do it, it would be somebody like Cimino, who—along with John Milius and Paul Schrader—is one of Hollywood's New Wave, fast-lane writer-directors. *Time/Newsweek* has hit the nail on the head. *The Deer Hunter* offers an escape from politics. It slices through all that tiresome debate about who was right and who was wrong to something that everyone can understand: plain old racism. It was Us—white American boys—against Them—yellow Asian savages. The Yanks versus the Gooks. That simple. Like the enormously successful *Midnight Express, The Deer Hunter* mines one of the richest seams in the bedrock of American mythology: the innocent abroad—the Jamesian heiress, Wilson at Versailles—beset, beleaguered, betrayed.

The Eden whence these pilgrims set forth is a steel town called Clairton tucked away in the hills of Pennsylvania. The first third or so of the film is devoted to a double celebration: A wedding party for Steven (John Savage) is also a going-away-party for him and the two friends—Nick (Christopher Walken) and Michael (Robert De Niro)—who are to ship out with him the next day for Vietnam. This wedding ceremony is so lavishly and lengthily rendered as to make the Corleone wedding that kicks off *The Godfather* look like a City Hall quickie. Every gesture is lovingly captured with majestic swooping camera movements; each ethnic tic of these Eastern European, working-class folk is relentlessly registered with such fidelity that the festivities become bigger than life, become heavy with symbolic weight. Such is the fascination that the artifacts of this subculture exercises over the camera that a can of Rolling Rock beer is invested with sacramental significance. This is America before the revolution, before the Fall. This is the final act of the postwar drama of power, innocence, and affluence, the end of the American century.

Cut to choppers hovering over a cluster of thatched huts in the dense green Vietnamese jungle. A Vietcong soldier tosses a hand grenade into the midst of women and children crouched in a bomb shelter. Michael, outraged by this barbarism, zaps the soldier with a flamethrower. The next moment, he, Nick, and Steven are captured. A Vietcong soldier facing the camera puts a gun to the head of a South Vietnamese prisoner to our right. We see a replica of the notorious UPI photograph of Nguyen Ngoc Loan, chief of South Vietnam's National Police, putting a bullet through the head of a prisoner, an icon of the depravity of the South burned into the minds of almost everyone who saw it. Only here, it is the Vietcong soldier about to shoot a South Vietnamese prisoner. About to shoot—he pulls the trigger and nothing happens, thus launching the metaphor which is to dominate the remainder of the film. The sadistic Vietnamese, like the slavering Turks in *Midnight Express,* shout gibberish at American boys and make them play Russian roulette, while they bet on the outcome. Meanwhile, more American boys, bloody and half-dead, are held prisoner in bamboo cages submerged in water. As they look on helpless, heavy gravid rats lumber across their bodies.

Michael survives all this, orchestrating an heroic, if improbable escape. Not only does he survive, he takes his pals with him, gulling, tugging, dragging them to safety. But it's too late. Steven loses both legs; Nick loses his mind, disappearing A.W.O.L. into Saigon to play Russian roulette for the amusement of bug-eyed Asians.

Michael goes home, but he had promised Nick before they left that whatever happened, he wouldn't leave him in Vietnam. So he goes back—searching through the human refuse of Saigon on the edge of defeat. Again, it's too late. As it began on Steve's wedding, the film ends on Nick's funeral. After the burial, the survivors—Michael, Steve, Nick's girl Linda (Meryl Streep), and their friends—sit around a table at the local bar singing "God Bless America." Not a bad image for the end of the Vietnam decade: Americans, older if not wiser, huddled together, chastened quiet, but still proud.

The Deer Hunter has to be judged harshly because of the boldness with which it upends the historical record and the power with which it manipulates its audience. It is a lie from beginning to end. True, the North Vietnamese and the Provisional Revolutionary Government (PRG) may have, on occasion, killed civilians, but no one claims that they could have won without the sympathy of the people. My Lai was, after all, an American atrocity. Bach Mai Hospital was bombed by Americans, not Vietnamese. It was Americans who used carpet bombs, anti-personnel weapons, defoliants, and napalm. The Christmas bombing of Hanoi was conducted by Nixon and Kissinger, not by Pham Van Dong. It was the South that used tiger cages, not the North. It was Nguyen Ngoc Loan who shot his prisoner, not the reverse. Judged narrowly, *The Deer Hunter* is little more than Pentagon propaganda. It is a criminal violation of truth; Michael Cimino, little better than the Nazi apologists who deny the Holocaust ever happened.

Some people defend *The Deer Hunter* with the argument that it is not about the war at all, but a retelling of Conrad's *Heart of Darkness*. It is certainly true that Cimino's film is not really anticommunist, since the South Vietnamese are as barbaric as the North Vietnamese. The film's racism is indeed apolitical, overwhelms ideology. Particularly memorable is the contrast between the scenes set in the final days of Saigon—terrified Asians frantically scrambling to board American planes and ships—and the scenes of Michael—careless of himself and motivated by the code of friendship—returning to Saigon.

To the extent that *The Deer Hunter* is a retelling of Conrad's tale, it could have taken place in Africa, New Guinea, or Brazil, anywhere there are savages. The Vietnamese and their war are merely a backdrop for the moral drama of white Americans, the only people civilized enough to matter. The Vietnamese are not only dehumanized, they are derealized, reduced to metaphor.

But *The Deer Hunter* is not about the "heart of darkness" either, or at least not only about it. The film fairly throbs with a passionate, deeply felt male eroticism, and if it is about anything, it is about doomed male love. Michael Cimino's first film, *Thunderbolt and Lightfoot,* is a boy-meets-boy bank-heist film in which there is also strong, barely submerged homoeroticism. Clint Eastwood and Jeff Bridges play male variants of Romeo and Juliet: These star crossed lovers can't get it on because they are both men. They care a lot more about each other than for any of the women in the film; indeed, the film is unusual for its frank and undisguised contempt for heterosexuality. Heterosexual lovers are repeatedly humiliated—bound and gagged together naked, ridiculed, and so on. Meanwhile, Bridges and Eastwood kid each other about being gay, snuggle up to each other in a drive-in to evade the cops, and tenderly exchange cigars before Bridges, half beaten to death by a jealous pal of Eastwood, dies.

In *The Deer Hunter,* women are entirely peripheral not only to the action, but to the feeling among the young men—the real emotional center of the film. Michael is markedly uninterested in women. Meryl Streep, who gives a good performance without much to work with, tries with indifferent success to arouse him, and there is one brief love scene distinguished less by its passion than by its awkward, perfunctory nature. Pushing this point a little further, it would not be too far-fetched to conclude that the reason Michael survives, and Steven and Nick don't, is that Michael is sexually most pure. Steven is married, and Nick has a girl. Michael's pal Stanley (John Cazale) is the only one of the group actively interested in women, and he's portrayed as a jerk. He's immature and undisciplined, a bit to one side of the male bonding that unites the others.

This theme is not hidden. Stanley accuses Michael of being a "faggot" on several occasions, and Michael finally tells Nick "I love you" in the climactic scene. The best, most moving moments are among the men: hunting, fighting, drinking. In one scene, Michael tears off his clothes and falls against a metal pole, finally ending up on the ground, naked, back-to-back with Nick. You don't have to be a Kraft-Ebing to know which way the wind is blowing. Nick dies and Steven is castrated (he loses his legs) not because of the Vietnamese, but because in Cimino's world, male love is doomed, the return to society, marriage, and family is death to these men. Michael will probably go on to wed Linda, but this will be an anticlimax. These were the best years of their lives.

One of the best things about this film is the resonance the relationships have. We recognize them and, especially if we are men, respond to the sense of lost innocence with which they are suffused. But we can't admire them, and the film never rises above the Hardy Boys virtues it celebrates.

One more point. Paulene Kael in *The New Yorker* has called attention to the Germanic flavor of *The Deer Hunter*. There are two hunting scenes in the film; after the first, the guys return to the bar, one of them plays a Chopin nocturne on the piano. "Beer sloshers savage breasts are soothed by music," Kael writes, "it's too much like those scenes in which roomfuls of Hitler's lieutenants all swooned to Wagner." All that's missing is the lederhosen. Meryl Streep, as Kael notices, "has the clear-eyed blond handsomeness of a Valkyrie." There's a steamy shower scene in the mill that is right out of G.W. Pabst's *Kameradschaft*. Michael cavorts on mist-shrouded mountain peaks, the slopes falling away around him in precipitous drops, while a heavenly chorus bellows Russian Orthodox chants on the sound track. He's like the romantic hero of Werner Herzog's *Heart of Glass*; the scenes recall the mountain films made in pre-Hitler Germany. According to German film historian Siegfried Kracauer, those films, with their enthusiasm for heights, rocks, glaciers, and dramatic cloud formations, expressed contempt for the ordinary mortals, the "valley-pigs" as they were called, who couldn't make the climbs. "In the opening sequence of the Nazi documentary *Triumph of the Will* . . . cloud masses surround Hitler's airplane . . . reveal[ing] the ultimate fusion of the mountain cult and the Hitler cult."

Michael indeed triumphs through will and discipline. Nick calls him a "control freak." He's not quite one of the boys, but a distant, somewhat myserious *Ubermensch*. If the term "fascist" weren't so threadbare, so overworked, it would be tempting to call Cimino (he worked on the script of *Dirty Harry*) our first, home-grown fascist director, our own Leni Riefenstahl. When Michael gets tired of telling war stories about the good old days in Nam to his drinking buddies, he just might amuse himself by organizing a Bund in the Pennsylvania hills.

All told, *The Deer Hunter* is a very distressing film. Its mixture of repressed homoeroticism, violence, and patriotism embrace the very worst aspects of American culture, those that led to Vietnam in the first place. Its popularity and warm reception by the critics indicate a failure to consolidate whatever progress was made in the '60s toward confronting the underside of our national life. *The Deer Hunter* resolutely turns its face from the lessons of Vietnam and marches backwards into the heart of darkness.

A BALANCE OF ERROR?

PBS'S *VIETNAM*:
WAIST-DEEP IN THE BIG MUDDY

Way back in 1974, when Peter Davis's Academy Award-winning documentary on Vietnam, *Hearts and Minds,* hit the screen, mainstream critics attacked it for taking cheap shots at Nixon and the Nixonoids, for tendentious editing, for insulting the intelligence of its viewers. They wanted more "balance."

Here at last is the film they called for, a thirteen-part, $4.6 million, six-years-in-the-making "definitive" examination of the war. (Complementing it are a 700-plus-page history by Stanley Karnow, transcripts, study guides and audio cassettes—a comprehensive educational package designed for home study and classroom use.) *Vietnam: A Television History,* a production of PBS's Boston affiliate, with help from Britain's Central Independent Television and France's Antenne 2, not only looks at the war from the American, South Vietnamese and North Vietnamese perspectives but within these gives us a spectrum of views ranging from policy makers and generals at the top to G.I.s and Vietnamese villagers at the bottom.

The principle of balance even dictates the film's structure and the editing strategy. Antiwar filmmakers of yesteryear made their points by juxtaposing official rhetoric with gruesome reality. In *In the Year of the Pig,* for example, Emile de Antonio cut from Gen. William Westmoreland claiming that prisoners of war were being treated in accordance with the Geneva Conventions to a Vietcong suspect being repeatedly clubbed with the butt of a rifle. *Vietnam* is much more restrained. Shot B more often illustrates shot A than contradicts it. And when B does contradict A, it doesn't mean that we are to question A, merely that reality is sufficiently complex to accommodate many points of view.

Vietnam has received rave notices in the press. Critics know balance when they see it, and they have praised the film for allowing viewers to make up their own minds about the questions it raises. On the face of it, this response seems right. It's not unreasonable to assume that a series released eight years after the war's end might be more informative and judicious than films made in anger at the height of the fighting. But do the multiple perspectives add up to the truth, or do they merely enable the film to hide behind a smokescreen of bogus "fairness," "impartiality," "objectivity"? Are the films really balanced? What are the parameters of the debate? Which participants and what points of view are excluded? And finally, is not the principle of balance itself an ideological artifact, a means by which the political center (which, after all, presided over the war) tries to defuse criticism from the "extremes," the right and the left?

For starters, let's take the centerpiece of the fifth show, the decimation of the village of Thuybo, near Danang, by American Marines in January 1967. British producer Martin Smith stumbled on the story during a visit to Vietnam in 1981. According to an account in *The Times* of London, Smith was told by his hosts that My Lais were a dime a dozen. They took Smith to Thuybo, where he interviewed a number of people who described the slaughter of about a hundred women and children. Smith apparently felt he had a scoop—a bloody massacre of My Lai proportions. But the American producers chose to present it from both sides—as experienced by the G.I.s and the villagers. According to Pvt. Jack Hill and his buddies, the Vietcong in the village opened up with .50-caliber machine guns, pinning down his unit in the rain for a day and a night. After three days without water, food or sleep, the Marines stormed the village. The surviving Vietnamese claimed they shot everything that moved.

"Some of the wounded people went to their beds to lie down," recalls Nguyen Bay. "The soldiers shot their ears. Blood was coming out in pools as they lay there. Then the soldiers shot at their stomachs and their insides splattered all over. Then they smashed people's heads, using the butts of their guns." According to Private Hill, on the other hand, "I know half of the guys in the squad didn't shoot no old ladies and kids." But, he continues, "I can't account for every Marine that was there and what they done at that particular time, because . . . that's what they had to do." As Sgt. Thomas Murphy puts it in the next segment, "An eight-year-old or a nine-year-old can kill you just as quick as a twenty-five- or twenty-six-year-old man." If the Marines did kill the kids, maybe they were right. Hill sums it up: "It's just normal procedure. . . . It was war."

Was it a massacre or not? We'll never know from this film, because it tries so hard not to take sides. The result? Leftists will hear the Vietnamese and conclude there was a massacre. Rightists will hear the G.I.s and conclude there wasn't, or if there was, it was justified by the circumstances of war. Centrists will hear both and conclude that since there was justice on both sides, it was a tragedy for which no one was ultimately responsible. As Karnow put it in an interview included in the press kit that accompanies his book, "Whatever you think of the war, whether it was right or wrong, you have to conclude that it was a terrible tragedy."

But the film's refusal to declare itself is suspect, to say the least. What, after all, constitutes balance? The numerical distribution of points of view, the placement of shots? It certainly can't be the former, because of the twenty-one statements we hear on Thuybo, sixteen are from the Marines and only five from the Vietnamese. Moreover, the Marines' stories frame the sequence, subtly tilting it toward their point of view.

The questions raised by this episode permeate all the films and seriously limit their usefulness. The best installments are the initial two, which deal with the French occupation of Indochina; first, because they contain rare footage and second, because they adopt a forthright anticolonial position. According to the narrator, the French simply "seized the areas near Saigon" in 1860 and established a "colony." There is no question that the French influence was malign. "Vietnamese society was reeling under the impact of Westernization," continues the narrator, who goes on to emphasize French "colonial repression." He accuses the French of "trying to transform Vietnam into a source of profit." "Cheap labor" enabled companies like Michelin Rubber to make "millions in profits from factories and plantations."

Vietnam's narrator suggests that the French collaborated with the Japanese in World War II, and says that in the nineteenth century they "staged public executions. The severed heads were photographed and printed on postcards which soldiers sent home to sweethearts in Paris 'with kisses from Hanoi.' " The film mocks a French newsreel that speaks of France bringing "peace, work, prosperity and joy" to "regions of hostility and misery."

Finally, in one of the few truly shocking moments in the thirteen long hours, we are presented with the spectacle of a French survivor of Dien Bien Phu describing how he was hit with a shell and woke up under the knife of a North Vietnamese surgeon, who was presumably saving his life. "You are badly wounded and we will take care of you," he recalls the surgeon saying. "From that moment," continues the officer, "I knew I had left the Greek, Latin, Judeo-Christian world to pass into the world of the Red termites."

Thus the French—brutal, arrogant and stupid—are allowed to convict themselves before the unforgiving gaze of the camera. There appears to be only one side to the story of French colonialism. Were viewers to watch only the first two segments of the series, they might be excused for accusing the producers of bias, simplification, even vulgar Marxism.

But when we get to America's Indochina war, it's a different story. Exit colonialism; enter anti-Communism. Whereas the former was incontrovertibly bad news, the latter was, well, reasonable. After all, Moscow had "dropped the Iron Curtain . . . on Poland, Hungary, Yugoslavia, Bulgaria," as a Paramount newsreel tells us (French newsreels are objects of fun; American newsreels provide information), the North Koreans had invaded the South and American G.I.s had fought the yellow hordes of China to a standstill. While the Vietnamese struggle had its own unique history, the film argues that the United States nevertheless could hardly be blamed for seeing the world in terms of falling dominoes.

Whereas the narrator referred to Ho Chi Minh and his followers as "rebels," "nationalists," or "the Vietnamese resistance" while they were fighting the French, once the Americans arrive they are invariably "Communists." Whereas Bao Dai is the "playboy emperor picked by the French," Nguyen Cao Ky and Nguyen Van Thieu are the "government." Whereas French troops just released from Japanese prison camps go "on a rampage, arresting and attacking Vietnamese," American troop's engage in the was-it-or-wasn't-it massacre at Thuybo. Americans, in both the military and the government, come off rather well. In *In The Year of the Pig,* there is a remarkable sequence in which the interviewer asks some big, healthy G.I.s how they like the beach they're cavorting on. "No American girls," they answer. "There are girls down there at the other end of the beach," says the interviewer, hopefully. "They're gooks. . . . slants . . . they're no good," the G.I.s reply. In *Vietnam* there is nothing to suggest the depth of the racism that infected America's attitude toward the Vietnamese. There is no Westmoreland saying, "The Oriental doesn't put the same high price on life as does a Westerner," as he does in *Hearts and Minds*; no Curtis Lemay threatening to "bomb Vietnam back to the Stone Age," as he does in *In the Year of the Pig*; no George Patton 3d praising his soldiers as "a bloody good bunch of killers," as he does in both *Pig* and *Hearts and Minds*. On the contrary, in *Vietnam,* Westmoreland, Rusk, Rostow and the others are all thoughtful, caring men caught up in circumstances beyond their control. William Colby is given all the time in the world to refute charges that the C.I.A.'s Phoenix Program, which he ran, was no more than an assassination campaign against suspected V.C. cadre, but only a few moments are available for rebuttal. Even Ky looks good. You'd never know from this film that he was an admirer of Hitler.

Why the difference between the film's treatment of the Americans and the French? Were the Americans better than the French? Was their war more just? Their bombs less lethal, their bayonets less sharp? Were the Vietnamese more deserving of death in 1964 or 1974 than they were in 1954? Surely not, and therefore it is hard to resist the conclusion that the producers, being American themselves, making the film in America for Americans, largely with American money, simply made the expedient judgment that if the American war was not more just, at least it was more "complex." Outrage is out; compassion is in. We're all a lot more mature now than we were ten years ago.

Not that the film pulls any punches as far as the prosecution of the war is concerned. It reruns the all-too-familiar footage of G.I.s torching "hooches," planes blanketing acres of forest with Agent Orange; it presents napalming, torture, disfigurement and ten different ways of dying. But the discrepancy between the enormity of the actions and the banality of the actors merely dramatizes the question the film never satisfactorily answers: Why did it happen?

Vietnam can't answer that question because it limits the debate over the war to "responsible" critics. With few exceptions, the film's treatment of domestic dissent is confined to those within the government. Hawks like Rostow and Rusk are disputed by doves like Ball, Clifford and McPherson, and occasionally by senators like Wayne Morse. Despite its palpable and dramatic inhibiting effect on the war effort, the peace movement is confined to a single installment, and to only part of one at that. The filmmakers appear to be so frightened of being accused of bias that much of the "Homefront USA" segment is bizarrely given over to pro-war demonstrators, even though they were insignificant until late in the game. Within the antiwar movement, the film dearly favors the McCarthy moderates, who stayed safely within the political system, over the radicals and long-hairs, who stepped outside it and took to the streets. (The treatment of the riots outside the 1968 Democratic Convention in Chicago, which basically follows Mayor Daley's line about police provocation, is a scandal.) It even attempts to discredit draft resisters with a snide aside from James Fallows, who claims they looked for "the painless way out."

Astoundingly, the phrase "American imperialism" is never once uttered in the course of the entire thirteen segments, except by the North Vietnamese. Where are the antiwar critics outside the government who could have challenged the cold war prattle of the foreign policy elite? Where are Noam Chomsky, I.F. Stone, Daniel Ellsberg? In their absence, Henry Kissinger becomes the only American authority on his own negotiations with Le Duc Tho!

This is not to say that the series contains nothing of merit. It has more than its share of moments. There is the remarkable admission by the C.I.A.'s Ray Cline that the second Gulf of Tonkin incident (the "attack" on the Turner Joy which occasioned the first American bombing of the North) in all probability never happened. "Many of the reports which seemed to relate to the second incident were proved either to be unsound or to relate to the first incident," says Cline blandly, adding, "Quite often the commanding officers—in this case the President of the United States—don't wait for the details to be settled if they feel they are in a critical situation with a danger of military conflict." Then there is Former Assistant Secretary of State for Far Eastern Affairs Roger Hilsman, excusing the Kennedy Administration's complicity in Diem's assassination by arguing, in effect, that Diem deserved what he got because he refused to follow American advice. Given America's notorious historical amnesia and the grave situation in Latin America today, it can't hurt to be reminded of our recent history in Vietnam, nor to hear what the Vietnamese have to say. As the series reminds us, Vietnam was the first television war, and if Reagan's news blackout of the Grenada invasion is any indication, it may be the last.

But if the film's stated goal is to answer the question asked by the narrator in the first segment—"Vietnam. A noble cause? A shameful venture?"—*Vietnam* is a failure. There is no debate, just the presentation of mutually exclusive points of view, as though the war could be boiled down to a failure of communication, the "tragedy" of Vietnam. The truth is that the war was a crime, not a tragedy. The tragedy is that this film lacks the conviction to say so. By trying to be all things to all people, *Vietnam* not only fails to educate its audience, it fails to fulfill its covert goal, which is to strengthen the center against the left and right. Ironically, the film confirms the right in its view that the United States should have nuked Hanoi when it had the chance in 1954; it confirms the left in its view that America is an amoral imperial power. We have come full circle.

Stanley Karnow's lengthy and inconclusive *Vietnam: A History* is a perfect complement to the series. Karnow was a *Time* correspondent in Paris during the 1950s and went to Southeast Asia for *Time* and *Life* in 1959—not, one would have thought, particularly good training for a book such as this one, given Henry Luce's notoriously unhappy influence on American policy in Asia. Luce's heavy hand is evident in the first paragraph of the book, in which Karnow writes, "With the young men who died in Vietnam died the dream of an 'American century.' "

Vietnam: A History contains a great many facts, little analysis and much waffling. For a political correspondent, Karnow has a surprisingly rudimentary grasp of politics. He piously describes the war as one "which nobody won—a struggle between victims." Tell it to the Vietnamese. "My general attitude, to the extent that I can sum it up succinctly," he writes, "has been one of humility in the face of a vast and complicated subject." Had Karnow demonstrated a little less humility and considerably more intelligence, he might have given us a real contribution to the literature on Vietnam instead of the oversized paperweight he produced.

AMERICAN FILM CRITICISM (POSTWAR)

There hasn't been much in the way of noise from Andrew Sarris and Pauline Kael for some time. It wasn't so long ago that they could have been depended upon to enliven many a dull movie season with their legendary feuding, the nipping and biting at each other's heels that we came to know and love, and even expect.

But both have been more or less put out to pasture by their respective publications. Kael has retired from *The New Yorker,* and Sarris was rudely shoved from his perch at the *Village Voice* and has set up shop, modestly enough, at the *New York Observer*. Meanwhile, their protégés, scattered about America's newspapers and magazines, don't seem to have the old fire. Maybe it's just that there isn't much to argue about anymore; maybe, in fact, there never was.

Twenty years later, it's hard to imagine that the silent groves of movie reviewing were once agitated by gnashing and wailing, that two generations of readers watched closely to see which one would emerge from battle intact, which more bloodied. Although it is difficult to recall just what the sound and the fury was all about, it is clear what purpose they served. They created an illusion of intellectual ferment when there was none, and disguised the extent to which the dead hand of ideological conformity ruled popular film reviewing and academic scholarship. The faux warfare between Sarris and

Kael also disguised the extent to which Sarris's auteurism and, for want of a better term, Kael's eclecticism, between them totally dominated the critical landscape. Even now, after academic film scholarship has inhaled the intoxicating fragrance of such exotic flowers of French culture as structuralism, semiotics, and Lacanian psychoanalysis, and auteurism has fallen into disrepute, we forget that to a remarkable degree it still determines the lay of the land, dictates which films will be examined from a semiotic, feminist, or psychoanalytic perspective, which directors will get monographs from the British Film Institute or will be included in the college curricula.

How did the world of postwar American film criticism come to be the way it is? Once upon a time, there lived a Frenchman called André Bazin. Bazin believed that the function of films was to "reveal reality." On these grounds, he broadly distinguished between two types of directors, those "who put their faith in the image and those who put their faith in reality." (*What Is Cinema?*, p. 24). The former embellished and distorted the object photographed either by means of editing or the manipulation of lighting, decor, makeup, acting and so on. The latter left reality alone in order to bring out its "deep structure" and hidden meanings. Whereas German Expressionist directors tricked out the image with bizarre sets, weird costumes, and dramatic use of shadow, and the Russians altered the significance of the image by means of close-ups and "montage," the directors Bazin preferred just stared long and hard at the real world. "Take a close look at the world, keep on doing so" (*WIC*, p. 27), Bazin advised. The best way to look at the world was by employing the long take in deep focus. Montage and deep focus called forth different, contradictory responses in the viewer. Deep focus implied "both a more active mental attitude on the part of the spectator and a more positive contribution on his part to the action in progress. While analytical montage only calls for him to follow his guide, to let his attention follow along smoothly with that of the director who will choose what he should see, here he is called upon to exercise at least a minimum of personal choice" (*WIC*, p. 36). The long take in deep focus presented a smorgasbord of objects and allowed the audience to pick and choose among them, decide for itself when and where to direct its attention. Montage, on the other hand, coerced the spectator's gaze, force-fed the audience a one-course meal. In short, deep focus was democratic, open, and pluralist; montage was totalitarian, closed, and monolithic.

Bazin's theory was tailor-made for the intellectual climate of postwar America, in which intellectuals of every stripe—historians like Daniel Boorstin, Richard Hofstadter, and Arthur Schlesinger, Jr.; sociologists like Daniel Bell and David Riesman; literary critics like Lionel Trilling—all agreed that the genius of America, as distinct from Nazi Germany and, more important, as it turned out, the Soviet Union, lay in its pluralism. In America, a variety of interest groups competed on a more or less equal basis for a piece of the pie. This competition was non-ideological) everyone agreed that it was "natural," "realistic," "commonsensical"), and was governed by compromise and the rules of fair play. The enemies of pluralism were political fanatics of the right and left, "extremists" who attacked the practical and pragmatic "center" in the name of ideology. Pluralistis of the center defended "culture" from "primitives," who attacked it in the name of "nature"; in the psychobabble that characterized postwar discourse, they privileged "adulthood" and "maturity" against the infantilism of "children."

Bazin's long take in deep focus was a perfect prescription for the pluralist style in film. (In the fifties, it would take other forms as well, particularly CinemaScope.) His emphasis on realism disguised and suppressed not only the ideological dimension of film, but the ideological dimension of criticism as well. And it just so happened that the practitioners of deep focus were American directors like Welles and Wyler, while the practitioners of montage were Soviet directors like Eisenstein. Before Bazin, Eisenstein's montage theory was the theory of film; Soviet cinema of the late twenties, the films of Eisenstein, Pudovkin, and Dovzhenko, were generally regarded as the pinnacle of film art. As the chill of the Cold War settled over East-West relations, Bazin put the skids under Eisenstein's reputation.

Needless to say, Bazin's ideological distinction between deep focus and montage didn't hold up. As Raymond Durgnat wrote many years later, in films like Wyler's *The Little Foxes* (1941) and *The Best Years of Our Lives* (1947), "Wyler had effectively determined which characters the spectators would be interested in, by the moral and emotional traits with which he endowed them, and which he balances against the other with just as much care and control as do such shallow-focus films as *Johnny Guitar* or *This Island Earth"* (*Films and Feelings,* p. 30). What we look at in the deep-focus long take is influenced by lighting, the composition of the frame, who's talking and who isn't, and numerous other factors. "The spectator is no freer," concluded Durgnat, "no more 'democratic,' in Wyler's films than in the others." But he appeared to be. Bazin was partly right. In the movies, as in society, pluralist techniques of control created the illusion of freedom; they manipulated, rather than coerced.

As the political spectrum in both post-war France and America moved right, French and American film criticism moved with it. Bazin roughly played the role in France that critic Robert Warshow played in America. As Annette Michelson acutely observed, "One can speak of Bazin's critical and theoretical work as providing an aesthetics of postwar Christian Democracy, and of Warshow's as both reflecting and reinforcing American liberalism in its Eisenhower phase." If Bazin was infatuated with "facts" and "reality," Warshow valued the "immediate experience" (the title posthumously given to his collection of essays).

In the late forties, when Warshow started writing (his articles appeared in *Commentary* and *Parisian Review*), American film reviewing was still dominated by men of the thirties and forties, of the Popular Front and New Deal, like John Grierson, Lewis Jacobs, Paul Rotha, Richard Griffith, Jay Leyda, Dwight Macdonald, Bosley Crowther, and James Agee. These men believed that film was Art, but what they had in mind were not Hollywood "movies," but the Soviet classics, the German Expressionists, and the films of D.W. Griffith and Charlie Chaplin.

The reputation of Charlie Chaplin was always a political bellwether. Agee considered Chaplin a true genius of the cinema. When *Monsieur Verdoux* came out in 1947, it was greeted with a storm of abuse, and its director hounded out of the country shortly thereafter by the witch-hunt. Agee, in a celebrated trilogy published in *The Nation,* sprang to the defense of the film, calling it "one of the greatest movies ever made," but Warshow, in an exquisite exercise in ambivalence and victim-bashing—of which he was a master—at once compared Chaplin to Swift, and also suggested it was all his own fault for not making *Monsieur Verdoux* more of a feel-good movie. "There was even an organized campaign against the movie which . . . could be successful only because *Monsieur Verdoux* was so forbidding," he wrote. "When this campaign culminated some years later in the Attorney General's suggestion that Chaplin, then in Europe, might not be permitted to re-enter the country, there were surprisingly few Americans who cared. We can say easily enough that this is a national shame: once again America has rejected one of her great artists. And Chaplin, no doubt, is only too ready to say the same thing; he has said it, in fact, as crudely and stupidly as possible, by his recent acceptance of the 'World Peace Prize.' But for him, who has asked so insistently for our love, there must be more to it than that; there must be the possibility that he has given himself away" (*The Immediate Experience,* p. 166).

Then there was the not unexpected revisionism on the subject of Soviet film. In Agee's opinion, writing in 1946, "Men like Eisenstein and Dovzhenko and Pudovkin [made] some of the greatest works of art in this century" (*Agee on Film: Review and Comments,* p. 195). He regarded Eisenstein as both a great artist and a victim of Stalinism. When Eisenstein died the following year, Agee wrote, "For years, as everyone knows, Eisenstein has been working as if in a prison, under the supervision of jailers who are . . . peculiarly dangerous and merciless . . . Everything that is meant by creative genius and its performance, and everything that that signifies about freedom and potentiality in general, is crucified in Eisenstein, more meaningfully and abominably, than in any other man I can think of . . . " (*AoF,* p. 250).

By 1955, however, Eisenstein was no longer a genius and victim of Stalinism, but a fraud and apologist for Stalinism. In "Re-Viewing Russian Movies," Warshow, making an invidious distinction between Dovzhenko's *Earth* and Eisenstein's *The General Line,* called the latter "the work of a skilled hack and philistine" (*TIE,* p. 211). But more interesting than the downward mobility of Eisenstein's reputation were the terms in which it was derided. Whereas for Agee, one of his strengths was his antirealistic stylization (in *Ivan the*

Terrible, Agee praised him for "go[ing] boldly and successfully against naturalism and even simple likelihood" (*TIE,* p. 249), this stylization, for Warshow, following Bazin, was a weakness, worse, a lie, confounded by the higher truth of "reality." "How utterly vulgar art and belief [read "ideology"] can be, sometimes, when measured against the purity of the real event," wrote Warshow. "There are innumerable examples of such vulgarity in the Russian cinema, moments when the director, taken up with his role as an artist who controls and interprets—few artists have put a higher value on that role than the early Soviet film directors—forgets what is really at stake and commits an offense against humanity" (*TIE,* p. 210). Again, attacking the celebrated montage by which Eisenstein evokes the awakening workers in *October* (three stone lions in the process of standing up), Warshow wrote, "This is another example of montage that is mentioned with honor in the textbooks, usually with the information that the three lions were not even photographed in the same city, a fact which is supposed to cast light on the question of whether the cinema is an art. The use of the stone lion is, indeed, a clever and 'artistic' idea, but it is also fundamentally cheap, and in both respects it is characteristic of Eisenstein, and of the Soviet cinema generally. What we want most, that cinema rarely gives us: some hint of the mere reality of the events it deals with. The important point about the lions is that all the 'art' of their use depends on the fact that they are not alive" (*TIE,* p. 204).

In attacking artfulness in favor of "reality," Warshow echoed Bazin, and moved the French critic's esthetic into the American mainstream. But what was the "pure reality," the "immediate experience" that Warshow employed to batter Eisenstein? In *The Liberal Imagination,* Lionel Trilling wrote that the future historian of the decade "will surely discover that the word reality is of central importance in his understanding of us." Trilling was right; it became a key concept in the ideological tug of war between pluralists and their enemies, and pluralists expended considerable energy attempting to secure the term for their own ends. Like them, Warshow was fairly clear about what reality was not, but somehow he never bothered to define exactly what it was, preferring to leave the impression that it was self-evident, or, if not, sufficiently "complex" to be in need of interpretation by experts like himself. Yet Warshow, who portrayed himself in his writing as something of a moral tuning fork, preternaturally sensitive to the crimes of Stalin, apt to quiver with pain at the slightest tremor of Zhdanovism, turned out to be, unlike Agee, astoundingly oblivious to the Soviet persecution of Eisenstein, and strangely unconcerned by the virtual expulsion of Chaplin from the U.S.

Warshow didn't attack the pre–Cold War, left-liberal, Popular Front critics directly; he shared many of their assumptions and spoke the same language, but nevertheless, he successfully undermined many of their assumptions, particularly the criteria of social significance, seriousness, and good taste they used to judge movies. He not only began the downward revaluation of Eisenstein and Chaplin, but he also had a taste for mass culture, and wrote well on the lowly Hollywood genre movies—Westerns and gangster films—which had hitherto been beneath contempt. In so doing, he made the old art-house gang look stuffy and foolish.

Warshow provided a bridge between Agee and Sarris, and when he died, suddenly, in 1955 (the same year Agee died), Sarris was just beginning his career. Drawing on the new generation of young critics and novice directors gathered around *Cahiers du cinéma* in Paris—François Truffaut, Jacques Rivette, Jean-Luc Godard, and Eric Rohmer—Sarris turned them to his own purposes. In their hands, Bazin's theory became a club with which to bludgeon the "Tradition of Quality," France's "official" film culture. This was a version of our old friend, Popular Front culture, and after the war, when *Cahiers'* Young Turks turned on their elders, they were turning on the left. Taking a hard line in France's cinematic cold war, Truffaut wrote in January 1954 that "peaceful co-existence between the 'Tradition of Quality' and the *'cinema d'auteurs'* was impossible." Attacking the films of France's most celebrated pre-war and postwar directors—Claude Autant-Lara, Henri Clouzot, René Clement, René Clair, and Yves Allegret—"He found them," as John Hess put it, "anti-bourgeois, anti-military, anti-clerical, opposed to all sorts of linguistic and sexual taboos, and full of profaned hosts and confessionals."

By the time Sarris began to write, the pages of American newspapers and magazines had been made safe for democracy. The

lefties, radicals, fellow travelers, independents, anarchists, paci-
fists, and general riffraff who had infected the press with their pink
prose in the thirties and forties had been flushed out by almost a
decade of witch hunting. It was all quiet on the Western front, save
for the click-clack of Westbrook Pegler or George Sokolsky goose-
stepping across the pages of the Hearst press. All Sarris had to do
was to conduct a mopping-up operation, and he saw to it that
auteurism would play the same role in America that it had played
in France; the American "Tradition of Quality" that it was used to
demolish was precisely the Jacobs, Rotha, Griffith, Macdonald,
Agee group that Warshow had already softened up. More so than
Warshow, Sarris saw them as a "tradition," and attacked them
directly. His strategy, borrowed from the French, was to dump the
silents, whether Russian or American, the "art films" so dear to
the old guard, and privilege "movies" instead, claiming they were
true "art." "The sociologically oriented film historians, Jacobs,
Grierson, Kracauer," Sarris wrote, "looked on the Hollywood canvas less as an art form than as a mass medium. Hollywood directors were regarded as artisans rather than artists. . . . Film historians have been misled by the sociological veneer of [*Birth of a
Nation* and *Potemkin*] into locating the artistic essence of cinema
in its social concerns. Realism and social consciousness thus
became the artistic alibis of socially conscious film historians, and
genre films without a sociological veneer were cast into the dust-
bins of commercial entertainments" (*The American Cinema*, p. 15;
The Primal Screen, p. 58).

If Hollywood films were Art, not artifacts, they could be
detached with impunity from the social and cultural context, from
the circumstances of production and consumption. According to
Sarris, sociological critics had a bad habit of "singling out the
timely films and letting the timeless ones fall by the wayside"
(*TAC*, p. 25). He intended to put a stop to that, substituting "timeless" for "timely." Arguing with Bazin about the impact of capitalism on film, he wrote, "I still find it impossible to attribute X
directors and Y films to any particular system or culture. . . . If
directors and other artists cannot be wrenched form their historical environments, aesthetics is reduced to a subordinate branch of
ethnography" (*TPS*, p. 45).

Sarris's 1962 auteurist manifesto veered wildly from the obvious to the obscure, but what it all boiled down to was that the films were judged on the basis of who directed them, and directors were judged on the basis of the presence or absence of personal style: "The distinguishable personality of the director [is] a criterion of value." He ranked some 150 directors from the "Pantheon" to "Others." The worst film of a permanent Pantheon pensioner like John Ford was more interesting than the best film of a director like Kazan for whom the Pantheon was full up. (As Dwight Macdonald remarked at the time, "This kind of grading is appropriate to eggs but not works of art" [*On Movies*, p. 305].)

Sarris led a one-man counterrevolution in film scholarship. He followed up on Warshow's attack on Chaplin by elevating Buster Keaton to the spot of #1 Silent Comic. Now it was the turn of "serious" films like *The Informer* to be carted out to the dustbin of social consciousness, while films once disdained like *Baby Face Nelson*, *Seven Men From Now,* or *El Dorado* were firmly ensconced in the Pantheon's bridal suite. Potemkin became the butt of dumb Cold War jokes ("What is black and white and Red all over?"—even Warshow would have turned over in his grave), and Sarris pretended to find (let's give him the benefit of the doubt) Ford's *Steamboat 'Round the Bend* "more interesting" than Ford's *The Grapes of Wrath*. Meanwhile, Ford's *The Man Who Shot Liberty Valance* became the subject of lyrical adulation: It "must be ranked along with *Lola Montes* and *Citizen Kane* as one of the enduring masterpieces of that cinema which had chosen to focus on the mystical processes of time" (*TPS*, p. 152).

This shift in the criteria by which films were judged had seismic consequences. Hollywood movies had always lagged embarrassingly far behind New York painting, Jewish and Southern fiction, and jazz as evidence of American superiority in the cultural Cold War with the Soviet Union. After Sarris, it was no longer necessary to apologize for "movies." Whereas Agee was a fierce critic of Hollywood, Sarris was a fervent admirer. Whereas the "sociological" critics and film historians once valued the German Lang, the English Hitchcock, and the French Renoir over the American films of the same directors, which were considered empty, glossy, and commercial, now the worm had turned, and the American Lang,

Hitchcock, and Renoir were suddenly as good if not better than their European films. The stock of directors like Aldrich, Fuller, Siegel, Hawks, Walsh, and even Karlson, whom no one aside from bleary-eyed cultists had ever heard of, shot up and off the scale. Auteurism marked the triumph of nationalism in film studies. Dismissing Murnau, Lang, Pabst, Renoir, Vigo, Cocteau, Rossellini, Mizoguchi, Kurosawa, Ozu, Satyajit Ray, and Wajda, not to mention the Russians, Sarris grandly declared, "Film for film, director for director, the American cinema has been consistently superior to that of the rest of the world from 1915 through 1962" (*TPS*, p. 48).

"Sociological" became an obscenity in the auteurist lexicon, a code word for "left" or "liberal," and was replaced by "aesthetic" as in "the criteria of selection for [the Pantheon] are aesthetic rather than social or industrial" (*TAC*, p. 16). Aesthetic was defined as "a commitment to formal excellence" (*TPS*, p. 69) and its use appeared to initiate a new era of formalism. But not quite. Sarris like Walsh better than Wilder, Hawks better than Huston (whom Agee championed), Cukor better than Kazan, Gregory La Cava better than Wise, Wyler, or Zinneman. Why? On closer inspection it turned out that Sarris's criteria weren't esthetic at all; they were ideological. The adoration of American film meant the adoration of American ideology. The action films auteurists liked were clean, mean, tough, and generally right wing. The films they didn't like were "liberal."

Take Sarris's review of Sidney Lumet's *Dog Day Afternoon*, written in the seventies. He was outraged that "once the robber gets started Pacino and Cazale begin more and more to resemble lovable non-conformists held at bay by a hostile, unfeeling society," and he pined for the movies of "the forties and fifties [when] the story would have been told in such a way as to make the audience root for the bank manager, his employees, the police, and the FBI . . . Under the aegis of Freud and Marx the perpetrator is transformed into a Problem we all should have solved a long time ago" (*Politics and Cinema*, pp. 35 and 33). After hundreds of column inches flailing liberals, he finally gets around to the "aesthetic value," seven lines from the end of the review, writing that *Dog Day Afternoon* "is not a bad job of moviemaking" (*TPS*, p.

36). But it was too little, too late. This was "sociological" criticism pure and simple. It suddenly became clear that there was good sociological criticism and bad sociological criticism. Good sociological criticism wasn't sociological at all; it was redefined as "aesthetic," and it was practiced by "us"; bad sociological criticism was practiced by "them." "Us" in this case meant centrists like Sarris. "My own political position," he wrote, is "rabidly centrist, liberal, populist, more Christian than Marxist . . . I believe more in personal redemption than social revolution . . . The ascending and descending staircases of Hitchcock are more meaningful to me than all the Odessa Steps . . . I never wept for Spain or Chile" (*TPS*, p. 61, etc.).

Despite his own oft-proclaimed "pluralistic" esthetic, "them," simply meant the left, with which Sarris conducted a career-long polemic, flinging about epithets like "the idiot left" with abandon. When Sarris looked left, he saw red; when he saw red he saw Stalin, and reached for his dog-eared copy of George Orwell. Sarris's rhetorical strategy followed the well-worn path trod before him by pluralist pioneers like Bell, Schlesinger, and Riesman. With a flourish of mock bathos, he portrayed the center as a helpless "muddled middle" beset on all sides by "extremists," a delicate flower set aflutter by the sound of approaching jackboots. He was a firm subscriber to the centrist doctrine that the left and right were essentially the same. "As a Centrist," he wrote in the sixties, "I am uncomfortable with both the Buckleys and the Berrigans. They are cut from the same absolutist cloth, and they would exclude the middle if they could."

Filled with paranoia himself, Sarris followed the lead of Richard Hofstadter's centrist classic, *The Paranoid Style in American Politics*, and called others paranoid, particularly his *bêtes noires*, the socially conscious critics of the thirties. Writing about what he calls the "forest" critics, he said, "It is the system that he blames for betraying the cinema. This curious feeling of betrayal dominates most forest histories to the point of paranoia" (*TAC*, p. 21). Following Bell's celebrated essay, "The End of Ideology," his enemy is "ideology," which becomes, like "sociology," a dirty word. In a characteristic attack, he wrote of "the ever mounting pile of idiotically ideological cinema"

(*PaC*, p. 81). The great beauty of pluralism was that it was indeed pluralistic, up to a point.

Not everyone bought auteurism. One critic who didn't was Pauline Kael. In a witty and stinging demolition job called "Circles and Squares," published in 1963 in *Film Quarterly*, she attacked Sarris's devotion to "distinguishable" personal style as the primary criterion of value: "The smell of a skunk is more distinguishable than the perfume of a rose; does that make it better?" (*I Lost It at the Movies*, p. 268). And she also attacked his attempts to isolate movies from their social context. "When is Sarris going to discover that aesthetics is indeed a branch of ethnography," she wrote. "What does he think it is—a sphere of its own, separate from the study of man in his environment?" (*ILIatM*, p. 280). But although Kael and Sarris went at it hammer and tong, they were both rocking, not tipping, in the same boat. If you didn't like Hertz, you could try Avis, to change metaphors in midstream, and still be assured of a smooth ride down the middle of the road.

Kael indeed attacked Sarris, but she did so in pluralist terms. Like him, she had scores to settle with the old-guard lefties, and in settling them, she used his techniques. When Richard Griffith, a noted film historian and curator of film historian and curator of film at the Museum of Modern Art, praised *La Grande Illusion* for its attempts to "influence" events, she complained that "the standard film histories still judge movies by the values of the 'Resistance'" (*ILIatM*, p. 255). Siegfried Kracauer, the left-leaning "sociological critic" whom Sarris savaged, fared no better in Kael's hands. Nastily reviewing Kracauer's book, *The Theory of Film*, in a pun worthy of Sarris's worst, Kael attacked the "Odessa-steeped film critics [who] tell us that Eisenstein's 'goal, a cinematic one, was the depiction of collective action, with the masses as the true hero'—and this battle hymn has become the international anthem of film criticism" (*ILIatM*, p. 254). Kracauer had a neorealist-influenced esthetic very much like Bazin's (and Warshow's)—he liked nonactors in real locations—and in attacking Kracauer, she was attacking Bazin, the granddaddy of auteurism. Despite her distaste for Eisenstein, she used him as a club against Kracauer, accusing the latter of disdaining "art" and artfulness in favor of "nature,"

111

defined as "a belief in progress," (p. 257) or "reality," defined as "poverty and mass movements" (p. 256). She draped Kracauer with all the unhappy qualities pluralists habitually attributed to extremists. He was guilty of "primitive . . . thinking" (p. 247), an adherent of a "monomaniac theory." "Siegfried Kracauer is in the great lunatic tradition" (pp. 244–45), she wrote, comparing him to a "religious zealot," and contrasting him to "relaxed men of good sense," presumably like herself, "whose pluralistic approaches can be disregarded as not fundamental enough" (p. 245).

When Kael turned to Sarris himself, she employed the same strategy against him she used against Kracauer and the others. Sarris was guilty of applying a "single theory" (by which she meant abstract preconceptions that get in the way of the "experience" of film), that overran the pluralist garden like a beserk "lawn mower" (p. 279). Auteurists were essentially loonies "united by fanaticism in a ludicrous cause" (p. 280). Worse, and this is the ultimate weapon in the pluralist arsenal, auteurists were implicitly toalitarian. Their esthetics were "an aesthetics for 1984" (p. 283). Sarris-the-Stalin-slayer was himself, implicitly, a Stalinist. His constant harping on directorial style convincted him of the crime of the "cult of personality" (p. 272).

Kael's prose in the fifties and sixties was full of echoes of Riesman (she called auteurists "inside dopesters"); like him (and Bell, Schlesinger, Trilling, et al.), she saw not only the democratic process but also reality itself in terms of the give and take of interest group politics. She spoke of "the real world of conciliation and compromise" (p. 295). Filmmakers she didn't like were not only bad, but undemocratic (un-American?). (She didn't sue "reality" as a criterion of value; she couldn't, after flaying Kracauer for doing it, but she tended to substitute "experience," as in "art is an expression of experience." Just what "experience" was, she, like Warshow, never quite said, falling back instead on the pluralist cant about "complexity.") Those who flouted reality were "neurotic" or infantile, allowing her to switch over to the derogatory psychologizing fashionable at the time. Thus, like Sarris, she was fond of calling her enemies "paranoid," as in "the accusatory, paranoid style of [Jonas] Mekas" (p. 285). (Mekas first published Sarris's auteur theory in his magazine, *Film Culture* in 1962–63.) And in the same way that Sarris opposed his "balanced" centrism to the paranoia of the extremists on the right and (especially) the left, so Kael opposed her calm, sane, "balanced" pluralist approach to the frenzies of auteurism. "I believe that we respond most and best to work in any art form (and to other experience as well) if we are pluralist, flexible, relative in our judgments, if we are eclectic" (p. 278). In fact, her own matter-of-fact, brilliantly colloquial, down-home conversational style went a long way towards establishing the ideology of the center as just plain common sense.

Kael misconstructed Sarris as a cultural radical. True, he first published in *Film Culture,* and then in the *Village Voice,* and it is also true that he affected a kind of populism, championing lowbrow commercial fare and baiting "coterie" art-house taste in "cinemah," as he was fond of calling it. But he turned on the avant-garde as soon as it became expedient, and it quickly became clear that he didn't want to demolish "cinemah" so much as redefine it to include the movies he liked best.

Both Sarris and Kael were, needless to say, entitled to their political views. Both had a keen eye for the weaknesses of Soviet cinema, the fatuousness of the "message" movies of the thirties and Forties, and the hollowness of the progressive film scholars who made themselves easy targets with their windy and sententious Popular Front rhetoric, labored Americanism, and sentimentalization of the "masses." Auteurism performed a real service in deflating the pretensions of the "montage maniacs," as Sarris called them, and making Hollywood movies respectable. Kael in particular played a key role easing the way for the New American Cinema of the seventies. Without her, the determined campaigns carried on in *The New York Times* and *Time* magazine against pictures like *Bonnie and Clyde* and *A Clockwork Orange* might have been successful. But both Sarris and Kael were beneficiaries of the witch hunt that cleared away the left-wing underbrush so that (centrist growths) like their own might flourish. The last chapter of Kael's *I Lost It at the Movies* is entitled "Morality Plays Right and Left," and, in it, Kael paid her ideological dues. First she dispatched an anti-Communist film, *Night People,* and then she joined the hue and cry against *Salt of the Earth.* She called it "Communist propaganda" (p. 298) and proceeded to chide the *New York Times* and

Los Angeles Daily News reviewers for not spotting the Commie line when it was being unreeled before their very eyes. "There are Americans," she asked in amazement, "who have not learned that Communist propaganda concentrates on local grievances?" (p. 298). Maybe these reviewers were themselves Red agents? Kael didn't say so; she was a centrist, so she only loaded the gun and aimed it, leaving it to others to pull the trigger.

Salt of the Earth may have been awash in Popular Front bathos as Kael charged, but she went further. At a time (1954) when the U.S. government had deported the film's Mexican star, Rosaura Revueltas, when Hollywood labs refused to process the exposed footage, when IATSE projectionists struck the movie, Kael delivered a blow for movie McCarthyism. Let-a-hundred-flowers-bloom centrist critics celebrated the variety and plenitude of the pluralist garden, but they were confined to the Hollywood mainstream, and nurtured in a climate of ideological conformity that would have made Stalin blush. And while they were busy pruning away the troublesome weeds on the American right and left, a whole new world of cinema sprang up with which they were totally unequipped to deal. It had become a jungle out there.

THE LAST CRUSADE

There's a dramatic moment at the end of the "origins" sequence of *Indiana Jones and the Last Crusade* where the young Indy, having seized the coveted Cross of Coronado from the ad guys, turns it over to the sheriff for safekeeping; the sheriff, however, is in cahoots with the bad guys and gives it back to them—much to Indy's astonishment. Indy, here played by River Phoenix, a child of the sixties (his parents were hippies), learns the *echt* lesson of the sixties: don't trust adults, particularly those in authority.

George Lucas and Steven Spielberg, who between them conceived, produced, and directed *The Last Crusade*, were also children of the sixties; their movies, despite their slick, formulaic sheen, are surprisingly personal (it's no accident that Lucas's hero is named Luke) and so are permeated by countercultural values. *Star Wars*, for example, was a generation gap drama that sided with the kids. With its conflict between the weak rebels and the powerful Empire, it couldn't help evoking Vietnam and the attendant moral and political crises amid which Lucas and his generation came of age. Lucas has said that the Emperor was modeled on President Richard Nixon, which makes the Empire equivalent to the United States, Darth Vader to, say, Henry Kissinger, and the rebels to the Vietcong. Or, on an even more personal note, as Dale Pollock pointed out in *Skywalking*, his book on Lucas, the Empire is the monolithic studio system that thwarted him at every turn, while the Emperor and Vader stood in for appropriate studio executives.

With the appearance of Yoda in *The Empire Strikes Back*, the Vietnam analogy, which functioned as a subject for the first film, became more intrusive. The gnomic Jedi master is wrinkled, old, and wise and lives in the jungle. When E.T., Gandhi, and Mr. Miyagi (*The Karate Kid*) made their movie debuts a few years later, the resemblance among them was striking, leaving little doubt who Yoda was: a closet Asian. After all, he was colored, small (under-developed), "ugly" (non-Western), and mysterious ("inscrutable"). If the Emperor was Nixon and Vader was Kissinger, Yoda had to be Mao or Ho Chi Minh, the Spirit of the Third World. (In a review of William Kotzwinkle's novelization of *E.T.*, social critic Ariel Dorfman described the pint-sized alien as "more like a small savage from the third world . . . than a Milky Way wizard. There is no [other] reason why . . . he should get drunk, why he never proceeds beyond pidgin English ["E.T. phone home"] such as . . . countless Indians have stuttered . . . ")

Lucas's idea of the Third World, however, was patterned on Northern California, where he lived, not Vietnam, where the war was fought; Yoda's cryptic Zen-speak recalls its dreamy, druggy, ecologically correct counterculture the same way Princess Leia's Guinevere hairdo and Pre-Raphaelite white gown suggests such quaint Northern California institutions as the Renaissance Faire, not to mention the ornate art nouveau concert posters of the six-ties. It was these values Lucas was trying to pass on to the next generation of teenagers, in the guise of Luke.

This Northern California ambience was most pronounced in the Moon of Endor sequence that concluded *Return of the Jedi*. With its dense forests of sequoias and its feisty, fuzzy-wuzzy Ewoks who defeat the Empire's technology with slingshots, crossbows, rocks, and homemade booby traps, Lucas gives us his most vivid picture of Vietcong guerrilla warfare, Marin County–style. The authorized novelization describes the Ewoks as "cadres" attacking in "human waves" and criticizes the Empire (the First World) for wrecking (aka defoliating) the greenery of Endor's moon, described as "dying from refuse disposal, trampling feet, chemical exhaust fumes." With the members of the Alliance and their teddy bear Ewoks gathered around a campfire at the end of *Return of the Jedi,* the Vietcong in the sky became Boy Scouts on the ground. The Empire is defeated by a children's crusade, an alliance of teenagers and teddy bears—in other words, the sixties. Nature, in the sixties equated with communes in the woods, Native Americans, and untrammeled innocence, defeats culture and civilizations, which were widely regarded as both corrupt and corrupting. *Return of the Jedi,* where these themes are most pronounced, represents the greening of *Star Wars.*

However, this Luddite, anti-technological strain was present in Lucas's films from the start. Apropos of his 1971 proto–*Star Wars, THX-1138,* Lucas once said, "I was fascinated by the . . . idea of rocket ships and lasers up against somebody with a stick. The little guys were winning and technology was losing—I liked that." Therefore, the trilogy pits the battered Millennium Falcon and the rebels' one-man fighters against massive Imperial Star Destroyers, Imperial Walkers, and the like, and, more important, the mysticism of the Force against the arid rationalism of the Empire, whose officers even sneer at Darth Vader's old-time "religion." When Luke is zeroing in on the vulnerable reactor core of the Death Star at the end of *Star Wars,* Obi Wan Kenobi's ghostly voice advises him to turn off his guidance system, close his eyes, and rely on the Force, which he does. These films prefer the heart to the head, feeling to thinking.

But it was, after all, 1976, not 1967, when *Star Wars* went into production, and times had changed. Lucas was nothing if not a creature of his era; if *Star Wars* was permeated by countercultural values, it embraced regressive values as well, attitudes that looked at once back to the old cold war of the fifties and ahead to the new cold war of the eighties. It was during the fifties, of course, that the Hollywood studios, along with their genres, began to crumble under the successive blows of the consent decree of 1948, television, the blacklist, and the increasing power of stars and talent agencies. Nevertheless, the conventions that governed Hollywood films survived well into the sixties. The ideology that underlay these conventions can best be described as centrist, which is to say, the films situated themselves within society and from that vantage point regarded the world. They preferred culture to nature, consensus and inclusion to polarization and exclusion, but quarreled among themselves over the best way to achieve these goals. By far the greater number of "corporate liberal" pictures (usually big-budget A-movies) espoused nonauthoritarian, persuasive (often therapeutic) methods of social control, while a smaller number of "conservative" films preferred force. At the extremes, a handful of right- and left-wing films attacked society as the enemy, often in the name of nature against culture, and resisted or actually fought social control.

As the sixties progressed, however, the Vietnam War split the consensus of the center into right against left. Fifties-style centrist spectacles like *Cleopatra* bombed at the box office, while anti-Establishment films like *Bonnie and Clyde,* whose politics would have made them marginal in the fifties, broke attendance records and redefined the mainstream. Suddenly it was okay to attack hitherto cherished values. On the left, killers (*Bonnie and Clyde*), bank robbers (*Dog Day Afternoon*), lunatics (*One Flew Over the Cuckoo's Nest*), draft dodgers (*Alice's Restaurant*), and hustlers (*Midnight Cowboy*) were regarded with sympathy, if not outright enthusiasm. Robbers and Indians were in; cops and cowboys were out. On the right, James Bond and Dirty Harry waged violent war not just on the scum who made the world a dangerous place for decent folk but on wimpy government bureaucrats who tied their hands with legal restraints. As cold-war liberals like Arthur Schlesinger, Jr., liked to put it, invoking William Butler Yeats, whom they oddly regarded as the poet laureate of consensus, the center had given way.

Since there existed no more than rudimentary alternative ideologies to support them, the newly respectable "extremist" films of the sixties—made by the so-called New Hollywood directors like Stanley Kubrick, Arthur Penn, Sam Peckinpah, Sidney Lumet, Robert Altman, and Woody Allen, some of whom had come up through television—most often made their points in a purely negative fashion, by picking apart mainstream genres that in any case had vanished when the consensus that supported them disintegrated. By the end of the fifties, sci-fi was no longer a viable genre, and it would be almost a decade before it momentarily reemerged in the form of *2001: A Space Odyssey.* War movies disappeared after the Korean Conflict, and when they finally surfaced in the guise of *Catch-22* and *M*A*S*H,* they were virtually unrecognizable. Westerns, traditionally the hardiest of Hollywood genres, were systematically dismantled by anti-Westerns like *Little Big Man, McCabe and Mrs. Miller, Buffalo Bill and the Indians,* and *The Missouri Breaks,* and even more conventional Westerns like *The Wild Bunch* and *Butch Cassidy and the Sundance Kid* were so pessimistic that the genre had no place to go. But this was a dangerous strategy in a narrative-based mass medium like movies, and when the counterculture itself began to wither away, and Carter won the presidency in 1976 on a platform that called for consensus and renewal, these "extremist" films gradually lost their audience, once that was fast growing younger and to whom the Vietnam War was rapidly becoming ancient history.

The next generation of directors, the "movie brats," were predominantly products of Los Angeles film schools. Lucas, Spielberg, and their young colleagues set out to restore or gentrify the genres they had learned to love in school. In the case of the *Star Wars* trilogy, this meant combat, sword and sorcery, Western, and, most important, sci-fi. Beyond specific genres, movies brat directors sought to revive the idea of genre itself. But to breathe new life into exhausted action formulas, it wasn't enough to put out the occasional sci-fi flick or Western (they invariably flopped); it was necessary to renovate the whole system that made genre possible, to restore, as Lucas put it, the naïve sense of romance, "awe," "wonder" that had accompanied the birth of the silents. If in *2001,* at least in its first half, Kubrick had demystified space travel by picturing space ships tricked out in humdrum HoJo décor, a drab extension of the friendly skies of United, Lucas not only wanted to remystify it, he wanted to remystify film itself.

Lucas achieved this goal by harnessing the dazzling, high-tech mega-effects pioneered by *2001* to the old action genres—really, the kids' matinee serials of the thirties—with their simple, functional narratives. He skipped at least a generation, turning his back on the anti-genre (and anti-war) films of the seventies, to old World War II films, with their unambiguous attitude toward combat. With what has often been called its "machine esthetic," *Star*

Wars was both a product and a celebration of the technology that had made the Vietnam War possible. Its spectacular depiction of bloodless dogfighting in deep space sanitized and aestheticized combat, in a manner all too reminiscent of the air war over North Vietnam.

The magic of the trilogy's effects lies precisely in their verisimilitude, and their success depends largely on creating the illusion that we are entering a futuristic world that actually exists. Whereas for many of the anti-genre directors of the late sixties and early seventies the screen was a mirror that reflected moving images back on themselves, in the *Star Wars* films the screen was a window on a world of spectacular "realism." According to effects wizard Richard Edlund, speaking of the all-important opening shot of the monumentally large and immaculately detailed Imperial Star Destroyer drifting into the frame from above, "If somebody sat down in the theater and saw this monstrous thing come over the screen and keep coming and coming, and they were awed by that, then we had our audience just where we wanted 'em. But if they laughed, we were dead." According to Pollock, "Edlund shot the opening sequence five times until he was sure nobody would laugh." Despite Edlund's success in achieving what appears to be photographic verisimilitude, however, the effects are rarely naturalized. Because of the dynamic play of scale and speed, they never appear commonplace or overly familiar.

Star Wars looked back to the golden age of movies in other ways as well. It rolled back the sixties by employing actors with square-jawed, Waspy good looks like Mark Hamill and Harrison Ford who had been relegated to the unemployment lines in the Nixon era by "ethnics" like Dustin Hoffman, Al Pacino, and Elliott Gould. In employing a new generation of relatively unfamiliar nonstars like Hamill, Ford, and Carrie Fisher, Lucas succeeded in creating the perception that the films were newly minted, that he had started over, reinvented the movies.

At the same time, the *Star Wars* films embraced the simple values of heroism and old-fashioned individualism and revived a kind of Manichean, back-to-basics moral fundamentalism suggestive of the Reagan era yet to come. "I wanted to make a kid's film that would strengthen contemporary mythology and introduce a kind of basic morality," said Lucas. "Everybody's forgetting to tell the kids, 'Hey, this is right and this is wrong.'" It's no accident that Lucas referred to the Empire's foot soldiers as "storm troopers," invoking a time when it seemed easier to tell good from bad. *Raiders of the Lost Ark* and *Indiana Jones and the Last Crusade* carried this further, portraying the bad guys as literal Nazis. The immediate past of the Vietnam War was presumably too complicated to deal with directly.

The Indiana Jones films were always to the right of the *Star Wars* trilogy. They shamelessly revived and relegitimated the figure of the dashing colonialist adventurer who plunders and pillages antiquities from Third World countries for First World collectors. The end of the title sequence of *Raiders*, with a white man (Indy) being flown out of the jungle a hairsbreadth ahead of a bunch of spear-chucking natives, not only brings to mind the myriad of naively racist jungle movies of the thirties but also evokes the "fall" of Saigon; this light-hearted, veiled allusion to what, after all, was the most painful and humiliating episode in recent American history was the screen equivalent of Reagan's soon-to-be-notorious flippancy about life-and-death world issues.

121

One of the basics Lucas tried to restore was the primacy of narrative, or at least an eighties semblance of the classic narratives of the thirties and forties. In 1968 Kubrick messed with narrative in *2001,* and in the seventies other directors like Penn, Altman, and Dennis Hopper followed suit. Penn experimented with a variety of anti-narrative devices, while Altman employed elliptical, dreamlike, and associative strategies. Moreover, as Richard Maltby argues in his book *Harmless Entertainment,* by the seventies the aesthetics of television, with its open-ended, soap opera/series–influenced anti-narrative orientation, which tended to privilege performances over storytelling, finally penetrated to movies, entirely transforming, say, a film like *Nashville* into a series of discrete tableaux whose order could be reshuffled at will without apparent damage to the narrative. At the same time, and to the same end, the enormous clout of stars ("bankability"), which had helped to destroy the studio system in the fifties, delivered the coup de grace to what was left of narrative in the seventies. Movies became little more than occasions for star turns: Woody Allen's monologs broke free of the story to address the audience directly in *Annie Hall* and *Manhattan,* and Marlon Brando's scene-stealing, baroque, and extremely mannered performances similarly became ends in themselves, like his wonderful, weird bounty-hunter-in-drag number in *The Missouri Breaks,* pushing the plot forward. As Maltby puts it, "in the New Hollywood, a star's enactment of him- or herself . . . became sufficient justification for a movie, and performance . . . assumed the cohesive function previously fulfilled by narrative." Movies in the seventies were not so much acted as performed; they were presentational, not narrative.

Presentational cinema like Altman's found favor with critics but not audiences. (Hollywood suffered from a box office slump throughout the early seventies.) And even the critics lost patience with films like *The Missouri Breaks.* At a point where the anti-genre movies had lost both their popular and critical following, Lucas came along and imposed two-dimensional performances on his actors, trying to subordinate both acting and effects to story, lending the films a stripped-down, streamlined feel. Mark Hamill was not about to disrupt *Star Wars* by lisping, wearing a dress, and upstaging the robots. After a decade of cinematic mannerism, audiences appeared to be relieved that the dog once again seemed to be wagging the tail.

Not only did Lucas attempt to reestablish the primacy of narrative; the kind of narrative he used was linear, direct, and traditional, which is to say, it gives the impression that it is transparent—the stories appear to tell themselves. They are straightforwardly chronological, without complicated flashbacks that weaken the narrative thrust or make the plotting hard to follow. Devices with which seventies directors had drawn attention to their narrative strategies were forsworn or suppressed. The artifice that, say, Francis Ford Coppola later used in *One from the Heart* is repudiated; artifice, like the kind displayed in the Jabba the Hutt sequence in *Return of the Jedi,* is decadent, associated with the bad guys.

In borrowing, combining, and recombining elements from both right and left, then, the *Star Wars* trilogy breathed new life into the ideological consensus of the center on which their conventions depended, and succeeded in doing in the realm of culture what the Carter Restoration had, with only partial success, attempted in the realm of politics. It was crafted (intentionality aside) to appeal to members of the disaffected Vietnam generation and draw them back into the fold. It created a new consensus that included both proto-preppies (Luke et al.) and, as junior partners, an assortment of outsiders and loyal "minorities": Chewbacca, R2D2, and C-3PO, and, in *Return of the Jedi,* an astonishing array of weird-looking aliens, as well as Lando, an actual (nonmetaphoric) black man who becomes a general in the rebel army, in the same way that the actor who played him, Billy Dee Williams, became one of the few black entertainment figures to play a role in the Reagan campaign during the 1980 presidential elections.

BOYS IN SPACE

AT THE END of *Close Encounters of the Third Kind*, Spielberg's second blockbuster, the blessed and much anticipated event finally occurs: the alien ship gently touches down in a panoply of colored lights, accompanied by a crescendo of orchestral music, as a bunch of dumbstruck Earthlings watch in silent amazement. Since this film, itself a much anticipated marvel of techno-movie magic, is on one level as much about its own construction and reception as about its ostensible subject—visitors from other worlds—it's not hard to equate the space ship with *Close Encounters*–the-movie, and the enthralled mortals with the blissed-out audiences who greeted the movie with similar awe.

123

For Lucas and Spielberg, those spectators in *Close Encounters* were the model audience. Although the agenda of *Star Wars* was nothing if not ambitious—to refurbish consensus for the seventies and after—the trilogy had other, bigger fish to fry, and its influence was vastly more profound. It attempted nothing less than to reconstitute the audience as children. Lucas said he wanted to make a film for "the kids in all of us." As Alan Ladd, Jr., put it, when he was head of Twentieth Century-Fox (which produced *Star Wars*), Lucas "showed people it was alright to become totally involved in a movie again; to yell and scream and applaud and really roll with it."

To infantilize the audiences of the sixties and empower the audience of the seventies, to reconstitute the spectator as child, Lucas and Spielberg had to obliterate years of sophisticated, adult moviegoing habits. *Star Wars* came on the heels of nearly a decade of wise-ass, cynical, self-conscious moviemaking. And it wasn't only Hollywood that thumbed its nose at mom and apple pie; after Vietnam, Watergate, and attendant traumas, parody and irony were running rampant throughout popular culture. Whether in reflexive, hip TV shows like *Saturday Night Live* and *Mary Hartman, Mary Hartman* (even the title was self-referential) or "adult" comics, both overground (*Spiderman* and Co.) and underground (*Mr. Natural* et al.), or punk music (the Ramones). But it was the New Hollywood, fueled by the influence of innovative directors like Jean-Luc Godard and driven by a gang of Young (and not-so-young) Turks working under the aegis of the so-called "baby moguls" eager to tap countercultural dollars (and score a few points for the "revolution" at the same time), that was most deliriously self-reflexive.

The directors whom Lucas and Spielberg were rebelling against characteristically distanced their movies from their audiences. Penn was fond of using spectator surrogates within his fictions, observers like the anthropologist in *Little Big Man* whose study frames the story, inevitably reminding audiences that they, too, are watching a "story." But there are few spectator figures in the *Star Wars* trilogy; in fact watching (and its ethical correlative, disengagement) is attacked as immoral. When Han Solo refuses to assist the rebels in the crucial battle that concludes *Star Wars,* when he becomes a spectator rather than participant, he's being selfish and is punished for it. Darth Vader, the Emperor, and the Empire's generals spend so much time watching the action on video screens that they're defeated by the rebels, the doers who act rather than look.

Likewise, in the *Indiana Jones* films there are precious few spectators, and those who do look quickly become participants, like the Cairo natives in *Raiders* who initially provide the passive backdrop for the chases in the bazaar but eventually intervene, saving Indy from the Nazis by surrounding and shielding him. Similarly, in the nightclub scene that opens *Temple of Doom* the distinction between spectators and performers breaks down in pandemonium, and Indy and Willie escape, one performer and one spectator indissolubly linked, their roles reversed, as performer Willie becomes spectator in Indy's world and spectator Indy becomes performer. And, as a spectator, Willie loses the inviolability her performance confers upon her, becoming increasingly at risk.

It's telling that in the climactic scene of *Raiders* the movie camera plays a cameo role, the first and only time it does so in the six movies, explicitly drawing a connection between making movies, possessing whatever it is Indy's looking for (in this case the Ark), unlimited destructive power, and guilty seeing, which must be punished. When the Ark does its thing, the camera is incinerated, the Nazi spectators have their eyes burned out, while Indy and Marion survive only by averting their gazes. Moreover, the unusual presence of the camera is a surprising bit of self-consciousness that can't help but allude to the cinema of self-consciousness that Lucas and Spielberg rejected.

Controlling, manipulative director figures in the *Star Wars*/Indiana Jones films are invariably bad. In *Star Wars* Vader is the director, choreographing complicated movements in space from his screen in the control room of the Imperial Star Destroyer. In *Raiders* the director is Belloq, the Cecil B. DeMille who orchestrates the unveiling of the Ark and is destroyed, while Indy, a potentially competing director, survives by dint of being immobilized, prevented from directing. In *The Last Crusade* the millionaire Donovan is the producer, who coerces a reluctant Indy into "directing," that is, conducting the search for Henry Jones and the Holy Grail. Dr. Else Schneider, not at all reluctant but an aspiring, wannabee director, is the villain. Lucas and Spielberg were, of course, real directors, and therefore the message of their movies disguises and contradicts the realities of how they were made and consumed. The demonization of metaphorical director figures within the movies creates the illusions that the movies are directed by no one. The movies are transparent.

This pattern of denial, or deniability, as it was called on the political level, operated in other ways as well. As we have seen, the *Star Wars* trilogy contained a pro-nature message, while at the same time it was both a testimony to and a triumph of technology. In *Raiders* the act of watching is rendered dangerous as the spectators within the movie who have the misfortune of seeing the Ark in action are killed, while (so that) the real spectators (the audience) can indulge in the pleasure of watching. Whereas the *Last Crusade* begins by offering up an origins sequence to reveal the roots of Indiana Jones–the-character, in reality Indiana Jones–the-movies concealed their origins. Lucas and Spielberg succeeded in contradicting the message by the medium, and, in so doing, they did in fact manage to remystify movies.

This is not to say that Lucas's and Spielberg's movies entirely rejected self-consciousness. The one vice that movie brat directors never could quite resist was making allusions to their favorite TV shows or classics from film school. Lucas bowed in the direction of *The Searchers* and glanced at *Dr. Strangelove* (Luke's mechanical arm). The kind of self-consciousness displayed by Lucas and Spielberg was most often self-congratulatory and narcissistic. As in *Close Encounters,* or the beginnings of *Raiders* and *Temple of Doom,* where the mountainous Paramount logo dissolves into reel mountains, it celebrated itself, whereas the self-consciousness of the seventies was self-critical and Brechtian. It deconstructed and demystified itself.

Lucas's new aesthetic of awe did succeed in infantilizing the audience, not only by overwhelming it with sound and spectacle, not only by attacking spectatorship within the films, but also, on a narrative level, by punishing cynicism, eliminating or suppressing elements that contributed to irony or critical self-consciousness. Lucas has always been quite clear on this score. He explicitly said he wished to exclude the traces of camp that had crept into the genre exercises that did persist in the sixties and seventies, most notably the James Bond films. "Lucas insisted that his cast never play a scene for camp humor, even if his script seemed to call for it," wrote Pollock. Said Lucas, "It wasn't camp, it was not making fun of itself. I wanted it to be real."

The most important part of this program involved attacking and discrediting adults while valorizing children and childlike qualities, particularly "innocence." By the post-Altamont mid-seventies, as the flower power revolution of the sixties had started to fade, a jaundiced view of childhood had become de rigueur among many of the older genre-bashing directors. Sam Peckinpah led the way in the late sixties with *The Wild Bunch,* a film that turned the traditional John Wayne Westerns upside down. In Ford's *The Searchers* (1956), primitive, seemingly amoral Indians massacre a family of settlers, who are identified with the values of civilization, and kidnap a girl (Natalie Wood). John Wayne, hell-bent on revenge, sets out to destroy the Indians. Years later, when he finally catches up with them, he tries to kill the girl, in the belief that she has been terminally corrupted by her Indian upbringing: nurture over nature. The film, however, partially repudiates the Wayne character, and sides with those who want to reintegrate the girl into the settler community, in the conviction that she is salvageable: nature over nurture. By the time *The Wild Bunch* was released, thirteen years later, the Indians had become an outlaw gang of senior citizens, now victims rather than killers, and (white) civilization had become totally corrupt, no more so than its children, little lords of the flies, who open the film by tormenting scorpions. But these same children were Lucas's primary audience, and when he alludes to *The Searchers* early in *Star Wars* (the massacre of the family farm in Tatooine), he's telling us that it's Ford's vision he's endorsing, not Peckinpah's.

If revisionist directors like Peckinpah, Penn, and Altman treated the legends Ford cherished as lies, Lucas wanted to reestablish their authority. And he brought children, often peripheral observers in the films of the seventies, to center stage. For Lucas, Spielberg, and the other movie brats, barely more than kids themselves, children were essentially good, adults generally bad. Adults behaved poorly in the sixties; they sent their children off to die in war. In the late seventies the children would have their revenge. Indeed, adults in the Lucas and Spielberg films are invariably either punished, like the ones in *E.T.* who, as Dorfman points out, are the real aliens, or redeemed through infantalization, like the hero of *Close Encounters,* who sheds his family (along with his adult responsibilities) to end up, in essence, playing in the sandbox, building towers out of mud and mashed potatoes.

In the *Star Wars* trilogy most of the adults are consigned to the Empire, certifiable heavies for whom death by blaster is too kind a fate. Like Darth Vader, Lucas's Ur-adult, grown-ups in these films are shrouded in darkness, in mystery; they're opaque and filled with secrets. (The fact that Lucas used James Earl Jones's voice for Vader and had Billy Dee Williams play the duplicitous Lando in *The Empire Strikes Back* makes a good deal of thematic, if not

127

racial, sense.) Luke even accuses kindly old Obi Wan Kenobi of lying to him on the subject of his father's true identity, and Obi Wan resorts to some lame adult double-talk in self-justification. The Empire typically exercises elaborate stratagems to trap the rebels, whereas the rebels are open and straightforward. When they do resort to trickery (spies misinform them that the Death Star II is not yet operational), they fail. When Luke is open and transparent (we can see from his face that he's pure of soul), Vader is hooded, masked and closed. When Luke finally removes Vader's helmet, his head looks like a white slug that's been living under a rock, a pale embryo, a proto-fetus. His good side, which Luke Claims he senses, the kernel inside the shell. The reality behind the appearance is an infant.

It's no accident that Vader's "real" self, his innocent self, is imagined as an unformed adult. In these films not all adults are bad; some, like Lando (and Natalie Wood in *The Searchers*), can be redeemed by nurturing their natures, that is to say, their child-like characteristics. The best example of this process is Luke himself, the films' teen-age identification figure. It is striking that although the *Star Wars* trilogy foregrounds the story of Luke's maturation and education in the mysterious ways of the Force (in other words, his development into an adult), the real significance of the films is the opposite: the way this process is thwarted, aborted, and denied. Or, to put it another way, to grow up in these films is to return to childhood.

The abyss that divides children from adults is—in Lucas's eyes—sex. Therefore, sex, like adulthood, is bad news. As Pollock points out, in Lucas's earlier *American Graffiti* "adolescence was the Force—hard to understand, even harder to control. 'This is a dangerous stage for you, Luke,' Ben [Kenobi] warns another teenager. 'You are now susceptible to the temptations of the dark side [of the Force].'" To resist the dark side of the Force, Luke has to spiritualize himself by subliminating (in war) and later suppressing his erotic and aggressive impulses (which tend to be equated) The measure of Luke's maturity, his light-sword, is, as Dan Rubey suggests, an all-too-obvious symbol of power and sexual potency. "You carry it in your pocket until you need it, then press a button and it's three feet long and glows in the dark." At the end of *Star*

Wars, Luke is confidently piloting his fighter, streaking through a correspondingly vaginal canal or trench so that he can launch his "missile" into the "womb" of the female Death Star.

But during *The Empire Strikes Back,* Darth Vader lops off Luke's arm, none too subtly "castrating" him; by the time Luke gets to *Return of the Jedi,* he gives up his light-sword and leaves the dogfighting to others while he attends more directly to his Oedipal needs—his struggle with his father. He's well on his way to becoming a monk (he's wearing sackcloth in his climatic confrontation with his dad and the Emperor), a passive Moonie, a First World Yoda. Although resolving this generational conflict is supposed to be the route to adulthood, it doesn't work out that way for Luke. He has merely learned to live with and internalize castration; when he renounces his light-sword, he voluntarily accepts what was earlier imposed by force from without. In the upside-down developmental framework of the trilogy, to submit to the dark side of the Force is to become an adult; Luke must resist, choosing endless childhood over childhood's end.

129

It follows from this imperative that, rather than becoming man enough to win Princess Leia from his rival Han Solo, Luke discovers that Leia is his sister. In the psychological universe of *Star Wars* she must turn out to be his sister, because Luke must be protected from even a hint of adult sexuality. In order to give this prohibition dramatic weight, sex must be, and is, portrayed as dangerous.

The Jabba the Hut sequence that leads off *Return of the Jedi* represents a striking intrusion of the sixties adult *Heavy Metal* magazine brand of sci-fi; and Leia, suddenly sexualized in her revealing Barbarella outfit, must be rescued not only from Jabba but from her own sexuality. (During the production Lucas strove to desexualize Carrie Fisher by binding her breasts with gaffer's tape. "No breasts bounce in space. There's no jiggling in the Empire," said Fisher.) The Jabba episode culminates in an explicit *vagina dentata* fantasy, as Luke and his pals have to walk a phallic gangplank into the pullulating maw—festooned with long, curved teeth—of the giant Sarlacc in its "nesting place." A more nightmarishly explicit image of threatening female sexuality would be hard to imagine.

When Luke renounces his light-sword, he not only relinquishes his sexuality, he gives up power as well. In the fifties power was a no-no; cold war ideologies associated it with Stalinism. Power had no place in a democracy; people did what they were supposed to do not because they had to but because they wanted to. In the sixties, when the culture shifted to the left, the spectacle of the world's strongest nation waging (near) total war against a small peasant society confirmed the bad rep force already had; it was no longer Stalinists who abused power but democratically elected American leaders, adults who burned Vietnamese with napalm abroad and crushed flowers with guns at home. In order to grow up into childhood, Luke must relinquish power. At the same time, however, despite this unsavory legacy, in the post-Vietnam period force had to be relegitimated. After all, when *Star Wars* was released, the Ayatollah was just about to precipitate a crisis that would go far toward the miraculous transformation of America from a bully to a victim, erasing testy hawks, impatient for the return of the cold-war martial spirit, dismissively referred to as "the Vietnam Syndrome." (There is even a hostage crisis in *Return of the Jedi* where Jabba holds Leia and Luke's robot pals.) So there is never any doubt that force is necessary to defeat the Empire; it is only that adults (Lando et al.) and extra- or subhuman aliens (the bug-eyed "monster" who commands the rebel fleet) must do the dirty work for Luke while he attends to more consequential matters. Moreover, Luke's solution is to forswear force in favor of the Force, i.e., relinquish personal power in favor of an impersonal power for which he bears no direct responsibility.

The last adult candidate for infantilization, and therefore redemption, is Han Solo. He is older than Luke (he calls Luke "kid"), more sophisticated, cynical, and self-interested. He is a right-wing Clint Eastwood–type individualist who rejects collective values, the claims of community—or contrarily, a left-wing (the two were often interchangeable) Jack Nicholson do-your-own thing free spirit (*One Flew Over the Cuckoo's Nest* won an Oscar for Best Picture the year before *Star Wars* was released). He's also the kind of person who could be expected to sneer at *Star Wars*. In other words, he's the adult viewer surrogate inside the picture. (Again, on a personal level, he is Luke/Lucas's "older brother" and mentor Francis Ford Coppola, by whom Lucas apparently felt betrayed when Coppola took *Apocalypse Now,* which Lucas had help develop and hoped to direct. Like Han Solo, Coppola often called Lucas "Kid.") As such, Solo is too powerful, his pursuit of Leia too threatening. He has to be immobilized by carbon freezing in *The Empire Strikes Back* before he can become a full-fledged member of the Alliance, which is to say, his development, growth, process of maturation have to be dramatically and demonstrably attested.

During the course of the three films the relative positions of Solo and Luke are reversed. In the beginning Solo is the dramatic focus of the story; he's the more powerful of the two, as indicated by the fact that he saves Luke's life. By the end Solo has almost disappeared from the plot, which now focuses almost exclusively on Luke. Moreover, Luke saves Solo's life, the boy becomes more powerful than the man. Even though Solo is eventually rescued from carbonization, he's learned his lesson. He has been turned into a wimp and is even obliged to apologize to Leia for a fit of jealousy.

BOYS WILL BE BOYS

IN THE INDIANA Jones films Indy is more like the older Han Solo than he is Luke. (There is no Luke figure in these films, but to compensate, *Temple of Doom* adds a kid, Short Round, to beef up preteen identification.) Like Solo (and Luke), he has to be prevented from growing up—instead of evolving into an adult, he has to devolve into a child. Early in *Raiders*, Indy accuses Marion (Karen Allen) of having come between him and her father, his mentor, inverting the usual Oedipal triangle in which the father comes between the son or daughter and the opposite sex. From Indy's point of view, in other words, the ideal relationship is one that only a girl can disrupt—presexual male bonding between father and son. Nevertheless, Marion is the perfect partner for Indy. She is a tough-as-nails, male-identified woman; that is, a presexual tomboy. In her first scene she wears pants, runs a bar, and beats a hulking Nepalese peasant in a drinking contest.

But as the plot careens along, Marion is divested of her "masculinity" by the lechery of the villainous French archaeologist Belloq. Whereas Indy treats Marion like an irritating kid sister,

Belloq treats her like a woman. In fact, so great is Indy's aversion to an adult romantic relationship with Marion that he virtually gives her to Belloq by refusing to rescue her when he has the opportunity. Belloq, who knows a good thing when he sees one, dresses her in a revealing gown and tries to get her drunk. But her burgeoning sexuality must immediately collide with the prohibition against adulthood that goes with the territory of these films; so no sooner does she flash a calf than she must be terrorized with a frightening fantasy of predatory masculine sexuality, the male analogue of the *vagina dentata* scene in *Return of the Jedi*. Marion, still dressed in Belloq's white satin dress (now an index of her vulnerability rather than of her sexual powers), dangles over a mass of writhing snakes, her panties blinking whitely in the dim light as her legs scissor back and forth. Spielberg presents Marion and the audience with a powerful equation of sex (again, read adulthood) and mortality in the striking images of snakes slithering first through the open toe of her shoe and then the eye sockets of a skull. The process of sexual awakening, in other words, has become a slippery slope leading to violation and death. Even when Indy and Marion merely play at parenting, it ends badly. Once in Cairo, they "adopt" a monkey and lightly allude to it as their baby. As it turns out, their monkey is a bad baby, a spy for the Nazis. Indy and Marion can't have children, of course, because they are children.

Belloq is the adult in *Raiders*. He's worldly, corrupt, and cynical—in short, a mercenary. The search for the Ark is nothing if not a Faustian quest for knowledge and power, and it is essentially Belloq's quest. Indy is Innocent of power, as he is innocent of sexuality. It's the chase itself that engages him; the outcome is unimportant. He's a process kind of guy, and he's always safest while he's looking. He can even excavate for the Ark right under the noses of the Germans, who don't, or can't, see him—until he finds what he's looking for and loses his innocence, at which point he's inevitably plunged into jeopardy: Belloq is there to seize whatever it is he's found. Belloq is always able to do this, of course, because while Indy is innocent, Belloq is not. He's allied to the Nazis and has no qualms about exercising power.

Indy himself is an adventurer, a guy who can punch out the heavies and read glyphs, too, the intellectual as man (rather, boy) of action, Richard Perle (or Pipes) as Andy Hardy. Belloq keeps insisting that he and Indy are alike, and he's partly right. In their climatic confrontation, where Indy demands Marion, the two men, ostensibly mortal enemies, call each other by their first names and speak a language of intimacy that only the two of them can understand. Belloq is the adult Indy and therefore makes the wrong choice (the Ark over Marion, power over love) and has to die because, once again, power is dangerous. (On the other hand, as in the *Star Wars* trilogy, power is hardly renounced, the good guys merely want it for themselves.)

In *Temple of Doom* Willie (Kate Capshaw) starts out in a dress, a femme woman plucked out of a nightclub and plunged into the jungle, thereby punished for her explicit adult sexuality. She's also culture, thrust unceremoniously into nature. She can't ride an elephant, can't stand the disgustingly primitive food, and so on. Indy treats her like a nuisance (à la Marion), but she teases him for not acknowledging that she is a woman and that he's attracted to her. It's the old battle of the sexes, or the sexless, in this case, and Willie has an uphill struggle. Sexual encounters between the two are characteristically interrupted and delayed, and, moreover, suffused with an aura of danger. One of their few sexually tense scenes, where Indy and Willie each wait for the other to make the first move, is interrupted by an attack on Indy, which then segues into another *vagina dentata* sequence in the underground Spike Chamber. In the film's final scene Short Round rains on Indy and Willy's parade by spraying them both with water (from a phallic elephant's trunk, yet) as they embrace, making the audience view the traditional romantic clinch from the point of view of a bored, playfully hostile, and suggestively jealous child. Worse, when Indy falls under the Thuggee spell, he nearly lets Willie die, and it's hard to resist the notion that this is his true desire, his unconscious wish. He'd rather see her dead than make love to her.

The dominant metaphor of *Temple of Doom* is the enslavement of children. In *The Disappearance of Childhood* sociologist Neil Postman argues that the idea of children as a distinct species, a breed apart, different in kind from adults, is a product of industrialization and the rise of schooling, of which laws prohibiting child labor were a by-product. The enslavement of children, which in

Temple of Doom consists of forcing them to work at the kind of adult hard labor prohibited by these laws is, in effect, an attack on the idea of childhood. Thus, when Indy frees them, he metaphorically rescues not just children but childhood. From another perspective, the child-slaves are the audience, made miserable by the serious adult films of the seventies, awaiting a director who will restore the innocence, joy, and laughter of old-fashioned, uncomplicated moviegoing.

The Last Crusade is said to be the final installment of the series, so it is fitting that in it Indy has at last grown up. Indy has been supplied with an instant childhood (in the "origins" sequence that leads off the movie) as well as a father with whom he ostensibly comes to terms, the implication being that he is now an adult. But, as in the *Star Wars* films, growing up in the worlds of Lucas and Spielberg is problematical at best.

The origins sequence is liberally studded with not-so-veiled allusions to the dangers of growing up. It opens like a Western in Monument valley, Spielberg's version of Lucas's homage to John Ford. But it quickly becomes clear that what we think are the cavalry are Boy Scouts. After a shot of a phallic rock formation that looks like Devil's Tower in *Close Encounters* (another example of the series' self-referential narcissism), the film suddenly cuts to a "primal scene" of sorts, redolent of forbidden voyeurism of taboo activities. It's reminiscent, even in its camera angles, of the scene in the underground cave in *Temple of Doom,* where Indy, hidden behind some rocks, looks down on the illicit activities of the Thuggees. Here little Indy, also in a cave, watches an older version of himself—wearing what will become, when he "grows up," his characteristic leather jacket and fedora—discovers the precious Cross of Coronado. Later, in an action sequence where Indy lies flat on his back on top of a circus car fall of rhinos, one of the animals pokes its horn through the roof; it comes right up between his legs. Having dropped in on a lion in another car, he fights phallus with phallus, grabbing what will become his signature bullwhip off a wall to defend himself. With this riot of battling phallic images, you don't have to be Freud or Lacan (or Joseph Campbell) to tell what's going on. In one scene he's got the Cross of Coronado stuffed into his belt. When a bad guy grabs for it, a snake (brother to the one that had crawled from his pants a moment earlier) slithers out of his sleeve. The suggestive proximity of Cross, snake, and private part makes explicit what the twp previous films had only implied; the power of the coveted object of the quest, be it Ark, Ankara Stone, Cross of Coronado, or Holy Grail, is the power of the phallus, or better yet, dad's phallus.

Enter dad, the new element in *The Last Crusade* formula. Although Indy's dad, Henry Jones, is more appealing by far than Darth Vader, he has been, like Vader, a bad dad, significantly "missing" throughout much of the picture, in the same way that Vader is "missing": Luke doesn't even know for sure he is his dad until the third installment of the trilogy. Here Indy and his dad haven't spoken for twenty years.

In *The Last Crusade* both father and son compete, after a fashion, for the same woman: Dr. Else Schneider. The state of grace (innocence) that protected Indy in the first two films is compromised. After two installments of coitus interruptus, Indy actually has sex with the female lead, played by Allison Doody. As we might suspect, both she and he have to be taught a lesson. Unlike Marion in *Raiders* and Willie in *Temple of Doom*, Else has a strong sexual presence and the moral ambiguity to go with it. In a script move of striking economy, she embodies the marriage of the Belloq and the Marion characters of *Raiders* (what would have happened if Belloq had succeeded in seducing Marion?), and in her the themes of power and sexuality converge. Like Belloq, she is obsessed by the quest for power; also like him, she has no scruples and will do anything to get her hands on the Grail, including allying herself with the Nazis. And, like Marion, she is, of course, a woman. But, unlike Marion (and Willie), as an archaeologist and adventurer herself, she is Indy's equal, more grounds for her eventual demise. Suggestively, she comes to life—animated and decisive—only when she reveals her Nazi colors. In the same way that going over to the dark side was to become an adult in the *Star Wars* films, so here (for Else, anyway) becoming a Nazi is to become an adult—or vice versa. After she slips from Indy's grasp and falls to her death, the same scene (in, for Spielberg, an unusual exercise in didacticism) is repeated, this time with dad in Indy's role and Indy in Else's role. Else's death has taught Indy a lesson; unlike her, he

135

chucks the Grail and grabs dad's hand with both his own, enabling dad to lift him to safety. In other words, he turns his back on the quest for power—but not, characteristically, before he's had a taste of it (the holy water has mended dad's wounds).

When Else, unmasked as the proto-Nazi, unreconstructed ends-justifies-the means-er that she is, falls to her death, the prelapsarian, presexual male bonding between Jones *père* and *fils* is restored. She is sacrificed to the sacred bond between father and son so that the two can live happily ever after. Giving up Else, Indy gives up the sexual competition with dad (much as Luke gives up competing with Solo for Leia) and renounces the quest for dad's phallus.

Has Indy finally grown up or not? He has saved his father's life, has gotten his dad to call him by his real name, "Indiana," instead of "Junior," as dad was prone to do. But the lesson dad teaches him—prefer process t product, leave the Grails to the Elses of the world, the Nazis—is not unlike the lesson Luke learns in the *Star Wars* trilogy when he renounces his light-sword: give up adult aspirations and return to childhood. It's as if once Indy made his point, made dad acknowledge his adulthood, call him by his real name, he is content to revert to the comfortable role of son. Like Luke, he has internalized castration, After all, Indy's last words in the movie are "Yes, sir!"

BACK TO THE FUTURE

THE *STAR WARS* and Indiana Jones trilogies, not to mention *E.T.* and *Close Encounters*, raked in an unprecedented amount of money. Most of these movies rank among the all-time top ten grossers. With their toy spinoffs ($2.6 billion to date for the *Star Wars* trilogy alone), their endless afterlife on video, and their enormous influence on the subsequent video game craze, they succeeded way beyond their producers' wildest dreams. They not only enshrined their aesthetic of awe, the changed the way Hollywood did business and, therefore, how it made movies. The blockbuster syndrome probably started with *The Godfather* in 1972 and got an added boost from *Jaws* in 1975 but really took off with *Star Wars*. Once it became clear that certain kinds of films could reap immeasurably greater returns on investment than had ever been seen before, studios naturally wanted to turn the trick again, and again, and again: enter the Roman-numeral movie, product of the obsession with surefire hits. Blockbusters were expensive to make, and the more they cost, the safer and blander they became, while the smaller, riskier, innovative projects fell by the wayside.

Nevertheless, despite the megaprofits of the Lucas and Spielberg movies, and despite the wide currency of their world view, in some sense the tow wunderkinder fell victim to history and to the contradictions within their own fictions. When Reagan's Strategic Defense Initiative (SDI) was introduced in the early eighties, its critics immediately dubbed it "Star Wars," meaning that it was no more than a silly screen fantasy. Ronald Reagan, blessed with a considerably keener appreciation of popular culture than his Democratic opponents, immediately understood that, given the infantilization of the electorate, this was a plus rather than a minus, and embraced the name. ("The Force is with us," he quipped.) Meanwhile, Lucas, whose consciously held politics, politics with a capital P, were still rooted in the sixties, quixotically sued to prevent the name of his movie from being used for the weapons system of choice of the newly revived cold war. He lost, of course, because the fit was perfect. There is an irony here of mammoth proportions: the culture of military/media/industrial complex that made SDI possible was the culture Lucas (along with Spielberg) had done much to create, and now it had turned around and bitten, so to speak, the hand that fed it. Moreover, Lucas had forgotten the lesson that inspired *Star Wars* and that little Indy learns so dramatically at the beginning of *The Last Crusade*: don't trust anyone over thirty.

Why was Lucas so surprised? Twelve years elapsed between *Star Wars* and the release of *The Last Crusade* in 1989, an eternity in the foreshortened hyperspace of American cultural history, and by the time Indy rode off into the sunset, ostensibly for the last time, a lot had changed. The propaganda of youth that fueled the sixties fizzled in the eighties. The high hopes of the sixties had been left in the dust of the Me Decade, and youth had become identified in the media with mindless self-indulgence. Pot had turned into coke, and then crack. The idea of childhood had changed radically from the Age of Aquarius to the Age of Reagan. One vehicle for this change, however unwitting, were Lucas and Spielberg's films. By attacking irony, critical thinking, self-consciousness, by pitting heart against head, they did their share in helping to reduce an entire culture to childishness, and in doing so helped prepare the ground for the growth of the right. The kids prevailed, but the ideals they stood for had been drained of content.

The seeds of the rightward drift were planted years earlier with Yoda and Obi Won Kenobi. They were the primary teachers or socializers of young Luke, because the generation gap of the sixties had stripped parents of the authority they need to properly raise their kids. *Star Wars* alluded to the loss of adult authority by eliminating the older generation altogether. Luke's father is apparently dead, his mother is never mentioned, and his aunt and uncle killed off. There simply is no Mr. And Mrs. Luke, Sr., to teach young Luke how to brush his teeth and drive his land speeder—there is only kindly old Obi Wan, Luke's spiritual, if not actual, grandfather. (In the same way, the movie brats of the eighties looked to the movies of the thirties and forties for inspiration, not to those of the sixties and seventies.) The trilogy creates an alliance of son and grandfather against the generation of fathers. Even at the beginning this alliance was deeply conservative. Despite the fact that Luke & Co. are referred to as "rebels," in essence they play a healing, restorative role, returning the galaxy to an earlier time, before the clique of Emperor/Nixon, Vader/Kissinger adults worked mischief in the galaxy by overthrowing the Republic. The earlier time was the pre-Nixon, pre-Watergate, pre-sixties golden age that Carter had pledged to restore, the period that Lucas had memorialized so well in *American Graffiti* in 1973.

As the ideological abyss between children and adults disappeared, there was no reason why young and old should any longer stand on opposite sides of the galaxy. If *The Last Crusade* begins with the don't-trust-adults lesson of the sixties, it ends with a lesson of the seventies and eighties: generational reconciliation. There is no father figure at all in the first two Indiana Jones films; the father is simply irrelevant. In the original sequence of *The Last Crusade* little Indy rushes into his father's office, clutching the Cross of Coronado to his breast. Instead of springing to his rescue, myopic Henry Jones, oblivious to the drama that has consumed his son, makes him count to ten in Greek. Dad is out of touch and, like his whole generation, has abdicated his responsibilities. Indy has to force his father to be a father.

The Last Crusade is about the rehabilitation of the over-thirty adults the sixties had written off. In it the renegade adults of the Nixon era became the avuncular, benevolent authority figures of the Reagan-Bush era. Reagan, in turn, wrapping himself in the mantle of FDR, tried to fulfill the promise of the Carter Restoration by visibly incarnating in himself the old verities from which the nation had wandered. The circle had closed; it was, indeed, back to the future.

As the politics of the movies changed, so did their deployment of basic, ideologically constructed categories. Although the *Star Wars* films endorse nature over culture, there is a distinct undertow pulling them in the opposite direction. Way back in the beginning, say, in *Star Wars* and *The Empire Strikes Back,* adults were portrayed as unemotional machines like the Imperial Guards, and Luke & Co., more than anything else, feared becoming robots like them. With his mechanical arm, Luke risked exactly this transformation into an automaton—the hard-edged Empire techies led by his wheezing, machinelike, respirator-assisted bad dad. However, in *Return of the Jedi,* released well into Reagan's first term and amid his campaign against sex in movies and softness in politics, the threat suddenly came from the opposite direction: formless organic matter, dissolution; burning and melting rather than freezing; Jabba rather than Vader. (The turning point in this battle between mechanical culture and organic nature came when Luke's fighter sank into the ooze of Yoda's swamp midway into *The Empire Strikes Back.*)

139

This change parallels a shift in attitude toward primitive and modern evident in the two trilogies. In the *Star Wars* films Third World figures like Yoda were gurus: in the Indiana Jones films the cultural backsliding of the Reagan years allowed them to revert to the traditional role of loyal sidekick (Short Round), pathetic victims (Indian villagers), or villains (the Thuggees). In the *Star Wars* films it is advanced civilizations like the Empire that have access to dangerous, unlimited power. In the Indiana Jones films it is ancient cultures. Primitive Judaism and Christianity and the Thuggees, that have access to such power. If the *Star Wars* films come down on the side of nature, the Indiana Jones films come down on the side of culture; high tech is better than low tech. The old tombs are invariably booby-trapped with ingenious primitive devices (recalling guerrilla warfare techniques of the Ewok-Vietcong). The films also present a generous sampler of nature's little horrors—poisonous snakes, spiders, scorpions and so on, and Indy-the-innocent-colonial-plunderer invariably leaves the tombs in ruins as he escapes by a hair.

The idea of the primitive in the Indiana Jones films, associated as it is with dangerous, out-of-control power, also stand sin for the unconscious, the id, and in the same way that sexuality has to be repressed, so does the unconscious, which, by extension, happens to be the Third World. Like the unconscious, the primitive has its own language; to the extent that Indy deciphers this language, reads maps, solves puzzles, and susses out cryptic symbols, he functions as an adult. Literacy is a product of culture, not nature. Schooling initiates children into the mysteries of adulthood, primarily by teaching them how to read. But in reading the language of primitivism, not only is Indy acting like an adult, he's acting like a particular kind of adult: a psychoanalyst plumbing the depths of the (nonwhite) unconscious. (He's Franz Fanon for the eighties.) In *Star Wars* adult secrets and mysteries are linked with villainy, while youthful transparency is equated with goodness; likewise, in the Indiana Jones films the search for the unconscious is, however, seductive, ultimately dangerous. The unconscious itself has to repudiated. It is better off left untouched and untapped, and the Third World forgotten.

We have seen that Indy is safest when searching for the Grails of the world and most at risk when he finds them. The pattern of innocent quest versus guilty possession parallels the patterns of innocent flirtation versus guilty consummation on the sexual level, which, in turn, parallels the pattern of innocent childhood versus corrupt adulthood on the development level. The structure provides an ironic commentary on the movie brats' own achievements. It cats a retrospective glow of nostalgia over the years of struggle and a cold, self-critical light on the success that followed. Success has its rewards, but it exacts a price, tempts fate, and courts the kind of apocalyptic retribution pictured at the end of *Raiders*.

On an emotional level the Lucas and Spielberg films are most deeply engaged over Oedipal issues, so it's no surprise that both trilogies boil down to explicit struggles between fathers and sons. For a much as Spielberg and Lucas tried to indulge their Peter Pan complex and deny adulthood, with its attendant anxieties of power and sexuality, they deeply longed for it as well and struggle hard to achieve it. And when they did achieve it, when their extravagant commercial success thrust them to the pinnacle of power in a studio system they half despised (Lucas installed himself in a bucolic fastness in Marin County, far from Hollywood, while Spielberg contented himself with informal power brokering behind the scenes), they turned around and denied it all over again in movie after movie because they were deeply uncomfortable with such success.

REVENGE OF THE DADDIES

FROM THE BEGINNING Lucas's and Spielberg's movies were preoccupied with the search for the father, "a strong revitalized father figure to fill a perceived void in the American nuclear family," as critic David Kehr put it. In *Jaws* the weak father emerges as the one man capable of dispatching the shark, while in *Poltergeist* "a weak-willed, childlike father finally steps forward to assume the disciplinary authority he needs to protect his family from evil."

For Spielberg the traditional father was the font of values, the storyteller, the "director." "Families [used to be] very, very close," Spielberg said, "They used to gather around the reader, or the seer, of the household, and in the twenties and thirties, usually it was the father. And then television replaced the father."

Thus, Lucas's and Spielberg's movies were disturbed by a profound contradiction. Much as they wished to infantilize their characters and their audience, they also wanted to re-create the characters and their audience, they also wanted to re-create the strong father; in fact, infantilization demanded the strong father. At the end of The *Last Crusade* Indy finally succeeded in re-creating his father, and it is precisely this that allows him to escape the uncomfortable role of an adult. Despite all the effort, Indy has expended on finding the Grail, ultimately he doesn't need to possess it, because he's found something more important: the father he never had. A newly powerful Henry Jones allows Indy to revert to infancy. He can indulge his talent for process (over product), relinquish his role as director, and afford to ignore adult preoccupations with power and responsibility. So powerful is this imperative that the moment of truth is dramatically equated with saving Indy's life.

It is no accident that Indy's dad is played by Sean Connery, whose James Bond movies Lucas and Spielberg grew up on. As far back as 1977 Lucas observed that "Steve said he'd always wanted to do a James Bond film . . . I said I had a great idea for a James Bond film. 'It's not James Bond. It's set in the '30's and is about an archaeologist . . . So Indiana Jones really evolved out of Steve's intense interest in James Bond." Like others of their generation, Lucas's and Spielberg's cultural tastes were much to the right of their political convictions. They were, as Godard put it, "children of Marx and Coca-Cola." (Or, to be more precise, children of Charles "the greening of America" Reich and Coca-Cola.) Spielberg once said, "I love *Rambo*. But I think it is potentially a very dangerous movie." While their cultural program—the infantilization of movies and moviegoers—was conscious and explicit, the political implications of their program were not, even (or especially) to themselves.

Ronald Reagan was the strong father Lucas and Spielberg didn't know they were looking for, the ideal president for the Age of *Star Wars*. Reagan presented himself as the precursor of children (particularly fetuses), and it was under his administration that child abuse became a major (non)issue, while his wife made it her business to protect kids from drugs. Like Obi Wan and Yoda, he was a blend of adult and child. (If Yoda began life in 1980 as Ho Chi Minh, he ended life in 1983 resembling Reagan more, thanks to Lucas's conflation of wisdom and Yoda's Zen-like simplicity and childishness.) As such, he transcended the ambivalence toward father, the twin feelings of fear and love, the need to rebel and the need to submit. He was the true ancestor of the movie brats, a man/child who had grown up in and on movies, for whom movies were as real as reality, a man who looked at crime through the eyes of Dirty Harry ("Make my day"), at Third World wars through the eyes of Rambo. Like Henry Jones, Reagan enabled the nation to revert to infancy, turn its back on the complicated reality of grownups in favor of the back-to-basics, black-and-white, heart-overhead, fighting-over-talking fantasy lives of children, a perspective that, ironically, had deep roots in the counterculture.

Reagan once said, "It is the motion picture that shows us not only how we look and sound, but—more important—how we feel." In his excellent book *Ronald Reagan, the Movie,* Michael Rogin suggests that the lack of box office success of the anti-communist films of the fifties meant that Ronald Reagan was wrong. Anti-communism was more a top-down than a bottom-up phenomenon; anti-Communist movies had not succeeded in colonizing our minds or showing us how to feel. He adds, as an aside, "Should movies fail in showing us how we felt, an emissary from Hollywood not altogether successful in them would have to enter politics and go to Washington." Reagan's journey from culture to politics represented a movement from buying tickets to marking ballots, suggestion to statement, covert to overt, unconscious to conscious. In this sense, politics was culture demystified.

Inevitably, however, culture found its way back into politics, as political parties turned to Hollywood for money, charisma, even candidates. In the same way that Lucas and Spielberg (re)mystified movies, the movies mystified politics. As Rogin points out, Reagan's national security policy, including SDI/Star Wars, was as much a fantasy as Lucas's movies. "It replaced the world it claimed to represent." (From Lucas's point of view, SDI amounted to Reagan's own, unauthorized sequel to the *Star Wars* trilogy. His crime was copyright infringement.) Like a movie, it didn't matter that it had no relationship to reality, because it was anchored in Reagan's personal authority. It was the man, more than the politics, people trusted. In the same way that in the mystified universe of Ronald Reagan the man belied the message. And, as Reagan understood, the electorate had become an audience.

Had Reagan not existed, Lucas and Spielberg would have had to invent him. As it was, he resembled a character in their movies. As Nancy Reagan once said, "There is a certain cynicism in politics. You look in back of a statement for what the man really means. But it takes people a while to realize with Ronnie you don't have to look back into anything." In other words, so far as Reagan was concerned, what you saw was what you got. Like Lucas's and Spielberg's heroes, he enjoyed a childlike transparency and two-dimensionality.

Reagan's career in movies petered out in the fifties, and he became the host of general Electric Theater on television. Reagan's relation to his policies, the man to the "movie," resembled the relationship of host to show; he "presented" his movie, directly addressing his audience in speeches and (rare) press conferences, and it was the presentation, not the movie, to which voters responded. "Ronald Reagan" was constructed as much by the logic of television as by movies, and his relation to his policies had more in common with the naïve television of the fifties than with the ironic movies of the seventies. As a presenter in a presentational mode, he was immune to the consequences of his actions.

As Maltby points out, television's open-ended, anti-narrative presentational structure diverts attention from the consequences of choice or actions to the choices or actions themselves. "Characters and audiences are required to make choices, but as they are immune from narrative, they are unaffected by the results of those choices." Thus, Reagan was able to dissociate himself from the results of his policies. In his neither-truth-nor-consequences administration he became the "Teflon president."

Nevertheless, as we have seen, Lucas and Spielberg tried to escape the presentational aesthetic. Whereas anti-genre films of the seventies were open-minded and unresolved, the *Star Wars* and Indiana Jones trilogies struggled to reassert the prerogatives of narrative and archive closure. But a funny thing happened on the way back to the future: countervailing tendencies within the films defeated their best efforts. Lacking the ideological and narrative structuring that characterized the age of consensus to fall back on, the films are permeated by ideological confusion, a legacy of the seventies and a testimony to the degree which both narrative and closure had been irremediably compromised. Although *Star Wars* has a conventional moral framework—the education of a young man—with regard to traditional areas of contestations, like nature and culture, it is, as we have seen, completely muddled. The premise of the Indiana Jones films is that Indy is a mercenary; older consensual films like, say, *Casablanca* would have brought him into the fold, sort of, but his education proceeds in fits and starts, and for reels at a time it is forgotten altogether.

In *Raiders* Belloq's relationship to the Nazis faintly echoes the ideological struggle between scientists and soldiers that characterized fifties sci-fi: Belloq, in his obsession with the Ark (he exclaims, "It's beautiful!" before his eyes are burned out), is not unlike the mad scientists, e.g., the naïve Dr. Carrington in *The Thing,* who sacrifice all to learn about the alien, and he's contrasted with the more level-headed Nazi officers. In the fifties, and even the sixties, there were important issues at stake: what principles would govern the coalition of the center—persuasion or force, reason or tradition? In *Raiders* the debate is carried on in a dilatory, inconclusive, spasmodic fashion. Although Belloq clashes with the Nazi officer several times in the course of the movie, sometimes he gets his way, sometimes he doesn't, and the issue is never resolved. This confusion and inconclusiveness are at least partly attributable to the weakening of the consequential, cause-and-affect structure of narrative by the wayward logic (or illogic) of the films.

Moreover, the story line of *Star Wars* often grinds to a halt entirely in order to display some astounding special effect that invariably overshadows audience concern with the fate of the humans, particularly because the actors' level of performance has been so severely scaled down. The observation often made about the film was true: not only was Mark Hamill not about to upstage the robots, but R2D2 and C-3PO continually upstaged him. Similarly, the story line of the Indiana Jones films is often interrupted by elaborate chase scenes that seem to last forever and do nothing to forward the plot. As audiences grew familiar with the special effects of the *Star Wars* films and the thrills of the Indiana Jones films, both directors were forced to pack more and more of the same into their pictures. Spielberg complained about this in 1982: "The thing that I'm just scared to death of is that someday I'm gonna wake up and bore somebody with a film. That's kept me making moving that have tried to outspectacle each other."

Spielberg's and Lucas's solution was to reemphasize conventional story values. Spielberg said, "You need good story-telling to offset the amount of . . . spectacle the audiences demand before they'll leave their television sets. And I think people will leave their television sets for a good story before anything else. Before fire and skyscrapers and floods, plane crashes, laser fire and spaceships, they want good stories." Indeed, the third installments of both these series are much more traditional than the first and depend much more on conventional character conflict and psychological realism than on thrills and special effects.

But psychological realism was never Lucas's and Spielberg's forte. Spielberg elaborated the much maligned "high concept" as a way out of this impasse. He was once quoted as saying that if the premise of a movie couldn't be boiled down to twenty words or so—the high concept—it wouldn't work. High-concept filmmaking, in which the idea drives the plot, was an antidote to the anti-narrative undertow in his movies.

Conceived serially, Lucas's and Spielberg's films also don't have the closure they might have had had they stood on their own, and the *Star Wars* films, in addition, are peculiarly presented as the fourth, fifth, and sixth of a series of nine. Spielberg acknowledged this problem and defended himself by arguing that he didn't have to provide "complete" endings. "I don't think in any of my films the end answers all the questions,' he said. "Why? Why spoon-feed? Why set out a buffet?"

Spielberg also recognized that part of the problem was television, and in combating the anti-narrative influence of the tube, he had to fight his own deepest instincts. Noting that he doesn't read much, Spielberg remarked, "I am really part of the Eisenhower generation of television." He came up through television, directing there before he made features. But he once described *Poltergeist* as his "revenge" against television. And if, as Spielberg observed, television replaced the father as storyteller and source of values, Indy's reconciliation with his father has to be seen as another metaphoric rejection of television in favor of an older tradition of storytelling, that is, of the movies. Hence, the ending where all the characters ride off into the sunset, à la the old Westerns.

Nevertheless, try as they would, Lucas and Spielberg were not able to whip their movies into conventional shape. Whereas other sequalizers had to come up with situations that allowed the stars they had created in the original to strut their stuff at the expense of a plot (*Lethal Weapon II* is a good example), their problem was not so much presentationalism, seventies-style, as spectacularism, eighties-style. The result, however, was the same. Narrative became hostage not to stars' wars, but to special effects. And just as Lucas's and Spielberg's insistence on infantilization had an unanticipated result—the rise of a new patriarchy inimical to many of the values these directors thought they believed in—so their attempt to restore traditional narration had an unintended effect—the creation of spectacle that annihilated story. The attempt to escape television by creating outsized spectacle backfired, and led back to television's presentational aesthetic.

Instead of rolling back the seventies, they, along with Reagan (following a somewhat different path), brought that decade to its logical conclusion. The movies of the seventies, however scornful of genre and consensus, were inevitably tied to that tradition, if only in opposition. Lucas and Spielberg cut loose entirely; they didn't restore narrative so much as empty it out. And, as usual, this contradiction had its roots in their own paradoxical attitudes toward filmmaking, growing up, success, and so on. For all their fear of seeing and insistence on punishing spectators, they were in love with seeing. Fear of sex and forbidden voyeurism implied its opposite: the rule of the unconscious expressed as spectacle, the erasure of self before the spectacle. Spielberg once said, "I want a movie to overwhelm me. I want an environmental experience, one that I cannot get from television." The striking resemblance of the last scene in *Star Wars* to the mass rallies of Leni Riefenstahl's fascist classic, *Triumph of the Will,* has often been noted; it's no accident that Lucas and Spielberg imagined adulthood as fascism, equated grown-ups with Nazis. In fact, the forbidden and explicitly demonized figure of the Nazi unexpectedly resolved all the contradictions that bedeviled these six films: the repressed unconscious finds expression as infantilizing spectacle created by the strong father, who at the same time is the director. Spielberg's most heartfelt scene is not the end of *Raiders* but its opposite, the end of *Close Encounters,* in which unlimited power is good and spectacle is enthralling. Which brings us back to Reagan and the odd cultural confluence between him and the two directors.

Lucas and Spielberg helped make the world safe for Reagan, only to find that reconciliation with the over-thirty generation turned out to be a pact with the devil. It was as if Indy had thrown in his lot with Belloq, run off with Else, and stayed in Berlin to parlay his Hitler autograph into a job with Albert Speer. In short, it was as if Luke had gone over to the dark side. Darth Vader had won.

147

• • •

In most ways the Age of *Star Wars* and Indiana Jones is over. New production and distribution formations—the internationalization of Hollywood—appear almost daily, while continuing technological innovation threatens to make the special effects work of Lucas's Industrial Light and Magic in the eighties look as dated as silent film. Neither Lucas nor Spielberg is promising another installment of their respective series; both have made noises about moving on, growing up, and so on. At the same time, and not coincidentally, the demographics of American viewers are changing. The baby boomers are growing older; the lock of the teenage audience has been broken. High concept, while not entirely dead, has given way to so-called "adult" movies whose plots do not lend themselves to one-sentence summaries. The blockbuster and the sequel are still with us—witness the record-breaking summer of '89—but the shape and the look of these movies are changing. Blockbusters still attempt to re-create the old consensual audience relinquished by television as it became Balkanized by the proliferation of delivery systems and specialized software, even as this audience becomes increasingly fragmented by age, geography, and class,

Nevertheless, however movies evolve in the nineties, they will have to take as their starting point the massive changes engineered by Lucas and Spielberg in the eighties, just as Lucas and Spielberg defined themselves against the movies of the sixties and seventies. Anti-genre filmmaking may reemerge, but it can never take the form it did in the seventies. It will be, like *Batman,* and *Robocop* before it, a kind of graft of the seventies onto the eighties, some amalgam of presentationalism and spectacularism, suffused by the apocalyptic glow of urban dread characteristic of the nineties: indeed, the world according to Darth Vader. Neither gentler nor kinder, these movies will likely be considerably more honest, and therefore more brutal, than anything in Lucas and Spielberg. If the 1930s found amusement during the Depression in fantasies of class reconciliation, the 1990s may find amusement in similarly egalitarian fantasies of mutual class annihilation.

REPORTS

THE WEATHER UNDERGROUND, TAKE ONE

Peter Biskind and Marc N. Weiss

> He's a real Weatherman
> Ripping up the motherland
> Making all his Weatherplans
> For everyone
> Knows just what he's fighting for
> Victory for people's war
> Trashes, bombs, kills pigs and more
> The Weatherman
> —[To the tune of the Beatles "Nowhere Man"]
> from the *Weatherman Song Book*

A lot of things have changed in Weatherland since that song was written in 1969. After five-and-a-half years, people have grown accustomed to them, used to seeing their faces on wanted posters when they were papered over by garden variety bank robbers and disappointed when the FBI took them off the Ten Most Wanted List. People have even grown used to their bombings of public buildings, used to reading their communiqués, which were eventually collected in a tasteful red volume suitable for coffee tables.

For a long time, it was their custom to detonate symbols of American power to damage those monuments which seemed in their ponderous solidity to guarantee American predominance forever.

They angrily retaliated against the savage displays of national arrogance from which the rest of us averted our eyes or protested in milder and more traditional ways. They bombed police cars in Chicago following the murder of Black Panthers Fred Hampton and Mark Clark in 1969. They bombed the Office of California Prisons in Sacramento after the murder of George Jackson in 1971. They bombed the New York State Department of Corrections after the Attica uprising in 1971. They bombed the U.S. Capitol in Washington after the invasion of Laos in 1971. They have carried out about twenty-five armed actions to date, most of them occurring in the period 1970 to 1972.

After 1972 they seemed to become less active. It looked like they were becoming just another faded feature of the sixties landscape, slowly disappearing from view like Huey Newton, or transformed beyond recognition like Rennie Davis.

Then, in July 1974, they clandestinely published and distributed 5000 copies of *Prairie Fire,* a 150-page analysis of changing U.S. and world conditions. It was an urgent invitation to groups and organizers throughout the country to respond in the form of political discussion and renewed action. Its flyleaf bears the inscription: "A Single Spark Can Start A Prairie Fire." In Spring 1975, they issued another 25,000 copies of *Prairie Fire* and published the first volume of *Osawatomie,* a quarterly "journal" named after the Battle of Osawatomie in which John Brown's abolitionists defeated an army of slavers in 1856. The Weather organization, in other words, is alive and well in underground America, perhaps more vigorous, extensive and together than ever before. The latest government estimate says there are thirty-seven Weatherpeople living underground; other sources place the figure much higher, but no one really knows.

The Justice Department, for all its million-dollar appropriations, computers, wiretaps, and grand juries, has been largely ineffectual in unearthing the members of the Weather Underground, which remains a perpetual embarrassment to the legions of agents who devote their energies to their apprehension.

The latest joke on the FBI is a documentary film about the Weather Underground produced by Emile de Antonio, Mary Pampson, and Haskell Wexler. The government was not amused. A congressman

151

from Georgia, Larry McDonald, no doubt expressed the Justice Department's sentiments when he read into the *Congressional Record* this statement: "Mr. Speaker, the Weather Underground organization terrorists have taken responsibility for a whole series of bombings, including one right here in the Capitol and one in the State Department earlier this year. Now a group of Hollywood's left-wing crackpots are planning to do a propaganda puff piece on these criminals. The ringleader of the Hollywood crew is the notorious Emile de Antonio, the maker of a number of pseudo-documentary left-wing propaganda films, including one smearing the late Senator Joseph McCarthy and another supporting the Communist aggressors in Vietnam."

De Antonio had indeed "smeared" Joe McCarthy in his first film, *Point of Order* (although McCarthy is a relatively attractive figure compared to the film's portrait of invertebrate congress people and craven Army officers). And he had shamelessly gone on to make *Rush to Judgment* (an examination of the John Kennedy assassination), *In the Year of the Pig* (the most comprehensive film study of the thirty-year anti-colonial struggle in Vietnam) and *Millhouse: A White Comedy* (a film about Nixon for which de Antonio was accorded the signal honor of being the only filmmaker on the former president's Enemies List).

No sooner had the FBI gotten wind of the film early this summer than it slapped the three filmmakers with subpoenas summoning them to appear, along with their negatives and tapes, before a grand jury in Los Angeles. They refused to cooperate and the Justice Department, somewhat mysteriously, withdrew the subpoenas ten days later.

The project itself began last fall, when de Antonio read *Prairie Fire*. "I had always been impressed with the tender loving care with which their bombings were executed. No one was ever hurt and they were all directed against the symbols of oppression and authority.

"I've always been a sort of half-baked radical most of my life. There was never anything to take hold of, to grab on to. What was left of the sixties was very little, frankly, just shards and fragments, attitudes of the counterculture with no program, no organization. These are the people who are the direct line to the sixties and to all those things in American society which are good. *Prairie Fire* impressed me. It represented a new phase, an attempt to extend the range of their politics, their activity, their influence."

If they were "coming out," de Antonio reasoned that a film would be the best way to do it. He sat at his typewriter and pounded out a proposal, part stream-of-consciousness, part machine-gun prose. It speaks of a "film weapon" that would reach millions of people on TV: "The mood should be defiant and revolutionary, but not wise-ass or cocky. It should be didactic in the sense that it should open eyes and point directions for others." It would combine the analysis of *Prairie Fire* with stock footage documenting the events of the sixties that generated the Weather Underground events almost forgotten in Gerald Ford's America. The film would sell on the strength of the Underground's undeniable dramatic appeal: "You have created a masterstroke of political theater which not only reveals the police state but that it's impossible to beat it." And then, scribbled in: "It belongs on film. BANG. BANG. BANG!"

The proposal finished, de Antonio set out to contact the Weather Underground. "In this case," he recalled, "I approached the project with a certain lack of confidence. Would these people cooperate? Would it be possible to get in touch with them? There were a couple of young radicals I know who I just assumed would have the contacts.

"The first time, I approached this guy and said, 'I know you can get in touch with them. Can you get the machinery in operation to get a letter to them from me?' And he said, 'Yes.'

"But I never knew how those letters reached them. I wrote a let-ter, gave it to somebody, and then a message came back saying that they were interested in the proposal and that I would be hearing from them.

"At that point, a person known to me but whom I had never thought of in that connection came to me and said, 'Are you inter-ested in meeting with these people?' And I said, 'Yes, I am.' That person then said, 'I'll meet you on the corner of so-and-so and so-and-so tomorrow afternoon.' "

The next day, de Antonio drove to the designated corner. He was not accustomed to taking security measures but he practiced a few elementary precautions that he had picked up from movies, like driving down a dead-end street and turning around to make sure he wasn't being tailed. The procedure he followed that first day established the pattern for each of the subsequent meetings, and once the pattern had been set up, the same intermediary was used again and again. The intermediary never knew where the meetings between de Antonio and the Weatherpeople were to take place. He or she merely took de Antonio from one designated corner to another, and then left. Each corner was observable from any number of different directions. There were instructions in that place that would lead him to another place, where there would be new instructions, and so on. Each step of the way he could be observed to determine whether or not he was being followed. "It took a long time to get there, even though I didn't travel far."

On that first day, de Antonio met two members of the Underground. "I expected to meet crazy people, mad bombers, fanatics. And the first things that absolutely overwhelmed me was that the people I met were so cool, relaxed. They were comfortable, self-possessed, light—everything I expected them not to be."

They discussed de Antonio's proposal over dinner. "Right away, it was obvious to me that there were conditions to this film that were not only different from any film I had ever worked on, but that were different from anything anybody has worked on. The main condition was security. They insisted, and I agreed at once because it was apparent that it was a legitimate request, that they be in charge of security all the way down the line: all the meetings, the conditions of filming, and more importantly, that they would have final cut in a security sense. Any shots that revealed too much would be eliminated. Now this came hard to me because I'm a free-wheeling, anarchistic type. I was always very bad at party discipline, wherever I was. But it was obvious that when you are dealing with people who are political fugitives, you can't flash their pictures around. Because you're simply doing the job of the police."

Later on, they arranged a system of direct phone contact. "Those conversations were very brief. We all had code names. In addition to their real names, they all had underground names, they had code names for this particular project, names that had not been used before and were never used again. Sometimes it got very confusing."

Subsequent meetings, like the first, were always held in public places—parks, restaurants, busy streets. The content of the film was worked out in detail, and they talked about who else would join the film crew. For a camera person, de Antonio had had Haskell Wexler in mind from the beginning. Wexler had several points to recommend him. He was widely acknowledged to be one of the best cinematographers in Hollywood (he won an Academy Award for *Who's Afraid of Virginia Woolf?*); he had solid political credentials extending back to the late Forties when he made films for the leftwing United Electrical Workers, and continuing through the last thirty years with documentaries on civil rights, torture in Brazil, Allende, several films on Vietnam and a feature, *Medium Cool*; he was able to contribute to the financing of the film (Wexler and de Antonio each put up $5,000).

Initially, Wexler was not thrilled with the idea of doing a film on the Weather Underground. "I wished it were something else. I'm basically a nonviolent person. I didn't know anything about the Weather Underground except what I read in the papers. They were strongly associated in my mind with violence."

Nevertheless, he agreed to meet with them and de Antonio. It was a more complicated logistical exercise than usual; the meeting was arranged in one part of the country and took place in another, some time later.

The meeting (Wexler described it as the "usual cloak-and-dagger kind of thing") was held in a park. They were sitting on a bench engrossed in conversation. Along came a stranger and sat down beside them. "My first instinct was to say, 'Let's get out of here,' " recalled de Antonio. "Haskell looked like he was about to say that too, when the Weather guy said, 'I'm very comfortable. Are you?' The filmmakers guessed that they were comfortable too, and the conversation continued on an innocuous level until the Weatherperson finally said, 'Don't you think it would be nice if we took a walk?' "

De Antonio told the story with a certain admiration. "The Weather guy was in total control of the situation. His instinct was correct. It wasn't instinct, it was training, discipline."

The Weatherpeople asked Wexler how he would shoot the film so that their faces would not be visible. Wexler explained: "We said we'd use every trick in the book except disguises. We felt disguise was untrue to the way they operate. They operate out in the streets, in the open, among people. So that we did not want to put ski masks on them, which are menacing, hostile symbols to begin with. We didn't want to make them look like they had just robbed the local A&P. We didn't want to camp them up with a lot of strange-looking makeup which would make them look grotesque and thereby confirm the government's caricature of them as crazed terrorists."

The Weatherpeople wanted the filmmakers to understand that they would probably be called before a grand jury when the film project became public knowledge. They wanted de Antonio, Wexler and later Mary Lampson to take a position of absolute non-collaboration with any investigation that might ensue. Even though they knew they were risking jail, the filmmakers readily agreed.

For their part, de Antonio raised the question of guns—what would happen if the police burst in during the filming. "I said, 'Look, are you people going to be armed? Because if you are, I would like to be too.' Laughing, they replied, 'Don't be ridiculous. We're not going to be armed. If we're surrounded, we'll just come out.' Here we were, good front people for them. The cops still don't kill filmmakers in this country. They do in Chile but not here. Not yet. Of course, I can't guarantee what the Weatherpeople would do in a different situation."

By the end of the meeting, Wexler was convinced. It remained only for de Antonio to bring a third person into the crew who would be responsible for the sound and editing and participate in the filmed exchanges.

Mary Lampson was a natural choice. She had worked with de Antonio on his last three films. She would be interested in the project, she could be trusted and at twenty-nine, she was roughly the same age as the Weatherpeople.

Nevertheless, it was a difficult decision for her. Although she had worked on some important films, including *Millhouse* and Cinda Firestone's *Attica*, she had never, by her own description, been a political activist.

Lampson recalled hearing about the Days of Rage in October 1969, when hundreds of Weatherpole took part in a series of violent attacks on police and property in Chicago. "I thought they were crazy, although I can remember sitting around with friends of mine and talking about doing that kind of stuff. We had gone on peaceful marches and not gotten anywhere. We had a tremendous sense of frustration and didn't know what to do with it. So although I don't think I ever would have gone out and done that, I understood what it was about."

The following month, she was at a massive antiwar rally in Washington. A group of several thousand people broke away from the marchers and moved toward the Justice Department to protest the continuing trial of the Chicago 7. Lampson recalled: "You knew that those people were going to get maced and tear-gassed and beaten and I can remember standing there and debating whether to go or not. I didn't go."

Now, five years later, Lampson stood nervously on another street corner thinking about which way she should go. To help her decide, a meeting had been arranged. There she confessed to the Weatherperson sitting across from her that she had never been a terribly political person. "I told him, 'I didn't agree with some of the things you did before. I still probably don't agree with some of the things. How do you feel about having someone involved in this that's certainly at a different stage?' That was a welcome thing, that's what they wanted. The film was to be a dialogue. They wanted us to challenge them and they wanted to challenge us. Once I saw what it was going to be like, well, then there was no doubt in my mind that I wanted to do it."

It had been six months since de Antonio had sat down to read *Prairie Fire*. Now all the arrangements had been made. Wexler, anticipating long hours of hand-holding a heavy camera, did his customary arm exercises.

The filmmakers were told to go to a certain place and wait for a phone call. The call would furnish them with instructions that "would set in motion a very carefully planned and elaborate series of moves," eventually bringing them to the "safe house" where the filming would take place.

Hours passed. "I was in a high energy state and irritable," de Antonio said. "Every time the phone would ring, I would run to pick it up. It would be somebody saying we hadn't paid the laundry bill."

157

The waiting continued through the night and into the next day. When the call finally came—after nearly two days—everything went like clockwork. The filmmakers piled into their car and drove to the first contact point, where they were told how to get to the rendezvous point. There they were picked up, given specially blackened glasses to wear and driven to the safe house.

"We were so heavily loaded down with equipment," recalled de Antonio, "that every time we made a turn, the tire would scrape against the body of the car. We wondered if we would make it or not. While we were driving I said to them, 'Don't you think any police-man who sees three people wearing dark glasses in a car is going to be suspicious of the car?' So they said, 'Okay, take yours off.' I took my glasses off and closed my eyes. I never opened them once."

When they arrived, the filmmakers were led from the car into the house. The equipment was unloaded and the car stashed.

A safe house is a house with no history. It is anonymous. Books had been put on the shelves, soap and towels in the bathroom, sheets on the bed—all the props necessary to make it look lived in and livable for the three days they would spend there. The windows had been sealed up so that nobody could look in—or out.

"That night," recalled de Antonio, "I don't think anyone slept too well. I mean, there we were in that strange safe house. Believe me, a safe house may be safe but it sure is strange."

The next morning, they set up a large piece of scrim—a gauzy material that would be used to conceal the details of faces but hopefully allow gestures and even lip movements to be seen. They taped up the posters they had brought with them—Ho, Allende, Fidel—and did those things that filmmakers do like look for the fuse box, figure out where to place the lights and so on. Everything was ready.

"We still didn't know who was going to be there," de Antonio said. "We never asked. We had placed ourselves implicitly in their trust. We knew they would do the right thing, so we anticipated it would be the national leadership of the organization. The door opened and in walked five people: Bernardine Dohrn, Bill Ayers, Cathy Wilkerson, Jeff Jones and Kathy Boudin."

"We shook hands," Lampson remembered. "Everybody was extremely nervous and we all sat down around this table. There was silence for a moment. Then, all at once, everyone just totally and spontaneously started to laugh and clap their hands. We were finally all together."

Was this the first time these five Weatherpeople had seen each other in a long while? "We tried to avoid knowing that," replied de Antonio, "so I can't give you an answer to that question. It's the kind of question I wouldn't answer even if I knew what the answer was. We were operating on a need-to-know basis. We never asked them if they belonged to the same collective or not. We didn't ask them how many collectives there were. All that kind of information is highly useful to the police.

"They themselves at the time described the filming as one of the most dangerous things they'd ever done. They had to anticipate that every mistake I made, or Haskell made, or Mary made, would be a mistake they made. Every mistake they make leads to their arrest or death."

There was an immediate good feeling in the room, Lampson recalled, and as they sat and talked about where to begin, she suddenly realized what an incredible moment it was. "We were sitting in this room with these people, doing this."

De Antonio felt it too. "You suddenly felt, you know, Christ, look at these people. You could almost see them on the wanted posters. There was a kind of thrill and excitement about being there with them.

"This was like sitting with Robin Hood. I mean, these people are fugitives, the whole state was against them. Now they themselves reject the myth that's grown up around them but people who live on the outside can't help but be aware of it. We had to break through that romance and show that their history is our history."

Take One

THE WEATHER UNDERGROUND has a keen sense of their own history. They speak for a whole generation when, in *Prairie Fire,* they describe their own development this way: "We inherited a deadening ideology of conformity and gradualism. Our first protests were law-abiding and peaceful. But we came to see that change is violently opposed every step of the way. We stood up and defied property, the state and the law, in street demonstrations and outrageous actions. Militant confrontation politics transformed us; we broke with a powerless past. As our own protest elicited tear gas, prison and bullets, we recognized the need to fight and the terrible cost of not doing all we possibly can."

In 1969, as SDS began to crumble, the Weatherman faction set out on a new and dangerous course. They singled out the Black Panthers and Third World guerrilla struggles as the vanguard; they came to believe in "the strategic necessity to build an underground movement, to learn to fight through fighting," in short, "to prepare and build the armed struggle."

The significant events of the early days, the Days of Rage (October 1969), the Flint War Council (December 1969), grew out of a reckless rage, a feeling that blind destruction was an expression of genuine revolutionary fervor.

In March 1970, because of a technical error, a bomb exploded in a townhouse in New York City, killing three Weatherpeople: Diana Oughton, Ted Gold and Terry Robbins. Two women, Kathy Boudin and Cathy Wilkerson, escaped the burning house and went underground. Within hours, the entire organization disappeared.

Now, five years later, a woman sat in front of a camera and said, "My name is Bernardine Dohrn. For a long time I watched the political developments of the sixties taking place, especially in the South. I thought about joining them but I knew that taking the first step would change my life. And I hesitated for a long time. The first demonstration I took part in was an anti-HUAC demonstration, and then increasingly I became involved in organizing work in Chicago. I joined the open-housing drives for equal housing rights that took place on the West Side of Chicago in 1966. I helped organize rent strikes. This was for SCLC when Martin Luther King was in Chicago. At the height of the student movement I joined SDS. This was long after I was a student myself. I was elected national officer of SDS and traveled for two years as an organizer and speaker. During this time, I had the opportunity of meeting with the Vietnamese and the Cubans. This experience in particular made me a full-time revolutionary and really changed my own idea of myself and what the revolution was going to be."

Cathy Wilkerson spoke next: "In my freshman year of college in 1962, I went to a picket line outside of Woolworth's, in Cambridge, Maryland. There I heard Gloria Richardson speak, and that was the beginning of realizing that there was a struggle going on that had deep importance for everybody's life, including mine. But I was still somewhat of a spectator until 1964 when I went on a picket line against segregated schools in Chester, Pennsylvania, and was arrested for the first time and found that even the jails are segregated. But mainly I found out that there are masses of black people in this country who are fighting for their freedom and that they are going to win." Each of the others spoke in turn. Bill Ayers and Jeff Jones described the events that had shaped their lives and given direction to their politics. Ayers had been arrested at a draft board sit-in and taught at a community school before becoming active on Ohio and Michigan campuses for SDS; Jones, an antiwar activist from Philadelphia, had traveled to Indochina in 1967 and met with representatives of the NLF. Kathy Boudin completed the introductions. "I think the turning point in my life came when I went to Cleveland with an SDS organizers' project in 1964. One of the kinds of work that we did there was to try to organize a movement of women who were on welfare, to demand adequate living, housing and food for children. We used to go down to the welfare department and ask people if they needed any help and wanted to see the caseworker because it was hard to do that alone. Being on welfare is like being in captivity. One day, a woman asked me to come down with her to the welfare department. I went to pick her up. She lived in Hough. Hough is the place where people were rioting because of lack of food, lack of housing. The day after the riots happened, I picked her up and her two children, and we drove down Hough Avenue. Hough Avenue was lined that day with jeeps, tanks, soldiers and rifles.

"She turned on the radio real loud and started to sing and we drove down through the middle of the tanks to the welfare department. She looked at me and she said, 'We're gonna get our welfare today and my people gonna get what we need.' I went to Cleveland to organize and teach, and it turned out that the people who I was working with, and in the struggle with, were people that taught me about the possibility of change in this country."

Take Two

The initial attempts at filming did not go well. Both the filmmakers and the Weatherpeople were nervous. "One of the problems in the beginning," recalled de Antonio, "was that we were being overpolite with one another. It would have been easy if we were the usual media. They would have been able to act as they have in the past with the media—very tough, everything on their own terms. But when there's any solitude involved, you're a little more careful of yourself, you're a little more hesitant, a little more withdrawn, and this applied to all eight of us. One of them put it better than anybody: 'We want it to be our best and we want you to be your best.' "

This situation was unnatural for everybody in the room. No one had photographed the Weatherpeople for five years; they were not accustomed to being looked at, particularly in the way a camera looks at you. The fact that the project had been in the planning stage for six months created an almost unbearable sense of anticipation, a feeling that a great deal was riding on each word.

Moreover, in years of meetings and collective work, they had developed a style of discourse that was contrary to the requirements of film. They were used to speaking at great length, to developing their ideas in a leisurely fashion without interruption. But a magazine of film only lasts ten minutes. As Lampson described it: "Ten minutes would go by and everybody's getting oiled up and then, boom. The roll was over, we had to stop, change rolls and start over again. It totally destroyed the atmosphere that had been built up. We always bounced back to the fact that here we were in this room with these machines and these lights."

De Antonio described the first frustrating attempts at filming. "We had a long horizontal mirror. Haskell shot into that, a long-slow pan across us, continuing to one of them, Jeff Jones, behind the scrim. The others were seated next to him. Jeff identified himself and then pointing to the others, identified them one by one. But in saying, 'I'm Jeff Jones,' he said more than 'I am Jeff Jones,' and as he said it, he realized he had made certain errors and he corrected himself. So we went back and did it again. By the time we were on the third round of filming ourselves and looking at ourselves in the mirror, there was a certain awkwardness that was extremely inhibiting. You know, it was the feeling that we were doing it for the fourth time. Finally, Jeff got so frustrated that, quite spontaneously, he hit out at the scrim with his hand and said, 'I'm not accustomed to talking with something in front of me.' We all felt that way, that we had a wall between us, both literally and figuratively."

As the atmosphere became more relaxed, they began to discuss Vietnam, a logical point of departure, since the war was a touchstone for the Weather organization as it was for other sectors of the New Left. They accused the media and liberals of aiding the Ford administration in rewriting the history of the sixties in order to convince people that a whole decade of militancy—from Selma to Mayday—had been a failure. They insisted that, on the contrary, the Peace Movement had made a material contribution to the Vietnamese victory.

According to the Weather Underground, the purpose of this effort to reinterpret our recent past is to call a halt to the revolution in consciousness that the New Left indeed achieved and to deflect attention from what they see as the terminal crisis of American capitalism. If Americans are to accept the new economic order—rising prices, loss of jobs, a lower standard of living—being imposed from above by the banks, corporations and their administration flunkies, they must be convinced that they are powerless to control their own lives, powerless to resist, powerless to fight.

The Weather Underground sees the sixties as a watershed in the American political experience. Racism was exposed and fought; women, youth, blacks, Indians and Latinos recovered their own identities and struggled to free themselves from the economic, political and psychic snares of male-dominated melting-pot liberalism; young women and men rejected the dominant values of conformity, materialism and security; white middle-class youth discovered that imperialism was not just a term in history books but that it could be used without quotation marks to describe the political qualities of mid-century America.

Moreover, all these revelations hung together. As *Prairie Fire* put it: "We also came to recognize that issues which once seemed separate had a relationship to one another. Imperialism was discovered as a whole, one system. This was a tremendous breakthrough—it made sense of the world and our own experience. The same school which tracked students by sex, race and class into the appropriate niche, turned out to own slums in the black community and to develop antipersonnel weapons and strategies against revolution—to be in fact a tool of the corporations and the military."

At the same time that it became apparent that imperialism was woven out of whole cloth, the cloth itself began to fray. Vietnam, according to *Prairie Fire,* taught us that "the U.S. imperial system is not permanently superior, not invulnerable even at the height of its power, not loved by the people of the world, not satisfying the needs of the great majority of the U.S. people."

After the morning session was over, they broke for lunch, which consisted of salads and sandwiches. "The Vietnamese influence on them was extraordinary," recalled de Antonio. "They used chopsticks and drank tea most of the time. You will hear slurping sounds on the sound track that sound like someone taking a leak. It's the pouring of tea from a distance."

While they were eating lunch and later during the filming, they were startled by sounds from the street. "We heard the noises that one ordinarily hears that have no meaning. Under the conditions of being in a closed space with the leaders of the Weather Underground, noises like backfires become magnified, as they must for anyone who's lived underground for a long time, let alone for the few days we were. In your mind, everything becomes something it isn't."

When they resumed the filming, the filmmakers posed certain questions that the Weatherpeople were hesitant to answer fully. De Antonio wanted them to give a detailed description of an action. He wanted to know how a target was selected, who was chosen to go, how the action was carried out, what kinds of mistakes were made, how the mistakes were remedied.

In response, they described the bombing of the U.S. Capitol Building in 1971. This sequence, edited for inclusion in the film, reflects the peculiar constraints of life underground which force the film into a modernist, almost Bressonian mold. The traditional documentary forms are turned inside out. The filmmakers, de Antonio and Lampson, are almost constantly in view, peering intently at the camera, while the visual center of interest is absent.

The Weatherpeople intrude almost like obstructions, as the backs of their heads obscure first one part of the screen and then another. The camera flits about the frame, picking up significant details. Like Dohrn's bracelet or Lampson's teacup, but avoids what we want to see: their faces. Meanwhile, on the soundtrack, Jeff Jones describes the Capitol bombing in matter-of-fact tones.

"The organization chose the Capitol," says Jones, partly to dramatize "the fact that Congress was completely in Nixon's pocket. There was nobody in Congress that was taking an honest, principled position against the war in Vietnam.

"Several people volunteered to do it. To get past security, they carried the explosive materials in on their bodies in a certain way." With the aid of a map of the building, they located an obscure room behind a barbershop where they assembled the bomb. "As they were putting it in the place where it was supposed to go, it fell. There was a slanted ledge where they thought there was a shelf. When they realized what had happened—and that they were still there—they took a couple of deep breaths and came out. That evening, members of the organization alerted the press that the action was going to take place. And then it didn't happen. It didn't go off. The fall had in some way affected it and there was no explosion. So, the organization made a series of quick calls around the country and came up with a plan, which was to take a much smaller device and go back in, and put in on top of the one that had been placed there the day before. Sort of like a little starter motor. The second time in was tremendously more dangerous and more difficult because they had called in and already claimed they were going to do it. The people who did it were really making a very strong statement about their commitment to ending the war. So they went back in and they put the little one on it. It worked. It ignited the big one."

165

Another potentially sensitive area was the role they played in helping Timothy Leary escape from prison, in view of Leary's current collaboration with the FBI.

According to the transcripts of their tapes, de Antonio said to the Weatherpeople: "I told you that if we ever made this film, I'd like to talk about something like Tim Leary, which is not exactly one of your high points, is it?"

Weather Underground: Laughter.

Bernardine Dohrn: "It was a lot of fun. To free anybody from prison is a wonderful experience; it is our intention to have the capability to do that a lot more."

De Antonio: "You sprung the wrong guy."

Bill Ayers: "I don't think you could spring the wrong guy. I think that freeing people from prison is a noble and a good thing to do, and something to be pleased with. Besides, it was a frame-up. He got ten years for one joint—maybe."

Jeff Jones: "Then he turned on us—under tremendous pressure from the state. And that's wrong."

Bernardine Dohrn: "I think that was his best self, that moment when he identified himself with the revolutionary forces in the world and actually risked his life to get out of prison, and he did that very self-consciously. And as an informer for the state, trying to save his own hide, it's pathetic, and so he's been made to be his weaker self. He lost."

Their moderation on the question of Leary is perhaps not surprising in the light of their generally conciliatory attitude toward other groups on the left and their strong emphasis on the necessity of unity. Mary Lampson put it this way: "They used to think that everybody who wasn't willing to do what they did was wrong and chickenshit, and they ended up cutting themselves off from the broad movement. It's not like that anymore. The townhouse explosion had a lasting impact on them; it made them rethink their exclusive reliance on armed struggle, which they referred to in their 'New Morning' communiqué as the 'military error.' There are lots of levels of struggle, from day care to filmmaking."

"In the course of preparing for armed struggle in late 1969," they wrote in Prairie Fire, "we began mistaking friends for enemies. We applied the strictest standards of willingness to risk everything; we attacked those who could not come along the whole way, sometimes just because they were not ready to support everything we said and did. We did not learn from meaningful criticisms from comrades." They now see their task as waging a two-front war against imperialism, both underground and aboveground. "Our goal for this period is to help build a mass anti-imperialist movement and to build the armed struggle, the guerrilla forces. Legal and clandestine struggle are both necessary; agitation and attack, peaceful methods and violent methods, sometimes organizing the people step-by-step and sometimes taking a leap through action to a new level. Mass work and armed struggle are united in revolution. Each needs to support and affirm and complement the other."

The first day's shooting lasted until early evening. After dinner, de Antonio, Lampson and Wexler evaluated the results. "I guess we were worried," recalled Lampson, "that the stuff we had gotten that first day was to rhetorical, too impersonal.

"We were afraid we were approaching the problems in a much too abstract way, that it was too much like a discussion of *Prairie Fire*. We felt that a lot of the conversation was stilted, that it took too long a time to express certain ideas and that it was very fragmentary: We knew they were really interesting people—from one personal contact with them, and I think we were unsure as to whether we had gotten that on film or not."

Haskell Wexler was frustrated because the film did not lend itself to a visual treatment. "Your whole idea ordinarily when you shoot people is to show people, show the eyes, show the mouth, show the expression. And the whole task here was to put yourself into reverse. Don't show this, don't show that. So for a while it was a good game, but then it got boring. There was nothing to shoot, nothing to see. A lot of times I just closed my eyes."

Chuckling, he went on: "We might as well have done a radio show! We could have gotten five dingalings from Hollywood Boulevard and photographed them behind a scrim and then dubbed in a sound track that the Underground would have sent us on a cassette. And not have risked anybody's life.

"You know, I was in Chicago for the Days of Rage, only I didn't know at the time that it was the Days of Rage. I thought it was going to be an ordinary antiwar march. I was near the front, walking behind some people who started all the fracas. One of the people who was there was one of the people we were filming. I told him that at the time I was really shocked, because I had marched in a lot of peace marches and wherever there was any violence, it had always come from the people along the curb and never from the marchers. But in this case, the people I was marching with all of a sudden looked like they went bananas. They started to throw rocks and they did it right in front of the police, too, which I thought was kind of dumb.

"But I changed my mind about a lot of things during the filming," Wexler continued. "They were good people, dedicated people, very sensitive to one another and to us as people and not just as political beings. And I sensed that it was not an act that they were able to turn on for special occasions. It seemed very much a part of the way they were all the time."

"The next morning when we got up it was dark," de Antonio said. "The sight of all that fucking film gear lying around was depressing as hell. We hadn't taken anything down. You see that camera and the tripod and the lights and all that stuff, and you think, 'Man, we're going to go through this all over again.'

"And that's when they came in from another room, where they'd slept, very much on the up—they were very big on the up— and said, 'Now we have to have a critique on everything we've done,' which apparently they had decided to do in a meeting they had held the night before while we were having ours."

They discussed what it had been like the first day. The Weatherpeople made it clear that it had not been what they anticipated. It was decided that the physical arrangement of the shots would be changed in order to dispense with the scrim. The Weatherpeople would face the film crew directly with Wexler shooting into a mirror, so that only their backs were revealed. This criticism generated a discussion of the filmmaking process during which it became clear that each group had, to an extent, different priorities.

One of the areas of disagreement was over the Weatherpeople's use of political rhetoric. "As any filmmakers would," Lampson said, "we kept pushing them to be more specific and not so rhetorical: 'Get more concrete, get more personal.' And they resisted because they didn't want the film to be an exposé of the Weather Underground. They didn't want it to be too personal—what kind of toothpaste or deodorant Bernardine Dohrn uses—the kind of thing that the media is always doing. They wanted the film to be about their idea, a tool around which people can organize and be organized.

"But I had always had an aversion to worlds like 'imperialism' and 'capitalism.' I had never really understood what those words meant and I had never trusted people who threw them around freely. But when you really know what you mean when you use those words—as I found they did when I listened to them—the words can be very useful. The struggle is to constantly redefine those terms and make them mean something. And that's the purpose of the movie.

"Of course, those words must be attached to life, to lifestyle, because that's where politics is finally measured. In what you do. That's why we felt that those personal things were very important. We tried to convince them that if they trusted us enough, we would not abuse that element, not sensationalize it. We felt that these were precisely the kinds of things it was important to get into, to explain to people where they came from, personally and politically."

De Antonio explained, "None of these people just dropped from the sky and said, 'I'm Lenin' or 'I'm Mao.' Every one of them has a long personal history, and when they finally did agree to speak about themselves, they talked about their childhoods, the kinds of homes they were brought up in. Every one of them speaks with a certain bitterness, about having tried to deal with the system, as they all did in the beginning."

One question seemed to bridge the personal and the political. "Haskell suddenly asked an overwhelming question," recalled de Antonio. "He said, 'When you go out on an action, are you afraid?' That was a big moment, because fear is an intensely personal thing and they responded in a uniquely personal way. They stressed the fact that you aren't politically mature until you recognize your fear and then you can both use it and understand it. It's the sort of mad person who pretends to experience no fear that becomes dangerous."

Jeff Jones answered Wexler this way: "Fear, yes. Every time, I think, for all of us. I know for me, every time I see a policeman I have this rush of adrenaline. And I take a defensive stance, in a martial-art type of sense. I mean, not a fighting posture but an alert posture. I remind myself who I am, what my name is, what my various numbers are, where I'm going, where I've been. That's an interesting way to live. There are risks every day. I wake up in the morning and I wonder how many times I'm going to be nervous today, 'cause it happens every day.

"Once about a year after I went underground, I was standing on the sidewalk next to this orange juice stand, and suddenly two police cars screeched to a halt in front of me. The cops jumped out with their guns drawn, grabbed me and threw me into the back of a paddy wagon. I didn't know if they knew who I was or what. We went a couple of blocks; the paddy wagon stopped, the door opened, a guy looked in and said, 'That's not him.' They'd mistaken me for somebody else. The cops were very apologetic and offered to drive me home. I said, 'No thanks,' and walked away.

"And then there's the other side of it, which is that we definitely feel good about what we're doing, what we've done, and right now it would be pretty hard to feel any better, 'cause we feel there's been a victory in Vietnam, which is a victory for the American people. We certainly identify it as a victory for ourselves. It's something that we fought for for ten years. I'd have to have my foot run over by a police car to feel bad today."

Cathy Wilkerson: "The other thing to say about fear is, I think, that because of the nature of American society, a lot of people wake up that way, like the people in Appalachia who fear the day that the strip miners are going to come by, or people who are in prison. The fear is everywhere. And the government means no good by the people. It only means bad, only means hurt."

Bernardine Dohrn: "I was a much more fearful person growing up in this society than I am now because now the fear is real fear; it's not paranoia, it's not fear of the unknown. It's a very tangible thing. And that doesn't make it go away at all.

"We have a strong ethic that has been very important in our survival; that fear is an open subject. When someone is afraid in a situation they have an obligation to say so because it's often based on a real thing, and we'll figure out later if it was right or not. We have really tried to discourage all the posturing kinds of things that might make you say, 'It's my problem, I've got to deal with it,' rather than this is probably a real thing and we should all act on it."

Wexler asked them what it was like to live underground. He associated the word with a claustrophobic existence, with someone hiding in a basement, fed through a slot in the door—a fugitive in essentially a defensive posture. The Weatherpeople stressed that this could not be further from the truth. They circulate freely.

Many have aboveground jobs and they do aboveground organizing as well.

"There is something that is not in the film," said de Antonio, "and that's the fashion in which we parted. We all held hands and they gave us presents. It sounds corny to say a group of people sat around in the middle of a room and held hands but it was a very moving experience. The most touching thing in the whole film for me was that the men and women of the Weather Underground had made a very beautiful quilt which they gave to me, a political quilt with a political message. It says: THE FUTURE WILL BE WHAT WE THE PEOPLE STRUGGLE TO MAKE IT. It is a message which I happen to accept and believe very strongly and it's one which they are believing and living.

"When we were done," de Antonio went on, "they loaded the car; then we were led out to the car and put into it. Again, they employed various methods to make sure that we did not observe which way we were going.

"When we arrived at the destination we all shook hands and kissed. Then our driver got out; there was an enormous ahhh, like the deflation of a tire, an audible gasp. And then we got the hell out of there.

"As we drove back, we all started laughing and making jokes about the funny things that had happened during the shooting. Like, I remember after it was all over, one of them offered me a joint and I thought, I can't smoke that, it's breaking the law!'

"We were very nervous because we had all the film, unsanitized. We had no idea that the film revealed anything but we knew that there would be mistakes. And Haskell kept saying, 'Look, I just know any number of places where Bill or Kathy would turn around and get a full shot, or I would drop the camera beneath the scrim and you get a shot of four or five people, crystal clear.' "

The next major problem was the lab, getting the film processed and printed without blowing the whole operation. "The lab represented a major security risk," continued de Antonio. "There's a kind of police mentality around labs because the FBI hangs around there. During the days of Vietnam, the largest single customer of the labs was no single studio or network; it was the U.S. government, turning out propaganda shit by the millions of feet.

Movielab, where my office was, had two whole floors where you
need FBI clearance to get on the floors. All you would need is some
executive who doesn't want to lose the business, to call it to the
attention of the LAPD or the FBI. Or a lab technician. Lab technicians are technicians. They want to see film the way they're accustomed to seeing it, especially when it's shot by Haskell Wexler.
They expect sharp, clear images. Now lab technicians don't look
at film unless it's porn, or unless it's weird. This would be weird.
'What is all this stuff?' they'd say. It would look like some sort of
fogging, or a light leak. What it was, of course, was the large piece
of scrim that we were shooting through.

"So the lab was a risk. When we got ready to have the film
processed, we thought of all the possible alternatives. It was too
dangerous to take the film out of the country, because what we
had, then, was one copy, the negative, unsanitized. If it got seized,
we'd be finished. We thought of taking it out of the L.A. area.
Where would we take it? Would we offer to pay cash, thousands
of dollars for developing? That was wild! That would draw attention to you at once. They would certainly look at the film carefully
because they would think it was some kind of superporn or something illegal. Only illegal people pay with cash. We live in a credit
economy.

"Going into a lab using a false name or somebody else's name
would be to set up another of those situations in which you were
unknown and therefore people would look at you. It seemed that,
finally, the most normal thing to do was to give it to Haskell's lab
in L.A. Haskell has a solid commercial reputation in L.A. That was
the main factor. He had a company that puts thousands of feet of
color film through the lab every week. It would be going through
so fast that, in the normal course of events, nobody would see anything. The secret of underground activity is, everything as normal
as possible. So, in this case, normal as possible meant putting it
through the lab as Haskell's film.

"That was *the* precaution," de Antonio said. "Any attention
brought to that film would have been a lack of precaution. Put
it through the way we would put through a Royal Crown Cola
commercial.

"Now, of course, a day or so after we put the film in, an executive from the lab called me and said, 'There's something radically wrong with this film. We just started developing it; the very beginning, where the people are looking into the mirror, is very clear, but everything after that is fogged. You can't see the faces.' So I said, my heart in my mouth, 'That's the way it's supposed to be. Just keep developing it in your normal way.' Then they got hold of Haskell, who of course told them the same thing. So we got away with it. Barely.

"When we finally got the stuff back from the lab and started looking at the fucking film, we almost died. Those people, from time to time, a glimpse here and a glimpse there, were clear as hell. Before we began shooting, Haskell looked through the lens. I looked through the lens, the Weatherpeople looked through the lens—and all of us felt that nothing could be revealed. We even shot some tests on videotape—and the quality of video being what it is, we were absolutely certain that nobody would see anything. But when we looked at the processed film, you could really see them. This was why the immediate priority was staying up day and night sanitizing the film.

"At this point we had the sense that the thing was just about blown and that the FBI was on to us. We found a place where there was an editing machine and Mary and I just disappeared and we went over it practically a frame at a time. And Mary would say, 'That's better than any mug shot!' We never emerged from the place we were in until all the film was looked at, cut and destroyed."

We asked de Antonio about the sound, which is a complicated problem, because in the editing process the sound has to be transferred from the quarter-inch tape on which it is originally recorded to 16mm magnetic track (basically recording tape the size of 16mm film). "It was hairy. Say I took the quarter-inch tape personally to a transfer house and said to the guy, 'Look, I want to transfer all this sound myself, with earphones, and I don't want anybody near me. I want your guarantee that you're not going to listen to it.'

"All the guy would have to do was routinely turn up the sound and there would be a voice saying, 'I am Kathy Boudin, I joined SDS in 1965.' But it was abnormal. It was weird. Why does a guy

173

want to go into a transfer house on a hot day and do this fucking thing himself, when he's paying the full rate?

"So I made up a story. I said, 'Look, there's a new kind of analysis. Existential Transactional Analysis. And we're under severe legal restrictions because this was a group session, in the charge of an analyst, and we could not get permission to finish the film unless we guaranteed absolute secrecy each step of the way. If anyone found out about the film, the doctor and the patients would withdraw and we'd have spent all this money. For nothing.' He understood it. It was convincing. There was no problem."

But about a week after the film came out of the lab, the filmmakers were sure the FBI was on to them. The FBI had staked out Wexler's house. "There was a car out front that was supposedly having its tire fixed," Wexler explained, "with a couple of guys looking so much like cops, you wouldn't believe it. They were just sort of working around the tire—so then I knew something was going on. And then later my son saw a guy out in front of the house taking pictures of the car, of the house, and so forth. Obviously an FBI guy, you know, the way he was dressed. And then I saw a guy up on the hill with binoculars, watching the house. It seemed like the FBI was sending people around just to make sure I knew they were watching. They didn't even bother to be surreptitious. If someone wanted to take a picture of the cars in front of my house, they could just go by with a Minox and click off a couple of shots, but to stand out in the middle of the street with a Polaroid—that's a little much!"

"We were sitting up at night biting our fingernails," continued de Antonio, "saying, 'Where the hell was the leak?' Everything seemed airtight. You know, you started getting those terrible ideas that the FBI was omnipotent and omniscient. Which we know is not true. There are two great mistakes: One is to think that they know everything; the other is to think that they know nothing. The truth is in the middle. The truth is they are very thorough. Every time you talk to them you make a mistake.

"We spent days and nights reconstructing how the FBI found out that we were up to something. We exhausted every possibility the human mind can think of. We worried that x, y, or z had happened. We even went into the realm of the insane, speculating that the sound studio was suspicious and that they had some kind of an outlet off the transfer machine, that they were making a secret quarter-inch tape for the FBI."

Their most likely mistake turned out to be something much more obvious. The day after they left the safe house, Lampson, Wexler and two Weatherpeople turned up at Martin Luther King Hospital in Los Angeles, where a doctors' strike was in progress. They only stayed for ten minutes, leaving when they were questioned by a hospital administrator, but that was apparently long enough. There was a rotating video camera on the hospital roof, scanning the crowd, and the chances are good that they were photographed by the LAPD as well. "My guess," said de Antonio, "is that the LAPD didn't know who they had. By the time they took the pictures to the Red Squad and the FBI, we'd had time to get the film processed and out of the lab."

The filmmakers thought the attempt to film at Martin Luther King was foolhardy but they were overruled by the Weatherpeople, who apparently felt the risk of discovery was small compared to the dividends—the chance to speak to striking doctors and the opportunity to show on film that they could move freely aboveground.

175

FBI surveillance continued after de Antonio and Lampson returned to New York. Friends and families were interrogated. De Antonio finally called the New York office of the FBI and told them, "Get your fucking gumshoes off my back." The next day, as if in response, he, Lampson and Wexler were subpoenaed before a federal grand jury in Los Angeles and ordered to appear on June 12. They were told to bring with them "any and all motion picture film, including but not limited to all negatives, working copies and prints, and all sound tracks and sound recordings made in connection with the filming of such motion pictures, concerning a group known as the Weathermen or Weather Underground."

The three filmmakers admitted to the press that they were, in fact, engaged in making a film on the Weather Underground but would refuse to cooperate with the grand jury, arguing that the subpoenas violated their First Amendment rights and constituted a particularly noxious form of prior restraint. For this act of defiance, they would risk a contempt citation and jail for the term of the grand jury.

They quickly gathered around them a formidable array of legal talent. Lampson's attorney, Leonard Boudin (father of Kathy Boudin), had successfully defended Daniel Ellsberg and the Harrisburg 7. De Antonio's attorney, Harvard law professor Charles Nesson, had worked with Boudin on the Ellsberg and Harrisburg cases, secured a parole for Daniel Berrigan and is currently working on the appeal in the Edelin abortion case in Boston. Michael Kennedy, Wexler's attorney, had represented members of the Weather organization in Detroit and San Francisco and defended Los Siete de la Raza. Boudin, Nesson and Kennedy were joined by ACLU attorney Mark Rosenbaum, who is currently suing the U.S. government on behalf of Jane Fonda.

Within two days, Eleanore Kennedy, film producer Bert Schneider and the ACLU of Southern California mobilized an impressive roster of forty-three Hollywood personalities to sign a statement in defense of the right of people to make a film about any subject, and specifically the right of these people to make a film about the Weather Underground Organization.

The list included Hal Ashby, Warren Beatty, Harry Belafonte, Peter Bogdanovich, Jeff Bridges, Mel Brooks, Peter Davis, William Friedkin, Shirley MacLaine, Jack Nicholson, Arthur Penn, Rip Torn, Robert Towne, Jon Voight, Robert Wise and Paul Williams, as well as Stanley Sheinbaum of the ACLU.

The subpoenas were withdrawn.

Four months later Assistant U.S. Attorney Robert C. Bonner said: "At this point it is extremely unlikely that new subpoenas would be issued to the filmmakers." Bonner declined to comment on the reasons the subpoenas were withdrawn.

Lawyer Leonard Boudin is of the opinion that the whole operation was poorly thought out. "They operated from the hip," he told us, "the way they did when they indicted Eqbal Ahmad for conspiracy to kidnap Henry Kissinger. Or when they filed a criminal complaint against Dan Ellsberg the night before the Supreme Court argument in the *New York Times* case. It's that kind of fast moving thing, without thinking what will happen if there's a fight back. I don't think John Mitchell ever thought that the *New York Times* was not going to capitulate, when those powerful calls came from Mitchell himself and Robert Mardian. The government did not anticipate the fact that its basic power would be challenged."

Michael Kennedy explained it this way: "In the good old Nixon days, a Weather grand jury like this one would have been handled by Guy Goodwin and his representatives from the Internal Security Division of the Justice Department. And what they would do is get a liaison in the local U.S. Attorney's office, wherever they happened to set the circus up. That was not done in this case. Bonner is a local man. We heard through two sources that Bonner got jumped on very hard by Justice for having moved so precipitously. There was a tactical fuckup by him and the local FBI office in that they should have waited, put on a very good surveillance instead of a sloppy surveillance, and not called a grand jury at all, hoping that the filmmakers would lead them to the fugitives."

The withdrawal of the subpoenas leaves Lampson, Wexler and de Antonio in a legal limbo, subject to a variety of possible indictments, including conspiracy to harbor fugitives. Although they will continue to remain under FBI surveillance, their lawyers feel that it is unlikely they will be resubpoenaed, because legal and political conditions are not favorable to a government victory.

Legally, the case is unusual because it is perhaps the first time that the federal government has attempted to suppress a documentary film, especially before it is finished. The government, of course, denies that it wishes to suppress the film, nor does it concede that First Amendment issues are at stake. But, as Charles Nesson put it: "Our situation was one in which, effectively, the government had put its foot on the typewriter. The subpoena was prior restraint that would really have stopped the production process." Or, as Haskell Wexler put it at a press conference in Los Angeles: "What the government is demanding is our notes. It's as if, as you leave here, someone says, 'Give me those little pieces of paper you're writing on. I want them to study what kind of an article you're going to write or what kind of film you're going to make.' "

Moreover, the case also raises serious questions about the government's use of grand juries for police, rather than investigative functions. Beginning with a grand jury in Tucson in 1970, the federal government has been using the grand jury system as the linch pin in its campaign to harass radicals and gather intelligence about those allegedly engaged in subversive activities.

It looked for a while as if the government had at last discovered a weapon to replace the discredited congressional investigating committees of the fifties. The Organized Crime Control Act, passed in 1970, contained the "use immunity" provision which enabled a prosecutor to coerce testimony in effect nullifying a witness's last line of defense, the Fifth Amendment privilege against self-incrimination.

Although grand juries were initially intended to protect the rights of the witnesses, the fact that they are free from most of the restraints and protections that we customarily associate with our legal system leaves them more open to abuse. The proceedings are held in total secrecy. An unlimited number of witnesses may be called. Witnesses have no right to legal counsel, or to cross-examination, or even to know the purpose of the grand jury. Whole categories of evidence which would normally be excluded from a court of law, like hearsay, rumor or tips, are freely admissible in grand jury proceedings. Selection of grand juries is skewed toward the conservative white middle class. The New Haven grand jury that indicted Bobby Seale and Ericka Huggins for the murder of Alex Rackley was composed solely of friends of the sheriff. According to Helene Schwartz, an attorney for the Chicago 7, four of the jurors had been acquainted with the sheriff for thirty to fifty years. A fifth was his barber. A sixth owned the barber shop. And two more were suggested by the sheriff's deputy.

These peculiarities allow ambitious and zealous prosecutors, armed with the immunity statute, to commit mayhem in the name of the law. The staggering number of abuses associated with the grand jury system includes, but is not limited to, the following list: 1) use of grand juries for intelligence gathering purposes; 2) use of grand juries to punish witnesses by coercing them into contempt or perjury; 3) use of grand juries to punish witnesses by whisking them thousands of miles from homes, families and jobs on short notice; 4) use of grand juries to "launder" tainted evidence like illegally obtained wiretaps.

The flood tide of grand jury activity was reached in 1973. Between 1970 and 1973, according to the *New York Times,* Guy

Goodwin and his minions presented evidence to more than 100 grand juries in 36 states. One thousand to 2000 people were subpoenaed. About 400 indictments were handed down. About 30 people were cited for contempt of court. In recent years, however, a number of factors including the government's notable lack of success in obtaining convictions from grand jury indictments of Movement people, the spirited resistance of the target community of activists and a number of unfavorable court decisions, like the prohibition on warrantless wiretaps, has created a lull in grand jury activity.

In the last few months, however, it has begun to look like this lull may be over. In addition to the Weatherfilm case, grand juries have been convened in Lexington, Kentucky, and New Haven, Connecticut, in connection with the Justice Department's pursuit of underground fugitives. Several people have gone to jail rather than talk. Jill Raymond, a feminist who refused to talk to a grand jury about women wanted by the FBI, has been in jail in Lexington since March of this year.

A new wrinkle in the grand jury game has appeared recently in New York City, where a state grand jury convened by Manhattan District Attorney Robert Morgenthau subpoenaed twelve people, including three lawyers, whose major offense seems to have been their presence in the courtroom when contraband material was allegedly found in the possession of the defendants, members of the Black Liberation Army. This case is distinguished by the dragnet subpoenaing of courtroom spectators (a challenge to the right to an open trial) and by the use of a popular local DA with a liberal reputation and a strong local constituency to do the dirty work of the FBI.

Michael Kennedy characterized the new grand jury strategy of the Ford Justice Department this way: "They're basically doing the same type of things, only they aren't doing them in as formalized a way as they did under Mardian. They are also more subtle. They don't want to go after high profile people such as Haskell, de Antonio and Lampson, who have a political base, not only ideologically, but also in terms of support people who will not collaborate, will make a big stink about it, embarrass the Justice Department and make more martyrs. They're really worried about that now. In the past, when they were terribly arrogant, they were ready to take on just about anybody. Now the way they do it is to got to these small areas, such as Lexington and New Haven, and try to find alleged Weather support personnel without a base of political support, isolate them and try to get them to turn or throw them in jail for contempt if they don't collaborate." In terms of this strategy, the subpoenas for de Antonio, Lampson and Wexler were clearly a mistake.

Although the use of grand juries against the Movement has been very destructive, Frank Donner, director of the ACLU Project on Political Surveillance, sees it as an expression of desperation. "The bureau is floundering about," he said. "They have a kind of American innocence. They don't have the kind of feel, for example, that the Czarist secret police had for the nihilists. There's no convergence between the areas in which the hunted live and sustain themselves and the areas of the police world. There are no FBI experts who were formerly Movement people and have any feel for the Movement. And, consequently, they're starting from scratch."

"It's pure guesswork," Donner continued. "What could you do? I suppose you could go to the wig shop and say, 'Who did you sell wigs to last week?'

"That's where the grand jury becomes useful, because pursuit of a fugitive is something quite complex, particularly when he lives in an alien habitat, has the kind of self-protective camouflage the Weather Underground has, who can make do with what they have or have some way of getting it. And have an overground support system.

"So, if you're the bureau, you attack the support network or a group that is related in some way by ideology or sympathy or parenthood to your target, and just go after it blind. All of American intelligence is based on the principle that they got from the Pinkertons in the nineteenth century, of the outer ring and the inner ring. The technique is, you go from the aboveground to the underground, from the support to the fugitives.

"That's what's happening with Lampson, de Antonio and Wexler in Los Angeles. The government says, 'We're really not interested in those people's film on the Weather Underground, we're interested in apprehending the fugitives.' And that's true. But they'd like to damage the outer ring at the same time. One is a cover for the other. They'd like nothing better than to take one of these middle-class people and really give it to them, in the hopes that that would force the whole support structure to crumble. They don't have the competence to catch the Weather Underground, so they've got to use this blunderbuss, the grand jury."

So far, the "support group" of the support group—the Hollywood stars who sprang to the filmmakers' defense—have shown no signs of wavering. Haskell Wexler was cautiously optimistic: "People are still sensitive enough to the way things are to know that if they come out to sign a public statement like this in our defense, the possibility exists of some kind of pressure being exerted against them. It did take a certain amount of courage. I don't think it was just because people learned the lessons of the fifties. I think they learned the lessons of the younger people who showed that defiance of the establishment isn't always death to those who defy. Sometimes you can come out and you can win."

And Bert Schneider, who made most of the phone calls to rally support, put it more bluntly: "The only way to fight oppression is aggressively. You should fight back right away. The government will harass people, will intimidate people, will fuck them over just so far as people will let them. We have to learn to mobilize ourselves to fight repression every step of the way. As soon as it shows its head, you've got to be there to chop it off."

The most notable exceptions to the enthusiastic declaration of solidarity were unexpected: Jane Fonda and Tom Hayden, who had worked with Wexler on *Introduction to the Enemy*. Hayden, one of the founders of SDS, felt that as a candidate for the Senate (running against John Tunney in the California Democratic primary) it was necessary to issue his own statement. He protested the "harassment" of the filmmakers and placed it in context of the government's other attempts to block the disclosure of embarrassing information like the Pentagon Papers. But he failed to mention the Weather Underground by name.

Hayden insisted he had never accepted the Weather analysis of the American political situation and still doesn't. "The original theory of Weatherman," he argued, "was that we were in a situation of virtual fascism, because of Nixon's policies and because of popular opinion being adjusted to these policies. And therefore, the only recourse, in their view, was resistance against this closed system. That's proven, I think, to be a fear that did not unfold. The democratic process came through.

"We're not living under a police state precisely because people can be reached by political methods, by organizing, by education and so on. So what's the sense of blowing up? If you're doing political work of a legal nature and you're identified with Weather politics, aren't you bringing grand jury and police heat down on you? The dilemma of those who politically support the Weather Underground is, how can they advocate both legal and illegal activity simultaneously without bringing enormous strains and contradictions to an organization?"

Hayden's optimism may be premature. It remains to be seen whether events of the last few years can be parlayed into any significant social change through electoral politics. Many of those who are identified with Weather politics would probably agree that the Weather analysis which predicted the imminence of fascism was incorrect. But they would argue that the breathing space we now enjoy was created by just those kinds of extralegal protests and resistance Hayden disparages. "We are up against the ruling class," they say in *Prairie Fire,* "and it makes no sense to ask them to reform themselves."

And what of the film now? Work was resumed after a brief interval pending assessment of the government's intentions. It is scheduled for a November 7 release.

We asked de Antonio what he anticipates. "Obviously, the main political aim is to get the film made," he replied. "What can the government do now but subpoena us again or come with a search warrant to get the film. We've gone through all this with our lawyers and we're prepared for any eventuality."

With mock indignation, he went on. "They'd be creamed if they came and took it. If the government were to destroy the footage, we would be outraged! This film is private property. I mean, are we living under capitalism or not?"

IN LATIN AMERICA THEY SHOOT FILMMAKERS

Some fifteen years ago, riding a wave of revolutionary enthusiasm, a new, vigorous Latin American cinema suddenly emerged. Glauber Rocha, working in Brazil's Cinema Novo movement, gave us films like *Antonio das Mortes* and *Black God, White Devil*. Fernando Solanas and Octavio Getino, working in Argentina's Cinema Liberation movement, produced *The Hour of the Furnaces*. Bolivia's Jorge Sanjines made *Blood of the Condor*, an expose of sterilization programmes carried out by the Peace Corps among Bolivian Indians. From Cuba there was Tomas Gutierrez Alea's *Memories of Underdevelopment* and Humberto Solas' *Lucia*. And from Chile, Miguel Littin's *The Jackal of Nahueltoro*.

Now, just as suddenly, this movement has vanished. With the exception of Cuba, the Latin American film scene has become a wasteland. National cinemas come and go, for a whole variety of complex reasons, but in the case of Latin America the cause seems fairly clear. Many of the most promising filmmakers are in prison or in exile or dead. In country after country, as right-wing regimes fought to retain or recover their power, governments have clamped down on cultural workers—poets, singers, journalists, playwrights, and filmmakers.

This is true because, in Latin America, culture is as much a battleground as are the factories or the streets. The experience of colonization has taught its victims that culture is an instrument of class domination. According to Andres Racz, a young Chilean filmmaker and former critic for *Chile Hoy,* "the government hates the artist as much as it hates the revolutionary, because it realizes that they are the same."

The plight of Latin American filmmakers is most evident in Chile, where the revolutionary process was furthest advanced and the reaction against it most brutal. The junta's attack on filmmakers must be seen as part of a larger effort to recapture Chilean culture for the middle class.

When Allende was elected in 1970, Chilean media were transmitting cultural images manufactured in the United States. More than half the programs on Santiago's leading TV channel, including *The Untouchables, The FBI, Mission Impossible,* and *Disneyland,* were produced in the U.S. Until 1972 over 80 percent of the movies shown on Chilean screens came from Hollywood. The USIA diverted students and intellectuals with festivals of avant-garde filmmakers such as Brakhage and Warhol.

When the United States imposed its "invisible blockade" of the Allende government, only two kinds of goods continued to flow into Chile: weapons for the military and cultural commodities for the Chilean media. As the revolutionary forces gained momentum, a vigorous popular culture, inspired by the example of Cuba, emerged to confront the official culture. Colorful wall paintings, songs performed by Victor Jara and Angel Parra, agit-prop posters, "people's" comics, a flood of inexpensive books from the newly nationalized State Publishing House, and home-produced films chased Donald Duck, Elliot Ness, and Dirty Harry out of the country.

The Allende government immediately recognized the importance of film. Chile Films, the state film company organized in 1941, ceased churning out ersatz imitations of Hollywood romances and turned to the production of documentaries, newsreels, and features intended to serve the process of social transformation. Miguel Littin, whose *Jackal of Nahueltoro* had been completed before Allende was elected, became head of the Chilean film industry and produced a stunning feature, *Promised Land,* completed in Cuba just before the coup. Films like *A Half Litre of Milk* (on a food program for the poor) or *Operation Winter* (on a project to help shanty-town dwellers whose shacks were washed away in winter rains) publicized government programs and showed the people to themselves, for the first time the agents of history rather than its victims.

Production was only the beginning. Newsreels and documentaries had to reach their target, in many cases people who had never seen a film before. Armed with portable generators and projectors, film workers traveled to shanty towns, factories, and mines. They showed Biberman's *Salt of the Earth,* Bunuel's *Los Olvidados,* Vigo, Eisenstein, Renoir, and Cuban and Vietnamese films. Even *Citizen Kane* was screened for factory workers.

With the coup, all this activity ceased. Filmmakers became the targets of arrests, detention, and torture. In June, during the first coup attempt, Argentine cameraman Hans Herman was shot and killed by right-wing troops attacking the governmental palace. Herman actually managed to film his own death; the footage has been used in several newsreels. An American filmmaker, Charles Herman, was taken from his home and shot to death in the National Stadium, where thousands of people were detained in the first days after the coup. Some workers in the film industry, such as Hugo Jaramillo, were killed. Maximo Gedda, Gladys Diaz, Jose Carrasco Tapia, and others are still in prison.

Over fifty filmmakers left Chile in the months after the coup. Some decided to remain and continue to work within the country, at great risk. Among them were Carmen Bueno and Jorge Muller, who have since "disappeared." The junta refuses to divulge their whereabouts or even to acknowledge that they have been arrested. Carmen Bueno is a twenty-five-year-old actress who appeared in the closing sequence of *Promised Land* where, in a strangely prophetic moment, she is cut down by troops, her naked body bathed in her own blood. Jorge Muller is a twenty-seven-year-old cameraman who worked on Patricio Guzman's documentary *The First Year,* Saul Landau and Haskell Wexler's *Brazil: A Report on Torture,* Raul Ruiz's *The Penal Colony,* Landau's *Que Hacer,* and Littin's *Promised Land.* In November 1974, while working on a documentary, Bueno and Muller were forced into a car by members of the Chilean secret police.

Two people recently released from Tres Alamos concentration camp have reported that both Bueno and Muller are being held at the camp. Both have been beaten and tortured with electric shock. One former prisoner reported that for several weeks Carmen Bueno "was taken daily to long torture sessions." Bueno's name has recently appeared on a list released by the junta of 119 Chileans allegedly killed in Argentina by security guards or by rival leftist factions. A report in the *New York Times* suggests that this story has no basis in fact. Observers fear that the list was fabricated as a cover for future executions, or for those already carried out.

Thousands of feet of newsreel footage in the Chile Films archives, showing the strikes, factory takeovers, workers' councils, land seizures, rallies, marches, and other manifestations of the political ferment of the Allende period, have been burned. Chile Films itself is to be sold to private investors. The new head of the Cinematheque of the University of Chile also works for the USIA. In the first ten weeks of its Chilean run, over one million people, one out of every ten Chileans, saw *Jaws*. American cultural hegemony has been resumed.

The grim tale of filmmakers in Chile is repeated in country after country. In Bolivia, Felix Gomez, cameraman for the UKAMAU film group which produced *Blood of the Condor,* was jailed in August 1971. Later that year the cameraman on *Hour of the Generals* was machine-gunned by soldiers while filming the army's takeover of a mine. Jorge Sanjines, head of the Bolivian Institute for Cinema from 1966 to 1968, went into exile in 1971 along with most of the UKAMAU group; there has been no significant film activity in Bolivia since. In June 1975, Antonio Eguino, director of photography for UKAMAU, was arrested for possession of a print of the Italian television documentary *The Courage of the People,* which he had shot.

In Uruguay, Walter Achugar and Eduard Terra, co-founders of the Third World Cinematheque, were arrested in 1972 as part of a government drive against the Tupamaros and their "urban network." Both were tortured. Achugar's wife was forced to listen to tape recordings of her husband's screams. Achugar was released after two months; Terra is still in prison. The film collection of the Cinematheque, one of the largest in Latin America, was destroyed.

Mario Handler, who directed six short films, left the country in 1973 after being targeted by the Death Squad, which is used by the government for unofficial executions. The team of filmmakers who made *In the Jungle There Is Lots to Do,* an animated short for children, were forced to leave in 1974.

In Colombia, four filmmakers, Carlos and Julia Alvarez, Gabriella Samper and Manual Vargas, were arrested in 1972 for making films "inciting to commit crime and violence." Their films were seized as "dangerous materials."

In Brazil, the entire staff of the Museum of Modern Art in Rio was twice arrested. The police destroyed the film collection in the museum's vaults, chopping films like *Battleship Potemkin* into small pieces. Filmmaker Glauber Rocha went into exile in 1969. He has since returned, but this probably has more to do with his recent kind words for the generals than to any mellowing of the regime.

In Argentina, Julio Troxler, featured in Solanas's *The Hour of the Furnaces,* was shot to death by the right-wing Argentine Anti-Communist Alliance (AAA). Solanas's group went underground for two months, then issued a statement in support of Isabel Peron.

On May 27, 1976, Raymundo Gteyzer, director of *Mexico: The Frozen Revolution* and numerous other films, was seized by the police. He is being held in a special torture center. According to sources quoted in *Cineaste* magazine, "like other detainees in this camp, [Gleyzer] is kept completely naked at all times and is dragged outside at dawn (where temperatures this time of year are below freezing) and subjected to continuous beatings, electric shocks, burns, and so on."

According to Rodi Broullon of Tricontinental Film Center, the largest distributor of Third World films in the United States, most Argentine films are heavily censored, both at the preproduction script stage and after completion. "Those that are not banned are bombed," said Broullon. The AAA and other right-wing groups attack theaters showing films that "insult the military." Film laboratories scrutinize material that comes in to be processed to make sure that it is not subversive.

Broullon says that repression in Argentina has reached such a point that it takes as much time and preparation to arrange a clandestine neighborhood screening of a film as it would to carry out an action against a bank. "Someone brings the projector, five more people bring little ten-minute rolls in their pockets, assemble the film on the spot, screen it, break it down again, and disappear," he says. "You need so much armed security to protect an audience of two or three hundred people that film is becoming a liability in mass struggle. Pamphlets and newspapers are cheaper to make and easier to distribute."

Despite the harshness of authoritarian Latin American regimes, they have been surprisingly responsive to international pressure. As Chilean filmmaker Racz put it, "they're lackeys of world opinion because of their dependence on foreign capital." In the past, letter-writing campaigns have been strikingly successful in obtaining the release of imprisoned filmmakers. European film personalities like Simone Signoret, Yves Montand, Costa-Gavras, Jorge Semprun, Chris Marker, Alain Resnais, Jean-Luc Godard, and others have frequently lent their names to appeals for clemency. In the United States, the Emergency Committee to Defend Latin American Filmmakers has been particularly active on behalf of Carmen Bueno and Jorge Muller.

Despite the repression, film-making in Latin America will continue. A few countries still provide relative freedom and safety for political refugees. Littin is working in Mexico, others in Peru, Venezuela, and Cuba. Clandestine filmmaking is still possible in Argentina and countries where the left is strong. And it is certain that, when the Chilean junta and regimes like it are destroyed, Latin American cinema will flourish once more, fulfilling the revolutionary promise of the popular movements that produced it.

PROMISED LAND
ON SUNDANCE

We of royal blood and noble intent like to think of Sundance as a home for ideas:
That is the illusion. . . .
It is a place with no luck, where birds refuse to nest, where there is no local support beyond lip service, where water dries up, snow avoids us like the plague, and unpaid bills pile up like soot on a city fire escape.
But by God I love it, and I love you, and that's all that counts.
Merry Christmas.
Robert Redford
   —From *Sundancer: The Sundance Community Newsletter*,
December 1988

Robert Redford's Sundance Institute is perched some six thousand feet up in the North Fork of Provo Canyon, near where *Jeremiah Johnson* was shot in Utah's Wasatch Mountains. The snow-covered granite cliffs sparkle in the sunshine. Dirt paths wind around rustic cabins that dot the hillsides of the Sundance ski resort and snake in and out of spiky stands of mountain pine and aspen that rise dramatically to the clouds. Young filmmakers wearing Sundance T-shirts, sweatshirts, and caps and drinking Sundance-brand sparkler are everywhere, working with actors, shooting videotape, huddling with Hollywood heavies like Sydney Pollack and world-class directors like Cuba's Tomás Gutiérrez Alea.

This is God's country, no doubt about it, and God here is Robert Redford. The star's elusiveness is legendary, but even in his absence, everything in this splendid corner of Utah speaks his name, from the rough-hewn architecture of the barnlike rehearsal hall and screening room to the Redford blend of coffee sold in the gift shop. There's a bubbling brook that tumbles down the mountainside, stops for a moment to form "Bob's Pond," and then continues on its course.

This year, Sundance celebrates its tenth anniversary. Over the past decade, Redford's enclave in the mountains has emerged as the most important of the Utopian experiments periodically initiated by Hollywood visionaries. It's had more staying power than Francis Ford Coppola's ambitious Zoetrope Studios and is considerably more influential and productive than George Lucas's Skywalker Ranch. Roughly one out of three scripts selected by Sundance reaches the screen, a development-to-production ratio significantly higher than that of the major studios. Sundance has materially enriched American culture with films as various as *El Norte, Smooth Talk, 84 Charlie MoPic,* and, more recently, *A Dry White Season, Impromptu,* and even *Pretty Woman.* Two yet to be released are *Dogfight,* directed by Nancy Savoca, and *Once Around,* directed by Lasse Hallstrom.

Although Sundance began as a film institute and was best known for its June Laboratory—which brings independent filmmakers together with Hollywood talent—it evolved into something of an all-around cultural center, with an annual producers' conference, a playwrights' lab, a film composers' lab (directed by David Newman), a choreographers' lab (run by Michael Kidd), and a children's theater (directed by Maurice Sendak). It has ties to Gabriel García Márquez's Cuba-based Foundation for New Latin American Cinema, and for the past year or two, Soviet and Japanese filmmakers have appeared at the June lab, while Sundance has been putting on a film festival in Japan.

The most public face of the institute is perhaps the wildly successful Sundance (formerly United States) Film Festival at Park City, Utah, which it took over in 1984. Since then, Park City has displaced Telluride as *the* hot festival, where wan and twitchy independents rub shoulders with the swarms of sleek Hollywood executives who descend every year to pick over the current crop of movies in hopes of finding the next Steven Soderbergh or Whit Stillman. (*sex, lies, and videotape* was "discovered" at the festival two years ago; *Metropolitan,* last year.)

More than a collection of programs, Sundance is an idea, a wish, a hope that for all its commercial success and international dominance, American film can contribute more to world culture than *Batman* and *Total Recall,* that there are genuine artists at work whose visions, if they can be nurtured and encouraged, can give film a substance and seriousness, a poetry of everyday life.

But Sundance is in trouble; all has not been smooth sledding on the slopes of Mount Timpanogos. The institute is in the grip of a chronic leadership crisis that has just seen the second director in two years forced out and a ballooning seven-figure deficit that required the elimination of nearly half the staff, a $1 million reduction of last year's $2.7 million budget, and the emergency amputation of all but the core programs.

Moreover, despite its lofty aspirations, there is evidence that Sundance has been compromised by the commercial realities of Hollywood. Behind its idyllic facade, the institute has been torn by staff backbiting and factionalism. Former employees have leveled charges of long-term mismanagement; even the specter of conflict of interest has haunted the enterprise, as a variety of Hollywood wannabes circle the fledgling filmmakers, who are often more interested in getting a foothold in the industry than in enjoying the ethereal pleasures of Sundance's famous "freedom to fail." As one veteran Sundance watcher put it, "It's hard to run a finishing school in the middle of a whorehouse."

Finally, there is what some staffers call the "Redford Factor." The success or failure of Sundance is closely tied to the personality of a man who has come to both love and detest the organization he created, who inspires a curious mixture of devotion and dislike in the people who work for him. Redford is a skeptic and a perfectionist, admirable traits that do have their downside; he has a way of turning victory into defeat. The final scene of *The Candidate* is classic Redford: his character has won the race for senator from California, but his last words are a querulous "What do we do now?" as the camera holds on an empty hotel room.

There is nothing more dangerous than a man with a dream, even a dream as benevolent as Sundance. Like many charismatic figures, Redford is gripped by millennial aspirations, not the least of which is an uncompromising notion of the importance of community. In

191

a divisive battle with staffers, he recently forced the Sundance offices to move out of Salt Lake City, where most staff members lived, into a new building on the resort grounds, which many felt the institute could ill afford and required of staffers a costly and possibly dangerous hour-and-a-half commute in winter snow. Ironically, during the round of recent cuts, the offices were closed down.

Redford founded the institute to "give back" to an industry that helped him. But some say he treats Sundance, a nonprofit run on other people's money, as his own, and that he's responsible to no one, least of all his board. As Howard Klein, a founding board member and former arts director of the Rockefeller Foundation, asks, "How do you keep the guy who created the toy from playing with it?"

To Redford, the dream of Sundance has become a nightmare of sorts: a child that has refused to grow up, returning again and again to the fold, needy and fractious, demanding attention, time, and money. "In the seventies, I made fourteen, fifteen films, and only four in the eighties," he says. "It was never my intention to quit my career and run Sundance."

Barefoot in the Park

REDFORD, PERHAPS HOLLYWOOD'S most glamorous and bankable star throughout the seventies, was always a maverick. He looked at the power that movies conferred upon him, and he didn't altogether like what he saw. He recognized that Hollywood had no place for the most creative filmmakers, who often toiled outside the industry as independents, and he also realized that if a filmmaker was brown, black, red, or female, his or her chances of getting a film produced were virtually nil.

At the same time, he had some firsthand experience with the problems faced by independents. "I knew what it was like to distribute a film that you produced," he says during a brief pause in New York on his way to Chicago to make a speech on the environment. He has recently completed a grueling four-month shoot of *Havana* in Santo Domingo, and he looks tired. "In 1969, I carried *Downhill Racer* under my arm, fighting the battles that most people face." He came to understand the dilemma of the "film-maker who spends two years making his film," he recalls, "and then another two years distributing it, only to find out he can't make any money on it and four years of his life are gone. I thought, *that's* who needs help."

In 1979, Redford dispatched Sterling VanWagenen, his friend and relative by marriage, to gather a group of people who would become the founding board of Sundance—a delicate mix of non-profit gurus like George White (president of the Eugene O'Neill Theater Center), Brian O'Doherty (of the National Endowment for the Arts), and Howard Klein; Hollywood folks like Mike Medavoy (then executive vice president of Orion) and Sydney Pollack; and independents Annick Smith (*Heartland*), Victor Nunez (*Gal Young 'Un*), Larry Littlebird (director of Circle Films), and Alan Jacobs (executive director of the Association of Independent Video and Filmmakers).

The founders decided to base the program on White's four-week National Playwrights Conference at the O'Neill, which became the model for the June lab. The assumption governing the lab process was that independents had something to say but didn't have the skills to say it, and that Hollywood had nothing to say but said it with great skill. The lab was supposed to be a place where the two could meet. Indies would come with promising scripts, which they would then proceed to rewrite, direct, tape, and edit with the help of top-flight Hollywood directors, producers, actors, and so on—otherwise known as "resource people." The hope was that the indies would pick up skills from the professionals, and the profes-sionals could recharge their batteries with the sparks given off by the indies.

VanWagenen began with $35,000 from the studios and solicited contributions from corporations, foundations, the National Endowment for the Arts, and individuals. Still, Sundance relied on Redford to raise money—an activity he despised. Once in the early eighties, he visited Marvin Davis, then owner of Twentieth Century Fox, to hit him up for a gift. Davis was watching football and seemed more interested in the game than in Redford. "He said, 'Hey, look, I'm going to give you the money, because you cared enough to come see me,' " recalls Redford, smiling. "He was very generous. Then he says, 'There's a few ladies out in the pool. Why don't you go jump in?' What's really bad is I did. But we needed all the help we could get in those days."

Redford was such a magnet for money that the institute became dependent on him. But he hated fundraising so much that he often—consciously or unconsciously—sabotaged those very efforts by being unavailable or inexcusably late for crucial meetings. Says former executive director Suzanne Weil, "You can't get him to go to a benefit, but you can't have a benefit without him."

Still, with Redford's help, VanWagenen and the board inaugurated the first lab in June 1981. For the first few years, there was a distinct utopian air to Sundance. A bunch of smart, dedicated, like-minded people struggled to realize a noble purpose. Every day was an adventure in improvisation as a ski resort was transformed into a jerry-built film facility. The ski-rental shed was used as a screening room. "We'd convert the restaurant into a place to stage scenes during the daytime," Redford recalls. "At night, we'd put the furniture back. We'd move the fire engine out of the firehouse and use it as a soundstage. A lot of the stuff was done outdoors, 'cause you just couldn't go anywhere else. It was really rough."

For the most part, the first lab went surprisingly smoothly, and the participants remember it fondly. Producer Michael Hausman was a resource person that year and at several labs thereafter. "I told them I'd never go back unless they promised me I wouldn't have to go to another Indian ceremony," says Hausman. "But I had fun. I made good friends there."

In those days, board members themselves screened applications for the lab. "You'd arrive having read about fifty scripts, and maybe you'd got three you'd like to talk about, while the other people would start waxing poetic about a bunch of scripts you'd never read," remembers a former board member. "You'd get so excited about what they were saying, you'd stay up all night reading *those* scripts."

Then reality reared its ugly head. In the beginning, VanWagenen had little more than the Redford cachet going for him. He was a charming, boyish-looking man with tousled blond hair and more passion than experience (he ran the eminently forgettable United States Film Festival in its pre-Sundance years). But he was a quick study—staffers quipped that he "gave good Sundance"—and that proved to be enough. According to one source, "Sterling was a very ambitious guy who understood from the beginning that the original board members, all of whom had considerably more experience in film than he did, were potential problems for him in terms of pulling together his power base. He suddenly made the board a three-year term. There was no way to fight, because Sterling was Bob's man. He was Redford."

The terms were renewable, but some were more renewable than others, and certain terms—the independents'—didn't get renewed. Nunez, Jacobs, and Moctesuma Esparza were off the board by the end of 1985 (Smith resigned because she had gotten a Sundance development loan), and the balance tipped in a corporate direction.

VanWagenen defends the changes as inevitable and necessary. "Like many organizations, as they evolve, the people who started them become passé," he says. "There was a lot of pressure to bring in people who could raise money. There was no contribution people like Annick Smith could make, except time and ideas."

"I thought it was a bad idea," recalls Smith. "Some of the life went out of the organization with the departure of the more political, idealistic independents. It became more Hollywood. But I understand the way institutions change. I'm not bitter." Others were. As a former board member put it, "All we got out of it was a silver-plated ashtray."

This Production Is Condemned

FROM THE EARLIEST days, the idea of producing films had considerable appeal. "Even in the first year, Bob was disappointed with the quality of the projects," recalls VanWagenen. "The scripts weren't good enough. That pressure was tremendously frustrating for me. I always felt that what was going to attract better material was making the link to production. It was the basic issue on which Bob and I disagreed. Bob said, 'Don't get involved.' His view was that studio involvement was a pact with the devil. But there was a great temptation to go back for money. Bob's leverage was too great to resist."

Redford felt that production would introduce the very elements he had tried to exclude from Sundance: money and competitiveness. Yet he was finally convinced it might be the solution to the script problem. "I'd heard filmmakers say, 'I need money,'" he says. "So I thought, maybe if we put more emphasis on the commercial aspect for a while, give them some incentive to get their picture made, that would allow us to go in and hammer them and make it more commercial. The thought was, 'Hey, if we can offer something more, we will get something more.'"

Redford did like one script, called *Desert Bloom,* a girl's coming-of-age story set in Las Vegas against the A-bomb tests of the fifties. It is one of the best films to come out of Sundance, and although it slipped into oblivion after a limited release in 1986, many thought Jon Voight should have been nominated for an Oscar for his role. Sundance assisted the project with development loans and helped director-screenwriter Eugene Corr get a green light from Carson Productions (which in turn had a deal with Columbia Pictures). The script was loosely based on the life story of Linda Remy, who was involved with Corr at the time.

Shooting began in November 1984, but even before that, the production had degenerated into a pitched battle among Corr, Remy, Sundance, and Carson president Richard Fischoff over locations and casting; later, they fought over editing. Eventually, Remy was banned from the Columbia lot because of her influence on Corr. The crowning blow came when, she says, "Redford took over the film from Gene and locked him out of the editing room. It was worse than a studio. I thought Sundance would protect us. I was utterly naive."

While Remy insists that Sundance didn't protect the filmmakers, Fischoff, who denies that Corr was locked out of the editing room, says Sundance failed to protect the studio. "I wanted to replace Gene," he says. "But Sundance wasn't prepared to fire the first director they had supported to make his own movie. It might have worked if only they'd honored their commitment to help Gene with the production, but they didn't. Redford never came to the set and never reassured the actors, who had taken pay cuts because of him, put themselves in the hands of an inexperienced director because of him. Instead, he went to Africa to work on *Out of Africa.*" (According to Hausman, the film's producer, Redford spent one day on the set.)

Sundance discovered that it could leverage lab projects into production but wasn't in a position to oversee those projects to the end. VanWagenen acknowledges that the institute "created expectations that Bob would be more involved than he was." When Sundance looked for a seasoned director to supervise Corr on the set, it couldn't find one. "At the lab, everyone was helpful," says VanWagenen. "When we were in the middle of that mess, no one would help. We went to one director who said, 'Why should I put money in Columbia's pocket? My deal's at another studio.' "

Desert Bloom spelled the end of the institute's foray into production. It was a no-win situation. If Sundance had to guarantee the quality of its films, it would find itself in the role of a studio, compromising its purpose. VanWagenen calls the dilemma Sundance's "heart of darkness."

Sterling VanWagenen and the Sundance Kid

VANWAGENEN LIKES to tell a story about the first time he drove to Sundance to discuss plans for the institute with Redford, back in 1979. "There used to be a rise in the road that you couldn't see over, just before you got to the parking lot. I gunned the motor right at the top and almost hit a jogger. I spun the wheel one way, the jogger jumped the other way. When I looked back, I saw that the jogger was Redford."

The tangled relationship between these two complex, intelligent, and ambitious men colored the early years of the institute's history and nearly paralyzed it. Redford and VanWagenen are too close in age for it to have been a father-son rivalry, but there was an Oedipal quality to it, with Redford's enormous power and prestige and his marriage to VanWagenen's cousin, and VanWagenen's dependent yet key position at the institute and his ambitions to strike out on his own in the film business. If VanWagenen fantasized about running Redford over, Redford returned the favor. "Bob used to undermine Sterling," says a source who knows both men. "He considered Sterling scattered and inefficient."

According to filmmaker Denise Earle, Redford and VanWagenen found themselves in competition as far back as 1981, after the first lab. The dispute arose over a script called *The Giant Joshua*, cowritten by Denise and her husband, John. They held an option on the book upon which it was based—a story about the Mormons, written in the forties. They brought it to the first lab, which Denise describes as a happy experience. But one week after the lab was over, she says, they got a call from a Redford representative, who wanted to buy the script. "His attitude was, 'The script is worthless; let us take it off your hands,'" she says. "It made us feel small."

The Earles refused. Then, according to Denise, along came VanWagenen, offering more money and participation for the Earles— for the same script. "Redford didn't want our participation," says Denise. The Earles made a deal. (VanWagenen remembers this story differently, claiming the Earles approached Wildwood Enterprises, Redford's production company, not the other way around.)

Meanwhile, VanWagenen, who had always wanted to produce, reportedly used his position as executive director of Sundance to develop contacts. In 1984, he resigned to produce *The Trip to Bountiful*, which won an Oscar for Geraldine Page in 1985. He had no intention of returning to Sundance. "I had been beaten up pretty bad," he recalls. "I was beginning to get stale." But Redford, despite his reservations, relied on VanWagenen and persuaded him to stay for another year.

During this period, their simmering quarrel over *The Giant Joshua* came to a head. John Earle died, and VanWagenen found himself unencumbered by prior commitments. Still, he was powerless to move ahead without Redford. "Sterling asked me if I would do the film," says Redford. "I said yes. He said, 'Can I work on the production?' And I said yes. After he got the rights, Sterling developed his own ambitions. This project was like a Merlin—it was like a sorcerer's tool—and what it did to people was sort of amazing. The next thing I know, it jumped from him wanting to develop it for me while I was busy on other projects, to him producing it with me directing it, to him directing it."

Redford's backing had enabled VanWagenen to put the financing together in the spring of 1987. "We got right to the edge—ten days before the start of preproduction," recalls VanWagenen. "Then Bob pulled the plug."

"Redford wanted to develop it himself," says Hausman, who was to have been the producer. "I think he was jealous of someone else directing a project he wanted to make."

Redford felt he was being taken advantage of. "I was suddenly out of it and being asked to have my company make it," he says. "So we had a disagreement about it. That's leveraging off of me, basically."

Denise Earle was the loser in the jockeying between Redford and VanWagenen, and she is bitter. "Redford never wanted Sterling to go out on his own," she says. "He only wanted him to do his thing, be his gofer." To this day, the project has not been produced.

Meanwhile, the tension between the two men took its toll on Sundance. With VanWagenen preoccupied by producing and his relationship with Redford (who was away in Africa for much of 1985) at a low ebb, the institute suffered. Redford led off a board meeting in June 1986, says a former staffer, by acknowledging that the institute faced a crisis in leadership, and he assumed full responsibility for it. Says Howard Klein, "No one was in charge in 1984, '85, and '86."

Racing Downhill

THE GIANT JOSHUA not only pitted Redford against VanWagenen, but if Denise Earle's account is accurate, it also put him in competition with the very independents Sundance was set up to nurture. Sundance is a minefield of potential and actual conflicts of interest. The institute was never intended to be a source of projects for Redford or any of its other principals. But sometimes the lines got blurred. For example, when board member David Puttnam was still head of Columbia, he got a Columbia script, *Stealing Home,* into the lab over the objections of several members of the selection committee. The studio reportedly paid its expenses. "Bob brought it in," says Tom Rickman, who was on the committee virtually from the beginning. "We thought it was a conflict of interest. Every year or two, we said, 'Let's sit down and make some rules about who can do what.' But it never got done." Says Puttnam, "Some people felt that the principle of young filmmakers paid for by a studio was in itself wrong, but I think it's an idea whose time has come. It's a way of developing talent while underwriting the institute."

Now board members may no longer be a part of projects while Sundance is involved with them, and there is a rule preventing producers from attaching themselves to more than one project.

Klein thinks the conflict-of-interest problems became more acute when the independents left the board and sees VanWagenen as one of the main offenders. "Sterling was serving a lot of masters, among them his own ambitions. He was unable to resist the conflict of interest that was open to him." Klein says a Sundance board member was a financial backer for *The Trip to Bountiful*. "Because they were doing the other stuff, conversations were held over dinner, deals were made."

However, Rickman feels that the conflict of interest was minimal. "Sterling would have to have taken a vow of celibacy," he says, not to have taken advantage of the contacts that came his way. In fact, one former staffer thinks *The Trip to Bountiful* represents the best Sundance has to offer, the opportunity for creative networking.

The tug-of-war over *The Giant Joshua* was not the only time Redford found himself in competition with the independents. In 1983, Annick Smith saw a script for *A River Runs Through It*, based on a book by Norman MacLean. Smith bought an option on the book from MacLean with a $15,000 loan from Sundance and brought in writer Bill Kittridge, director Dick Pearce (*Heartland*), and producer Hausman. Smith brought a treatment to the '85 lab.

In 1987, when Smith's option was running out, Redford went to MacLean and bought the rights. "When Redford gets control of a project, it's his project;" says Smith. "He took over the show." With Redford as director, Pearce was out. (Smith is supposed to get a coproducer credit and Kittridge a coproducer and/or cowriter credit.)

"Redford works in such an Olympian fashion, says Pearce. "I don't know if he had any idea how much I wanted to make it. A friend told me something that helped me make sense out of it. He said Redford is like a beautiful woman who has no idea of the chaos she creates when she moves through the world. But I will say one thing: if I had a project that one of Redford's companies would love, I'd be hesitant to send it to them, because of what happened on *A River Runs Through It*."

Smith is more resigned than anything else. "There's nothing sinister in it at all. He's not obliged to keep his hands off everything that's mentioned at Sundance." Redford says he plans to go into production on the film in the summer of 1991. Norman MacLean died in August 1990.

"I had a rigid standard at Rockefeller when I was making grants: I never accepted a piece from an artist," says Howard Klein. "But I'm not sure it was clear in Bob's mind what the protocols were. I'm not sure he knew he wasn't supposed to touch the merchandise. There were so many gray areas, and he came from another world."

Redford listens to the charges of conflict of interest and dismisses them. "This issue has been haunting us for ten years," he says. "There's been a lot of rumors about things we've done that I don't think are right or fair. They say, 'Well, Redford is taking the projects for himself.' I bend over backward not to try to get any of these projects for my own use."

But it's less clear that he really hears the accusations. "I wasn't aware of moving anybody out," he says about *A River Runs Through It*. "We all joined forces. Now, in truth, I don't have a lot of success working with a lot of people. So I said I'd just like to develop this myself. So am I going to be able to do that or not? Annick was very good about it and said, 'Yeah.' "

Legal Eagles

THE THREE-YEAR leadership vacuum in the mid-'80s allowed a former Washington politico named Gary Beer to emerge as a newer and better Sterling VanWagenen. Beer came to Sundance after working on Salt Lake City mayor Ted Wilson's unsuccessful Senate campaign against Orrin Hatch. "He was funnier and hipper than most of the people on the staff," recalls Suzanne Weil.

In 1985, Beer became executive vice president, and the inevitable contradiction between the Hollywood ambience of Sundance, with its celebrity-owned condos, and the realities of running a nonprofit institution became more acute.

According to several sources, Beer displayed the habits of a studio head. "He treated the place like a big expense account," says one former staffer. Beer's home phone bills were a constant source of contention between him and the general manager, Maria Schaeffer, says Schaeffer's assistant, Gary Burr, who had worked on accounts payable. Beer charged the institute for "flowers and catering expenses for parties," says Burr. There were "huge entertainment bills, two hundred to three hundred dollars a night," two or three nights a week, at the Tree Room, a resort restaurant. "The restaurant would bill the institute for the food," he says, adding that the monthly charges owed the resort would at times approach $20,000, and "Beer's expenses were a large proportion of them. And this would be during off months, when there were no programs." (Most are held during June, July, and August.) "By the time the summer came around, there wasn't enough money for the programs, to pay for food and housing," says Burr. Adds another former staffer, "Gary didn't understand that he was working for a nonprofit and the people under him were working for almost nothing."

The institute had to pick up the tab on Beer's resort bills as a result of the peculiar relationship between the nonprofit Sundance Institute and the for-profit Sundance resort, which is wholly owned by Redford. Originally, the idea was that the resort would support the institute. But the resort had never been a big money-maker, so in the end, it turned out that the institute was the resort's single biggest customer, paying a little less than half of its annual lab budget (about $225,000 in direct costs) for rental of cottages and food services. Thus, a nonprofit institution helped support an unprofitable business.

Some staffers also resented the fact that Redford gave so little of his own money to the institute. Of Sundance's annual budget, which had grown to $2.7 million by 1990, Redford donated only $50,000 a year, and this was often earmarked for bills the institute owed to the resort. Thus Redford got a tax write-off for money that went from one pocket to another. (With the current crunch, Redford is doubling his contribution. His lawyer, Robert "Reg" Gipson, says earmarking the money for the resort was his idea, not his client's.)

The institute's financial constraints led to some bookkeeping legerdemain. The Production Assistance Fund, which was set up in the mid-'80s to make small loans to filmmakers and included at least $250,000 in public money in the form of an NEA grant, was frozen as security for a bank loan to defray the cost of the festival and to pay for the West Coast office, among other expenses. "The Production Assistance Fund was raped to finance the deficit," says an authoritative source.

Worse, there is a report that no more than about $180,000 of a fund that totaled $1 million at its height ever reached the film-makers. Gipson says there was nothing wrong with using the money for general operating expenses.

The source charges that what was true of the Production Assistance Fund was true of the whole institute. "The bottom line is, the total amount of money that goes to help the constituency is minimal. Most of it goes to overhead. All we were doing was maintaining the infrastructure."

There was nothing illegal about any of this, and Johann Jacobs, a former Sundance financial officer, argues that the problem was not so much Beer as that "it was never clear where the difference lay between the institute, the resort, and the Sundance Group [a separate entity set up to develop commercial business opportunities for Redford]. It was hard to say, 'Yes, this is right; no, this isn't right.' "

Beer emphatically denies that he charged Sundance for any personal expenses. "The institute has never paid for anything of mine that was personal. These things are audited every year, and nothing ever came up." He adds that the institute "is not like one of these organizations where 90 percent of the budget goes to overhead. It's way under the national average of 15 or 17 percent."

The expenses and accounting procedures are probably justified, but the essential point here is that, right or wrong, "there was a general perception of misuse of funds; it was a huge morale factor," recalls a former staffer. Many blamed Beer. "Bob had blinders on about Gary," says the source. Beer was like "the hunchback who manipulates the handsome prince."

A chasm opened up between Sundance's upper echelons and its young, idealistic staff. Redford was aware of the discontent. "It drove me crazy," he says. "The whole point was to have an egalitarian tone. I don't take kindly to fat-cat behavior. I'd caution Gary about it." Regarding the Production Assistance Fund, he reiterates that he was against production in the first place and didn't know where the money went. But he's not surprised that much of it may have gone to defray the costs of the Sundance bureaucracy. "That's just the kind of thing I was afraid of; that's why I hate bureaucracies."

The Provo Beanfield War

IN OCTOBER 1987, VanWagenen left for good. Tom Wilhite, who had been vice president of production at Disney, was appointed executive director, and Beer was eventually moved over to the Sundance Group, apparently because so many program heads had complained to Redford about him. It is generally agreed that the institute prospered during Wilhite's tenure. Although the actual figures are in dispute, several sources say that the debt level when Wilhite took over from Beer had reached about $850,000 and that he reduced it to about $400,000 while expanding the programs. But Wilhite and Redford differed on a number of issues, and just two years after he was hired, Wilhite was out.

The final straw may have been the highly successful "Great Movie Music" fund-raiser, which was organized in the spring of 1989, by Wilhite and composer David Newman and raised $600,000. By all accounts, what should have been a fund-raising watershed turned into a traumatic and divisive situation that still haunts the institute. Charlton Heston and Christopher Reeve were on hand at the glittering event at New York's Lincoln Center, and such composers as Maurice Jarre, Marvin Hamlisch, and Henry Mancini donated their services.

But Redford was unhappy. He reportedly had a fit because he didn't want to wear a tuxedo. He refused to come out of the greenroom at Lincoln Center to greet donors—including then–Columbia Pictures CEO Victor Kaufman, a board member who had personally raised a huge proportion of the total by selling tables and, in addition, had gotten Columbia to pick up the $65,000 tab for the dinner that followed. Afterward, Redford tried unsuccessfully to cancel a similar event in Los Angeles and did cancel one in Chicago.

Redford had his reasons, both for pushing out Wilhite and for undermining the fund-raising events. He says Wilhite was a good executive but wrong for Sundance. He was too aloof, too mainstream, too divisive—and he lived in Los Angeles. "I woke up one day, and there were vice presidents all over the place—vice president this, vice president that. I'm not big on titles." According to VanWagenen, Wilhite "struck out on his own. He didn't make a serious effort to set up personal contact with Bob. He resisted making himself accessible." (Wilhite refuses to comment.)

Redford was increasingly coming to see himself as a drag on Sundance and Sundance as a drag on him. He struggled to find a way out. "A lot of people were talking about what an asset I was. I began to see it differently, that I was a distorting force, a liability. If someone says this guy is a dilettante, and he's out there in Utah trying to use this as some tax write-off, then they aren't going to be anxious to contribute. So I purposely tried to step back, because I didn't think it was healthy."

When he did step back, he says, he was misrepresented to the staff. "If I didn't show somewhere, they'd say, 'He was supposed to come, but he didn't.' The truth was, I'd said I wasn't coming. And suddenly I found out that the staff is upset because they think I let them down. It's upsetting stuff."

The "Great Movie Music" event was a perfect example, he says. "I did not agree with Wilhite about Lincoln Center. I said, 'Don't put me in the center of this evening.' And I suddenly found myself smack in the center of it. I resented it. Some people view that as schizophrenic leadership. It's not true. It's been conscious. I decided three years ago that I've got to go back to doing my own work. There are things I want to do and films I want to make."

Whatever Redford's motives, staffers, proud of raising $600,000, regarded his behavior as "a slap in the face," says former accountant Burr. According to Mary Cranney, former associate director of development, Redford's attitude was often perceived this way: "It was like Bob was saying, 'This is my dream. I want you to fund it, but don't bother me.' " Staffers charged that Redford couldn't or wouldn't run Sundance himself and wouldn't let anyone else run it either.

All the President's Men

IN FEBRUARY 1989, Redford hired Suzanne Weil, perhaps hoping to find a more congenial director, but history repeated itself—this time as farce. If Wilhite was a good administrator with a poor relationship with Redford, Weil was the reverse. She cultivated Redford but was by most accounts an indifferent administrator. Her method was described by one veteran staffer as "management by crisis control." She had good ideas that required a strong support staff. Yet one of her first moves was to fire the head of that staff, Maria Schaeffer, who had been at the institute for four years. Just a few days after she started, Weil hopped on a plane for a two-week trip to Japan, leaving her staff to wonder what was next.

When Redford returned from the *Havana* production in Santo Domingo, Sundance's deficit was about $1 million, more than double what it was when Wilhite left. "I just couldn't have it," he says. By the fall of 1990, Weil too was gone.

Weil says she was unpopular because she tried to make changes. She says she had a three-year game plan and didn't have time to complete it. "I had a chance to mess it up, but I didn't have the chance to put it together again."

With Weil gone, Sundance was again without a director. "If you say there's a leadership problem at Sundance," says Redford, "it's my responsibility to find someone who will run it. I haven't done it. It's as simple as that. But there's somebody who has moved into the picture right now who I think has a very good concept for raising a lot of money: Gary Beer."

Redford says he brought Beer back on a temporary basis to get the finances in shape. Beer has a particularly strong relationship with the trustees. "We were all thrilled. He's an excellent piece of manpower," says ICM president Jim Wiatt, a board member for two years.

For some staffers, it was a different story. Within two months, Cinda Holt, the director of program administration and an eight-year veteran, had resigned. She had complained to Redford about Beer in the past, and reliable sources say her resignation was not voluntary. According to Alberto Garcia, festival competition director, "Some of the firings were completely political. I would wish, if I'd spent years of my life with a nonprofit arts organization, to get a nice good-bye rather than a hefty boot."

In essence, it appears that the institute is now run by Redford, Beer, and Gipson, Redford's lawyer, who is secretary treasurer of Sundance. This is a far cry from the days when it was run by

Redford and a board composed of people who were passionate about independent film.

Not only did some board members reportedly first learn about Weil's appointment from the trades, they didn't even know that Wilhite had left. (Wiatt, for one, denies this.) The board did bestir itself when the magnitude of the deficit became clear: it reportedly pressured Redford to get rid of Weil. "I find it highly ironic that the institute was created to shelter independent filmmakers from the lawyers and the money people so that they could focus strictly on the material," says Garcia, "yet now Sundance is being run by those same people, the bean counters."

Situation Hopeless—But Not Serious

ODD AS IT may seem, despite all these problems, Sundance's core programs have survived, and there is reason to be optimistic about the future. The June lab, the January screenwriters' lab, the producers' conference, and the festival are all going strong; other programs have been eliminated; and the playwrights' lab has spun off and combined with the children's theater. Says Wiatt, "I think the institute is in very good shape."

Much of the credit for the June lab must go to feature-film head Michelle Satter, a ten-year veteran who has successfully steered her program through the treacherous shoals of Sundance politics. She feels the reorganization will do the job. "We're focused on what we do best," she says. Satter's specialty is simple but important: helping filmmakers get their films made. Jill Godmilow had a project at the '85 lab, *Waiting for the Moon*, loosely based on the relationship of Alice B. Toklas and Gertrude Stein, that was later produced and released. "We had Linda Hunt, but we couldn't find a Gertrude, and we'd run out of money," says Godmilow. "I called Michelle, who gave us the name of Laura Kennedy, a West Coast casting director. Laura sat down three days a week for three months—for free—and we saw every possible Gertrude on the West Coast. People will do that for Sundance."

Until recently, Sundance has been entirely script-driven, and those scripts have followed a down-home, regional formula for what even staffers call "granola films." According to John Pierson, a producers' rep who has sold such films as *Roger & Me, She's Gotta Have It,* and *The Thin Blue Line,* "No one at Sundance would give these films the time of day on the basis of their scripts. They wouldn't know what to make of *Roger & Me* if they tripped over it." But from now on, finished scripts will not be required, and selection committee members, some of them hoary with age, will be limited to one-year terms (ditto the artistic director).

It is remarkable that the lab works as well as it does. "Even in the early years, I felt it was an extraordinary place, and I don't use that word lightly," says director Ulu Grosbard, who has attended labs as a resource person. "I'd gone to the Actors Studio years ago, when Strasberg was running it, and there was always an enormous discrepancy between what it wanted to be and what it was. This is not true here."

By all accounts, the last lab was one of the best yet. The selection of projects suggests that Sundance is trying hard to shed its regional image and reduce its emphasis on scripts. *Spring '61,* a quirky project about a girl with hooks for hands, and *Suzi and the Mechanic,* written and directed by Everett Lewis and set in an L.A. art world filled with sex and violence, were projects that would never have reached the lab five years ago. According to Satter, *Suzi* will go into production this year, and Tom DiCillo's *Johnny Suede,* another recent project, is already being shot.

Sundance is also now going to filmmakers and asking them what they need rather than trying to force them to conform to the lab structure. Gregg Araki is an Asian filmmaker whose avant-garde 16mm films often include gay relationships. He is the kind of marginal filmmaker that many staffers would like to see Sundance take more interest in. Araki didn't attend June lab but was offered support in other ways.

Yet there are still pitfalls. Feeling burned by first-time directors, Sundance is stressing so-called "transitional" filmmakers (such as Carl Bernstein, Bill Irwin, Martha Clarke, and Twyla Tharp) over "emerging" filmmakers. But this sounds like little more than a copy of the Chanticleer Films Discovery Program and uncomfortably close to abandoning the institute's original raison d'être in favor of celebrity filmmaking. Peter Weller is a good actor and a serious guy, but is he so without resources that Sundance money should be used to teach him how to direct, as it did in the '89 lab? Redford's words on the subject are not entirely reassuring. "Maybe it's time to say, 'Are we making a mistake using the word 'independent' quite so much?' Should we not just say, 'Film is film'?"

The Way They Are

HAS SUNDANCE SUCCEEDED or failed? There is no simple answer to that question. If its goals are interpreted grandly, it has undoubtedly failed. As Hausman puts it, "If there were twenty of them, it would be okay. But there's only one. It's like the Statue of Liberty—everybody looks to it. Everyone's pinning their hopes on it." Or, as another observer says, "Sundance has never been the visionary vanguard organization that it clearly wants to be, in terms of changing the face of American independent cinema."

But Sundance does not want to be judged by those criteria. And in this, it may well be right. "Sundance works best as a facilitator," says Tom Rickman. "If it can bring the filmmakers together with people who can get their films made for them, that's terrific."

However, the question of Sundance's past performance has been eclipsed by a more urgent question: Can it survive? There is not much chance that it will founder on the rough seas of financial hardship. Serious fund-raising could erase the debt, although dismantling the development department won't make that any easier. More serious is the toll on morale and spirit inflicted by the years of drift and poor management. "We're moving into the tenth year," Redford says gloomily. "No matter how hard you try, somebody gets pissed off. It's time now for me to step back and see if this thing can go on its own or not. If it can't, it shouldn't." He pauses. "I'd hate to think that ten years of my life have been wasted. You know, it's a good idea, and Hollywood needs it."

The key, of course, is the enigmatic figure of Redford himself. He is an intensely private and somewhat lonely man, enormously powerful but unsure of himself at the same time. He is intelligent but not particularly well educated. As a former colleague put it, "You can take the boy out of Van Nuys, but can you take the Van Nuys out

209

of the boy?" In Sundance, he has indeed created an instant family, an artistic and intellectual community where he can rub shoulders with Gabriel García Márquez, but he (or his surrogates) often treat it with the cavalier disregard reserved for loved ones.

Paradoxically, Sundance may be doing better than it knows. The fact that the festival has emerged as the institute's most spectacular achievement suggests that the independents who are really passionate always find a way to make their films, and that the real need now that the movement has achieved a degree of commercial respectability is not so much production aid as help in distribution and exhibition—two areas that Sundance ought to address seriously.

Moreover, partly because of Sundance, studios now routinely scour film schools for fresh talent and are much more open to giving promising filmmakers a shot than they were a decade ago. At the same time, the vast majority of filmmakers are just dying to get that studio assignment The Gus Van Sants and Jim Jarmusches are getting more and more rare. But there are still emerging filmmakers who need and deserve help, and Sundance's original purpose remains as compelling as ever. Film is not just film; it can't be in an "industry" dominated by a handful of studios. If Hollywood is the be-all and end-all of American film culture, we will all be impoverished.

Redford is hanging on to the basic vision of Sundance, and he is optimistic. "I know it's good," he says. "I've heard that from the filmmakers. There have been times in the past ten years when it would have been easier if I'd been sitting by a pool in Beverly Hills—but then you see a resource person who's rich and fat get recharged, or you see a piece of work that wouldn't have been made without Sundance, and it's like an electric shock. That's what it's all about."

AUTEURS

ANY WHICH WAY HE CAN

It is 6 P.M. on a Saturday night in Alberta, Canada, on the set of *Unforgiven*. Clint Eastwood likes to shoot westerns in the autumn, so the production descended on the town of Longview just as the leaves were beginning to turn. But now it's four weeks later. The trees are bare, and the production is bumping up against winter.

The cast and crew are expecting to break for their day off, Sunday. But there's a storm coming in. The weather service in Calgary says it's supposed to snow twelve inches on Monday, with freezing weather the rest of the week—meaning the snow won't melt.

They still have half a day's shooting in the town. Then, on Monday and Tuesday, they're scheduled to do a pivotal exterior scene, the one under the pine tree where the whore rides in, tells Eastwood's character, William Munny, that Little Bill Daggett has beaten his partner Ned to death, and Munny takes his first, long pull from the bottle of whiskey that will send him on a rampage of killing. There are eight and a half pages of dialogue. Eastwood wants to see the town in the distance—with no snow on the ground.

Executive producer David Valdes comes up with a nutty idea: shoot into the wee hours of Sunday morning; wrap at 2 A.M.; go back to the hotel, an hour away; let the crew grab four hours of sleep; on Sunday, go up to the hill, without breaking for meals, and do the

Monday and Tuesday sequence till the sun goes down; then film the scene where Munny emerges from the bar in the rain, through the night into Monday morning. Had Valdes called the studio, they would have gone ballistic—Eastwood and Co. were about to break every rule in the book: double time for working the crew on Sunday and a hailstorm of penalties for not feeding the crew when they're supposed to be fed. The weather report has been wrong before. Valdes is not going to be a popular guy in Longview (or in Burbank, for that matter) if the storm passes a little to the east or a little to the west of them. But the alternative is to risk having to shoot the scene in California later, which would cost hundreds of thousands of dollars more and forfeit the tie-in to the town.

They complete the eight and a half pages on Sunday and continue on into the night, twenty-one hours straight. It's so cold, the water from the rain machines is freezing, making for a treacherous purchase on the muddy ground. The horses are slipping and sliding all over the ice, and the people aren't doing too well either. It's so cold, Eastwood's teeth are chattering. At about 2 A.M., pissed-off crew members are demanding pizza. "We're in Bumfuck, Alberta," Valdes screams back, "and there's no Domino's around the corner."

At 5:30 or so Monday morning, Jack Green, the cinematographer, turns to Eastwood and tells him there's time for only one more shot before dawn. Fifteen minutes later, they're finished. The first snowflakes begin to fall—and don't stop until the following evening. A foot of snow arrives on schedule. Winter in Alberta has begun.

Clint Eastwood hasn't been to the Oscars since 1973, when he was asked to present the Best Picture award and ended up subbing for host Charlton Heston, who was stuck on the freeway. "Howard Koch said, 'Here's the script,' " recalls Eastwood. "It was a parody of Moses, *The Ten Commandments,* thou shalt not be this and that, all relating to movies. Bad material, even for Moses. I said, 'You gotta be kidding. Never invite me again.' 'Will you come back if you're nominated?' 'Yeah, I'll do that.' Koch says, 'Then I don't have to worry.' "

Well, Eastwood might have come back with *The Outlaw Josey Wales,* and most certainly with *Bird,* but as it turned out, he stayed away for nineteen years. In the twentieth year, the Man With No

Name finally rode into town with a clutch of nominations for *Unforgiven* in his saddlebag: Best Picture, Best Director, Best Supporting Actor, Best Original Screenplay. Not bad for a guy who used to be dismissed as a cowboy, one of whose films was derided by Rex Reed as a "demented exercise in Hollywood hackery."

It's been a long and twisted trail from *A Fistful of Dollars,* the first spaghetti western Eastwood did for Sergio Leone, in 1964, when Lyndon Johnson occupied the White House, to the Dorothy Chandler Pavilion in this, the spring of the Clinton presidency—thirty-nine pictures, with another, *In the Line of Fire,* in the can and scheduled for a summer release, and still another, *A Perfect World,* which he directs and co-stars in with Kevin Costner, set to begin shortly. Sixteen of them he directed himself. Eastwood, always philosophical about the Oscars, once said, "I figure that by the time I'm really old, somebody at the Academy Awards will get the bright idea to give me some sort of plaque. I'll be so old, they'll have to carry me up there. . . . Thank you all for this honorary award and SPLAT. Good-bye, Dirty Harry."

Standing around the Westin Bonaventure hotel, in downtown Los Angeles, watching director Wolfgang Petersen shoot inserts for *Line of Fire,* Eastwood is uncomfortable talking about his Oscar prospects. *Unforgiven* is the front-runner, after grabbing a slew of critics' awards, and it makes him nervous. Or maybe it's the inserts, pickups, bits of business, whatever, that make him impatient. He is legendary for working quickly, coming in ahead of schedule and under budget. It's a matter of pride to him—more, a way of life. Recalls Frank Wells, who was president of Warner Bros. during the '70s, "His favorite time was the last day of a picture. He would call me, and I would guess how much under budget he was." Eastwood is fond of saying things like, "The more time you have to think things through, the more you have to screw it up."

In the Line of Fire boasts a very good script, by Jeff Maguire, a bit along the lines of *Tightrope,* or even *Unforgiven*—films in which the character Eastwood plays is less a superhero than an ordinary guy with a Past, a guy who's been damaged by life, a guy who has to live with something he'd rather forget. Here he's an aging Secret Service agent who is convinced he let John F. Kennedy die, those many years ago in Dealey Plaza, by not moving fast enough, perhaps paralyzed by a flaw in his character. It is a story of Conradian dimensions—whether the execution matches the ambition remains to be seen. Like *A Perfect World, Line of Fire* represents a more commercial, less personal choice for him than *Unforgiven*.

Eastwood, who had director approval, selected Petersen, best known for *Das Boot*. People in advanced stages of megastardom often hire flunkies for the express purpose of second-guessing them and making their lives miserable. But Eastwood, it is said, does not operate that way. When he decides his employees can perform the jobs they've been hired for, he leaves them alone, relies on their judgment, and if they come through, he hires them again—and again. Glenn Wright, his costume designer, has been with him since the *Rawhide* days. Eddie Aiona has been his prop master for some twenty-five years. Joel Cox, his editor, started working for him eighteen years ago. Valdes began as a second assistant director thirteen years ago.

Listening to the people who work for him saves Eastwood enormous amounts of time. He doesn't audition actors; he looks at tapes supplied by his casting director. When Valdes or the production designer chooses a location, he often won't see it until the day before the shooting begins. The look-of-show meeting is usually over in ten minutes, because he can count on cinematographer Jack Green (twenty-two years) to react to a script the way he does. Eastwood lets Cox put the first cut together himself, from rushes of Cox's selection. Five to six weeks after the film wraps, the editing is finished.

Eastwood's people have a refreshingly casual approach to making movies. "It's fun," says Valdes, "and everyone realizes we're not curing brain cancer." Cinematographer Bruce Surtees, who worked on a number of Eastwood's pictures, once said, "There's no trick to lighting. You turn on a light, and if it looks good, you use it. If it doesn't, you turn it off and put it some other place."

No one sits around waiting for the sun to go in or out of the clouds on an Eastwood set. His luck with weather is a legend in the business. If he needs snow in the Mojave Desert in July, it will snow. But it's not all luck. He moves so fast, he doesn't have to worry about matching one part of a scene with another. "Once you get that kind of velocity, suddenly weather doesn't matter," says gaffer Tom Stern, the baby of the group, who's been with

Eastwood for a mere eight years. "Instead of calling it adversity, you call it serendipity."

Eastwood hates overlighting, which he associates with television, especially in his thrillers. He prefers a *noir*-ish, chiaroscuro effect. Pauline Kael once wrote, apropos of *Bird,* "The picture looks as if [Eastwood] hasn't paid his Con Edison bill." On *Firefox,* which is a bit on the murky side, there is a shot that is so dark, only Eastwood's elbow is visible. The cameraman wanted to do another take. Eastwood said, "Am I in the frame?" "Yeah." "Can you hear my voice?" "Yeah." "They know who I am. Let's print it and move on."

In an industry where first takes are virtually always rehearsals and actors don't get serious until the fourth or fifth, where it is not unheard-of to shoot thirty, forty, fifty takes of the same scene, Eastwood is famous for shooting rehearsals—and not just rehearsals, but first rehearsals. He walks the stand-ins through the scenes, to get a rough sense of blocking, light placement, and so on. Then, says Green, he brings in the actors. "They're working with the words for the first time, and we're rolling. They have to paraphrase or deal with props in a naturally awkward way. If they do hit the light, we're lucky; if they stay in the frame, we're really grateful." On the other hand, says Jeff Fahey, who played the writer in *White Hunter, Black Heart,* "he'll never walk away from something until he has what he wants."

Usually Eastwood will do no more than three to five takes, and print two. On *Bronco Billy,* Scatman Crothers had just come off *The Shining,* where Stanley Kubrick had put him through something like fifty takes on one scene, and he was almost paralyzed with fear. Eastwood did one take and printed it; Crothers nearly burst into tears.

Eastwood's method works. It lends his pictures a fresh, improvisatory, realistic flavor. The extraordinary first scene of *Unforgiven,* in the whorehouse when the woman is cut, is a first rehearsal. It has the impact of real violence; it's over in an instant, and we're not really sure what has happened. We feel like voyeurs, as if we walked down the hall, passed an open door, looked in, and saw something unspeakable.

Eastwood has never believed, as Sam Peckinpah did, in drawing out violence, aestheticizing it, and indeed, these two masters of the western never worked together. "One time I was talking to a class at USC and somebody said, 'How come you never worked with Peckinpah?'" recalls Eastwood. "I said, 'Well, he's never asked me.' And all of a sudden some guy got up in the, back and said, 'I'm asking you now!' I look up and it's Peckinpah sitting in the class. He was so wild; he'd go off and live in whorehouses. Some of those guys were amazing—John Huston, staying up to all hours doing whiskey and then directing the next day. I can't do that. I always have to train up, run, like it's an event."

The bonaventure, where the endangered president makes a campaign stop, has a cold, inhospitable lobby consisting of cavernous atrium punctuated by concrete columns. Someone has spent a good deal of money to create a series of small concrete pools filled with stagnant-looking water covered with a dull gray film. One finds oneself looking in vain for floating condoms. Watching Petersen do take after take of his insert, it's clear what Eastwood is thinking, but he would never say anything. Nor will Petersen, a short, lively man with shaggy blond hair and an engaging smile, admit to being intimidated by his star, who could get an Oscar for directing. And maybe he isn't. "Clint knows if I'm directing the film, to let me alone," says Petersen. "He's not a guy to step up and say, 'Shoot it this way.' Still, sometimes, when I say, 'Clint, this was great, but please, let's do it again,' he says, 'If it's great, why do it again?'"

Despite the fact that *Dirty Harry* was made more than twenty years ago, Eastwood is constantly beset by fans asking him to make their day. Once a cop lurked about the Eastwood-owned Hog's Breath Inn in Carmel, California, for a week, waiting for the actor. Eastwood finally showed up; the guy entered and in one sudden sweeping movement pulled an enormous .357 magnum from the small of his back. The customers hit the floor. But he only wanted Eastwood's autograph on the barrel—he'd brought along his etching tool. Eastwood signed it, thought for a moment, and said, "Don't go leaving this around anywhere," like the guy might do a liquor store and drop the gun on the floor.

Now a large, buxom woman pushes her way through the crowd of onlookers and tourists surrounding Eastwood on the *Line of Fire* shoot. She is yelling "Clint, Clint, let me at 'im." She heaves up in front of him and bellows, "East Clintwood! I got all your records!"

Eastwood was born on May 31, 1930, in San Francisco, right in time for the depression. His father scratched out a living at odd jobs before ending up in Oakland at Bethlehem Steel. After high school, Eastwood traveled around, mostly in the Northwest, working at Boeing, Bethlehem, fighting fires for the Forest Service, hauling lumber at a Weyerhaeuser pulp mill, baling hay, and so on. He once described himself as a "bum and a drifter," but he later attributed his sure feel for the blue-collar audience to these experiences.

After a stint at Fort Ord as a lifeguard during the Korean War, he went down to Los Angeles to find work as an actor. Every day, he said, was like getting slapped in the face with a wet towel.

In 1954, he got a job driving a truck around the Universal Studios lot and eventually hired on as a contract player for seventy-five dollars a week, acting in a couple of cheapies that later became shlock classics. *Tarantula* and *Revenge of the Creature* (from the Black Lagoon). Eventually, Universal let him go (because his Adam's apple was too big, his buddy Burt Reynolds once joked).

For two years, he scrambled, digging swimming pools, pumping gas. Then, in 1958, through a chance encounter, he got the part of Rowdy Yates, the sidekick of Eric Fleming's Gil Favor in *Rawhide,* a TV western that ran on CBS for seven years. In 1965, Fleming left the show (a year later, he was killed by a crocodile while on location in South America, according to director Ted Post), and Eastwood had the series to himself.

In 1964, his agent asked him if he was interested in starring in a western to be shot in Spain by an Italian named Sergio Leone. "I had questions, normal questions, like who is Sergio Leone? It wasn't like Fellini was offering to do it." For $15,000, he agreed to go over to Spain during his hiatus from *Rawhide*. He even brought his own cigars, which he found at a tobacco shop in Beverly Hills. "They were about that long," says Eastwood, placing his hands about a foot apart. "I said, I'll chop 'em in threes.' Boy, they tasted ugly. Put you right in the mood for killing.

"Leone knew 'good-bye,' and I knew *'arrivederci,'* " says Eastwood, and they communicated through gestures and intermediaries. The script was wordy, and Eastwood cut out dialogue by the mouthful. "Whenever I had a problem, I'd use my street psychology, Psych 1-A. I'd just say, 'Well, Sergio, in a B western, you'd have to explain. But in an A western, you just let the audience fill in the holes.' He'd say, 'Okay.' "

Eastwood did two sequels to *A Fistful of Dollars*. When the first of his spaghetti westerns arrived in America, in 1967, the critical reaction was mixed. The films were acclaimed—and disdained—for their hip, surreal cynicism.

The trilogy established the formula for the Eastwood western: the Man With No Name squinting in the fierce midday sun, laconic, cool, and laid-back but remorseless and vengeful at the same time, coming from nowhere, going nowhere, without a past, without a future. He was the antithesis of the liberal Freudian western hero of the '50s—Paul Newman's Billy the Kid, say, in Arthur Penn's *The Left-Handed Gun*. "I was the king of cool," says Eastwood.

The western was *the* American genre, as critic J. Hoberman has said, the one in which America stared itself in the face and asked the big questions: What is good? What is bad? What is law? What is order? Eastwood's westerns were no exception. The pasta pictures were the cultural Muzak for the post-Kennedy era; the Man With No Name became the big-screen version of J.F.K., who forced Khrushchev to back down over the Berlin Wall and the Cuban Missile Crisis, launched the Bay of Pigs, and cultivated the Green Berets. Along with the James Bond pictures, Eastwood's films ushered in a new era of cinematic violence. Some fifty people are killed in *A Fistful of Dollars*. The line between the hero and the heavy was becoming blurred. With the war in Vietnam heating up, there was no time for niceties.

"In *Josey Wales,* my editor said, 'Boy, you shot him in the back,'" recalls Eastwood. "I said, 'Yeah, you do what you have to do to get the job done.' I think the era of standing there going 'You draw first' is over. You don't have much of a chance if you wait for the other guy to draw. You have to try for realism. So, yeah, I used to shoot them in the back all the time."

Eastwood and Leone changed film history together, but they

barely knew each other. After *The Good, the Bad, and the Ugly,* Leone wanted Eastwood to do *Once Upon a Time in the West,* but Eastwood had had enough. "I went home, and I didn't see him for a lot of years. I think he was resentful—I had started becoming successful. And he didn't do a lot of movies. Many years later, when I went over to Italy for *Bird,* he called. We went out together one evening and got along better than in all the times we had worked together. I left, and he died. It was almost like he had called up to say good-bye."

Eastwood's first American western, *Hang 'Em High,* in 1968, for United Artists, was in the spaghetti mode. His next picture, *Coogan's Bluff,* began a lengthy collaboration and friendship with director Don Siegel. "When we met, it was a very sort of surly relationship," says Eastwood. " 'I don't like your suggestion for this.' 'I don't like yours.' Finally, we just zeroed in, started agreeing on a few things, and then we became fast friends."

Eastwood had always wanted to direct, and he picked a small story, *Play Misty for Me,* to start with. The studio, Universal, preferred he stick to his six-guns. This was a sort of proto–*Fatal Attraction,* in which a disk jockey gets involved with a psychotic woman. Eastwood prepared well, perhaps too well. The night before the shoot began, "I was lying in bed, going over the shots in my mind. I had them all planned out. I turned out the light, thought, 'I got this now.' All of a sudden, I went, 'Jesus! I got to be in this thing!' I turned on the light and started approaching the scenes all over again from the actor's point of view. Needless to say, I didn't get much sleep." The critics were not nice, Eastwood recalls. "They said, 'We're not ready for him as an actor, much less a director.' "

Misty was a modest hit. And then came *Dirty Harry.* The tenor of the film was evident from a tag line that was never used: "Dirty Harry and the Homicidal Maniac. Harry's the one with the badge." But the critics were not amused. In the highly polarized political climate of 1971, many people felt that *Dirty Harry* said it was okay for cops to trample civil liberties in the pursuit of crooks. Plus, the Scorpio Killer wears a peace sign, as if Siegel and Eastwood were turning a whole generation of kids who fought for social justice and an end to the war in Vietnam into a bunch of

Charles Mansons. Kael was particularly vocal. She wrote that Dirty Harry is a man who "stands for vigilante justice" and termed the picture "fascist." Eastwood answered his critics by insisting it was just a defense of victims' rights. "The general public isn't worried about the rights of the killer; they're just saying get him off the streets." So far as the peace sign went, "that was a thing where the actor wanted to do it and everybody just thought, 'Well, that's irony. A lot of people hide behind the guise of being peaceful, and they'll be the first ones out there advocating violence.' "

After *Dirty Harry,* Eastwood was given considerable freedom at Warner's. "The guy had a story sense about his own persona that nobody else had," recalls Wells, who is now president of the Walt Disney Company. "You'd make the deal and not see him again until the preview—of an under-budget movie. We always did what he wanted to do." Except in the case of *Dirty Harry.* Eastwood did not want to do a sequel, but the studio was implacable. Ironically, *Magnum Force* was based on an idea spawned by the febrile brain of wild man John Milius. Eastwood considered it a liberal riposte to *Dirty Harry.* "It showed that just because these guys were killing people who deserved to be killed doesn't mean that's the way society should go about it."

221

"Eastwood was typed early on as a guy who could do only one thing—Harry—over and over, and he was the only guy in the mix who thought, 'I can do better than that,' " says Dennis Shryack, who cowrote *The Gauntlet* and *Pale Rider.*

In real life, Eastwood was far different from the character he became identified with. He did collect guns, but he didn't care much for hunting. It's said he once stopped his daughter from stepping on a cockroach. "I don't like killing," he says. "It's one thing to fantasize about it in a movie, but I never saw the sport in removing a life from the planet."

In 1976, he directed himself in *The Outlaw Josey Wales,* another tale of revenge and his best western up to that time. Even though critics constantly compared him to John Wayne, Eastwood—and the Duke—knew different. Wayne wrote him a letter after he saw *High Plains Drifter* (1973). "He said, 'That isn't what the West was all about. That isn't the American people who settled this country,' " Eastwood later recalled. Eastwood's westerns were more akin to Elizabethan revenge tragedy than to John Ford. "I was never John Wayne's heir," he once said.

Ford believed deeply in the civilizing impact of society, the transformation of the jungle into the garden. In Ford's dusty towns, there is always a church or a school going up, the frame building standing starkly against the raw landscape. Eastwood's westerns are about darkness and pain, and even when the evil has been avenged, the wounds rarely heal. In *Unforgiven,* there is a house going up, built by Little Bill Daggett, Gene Hackman's sadistic sheriff. At the end, with Mutiny's weapon aimed at his head, Daggett says: "I don't deserve this . . . to die this way. I was building a house." Munny replies, "Deserve's got nothin' to do with it," and pulls the trigger. Ford westerns are about deserving, and this scene would never have happened.

Until 1976, aside from the Dirty Harry movies, Eastwood for the most part worked for Universal. But he had long been dissatisfied with the way the studio was marketing his movies. The Universal tour was the last straw. "I had a really nice bungalow, a very comfortable place to work," he recalls. "But I'd walk out of my office and the bus would be sitting there with people yelling. So finally I called Frank Wells [at Warner's] and said, 'I'll move over there if you've got a space for me, but if you ever have a tour, I'm leaving.' He said, 'We're not in the tour business.' "

Moreover, Eastwood had an itch. His career has always gone against the grain. He was making genre movies in an era when the most interesting work was devoted to subverting genres, particularly the western, which more or less died under him. He was riding tall in the saddle in an age of antiheroes; he was the laconic star for Nixon's silent majority. If Dirty Harry was a decade ahead of itself, when the Reagan-era Zeitgeist caught up with him, in 1980, Eastwood had already moved along. While George Lucas and Steven Spielberg were busy reinventing the old formulas that Penn, Scorsese, Airman, and others had buried, one thought, for good, Eastwood started tinkering with his image, journeying into the shadows of his own persona.

He told writers Shryack and Michael Butler that he regarded their script *The Gauntlet,* in which he plays a feckless cop, as a bridge to a new kind of character. In 1980, the beginning of the Reagan era, he further cut the ground out from under himself in the self-mocking *Bronco Billy*, where cowboy Billy is a purveyor of illusions. While Reagan was using the symbols of the West to promote the illusion of a heroic America that no longer existed, Eastwood was increasingly obsessed by the limitations of the human condition. "Exploring the dark side sort of came about when I started doing things like *Bronco Billy*," he says. "I've played winners, I've played losers who were winners, guys who are cool, but I like reality, and in reality, it's not all like that. There's sort of that frailty in mankind that's very interesting to explore. Heroics are so few and far between."

When *The Gauntlet* didn't do as well as hoped, Warner's became concerned that Eastwood was making the wrong choices. He always had a streak of Burt Reynolds redneck humor about him, and when he wanted to play opposite an orangutan in *Every Which Way but Loose,* Warner's did some market research that indicated a negative reaction to the title, to the orangutan, and even to the idea of Dirty Harry in a comedy. But Eastwood doesn't have much truck with market research and went ahead anyway. It cost about $8 million and grossed about $85 million (about $150 million in today's dollars), making it his biggest film. Even *Bronco Billy* grossed $33 million. Finally, the East Coast establishment climbed aboard. In 1980, the Museum of Modern Art in New York gave him a retrospective. Two years later, Robert Mazzocco wrote a widely read appreciation in the *New York Review of Books,* calling Eastwood "the supply-side star." The essay registered his anointment by Upper West Side "neos"—both liberals and conservatives. Then, in 1985, the French, who had always lauded Hollywood directors without honor in their own country, gave Eastwood a retrospective at the Cinémathèque, as well as a Chevalier des Arts et Lettres decoration.

Mazzocco was right. Eastwood had indeed benefited from the Reagan-era cultural shift. But liberals applauded him, too, falling all over themselves to find the bleeding heart behind the "fascist" veneer. His acting, previously "stiff," became "spare and stylized." *Honkytonk Man* was compared with *The Grapes of Wrath*. The *Los Angeles Times,* doubtless with *Sudden Impact* in mind, called him "the most important and influential . . . feminist filmmaker working in America today."

223

But just as Eastwood was never a fascist, his new liberal threads did not quite fit him either. In the early years of the Reagan administration, he gave a reported $30,000 to a former lieutenant colonel in the Special Forces named James "Bo" Gritz to launch an "incursion" into Laos, and then agreed to act as Gritz's liaison with Reagan.

"I said, 'If there's a possibility of saving just one person, I would certainly spend any amount of time and effort necessary,'" recalls Eastwood. "But it wasn't *The Dirty Dozen*—I think they ended up spending most of the dough hanging around Bangkok. They brought back a bunch of bones—some of them weren't even human. Remains weren't worth risking lives for." (Gritz denies dribbling the money away in Bangkok and insists that the remains were human.)

A registered Republican for most of his life, Eastwood criticized Reagan for visiting a military cemetery in Bitburg, Germany, where SS troops were buried. He ran for mayor of Carmel in 1986 and won—but spent $25,000 to land a job that paid $2,400 a year. Although Eastwood feels his two-year term was plenty, his editor, Joel Cox, says, "I think it was the best thing that ever happened to Clint. He's always been a loner. It sort of opened his personality a little bit."

Eastwood rejected George Bush's request for help in the last election. "I think what the ultra–right wing conservatives did to the Republicans is really self-destructive, absolutely stupid." He voted for Ross Perot. "Perot was kind of out there, with dirty tricks and all. But in the final analysis, he's the only one I believe. I would have loved to have seen four years of the little guy from Texas rolling his eyes, screaming and yelling, 'Time to bite the bullet.'"

In the last ten years or so, Eastwood has chosen more personal, character-driven projects: *Honkytonk Man; Bird; White Hunter, Black Heart;* and *Unforgiven.* He gets away with it because he is so financially responsible. Asking Warner president Terry Semel about Eastwood is like asking a kid about Santa Claus on Christmas morning: "Clint is the best producer I've ever worked with. He is more careful with our money than he is with his own." Warner's is not going to lose much on an Eastwood picture, no matter what it's about. Says Valdes, "I think if Clint Eastwood wants to make a cooking show, he will call [Warner chairman] Bob Daly or Terry Semel, and we'll be doing a cooking show." *Bird* is a period drama about a black jazz musician—an alcoholic, a smack addict, and a wife beater—who dies at the end. But Eastwood knew he could bring it in under $10 million, including his fee, at a time when an average picture cost $18 million. And he did.

At the same time, Warner's counted on him to deliver commercial product. The problem was that *Heartbreak Ridge, The Dead Pool, Pink Cadillac,* and *The Rookie* were not that commercial. For the first time, Eastwood's career looked as if it might be in trouble. Then came *Unforgiven*—not, on the face of it, much more of a box office draw than *Bird,* a risky project for someone who hadn't had a real hit in nearly ten years. But as with *Bird,* he kept the costs down. He brought it in in fifty-two days for $14.4 million, excluding his fee. With some exceptions, Eastwood always had trouble getting marquee names for his movies; they were seen as *his* movies. "You'd start talking about Meryl Streep and end up with Patty Clarkson," says Marco Barla, Eastwood's project coordinator. Hackman didn't want to do *Unforgiven.* "The violence of the characters I portrayed had begun to wear on me," he says. But Eastwood convinced him that the film made a statement *about* violence. "He was very explicit about his desire to demythologize violence," adds Hackman. Later, Hackman quipped, "I'm really glad Clint convinced me this was not a Clint Eastwood film."

"When *Unforgiven* came out and started doing business, I was shocked," says Eastwood. "Because I never try and romance the audience. You've got to forget that there's somebody out there eating popcorn and Milk Duds. I figured that if people want to see it, they'll see it. If they don't, screw it." Eastwood, sitting in his trailer between takes on *Line of Fire,* is dressed in a conservative gray Secret Service suit, scuffed and ripped in places from his exertions in the name of national security. He looks tired. There is a half-pint container of milk on the table. "Better get rid of that," he says softly to Frances Fisher, whom he has been seeing for some time and refers to as "Bad Fran." "Else you'll be *Big* Bad Fran."

Eastwood has said he doesn't know if *Unforgiven,* which has now grossed more than $100 million worldwide, will be his last western, but it should be. He's come full circle. *Unforgiven* is *Dirty Harry* turned on its head. After two decades, Harry, still above the law, has become the sadistic sheriff, Hackman's Daggett, while Scorpio has evolved into Munny, the killer now reformed. By killing Daggett, Eastwood purges the identity that has imprisoned him throughout his career.

Richard Schickel once said that Eastwood is a man who works in the American vernacular, an artisan whose art emerges from the craft. As Barla puts it, he is like a body-and-fender man who's been beating out dents for thirty years and then builds his own car. Everybody oohs and aahs, and it goes in a museum. Eastwood, of course, will never make any extravagant claims about his own work. "I sort of just do my thing and make films, and the body of work just sort of adds up year after year," he has said. "Eventually you do something someone thinks is okay."

More than okay, and the beauty of it is, he's still working. *In the Line of Fire* is not *Unforgiven*. But neither is it *Dirty Harry*. Yet the executives at Columbia Pictures just can't get *Dirty Harry* out of their minds.

Line of Fire's killer (played by John Malkovich) has been taunting Eastwood's character, Frank Horrigan, insisting that history is about to repeat itself. There's a scene in which Horrigan stands by Kennedy's grave, staring at the flame, and mutters to himself, "It's not going to happen."

When the execs heard that, a light went on: if he spits out "It's not gonna happen," it could resonate like "Make my day." They could use it in the trailer.

They ask the screenwriter, Jeff Maguire, to add the line during the climactic fight between Eastwood and his doppelganger. There's no way to do it, unless Maguire makes the killer—a clever fellow, and by no means a cardboard villain given to thundering imprecations—shout something like, "I'm gonna kill you," or "You're a dead man." Maguire doesn't want to do it. But he's only the writer, and, worse, this is his first script. So it's up to Eastwood to draw a line in the sand, tell Columbia, "It's not gonna happen." But it's not his picture.

Under pressure, Maguire rewrites the dialogue. Malkovich looks at the new pages and says, "Why would I say that?" One day, while they're shooting the fight, Eastwood says, "Let's do it." They shoot the scene. Malkovich threatens; Eastwood fixes him with that cold stare and retorts, "It's not gonna happen." But he doesn't pause for effect. He says it quickly, swallows the words. They are nearly inaudible (they ended up reshooting the line so it can be used in the trailer). But no one can say Eastwood is hard to work with, or throws his weight around, or is on a star trip, or acts like Dirty Harry. He doesn't. He's not.

CHAMELEON MAN

Woody Allen's latest film, *Zelig,* is a pseudodocumentary about a human chameleon who is so adaptable that he can even take on the physical characteristics of those around him. By setting the film in the '20s and playing loose with actual newsreel footage, Allen and his collaborators are able to let the star (Allen, of course, plays Zelig) brush shoulders with such historical personages as Babe Ruth, Eugene O'Neill, and Adolf Hitler. *Zelig* is enormously clever and very funny—a cross between *The Elephant Man* and *Dead Men Don't Wear Plaid*—but it is also, even more than Allen's other films, a complex comedy of ideas and ideologies.

Allen himself has worn various guises in the course of his artistic career, and has been many things to many people. In the '70s, with such autobiographical sex comedies as *Play It Again, Sam, Annie Hall,* and *Manhattan,* he became a celebrant of the singles scene, an apostle of men's liberation, the poet laureate of what Christopher Lasch called "the culture of narcissism." In *Manhattan* we had Allen as Ike Davis, a doubly divorced, unemployed writer in love with Mary (Diane Keaton), a brainy, self-declared neurotic who gave good conversation, and at the same time involved with Tracy (Mariel Hemingway), a stunning high school senior who gave good sex. Not a pretty picture, especially for those who, like Allen, had been raised in the '50s on a steady therapeutic diet of maturity, adjustment, and responsibility—ideals which required, at least in the movies, that errant bachelors like Frank Sinatra in *The Tender Trap* or Rock Hudson in *Pillow Talk* shape up and settle down.

But an ocean of psychobabble had flowed under the bridge by 1979, when *Manhattan* was released. Like Alvy Singer in *Annie Hall*, Ike was forever in therapy, though it wasn't the same kind as that practiced by the sober Freudians of the '50s. It didn't enslave him to the breadwinner ethic, indenture him to the wife and kids, or yoke him to the office on weekdays and the barbecue on weekends. With its emphasis on personal growth rather than adjustment to responsibility, this new kind of therapy freed him from domesticity. As critic Mark Shechner wrote, therapy came to take the place of marriage, therapist of family. Ike found not a cure but a lifestyle. He may have been "old-fashioned," may have disapproved of extra-marital affairs, but he was into serial monogamy with a vengeance.

Appearances to the contrary, Ike was not unemployed: he'd merely chucked an "inauthentic" job churning out TV scripts so that he might give some attention to the book he'd always wanted to write. His twin divorces were not a sign of failure: both of his ex-wives—one a lesbian, the other a Moonie living in San Francisco—victimized men. His infatuation with Mary was not "immature": it was just another "growth" experience. And his affair with Tracy, far from being self-indulgent, was sanctioned by two decades of *Playboy* advice to swingers. In other words, it wasn't Ike's taste for jailbait that screwed him up, but the long, lingering shadow of Freud. Crippled by guilt, Ike was mortified by the idea that a forty-two-year-old man could find true love in the arms of an under-educated seventeen-year-old mannequin. But in the end he'd learned his lesson: seventeen was old enough for him. The triumph of Tracy over Mary represented a triumph of the '70s over the '50s, *Playboy* over Freud, the id over the superego. *Manhattan* was a thinking man's *Porky's*.

Woody Allen and his message were welcomed by such critics as Richard Schickel, who had been one of the first to "discover" him, way back in 1973, around the time of *Everything You Always Wanted to Know About Sex—But Were Afraid to Ask*. In an influential article that appeared in *The New York Times Magazine* in

January of that year, Schickel called Allen "the most important comic talent now working in the country," and went on to say that Allen's films gave a "nudge of recognition" to the "psychoanalytic" generation contemplating "the wreckage of sundry relationships." When *Manhattan* appeared, Andrew Sarris called it "the only truly great American movie of the 1970s."

But by treating Allen and his work as a sort of cultural barometer, Allen's admirers were asking for trouble; and trouble they got, from Joan Didion, who inaugurated an anti-Allen backlash in 1979. Didion ridiculed Allen's schnook-chic, complained that his films displayed "hermetic self-regard," and, worse, accused his characters of being "morose" and having "bad manners." With an exasperation equal to that of the character portrayed by Keaton in *Interiors,* who tells her simpering husband, "I'm sick of your needs," Didion went on to scoff at the growth industry's notion of "oneself as a kind of continuing career—something to work at, work on, 'make an effort' for and subject to an hour a day of emotional Nautilus training, all in the interests not of attaining grace but of improving one's 'relationships.' "

Pauline Kael, for her part, eviscerated *Stardust Memories* a year later in *The New Yorker* with a review in which she took Allen to task for grotesquely caricaturing his Jewish fans, and claimed that Jewish self-hatred spilled out of the film. " 'Woody Allen *c'est moi,*' any of us could say," Schickel once wrote, and it was now suddenly apparent that the "us" in question were men—urban, hip, liberated men—who saw Allen as a borscht belt Werner Erhard.

Ironically, Allen's fans began to derogate his early films as "chaotic" while praising his new ones in the name of the very values—such as maturity and control—the films repudiated. On the other hand, Allenophobes would praise his early films for their "spontaneity" and "vitality," denouncing his new films because they endorsed, but allegedly did not embody, those same values. While rhapsodic pro-Allen paeans appeared, with clunky but reassuring titles like "The Maturing of Woody Allen" (the *New York Times Magazine*), anti-Allen broadsides dismissed him as a practicing adolescent. Was he a grown-up or a kid? Only his mother knew for sure.

Schickel was right on one count, at least: Allen had come to stand for the ideology of therapy and for the urban lifestyle as defined by the culture of narcissism. The fight over Allen's films was really a fight over those values. In *Zelig* Allen attempts to defuse this debate, employing a strategy of preemptive disinterpretation. The film is so self-conscious that it's difficult to say anything about it that it doesn't already say about itself. In a wicked parody of *Reds*, *Zelig* incorporates several "witnesses," who provide a chorus of commentary. "All the themes of our culture were there," says Irving Howe, who sees Zelig's life as a metaphor for the "Jewish experience." According to Bruno Bettelheim, Zelig was the "ultimate conformist"; for Susan Sontag, his cure represented the triumph not of psychotherapy but of "aesthetic instincts." At one point the narrator notes that French intellectuals found in Zelig "a symbol for everything." Everything and nothing. This *Rashomon*-like smorgasbord of interpretations parodies not only the witnesses' own work but the work of interpretation itself. Indeed, Sontag is identified as the author of *Against Interpretation*. If Zelig the Great Imitator is really Allen the director (often accused of mimicking his betters—Fellini in *Stardust Memories* and Bergman in both *Interiors* and *A Midsummer Night's Sex Comedy*), then Allen's art, like Zelig's life, is being placed beyond analysis.

231

Kael has written that "*Stardust Memories* doesn't seem like a movie, or even like a filmed essay; it's nothing. You see right through it to the man who has lost the desire to play a character." *Zelig*, in a sense, is Allen's response, a film about a man who does nothing but play characters, a man who would be everyone. It is his attempt to throw a bone to his critics while remaining himself.

Politically, Allen has positioned Zelig safely in the center. Despite his flirtation with the comedic styles of Mort Sahl and Lenny Bruce, Allen has never been an issue-oriented comic; he prefers to exploit private, not public, life and recommends the politics of expedience, avoiding the risky business of taking stands. His stand-in in *Stardust Memories*, Sandy Bates, says, "I find-I-I find it very, very difficult to have a-a-a commitment . . . I feel . . . to survive in life you want to stay loose, you want to keep flexible . . ." There is one political issue to which Allen obsessively returns, however: the blacklist. After all, he played the lead in *The Front*; and in *Manhattan* Ike confronts his pal Yale (Michael Murphy) with: 'The next thing you know, you're in front of a Senate committee and you're naming names! You're informing on your friends." Zelig's struggle to "become his own man," to find his own shape, is in part a struggle not to become an informer. But he doesn't want to become a radical either, and he fights against becoming too much his own man, too opinionated, too outspoken. Vilified by "extremists" of both the Left and the Right, the Reds and the KKK, Zelig is the centrist as martyr, the moderate as hero.

Zelig is not only a political moderate; he is ethnically balanced as well. In the same way that Allen has vacillated between commitment and disengagement, he's vacillated in his attitudes toward Jews and gentiles, one moment sentimentalizing Jews as lifesaving agents of passion and vigor, capable of revitalizing desiccated WASPs, as he does in *Interiors*, the next denigrating them for their vulgarity, as he does in *Stardust Memories*, or romanticizing WASPs as vessels of truth and beauty, put on earth to redeem eternally ambivalent Jews, as he does in *Manhattan*. In *Zelig* Allen does all of these. On one level, as witness Irving Howe implies, the film is a tract against Jewish assimilationism. Zelig, haunted by right-wing anti-Semitism ("Lynch the little Hebe," concludes one radio broadcaster), magically carries off a whole-body nose job and takes the ultimate step toward cultural assimilation: he becomes a Nazi. On another level *Zelig* sees assimilation as something, however ultimately self-destructive, to which the Jews' own ethnic heritage offers little alternative. Following in the footsteps of anti-ethnic melting pot films about Italians—*Saturday Night Fever, Bloodbrothers,* and *The Godfather Part II,* for example, all of which endorsed assimilation and upward mobility—*Zelig* heaps scorn on the old-world family and neighborhood, portraying them as little better than a jungle in which kids beat one another, parents beat kids, and neighbors beat them all. Because the ethnic enclave is this bad, Zelig has no choice but to escape into WASP country, which he does by marrying his New England-bred shrink, Eudora Fletcher (Mia Farrow), and retiring into a sunset of tennis whites and parties at San Simeon. In other words, the Jew who learns to refuse assimilation is rewarded—with assimilation.

Finally, *Zelig* deals with the complaints of women on both the Left and the Right. For feminists it offers no-nonsense Dr. Fletcher, the bespectacled pioneering psychiatrist who wears her hair tightly braided, drapes herself in ratty cardigans and boxy jackets, and is an airplane pilot to boot—*the* cinematic metaphor for the liberated woman ever since Katharine Hepburn took off in *Christopher Strong* in 1933. It is Fletcher who "cures" Zelig, who "molds" and socializes him. Through Fletcher, it seems that Allen has come to terms with the brainy women he put down in *Manhattan*. As the narrator of a "newsreel" says, Zelig's cure is a "resounding success for psychiatry. Who says women are just good for sewing?" But Allen also makes concessions to those who don't care a fig for feminism or would complain, like Joan Didion, that consumer culture, aided and abetted by the ideology of therapy, is destroying the family. By having Zelig announce his intention to marry Fletcher, Allen in one swift stroke has united the therapist and the family. It's the end of the Me generation, a return to the couple.

However, Zelig can't simply marry Fletcher: he's got to be chastened first for his swinging lifestyle; he's got to put his past behind him. Unfortunately it catches up with him. All the time we thought Zelig was harmlessly aping celebrities, slipping into the frame with Babe Ruth or squeezing in with Coolidge and Hoover, he was also marrying women in droves and breeding like a rabbit—the amorous Alvy Singer or Ike Davis of the pre-Pill '20s. When he announces his engagement to Fletcher, his wives pop up like mushrooms, toddlers in tow. Zelig can't expect any relief from the courts, which treat him like a criminal rather than a patient. As the narrator puts it, "The American legal profession has a field day. Despite Dr. Fletcher's insistence that he cannot be held responsible for his actions while in his chameleon state, it is no use." Liberal docs lose out to conservative cops, and Zelig is found guilty. On the eve of his sentencing he flees to Germany to hide out among the Nazis, but in keeping with Allen's new moralism, he can't just run away; he's got to return to face the music.

It is Fletcher, of course, who brings him back, and in the process they change places. As Zelig becomes stronger, she becomes weaker. Feminism in *Zelig* has its limits. Midway through the film, when Fletcher tries to analyze Zelig, it doesn't work; he pretends to be a therapist himself. He's not imitating her so much as competing with her. The only way she can get him to accept the fact that he's the one under treatment is by relinquishing her authority as doctor and pretending to be him, the patient. Near the end of the film

233

Fletcher steals an airplane and rescues Zelig from the Nazis. But once in the air, she's stricken with fear of flying. Zelig takes over, having become a pilot like her. He saves them both, at the same time setting the world record for flying nonstop across the Atlantic upside down, and arrives home to a ticker-tape parade in New York. Although the end titles tell us that Fletcher continued to practice psychoanalysis after they married, this scene makes clear that, feminist or not, her place isn't in the cockpit. It is *Zelig,* after all, who becomes the hero, though an upside-down hero—a Jewish Lindbergh. His is the best of all possible worlds.

All along, Zelig has been assaying men's occupational roles— butcher, baker, candlestick maker—trying them all but adopting none, an oblique slap at the male striver. The film's comforting message, however, is that it's okay not to achieve—you can be a hero by being yourself. In other words, just as the reward for renouncing assimilationism is true assimilation, so the reward for renouncing the self-indulgent, "immature" side of men's lib is true liberation. Zelig doesn't have to be a striver to be successful; he doesn't have to be Lindbergh to be Lindbergh.

234

Zelig's true self, of course, is that of a patient. As witness Saul Bellow states, "His sickness was also at the root of his salvation. It was his very disorder that made a hero of him." Shorn of its worst narcissistic excesses, chastened by its run-in with the law, and securely wedded to the family, therapy emerges bloody but unbowed. At a reception in New York, Zelig's feat is called "an inspiration to the young of this nation who will one day grow up and be great doctors and great patients."

Zelig works as well as it does because it is spectacularly original and tells us what we want to hear. It is the perfect vehicle for Allen's intentions. His penchant for black-and-white in an age of color, previously merely the badge of his pretensions, is just right in *Zelig* and natural in a mock compilation film about the '20s. The callow world-weariness, arrogance, and self-pity that rub the wrong way in his clearly autobiographical earlier films are here held in check, distanced and attenuated by the film's conceit. Like Zelig, Allen has succeeded at being his own self, and everything to everyone at the same time.

SLOUCHING TOWARD HOLLYWOOD

Martin Scorsese is killing time. Dressed in a crisp khaki shirt and pressed blue jeans, with a tiny white bichon fries named Joe tucked under his arm, he is waiting for the sun to go behind a cloud so the next shot will match the last one. He is near the end of the *Cape Fear* shoot in front of a produce stand just outside Fort Lauderdale, Florida. With him are Nick Nolte, Jessica Lange, and Juliette Lewis playing a married couple and their daughter fleeing from a psycho who is stalking them.

While he waits, Scorsese's hand rarely leaves the side pocket of his custom-made jeans, where he works his watch chain like worry beads. He used to have Armani make his jeans, but he felt guilty wearing them. He orders new ones every two years, and since he can't bear to throw away even the most threadbare, his collection goes back fifteen years.

The sun finally goes in. Nolte is on his mark in an instant. Lange is immersed in the *New York Times*. "You can do it, Jessica," Nolte calls. "Just put one foot in front of the other." (They've been ragging each other throughout the shoot—Nolte dropping his pants, Lange refusing to go to the set until "everything is put away.") Lange finally arrives at her position, and they walk through the scene.

"Nah, nah, nah—too long!" snaps Scorsese with his trademark machinegun delivery. "We've gone through four bars of the theme of *Psycho*. Start them closer to the car."

"I've moved them from pepper to lettuce," says an assistant director.

"Start them at the okra."

"You know okra?" the A.D. inquires of Lange.

"Yeah, I know okra."

Starting from the okra, Lange, Nolte, and Lewis walk quickly to their Jeep Cherokee. The scene is wrapped.

For most directors, this shot would be a throwaway. But for Scorsese, there's no such thing as a throwaway. "The hardest thing to do is get people into a car—to make it interesting," he explains. "It's all about the philosophy of the shot. Those people were beaten into the ground. They didn't want to talk to each other." So he decided to start wide. "You have to see the family as a unit, broken up and terrified as it is, and then move into Nick's face, pan to Jessica, and pan back over. Then actually zoom into Jessica looking out, pan across the kid onto Nick's face, so determined to get his family out of there. That's finally the move I used."

Cape Fear is Scorsese's fourteenth feature. With a budget of approximately $34 million, it is the most expensive picture to date from a director who has always pinched pennies. It is the first fruit of a comfortable six-year deal with Universal Pictures for a director who has never had better than a two-year picture deal anywhere. The film was initiated by Steven Spielberg and is being co-produced by his company, even though no one could be further from Spielberg's sensibility than Scorsese. And it is a remake of a 1962 studio thriller, from a director who disdains remakes. This project, in other words, is very much a paradox, a bow in the direction of the mainstream from the ultimate outsider.

Shot in CinemaScope, *Cape Fear* is emblematic of Scorsese's love/hate relationship with Hollywood, an ambivalence the industry is more than happy to reciprocate. He is widely considered one of America's most brilliant directors, one of a select circle of contemporaries that includes Stanley Kubrick and Woody Allen, within shouting distance of masters like Akira Kurosawa. His greatest film, *Raging Bull*, was selected as the best film of the '80s by an outstanding array of critics. Yet Scorsese has been mocked and reviled in Hollywood.

Last year, he came back from a ten-year drought with *GoodFellas*, selected as best film of the year by the New York, Los Angeles, and National societies of film critics. Since then, Scorsese has been showered with honorary degrees and has been the subject of books and documentaries too numerous to mention. He has virtually become a national institution. It's a heavy burden to shoulder, and no one is more aware of that than the director himself.

"You have more to lose," says Scorsese, gazing at the view from his apartment window, seventy-five stories over midtown Manhattan. "Would it be a different risk if every picture I made was about Italian Americans in New York? I don't think so. Because they'd say, 'That's all he can do.' So I'm trying to stretch." His next picture is a good example. *The Age of Innocence* is based on an Edith Wharton novel and set in the very unmean streets of upper-crust New York, circa 1870. It's not the movie of a man content to rest on his laurels.

"I've always said the way I learned how to make movies was by being a wise guy in the theater when I was a kid," says Scorsese, who was raised in Manhattan's Little Italy. He grew up, frail and badly asthmatic, among priests and mobsters—flicking images on the screen. "We were merciless, my friends and I. You know, picking out clichés, saying the line before the actor said it."

Scorsese had planned to go to go into the priesthood, but in 1960 he ended up at New York University. There he fell under the spell of a charismatic professor, Haig Manoogian. "When I heard him lecture, all the passion I had for the seminary was somehow transferred over. I said, 'I want to be talked about in that way, because my appreciation of the people he's talking about is so strong.' I knew I was a director. Other people didn't know it, though." He laughs. "What was the matter with them?"

At the time, Scorsese was collaborating with NYU classmate Mardik Martin. "Our wives hated us," Martin remembers. "We couldn't go home, because they would pick on us. We weren't earning a living; they thought we were wasting our time. We'd sit in my Valiant and write *Mean Streets*."

In 1970, Scorsese moved to Los Angeles, where he helped Thelma Schoonmaker edit Michael Wadleigh's *Woodstock*. There, he met a young woman named Sandra Weintraub, whom he lived and worked with for the next four years. His first big break came when Roger Corman hired him to direct Barbara Hershey in *Boxcar Bertha* in 1971.

While he was editing *Bertha*, he resurrected the *Mean Streets* script and showed it to Weintraub. "There was a man talking to God about everything," she remembers. "I said, 'What is this about?' 'It's about growing up.' I said, 'You have the most incredible stories in your head about growing up. Put them in!' " He did. Jonathan Taplin, an ex-road manager for Bob Dylan and the Band, arranged the financing.

Scorsese met Robert De Niro at a party and eventually gave him the part of Johnny Boy. "What they did together, they did in private," says Weintraub. "Definitely no women allowed." One night, after a screening of the rough cut of *Mean Streets,* Weintraub, Scorsese, De Niro, and a few others went out to dinner for what Weintraub assumed would be a group dissection of the film. But De Niro and Scorsese disappeared into the men's room for two and a half hours and hashed it out between themselves.

After the film was completed, it was shown to the majors, and instantly turned down by Universal and Paramount Pictures. At Warner Bros., John Calley, head of production, and two other executives—"all New York guys"—attended the screening. "After fifteen minutes," says Taplin, "a waiter comes in, stands right in front of the projector, and yells, 'Who's got the tuna on rye?' They're not even watching. And Marty is dying. Finally, they settle in, start to laugh, enjoy the New York humor. Then Calley gets up. I think we're lost. He says, 'This is the best movie I've seen all year, but would you mind shutting it off? I've got to take a leak.' "

Calley bought the picture. *Mean Streets* was a critical hit and instantly established Scorsese as a major talent.

"The period from '71 to '76 was the best time, because we were just beginning," says Scorsese. "We couldn't wait for our friends' next pictures—Brian De Palma's, Francis Coppola's—to see what they were doing."

Scorsese, Coppola, De Palma, Spielberg, Paul Schrader, George Lucas—these were the so-called movie brats. The first generation of directors to go to film school, they took Hollywood by storm, wresting control of the industry from the old men.

The late '60s and early '70s were the golden age of postwar film in America, a time when directors, newly legitimized by the auteur theory—particularly young directors, riding the crest of the countercultural new wave—were given a degree of power and autonomy unprecedented in the history of Hollywood. They used their new power to produce a corpus of startlingly original work that deconstructed traditional genres and by implication asked troubling questions about American life. This was a film-intoxicated generation for whom movies were more than escapism, more than a job or a new Jaguar or a choice table at Spago. Movies were a way of life, a religion, a means of salvation. As Schrader once put it, "Somehow we knew the world was ours. We were going to go out and make a difference. You know, films of importance had to be brought to the marketplace, and we were going to do it."

In 1973, Warner's asked Scorsese to direct one of these movies, *Alice Doesn't Live Here Anymore,* about an independent woman who must find her way when she loses her husband. It was one of the first films with a whiff of feminism about it. Scorsese was reluctant. "Marty said, 'I don't know anything about women,'" recalls Weintraub. I said, 'Women are people, too.' "

Alice did well, although the upbeat ending, in which the heroine (Ellen Burstyn) falls for a handsome rancher (Kris Kristofferson), was considered to be politically incorrect. "We tried to work as truthfully as possible within the conventions of the genre," explains Scorsese. "And within the conventions of the studio chief telling me, 'Give it a happy ending!' I said, 'All right.' But the last line is the kid saying, 'Mom, I can't breathe.'"

While working on *Alice,* Scorsese read Schrader's screenplay for *Taxi Driver,* the story of a terminally alienated and deranged Vietnam vet who befriends a preteen hooker and then wastes her pimp and his pals in a bloodbath of Peckinpavian dimensions. He loved it, but, says Weintraub, Schrader told him "he was looking for a 'Tiffany director.' [Marty] was really upset by the word 'Tiffany.'" But when Burstyn won an Oscar for *Alice,* Scorsese's stock went up, and producers Michael and Julia Phillips—with financing from Columbia Pictures—were happy to hire him.

Jodie Foster, who played the hooker and was all of twelve at the time, remembers what it was like to be directed by Scorsese: "There's a big difference between somebody who performs with you and somebody who asks you to perform for them. He is there. Marty gets behind your eyes."

Weintraub also recalls Scorsese in those days: "He was tempestuous, volatile. One time I was on the phone, angry with Taplin. Marty grabbed the phone out of my hand, yelled at Taplin, threw the phone and broke it. Then he went down to the street, put a dime in a pay phone, and continued to yell at Taplin." Taplin remembers that "he was always throwing things. For Marty's birthday in 1977, his office gave him ten breakaway glasses and four breakaway chairs. He had a telephone man on constant call because he would regularly rip the phone out of the wall."

"He always had a lot of superstitions that were a melding of Catholicism, general superstition, and some of his own making, forebodings from dreams," Weintraub says. "He had an unlucky number that really bothered him. He wouldn't travel on that date, wouldn't travel on that flight, wouldn't stay on that floor."

It was an exciting but stressful time for Scorsese. His asthma was still a constant problem. "It was the way he manifested his feelings," says Weintraub. "When things would go wrong, he'd reach for the spray. It was a way to get people to feel sorry for him—the man was barely breathing."

Things went wrong a lot. "For me it was just the beginning of going into an abyss for about two years and coming out of it barely alive," says Scorsese. "It was a few weeks after *Taxi Driver* opened that I started playing with drugs." Toward the end of production, he had split up with Weintraub and soon connected with writer Julia Cameron, whom he married.

"It's hard to live with someone when every day people are telling him what a genius he is," says Weintraub, who today is a producer. "If you weren't there for the movie, you couldn't be with him. I would tell him my dream, and he would tell me what movie he had seen on TV the night before." "But," she continues, "he gave me a career. If I had fallen in love with a garbageman, I might be collecting trash today. He gave me my love of film."

When *Taxi Driver* was nominated for Best Picture and Best Supporting Actress of 1976, Scorsese got a letter threatening his life. One of his pals unthinkingly called the FBI, creating a sticky situation. "They smuggled the stash out before the FBI got there," says Taplin. "It was that kind of scene." FBI agents disguised as guests attended the awards ceremony that year to protect Scorsese. "Imagine ducking into the bathroom with FBI all over you," says Taplin, laughing.

Taxi Driver did surprising well at the box office and won the Palme d'or at Cannes in 1976. Perhaps it was the success, perhaps it was the drugs, but Scorsese was setting himself up for his first failure. *New York, New York* was a big-budget homage to the old Hollywood musicals, starring De Niro and Liza Minelli, in which the music overwhelmed the story. "I will always thank the French for giving me that grand prize to allow me to allow me to reveal to myself what a total failure I could be," he says now. "You get a big head. You think, 'Oh, I don't have to make up a script, I can work it out on the soundstage when I'm there.' Sure. A lot of guys work that way. Evidently, I couldn't."

241

Still, the word on the street about *New York, New York*—with its lush sets, big production numbers, and daringly unconventional unhappy ending—was very good. Marcia Lucas edited the film, and every night she would return home to her husband, George, full of the promise of the movie. George, in postproduction on his own movie, was depressed that it was over budget and certain it wasn't going to make any money, according to Weintraub. When *New York, New York* came out, it flopped. Lucas's picture, *Star Wars*, transformed the industry.

The year 1977 was a watershed for American movies. Simply put, it was a moment when the kind of movies Scorsese made were replaced by the kind of movies Lucas and Spielberg made. Scorsese's films came out of the '60s. Despite (or more likely because of) the fact that they were so artfully crafted, they delivered a shock of documentary rawness, energy, and violence that spoke to the Vietnam generation, with its frantic mixture of idealism and destructiveness. But by the mid-'70s, with Jimmy Carter in the White House looking to bind the wounds of Vietnam and Watergate, people were tired of all that. The personal and critical "cinema" of the '60s was dying. Movies like *The Missouri Breaks* and *3 Women* bombed, while directors like Sam Peckinpah retreated to the bottle and Robert Altman eventually stopped trying.

For Scorsese, the consequences of these changes were still to come. While *New York, New York* was in production, he met musician Robbie Robertson, who asked him to shoot a documentary on the Band's last concert, which became *The Last Waltz*. "He was overjoyed," says Taplin—the pressure on *New York, New York* was unbearable. Taplin recalls the day when 150 fully dressed extras stood around while Scorsese spoke to his therapist from his trailer.

Scorsese was spreading himself thin. He had split up with Cameron and was trying to finish two films simultaneously. It was at this point that Robertson moved into Scorsese's Mulholland Drive house. Says Robertson, "We were the odd couple—looking for trouble."

Scorsese, Robertson, and friends like Mardik Martin and actress Genevieve Bujold would sit in Robertson's bedroom, which doubled as a projection room, and watch four or five movies a night. "We had two problems," says Robertson, "the light and the birds. Marty had the house blacked out with shades, and he installed a soundproof air system so you could breathe without opening the windows."

"We were like vampires," recalls Martin. "It was like, 'Oh, no, the sun is coming up.' We never got to sleep before seven, eight A.M. for six months. We did all kinds of crazy things in those days."

Taplin recalls the first time they projected *Waltz*, and the face of Neil Young, looking wasted and very big, appeared on the screen. "There was a rock of cocaine falling out of his nostril. His manager was freaking out—'I'm refusing to let you put this song in the movie!' I went to an effects house run by these older guys who didn't know cocaine from . . . a booger. I told them, 'This guy has got a booger in his nose. Can you fix it?' They called back in a couple of days and said, 'We've invented a traveling booger matte.' "

"There was a lot of high living," remembers Scorsese. "At first, you felt like you could make five films at once. Then you wound up spending four days in bed every week because you were exhausted, and your body couldn't take it." He was in and out of the hospital with asthma attacks. "The doctor would say, 'Take these pills. You're suffering from exhaustion,'" says Robertson. "But we had places to go, people to see." Martin remembers De Niro, who was not part of this scene, coming over one day and saying, "What's the matter with you boys? Don't you want to live to see if X gets married to Y?"

It all came to a crashing halt on Labor Day 1978, when Scorsese ended up in the hospital with internal bleeding. "Finally," says Robertson, "Marty got a doctor who conveyed the message that either he alter his life or he was going to die. We knew we had to change trains. Our lives were way too rich. The cholesterol level was unimaginable."

During the same period, De Niro and Martin tried to persuade Scorsese to do *Raging Bull.* "I had to find the key for myself," says Scorsese now. "And I wasn't even interested in finding the key, because I'd tried something, *New York, New York,* and it was a failure." He couldn't bring himself to read the script. "I didn't want him to say no," says Martin, "so I catered to his whims and bullshit. This went on for months. It was driving me crazy. But he was not himself." Finally, Schrader did a rewrite, and De Niro, visiting Scorsese in the hospital, made one last stab. " 'Are we doing it or not?' Bob asked me," says Scorsese. "I said yes. I finally understood that for me I had found the hook—the self-destructiveness, the destruction of people around you, just for the sake of it. I was Jake La Motta."

As luck would have it, United Artists released *Heaven's Gate* ten days after *Raging Bull,* and the roof fell in. Scorsese's movie bombed. He admits it was a hard picture to sell. "The poster with the picture of Bob's face all beaten and battered—I mean, if you're a young girl, I don't know if you'd say, 'Let's go see this one.' "

The commercial failure of *Raging Bull,* on top of *New York, New York,* was a crushing blow. "Marty wanted the kind of success that Lucas and Coppola had," recalls Weintraub. "He was afraid he would always be the critics' darling but the American public would never love him." He was terrified that he wouldn't be allowed to continue making movies if he didn't make money. "There was nothing in his life besides movies," Weintraub adds. "What would he do?"

Scorsese likes to tell the story about how his first feature, *Who's That Knocking at My Door?*, whose priest-ridden hero couldn't bring himself to sleep with his girlfriend, went against the grain of the sexual revolution of the '60s. Now, again, he was out of step with the public and an industry that was largely given over to the search for blockbusters. He says he made *Raging Bull* with the conviction that it was his last movie. And yet he continued to pursue his personal vision with single-minded persistence.

Somehow, Scorsese got the backing to make *The King of Comedy*, which turned out to be another troubled production. Scorsese had always had difficulty controlling his temper on the set. He did not suffer fools kindly and was easily frustrated. "I'm just an angry guy, anyway. I look out of the window," he gestures to the twinkling lights in the distance, "and I'm angry about the smog. I'm angry about—you name it, I'm angry. You get to a point where the anger in you can explode. You go into little pieces. And then what— you're dead. Finally you realize that it's probably not worth it."

During the editing, Scorsese hit a brick wall. From December 1981 to March 1982, he couldn't work. "I got myself into such a state of anxiety that I just completely crashed," he continues. "I'd come downstairs from the editing room, and I'd see a message from somebody about some problem, and I'd say, 'I can't work today. It's impossible.' My friends said, 'Marty, the negative is sitting there. The studio is going crazy. You've got to finish the film.' "

This episode taught Scorsese a lesson. "It was up to me. Nobody cared, ultimately, even your closest friends. You're gonna act crazy? You're gonna get in a situation where you can't work? Nobody gives a damn. And you wind up alone. You face yourself anyway. It's Jake La Motta looking in the mirror at the end of *Raging Bull*."

The King of Comedy was plagued by negative word of mouth. "A close friend of mine told me, two months before the film was finished, 'The buzz is bad.' I hate that. When the buzz is bad, people don't want to be associated with the picture. You feel totally abandoned. I must say, that was painful. Because the film came out and died in four weeks, and they were right—the picture was a bomb. It's called *The King of Comedy*, it's Jerry Lewis, and it's not a comedy. I mean, already it's a problem."

Scorsese plunged ahead with *The Last Temptation of Christ*, a pet project he had been gestating since Barbara Hershey gave him the Nikos Kazantzakis book in 1971. But it made him an object of ridicule in the Hollywood–New York party axis. "Big people in the business were saying, 'Yeah, I know the pictures you make,' " he recalls. "One guy introduced me to someone who was the head of a company. He says, 'This guy's gonna make *Last Temptation*.' The guy looked at me and laughed in my face. 'Yeah, right. Call me next week.' I mean, I'd come through all those years to get that? It was like a kick in the heart."

Finally, Scorsese set it up at Paramount, only to have the studio pull the plug well into preproduction. "I had to make up my mind whether I really wanted to continue making films. There was such negativity. So what do you do? Stay down dead? No. I realized then, you can't let the system crush your spirit. I'm a director, I'm going to try to be a pro and start all over again. I'll make a low-budget picture, *After Hours*. And then went a couple of notches up the ladder with *The Color of Money*, working with major stars and that sort of thing."

Neither *After Hours* nor *Last Temptation*, when it was finally made in 1988, was successful, critically or commercially. Scorsese, who had feared never being more than the darling of critics, was in danger of losing that slim solace. He had still to learn how to subject his vision to the requirements of the industry. Searching for a new film, he turned down *Sea of Love* and *White Palace* from Universal. It wasn't until 1989, with his episode of *New York Stories*, generally recognized as the best of the three (Woody Allen and Francis Coppola supplied the others), that he regained a piece of critical ground.

Then, in 1990, a decade after his masterpiece, *Raging Bull*, and thirteen years after his last critically acclaimed hit, *Taxi Driver*, *GoodFellas* proved that he could make art and money at the same time. Martin Scorsese had returned from Gethsemane.

245

• • •

Now the days of drugs and even asthma are behind him. "I haven't had a serious attack in more than a year," he says. With the relative security of his Universal deal and his apparently unassailable critical status, life seems to be looking up. Or does it? He's worried about the perception of him as a film artist—the "*a*-word," as he calls it—and corrects himself when he inadvertently uses the term "cinema" instead of "movies." "I don't want anybody to think we're talking about art," he says. "It's a stigma in the commercial area of movies. A stigma."

He's angry and disappointed that he didn't win an Oscar for *GoodFellas*. "I wish I could be like some of the other guys and say, 'No, I don't care about it.' But for me, a kid growing up on the Lower East Side watching from the first telecast of the Oscars, and being obsessed by movies, there's a certain magic that's there. When I lost for *Raging Bull*, that's when I realized what my place in the system would be, if I did survive at all: on the outside looking in. The Academy sent out a very strong message to the people who made *GoodFellas* and *The Grifters,* no matter how talented they are, that they may get some recognition, but they will not get the award. It just turns out that I produced *The Grifters*. And I certainly got the message."

Scorsese is philosophical about it, sort of. But his friends and collaborators are not. Says Jodie Foster, "When you look at the ten old ladies who put down *Dances With Wolves* instead of *GoodFellas*—I don't know. The Oscars are like bingo. Who cares?" And Paul Sorvino, who played Paul Vario in *GoodFellas,* says, "It's an outrage and a scandal in my mind. What does the man have to do?" Harvey Keitel sums it up: "Maybe he got what he deserves—exclusion from the mediocre."

With his recent success and his virtual canonization, the pressures upon him have, if anything, increased. Bigger budgets, more responsibility (he's producing *Mad Dog and Glory,* from a Richard Price script, starring De Niro and Bill Murray). He's joined force with Spielberg on *Cape Fear,* and he's moving from his cluttered office in the historic Brill Building on the seedy West Side of New York to MCA's sleek East Coast corporate headquarters on Park Avenue.

The move across town is as much symbolic as physical. It could well be the beginning of Marty's Excellent Adventure, his attempt to enter the mainstream on his own terms. The risks are great: commercial failure on the one hand, selling out on the other. "You wanna audience," says Price, who wrote *The Color of Money,* "you gotta play ball. He wants to make big personal movies—the best actors he can get, the biggest audience he can get, to make the smallest films he can make."

Schrader speculates about the direction of Scorsese's career: "*Cape Fear* is the first time he's worked with such a large budget since *New York, New York,* and it demands an audience level and a mainstream sensibility that he's not completely comfortable with. Marty's a conglomerate now. But I think at the end of the day, no matter how hard he tries to sell out, he can't really do it. The thing with Spielberg is a marriage of convenience. We're talking about Warren Beatty and Madonna."

Scorsese tried very hard not to get involved with *Cape Fear.* "Bob De Niro and Spielberg asked me to read the script while I was finishing up *GoodFellas,*" he recalls. "And by the end of the editing of the film, I had read *Cape Fear* three times. And three times I hated it. I mean really hated it." The original script took its cues from the 1962 movie, which starred Gregory Peck as an improbably virtuous family man and Robert Mitchum as the psycho, Max Cady, who gets out of jail and goes after Peck for testifying against him. "I thought the family was too clichéd, too happy," says Scorsese. "And then along comes the bogeyman to scare them. They were like Martians to me. I was rooting for Max to get them." But Spielberg and De Niro, who wanted to play Cady, wouldn't take no for an answer. "Finally, Steve says, 'Marty, you dislike this version of the script?' I said, 'Yes! Whaddya want from me?' He said, 'Why don't you rewrite it?' And I said, 'Of course!' "

Scorsese Freudianized—or, as he prefers to think of it, Catholicized—the script. It became a drama of sexual guilt and punishment. He shifted the focus to the emotional pathology of the family, with Lange suffering from the aftereffects of Nolte's infidelity and Nolte trying to deal with his daughter's emerging sexuality. "Cady was sort of the malignant spirit of guilt, in a way, of the family—the avenging angel," Scorsese says. "Punishment for everything you ever felt sexually. It is the basic moral battleground of Christian ethics."

Scorsese pauses, laughs. "This sounds like every other picture I've ever made. I could talk this to death. It's ridiculous, but I've got to be careful. Otherwise, people say, 'It's some sort of religious film. I don't want to see it.' Don't listen to any of this! It's a thriller. Go see it! Enjoy yourself!"

When all is said and done, Scorsese has been fortunate. Despite, or rather because of, his failures and struggles, his wanderings on the wild side, he is perhaps the only filmmaker from that enormously hopeful generation of the '70s to have truly fulfilled his promise. Some, like Coppola, have made great movies—*The Godfathers*, *The Conversation*, *Apocalypse Now*—but Scorsese has done more than that. He's made a career. He's survived in a business notorious for burning out talent and has arrived at the '90s at the peak of his creative powers. *GoodFellas* was so assured, so perfectly realized, that it is hard to imagine he will stumble as badly as he did in the '80s. "Maybe it was because I fell from grace earlier," he says. "Maybe because other people went through the terror later, so it was harder for them to come back."

The movies have always been Scorsese's life. But along the way he picked up a considerable amount of baggage, including four wives and two daughters. Now approaching fifty, he has had to make difficult choices. "I just started divesting myself of all these complications. Your personal life, you know, you deal with as best you can. But you even divest that.

"All the way up until, I'd say, '84, '85, every Sunday my mother and father, my friends would come over. We'd have a big Italian dinner. Whatever different marriages—whatever was going on. It was really good, like the Italian family I remember growing up. But I don't expect much from people anymore, and I don't really want them to expect much from me. Except when it comes to the work, [where] you're gonna get the best from me. You're alone. That's the way it goes."

The thing that may save Scorsese, finally, from the vertigo of fame is his humility before the shrine of "cinema." As much as he serves as mentor for struggling young directors, as much as he has become a force on the film-preservation scene, as much as he has matured into a disciplined director, he is in many ways still a student. As Barbara Hershey puts it, "His love of film over himself is the great leveler."

"You've gotta be careful," says Scorsese, "because you hear talk: 'Well, Marty, people say in Hollywood, your films are really good and you're one of the best around . . . ' It's an odd thing. You can't believe it, first of all. I think a lot of the pictures I've made are good. But they're not *The Searchers*. They're not *8 1/2*. *The Red Shoes*. *The Leopard*. What I'm saying is I have my own criteria in my head that's private. There's constantly a test. Constantly a final exam every minute of my life. Literally, I have the image of myself always keeping my nose right above the water, the waves always getting to me and about to sink me . . . I just hope that, you know, *Cape Fear* makes money."

THE MAKING OF "BLATHERLANDS"

AN IMAGINARY CONVERSATION BETWEEN SISSY SPACEK AND TERRENCE MALICK

Peter Biskind and Michael Silverman

I told Terrence that the script was awful, that it sounded like a *True Confessions* magazine, but Terrence said it was supposed to sound that way, that I was supposed to make a running commentary on the action that I wouldn't know the meaning of because I was a limited character, but the audience would understand. Terrence called that irony and said he oughta know because he went to Harvard and he had put one of his old professors in the film to prove it, only no one would know but his friends. Besides, he said, even though I sounded dumb I could be poetic at the same time because there was something he called a mythic splendor in the ordinary language of the Midwest, and the critics would be sure to recognize that. He said he counted on this mute splendor a lot. He said we could have it both ways—we could sound dumb but be heroic at the same time. He said all directors did that—they condemn violence and exploit it at the same time. He said he could mystify us and demystify us, both at once.

I told him I didn't know what that meant, but I was sure those people at Ms. and those female critics in New York were going to be angry if he made me sound so stupid. Terrence said they might be mad for a while, but when they reflected they would see that our very inarticulateness made us moving, and they would like the fact that Holly pulls away from Kit in the end—she grows. He said I should stop worrying about it since Kit and Holly's language was perishable anyway, and that's why Kit keeps leaving messages like on the record and the Dictaphone. He asked me if I remembered in *Bonnie and Clyde* how Faye and Warren were worried about their legend and how Faye was always writing poems about themselves to the newspaper. He said he was doing the same thing in *Badlands*, but that he wasn't copying Arthur Penn. Arthur was an influence he'd assimilated. I asked him if the mute objects like the stuff Kit gives away to the troopers at the end wasn't a sort of language and less perishable than words. Terrence said to forget about that—that his film was the ultimate testimonial to the meaning of their lives.

251

Then he thought for a while and asked me if I'd noticed that Kit was always trying to commemorate occasions with piles of stones, and asked me if I'd noticed that Kit was obsessed with objects from the very beginning when he was a garbageman and when he shoots his garbageman pal he looks around at all the things and says they're junk. He said if I didn't notice, the critics would, and that the struggle to create permanence was a terrific theme, that it comes out in Shakespeare's sonnets and all through literature and there are garbagemen in *Weekend*, too. Terence said he wasn't copying *Weekend*. *Weekend* was an influence he'd assimilated. I asked him how come Kit says all that stuff was junk if he's so into objects. Terrence patiently explained that it was all relative, and that the objects only mean something to the person who collects them, and that's why it's so hard to create significance.

He said Holly and Kit had different attitudes towards time from each other, too. Kit was always trying to create a world outside time. That's why he buries those objects in a sort of time-capsule, even though he knows his gestures are doomed. Terrence said Kit tries to include Holly in this timeless realm. When he kills her dad, he's really trying to annihilate her past. Terrence said that even the dumbest critics would see that—that if the daily reviewers missed it, Time would be sure to pick it up. Speaking of time, I asked what it meant when Holly looked through that stereopticon they took from her dad. Terrence said he was really proud of that part and asked me if I noticed that the color of the slides was the same as the sepia tones in that part that was supposed to be newsreel but really wasn't. He asked me if I knew what that meant, I said I thought it probably had to do with old pictures and the Past but I wasn't sure what. Terrence smiled and said that when Holly looked through the stereopticon she falls back into time—she recalls the fact of her past and imagines a future without Kit. Once she includes him and his hopeless project in a larger temporal context, things can never be the same between them.

I was sad about that, but Terrence said it had to be that way, and that the tension between her consciousness of time and his attempt to transcend time was the central paradox of the filmmaker today. I asked him what paradox he was talking about. He said it was the paradox of cinematic history, that old movies are better, that everything's been done already, but that young directors had to keep on making films anyway. I asked him what he meant by old movies, if he meant silents like the sepia sequence reminded me of, or did he mean the movies about Godard that he's always talking about, or even one I liked like *Glen and Randa*. That movie made Terrence nervous. I remember, but the treehouse reminded me of it, even though Terrence says it's from Godard. Terrence agreed that these movies were history, and also the old Bogart flicks like *High Sierra* he used to see at the Brattle, where Bogie goes towards the mountains for the final shootout just like Kit does in *Badlands*. I remembered that Bogie makes it to the mountains, while Kit never does get there. Terrence became agitated and shouted that's the point, that's the point—it's an acknowledgement that we younger directors live in the shadow of the classics. We're doomed to fall short of our inherited destinations. In some ways, he said, I'm like Kit, and *Badlands* is as much about old movies as it is about killing. Like Kit killing all those people the only way I can make movies is to vampirize old ones, and like Kit, I know I'm doomed to fail. We can't go home again, as it were, he said quietly. The old genres are gone and we have nothing more to say.

252

I asked if that was why *Badlands* was so boring, why it dragged on and on with nothing but pretty pictures of dust clouds following Kit's car. Terrence became angry and said he had been trying to explain to me that it wasn't his fault that his film was boring, but it was because the genres were exhausted, were used up. He said if I thought *Badlands* was boring, had I seen *Thieves Like Us,* which he said was like a spaced-out *Bonnie and Clyde* and was only redeemed by good acting. He said that American films were facing the same crisis that European films faced at the end of the sixties when they exhausted the veins they had worked with so much success. He pointed out to me that Antonioni had solved the dilemma by turning away from personal neuroses to deal with the problem of acting in the world, like in *Blow-Up* and *Zabriskie Point,* and that Godard had found ideology, or something in *Wind from the East* and all those other films, while Fellini is content to explore his own navel. Terrence said Hollywood never card much for social observation or analysis of motive, and so American directors had no place to turn at all except to lyrical camerawork, since technical skill was all that Hollywood had to offer after the genres gave out. He said that everybody saying that Kit looked like James Dean symbolized what he meant by the genres dying out and reaching a dead-end and all. And he said if the film was boring it wouldn't hurt it at the box-office because the critics would say that its aesthetic and spiritual emptiness reflects the bankruptcy of American society. They would say that the destruction of constricting cultural and social forms symbolized by the burning of Holly's dad's house and the doll house inside it is no solution but just leads to the nothingness and moral confusion suggested by the vast featureless space of the American Midwest. They would see that we can neither live within society nor without it. There's no escape. And besides, even if it was boring, it was pretty to look at, and he had me there, because it was pretty to look at.

I remember how angry he was when the camera-operator dropped the telephoto lens and I forgot the vaseline at the motel. But then he said he didn't care about the vaseline, because everybody would say he was copying Altman, and he could use Noxzema instead. In the end, he decided not to use anything on the lens and go with composition and sunsets instead. That was ok with me

253

because I was getting vaseline all over the script and the pages kept getting stuck together. But I said didn't people want more from movies than pretty pictures—that if that's all they wanted they could buy the new Polaroid camera or go look at the eighty-foot Kodachrome slide exhibit at Grand Central Station if they lived in New York. Terrence didn't say anything for a long time after that. Then he looked deep into the lens of the Panavision camera and shook his head and said again as if I weren't there that we have nothing more to say and all we can do is say that over and over again and hope no one notices. Then he looked at me and said that it wasn't only him that felt that way but that Bogdanovich and Altman were in the same boat, and if it weren't for the cameramen they'd all be sunk. He said he felt a lot like Holly when she sits huddled to one side when Kit is yelling at her to meet him at the Grand Coulee Dam when her new consciousness of time paralyzes her. The only reason Kit can act is because he remains naïve. Terrence said he kept thinking of the old film classics, and that his total consciousness of film history is a special consciousness of time like Holly's, and that he felt immobilized too. He said it's only the real action directors like Don Siegel who haven't acknowledged the passage of time, who can keep on firing away like Kit. He really admired them. But, I said, Kit gives himself up at the end. He doesn't keep on firing. Terrence looked away and then asked me to get my make-up on since we had some more shooting to do that day and we couldn't spend all our time bullshitting.

THE RUNAWAY
GENIUS

When *The Thin Red Line,* a tale of World War II, unleashes its artillery—including an all-star cast of Sean Penn, Nick Nolte, John Travolta, Woody Harrelson, John Cusack, Bill Pullman, Gary Oldman, George Clooney, and others—in December, expect a twenty-one-gun salute to a hero who seems certain to remain an unseen soldier. The project marks the return, after exactly two decades, of the mysterious director Terrence Malick, whose *Badlands* (1973) and *Days of Heaven* (1978) are classics. Malick, who declined to speak for this article, has established himself as a sort of cinematic Salinger, as silent as Garbo, as evasive as the Fugitive. A fleeting presence, like the rare birds he loves to watch, Malick is the kind of seductive talent sought after as much for his elusiveness as for his eye. He has always been an enigma, one of modern Hollywood's genuine myths. Nobody knows why. At the height of his powers, after those two unforgettable films, he walked away from directing. And nobody knows why he came back. But one thing is definite: offscreen a battle rages about who deserves the credit for bringing Malick home.

Bobby Geisler first met Malick in 1978 when he approached the filmmaker to direct a movie version of David Rabe's play *In the Boom Boom Room.* Geisler—short and cheerful with long, thinning locks and an accent that softly suggests the South—was a novice producer who had been deeply impressed by *Badlands,* which starred then unknowns Martin Sheen and Sissy Spacek in a story loosely based on the bloody career of spree killer Charles Starkweather and his girlfriend, Caril Ann Fugate. With its stunning mix of psycho and pastoral, *Badlands* inspired subsequent lovers-on-the-lam films, culminating in Oliver Stone's notorious homage, *Natural Born Killers,* in 1994. *Badlands* made its debut at the New York Film Festival in 1973, overshadowing even Martin Scorsese's *Mean Streets.*

Malick turned down the Rabe project. Still, he and Geisler had hit it off and began meeting at Los Angeles restaurants little frequented by celebrities, such as the Hamburger Hamlet on Sunset and Doheny, where they sat in back batting around ideas. Malick, about thirty-five then, was bearish and bearded. He had the beef-eating habits of a boy raised in Texas and Oklahoma; as he talked he wolfed down hamburgers, two at a time. Malick invariably wore jeans and a seersucker sport coat a little too small for him. It gave him a slightly Chaplinesque air. Geisler kidded him that it looked like the seersucker jacket that Kit Carruthers—Sheen's Starkweather surrogate—stole from a rich man's house in *Badlands.*

"For eighteen months or so, well into 1979, Geisler and Malick worked on a project based on the life of Joseph Merrick, the nineteenth-century British sideshow celebrity who suffered from a rare, debilitating disease. One day Geisler was stunned to receive an invitation to a screening of *Days of Heaven,* Malick's new picture. The director had never mentioned it.

Featuring Richard Gere in his first big role, along with Sam Shepard and Brooke Adams, *Days of Heaven* was a brutal shoot, complicated by conflict between the director and its temperamental male lead, as well as by savage battles between Malick and the producers, Bert and Harold Schneider. Linda Palevsky, then married to Malick's friend and patron, computer millionaire Max Palevsky, recalls, "Terry's quite mad, and he had this notion of wanting to make the perfect movie. He used to describe the kind of purity he wanted—he would say things like 'You have a drop of water on a pond, that moment of perfection.' That's the kind of quality he expected from the work he did, and if he couldn't do that, then there was no point making a movie. "You'd say to Terry, 'You really ought to go into therapy,' and he'd say, 'If I go to therapy. I'll lose my creative [juice].' "

The picture languished in the editing room for nearly two years, partly because Malick wouldn't or couldn't make decisions. Says Paul Ryan, who shot second unit on the film, "Terry's not one to draw things to a close." Confounding the doubters, *Days of Heaven* emerged as a testimony to Malick's artistic persistence, a dark jewel of a film, acclaimed for its stunning imagery, even by critics who found his meager narrative elliptical. The movie was nominated for four Oscars (winning the best-cinematography award) and impressed Charles Bluhdorn, the colorful head of Paramount's parent company, Gulf & Western, who fell in love with Malick's melancholy tone and dreamy landscapes. Bluhdorn gave him a production deal. Still, Malick seemed to feel he had failed at what he had set out to do.

Geisler's Merrick project never wound up on Malick's Paramount agenda. When director David Lynch announced *his* Merrick project, *The Elephant Man,* Malick and Geisler shelved theirs—and quickly lost touch. Still, Malick had made a lasting impression on the producer. "I thought Terry was a genius, an artist, and I was completely mesmerized by him," Geisler says. "I felt better when I was with him and more than anything I wanted to learn from him, swore that I would produce a play or a movie of Terry's if it was the last thing that I did."

Exhausted and bruised by *Days of Heaven,* Malick spent considerable time with his girlfriend. Michie Gleason, in Paris. While she directed a film called *Broken English,* he labored in their Rue Jacob apartment on his new script, tentatively entitled *Q.* Its prologue, which dramatized the origins of life, became increasingly elaborate and would ultimately take over the rest of the story.

Malick shuttled between Paris and Los Angeles, where he hired a small crew, including cameraman Ryan and special-effects consultant Richard Taylor, who worked intensely for a year or so to realize Malick's vision. "He wanted to do something different, get images nobody had ever seen before," recalls Ryan. In one version, the story began with a sleeping god, underwater, dreaming of the origins of the universe, starting with the big bang and moving forward, as fluorescent fish swam into the deity's nostrils and out again.

"Terry was one of the coolest guys I ever worked with," says Taylor. "He had a passion for trying to do things from the heart. The amount of work we produced was phenomenal." Malick dispatched cameramen all over the world—to the Great Barrier Reef to shoot micro jellyfish, to Mount Etna to shoot volcanic action, to Antarctica to shoot ice shelves breaking off. "He was writing pages of poetry, with no dialogue, glorious visual descriptions." Ryan continues. "Every few months. Paramount would say. 'What are you doing?' He'd give them thirty pages that would keep them happy for a while. But eventually they said. 'Send us a script that starts with page one and at the end says, "The End." We don't care what it is, but do something.' Terry's somebody who always functioned very well from the underground position. Suddenly, everybody was looking at him. . . . He did not work well under those conditions. He didn't want to be on the spot."

Taylor adds: "Then one Monday, Terry never showed up. He didn't call anybody, we couldn't find him—we got worried that maybe something had happened to him. Finally, after about two weeks, we got a phone call. He was in Paris, and he said, 'I'm not sure if I'm going to make this picture. Maybe you should just pack all that stuff up. He just stopped. It was disappointing. I had never put my heart into a project as much as I did that one."

Malick's relationship with Gleason ended, leaving him as bitter and disillusioned personally as he had become professionally. Still, he liked Paris and was spending more time there. Every now and then he called friends. On one occasion he exclaimed to Ryan, "I have a great idea. We're gonna give cameras to people who are just coming out of insane asylums, and let them film. You think that's nuts, but it's not. I'm deadly serious about this."

One day in 1980 or 1981, Malick's landlord introduced him to Michèle, a tall, thirtysomething blonde Parisienne who lived in the same building. She had a young daughter, Alexandra. Michèle had never met anyone like Malick. "He takes you places where you never go with regular people," she says. "He's interested in everything from ants and plants and flowers and grass to philosophy.

And it's not superficial. He reads all the time and remembers everything. He's got this incredible charm . . . something interior."

Malick, friends surmised, was trying to fashion a normal life far from Hollywood. Michèle had become part of that. She thought of herself as average, unglamorous. She cooked and did dishes while Malick played father to Alex. Occasionally, they attended Mass. Always preoccupied with faith and religion, Malick knows the Bible well.

In a year or two, the trio moved to Austin, Texas, where Terry had attended prep school, St. Stephen's Episcopal, in Westlake Hills. He had been a star football player and outstanding student. His parents, whom he and Michèle visited often, lived by then in Battlesville, Oklahoma. Terry's father, Emil, was an oil geologist of Lebanese extraction ("Malick" means "king" in Arabic) who worked for Phillips Petroleum. His mother, Irene, is Irish and grew up on a farm in the Chicago area.

The Malicks were a family of secrets, marked by tragedy. Terry was the oldest of three boys. Chris, the middle son, had been involved in a terrible automobile accident in which his wife was killed. Chris was badly burned.

Larry, the youngest, went to Spain to study with the guitar virtuoso Segovia. Terry discovered in the summer of 1968 that Larry had broken his own hands, seemingly despondent over his lack of progress. Emil, concerned, went to Spain and returned with Larry's body; it appeared the young man had committed suicide. Like most relatives of those who take their own lives, Terry must have borne a heavy burden of irrational guilt. According to Michèle, the subject of Larry was never mentioned.

Malick was worshiped by his family. He was devoted to his mother. (For years he wouldn't allow her to read the script of *The Thin Red Line* because of the profanity.) But he had terrible fights with his father, often over trivial issues. Even at the age of fifty, according to Michèle, he still argued with Emil over whether he should wear a tie to church. Another bone of contention was family photographs. Malick's father loved to take pictures, but it made Terry uncomfortable. (Malick's contract with Twentieth Century Fox prevents his likeness from being used to promote *The Thin Red Line*.)

Michèle did her best to adapt to Austin. Malick took her on bird-watching expeditions to Big Bend National Park in south Texas. But she was out of her element. Although Terry, who spoke softly and slowly, tried to avoid confrontations, he shared his father's temper. According to Michèle, Terry loved to debate abstract intellectual issues but had very rigid ideas about how domestic life ought to be lived. He did not brook contradiction.

The first real fight he and Michèle had was over buying a television, which she thought Alex, who was eleven or so by then, needed to help acclimate her to a foreign country. Malick, who has the habit of casting his likes, dislikes, and personal eccentricities as matters of principle, argued that TV was trash, that it would ruin the child. (When traveling, Malick often had the TV removed from his hotel rooms, and when that wasn't possible, covered it.) Michèle wouldn't relent—and there was a blow-up. At difficult times like these, Malick would often just leave, for hours, days, or weeks. She never knew where he went, and it made her crazy.

Malick had other eccentricities. He was compulsively neat and possessive about his things. Michèle says she was not allowed to cross the threshold of his office. If she wanted to read one of his books, he preferred to buy another copy rather than lend his own. It was difficult for her to figure out what he was reading, anyway: he always placed books cover down. When he listened to music, he used a Walkman and rarely left cassettes faceup.

Malick didn't discuss his film work with Michèle, telling her, "I want my personal life to be completely separate from the movies." Although once in a while she read his scripts, mostly he wouldn't tell her what he was working on, and she was not supposed to ask. Occasionally, Malick went to Los Angeles, and every so often he took Michèle along. She met a few of his friends. Malick and Michèle had married in 1985, but no one in L.A. had known of the wedding, or even of their relationship. She felt she had ceased to exist.

Alex had become sassy and rebellious. But Malick was very strict. Not only was there no TV, there was no candy, no telephone. The stricter he became, the more the teenager acted out. Michèle was not strong enough to protect her. One day, Terry and Michèle found Alex gone. She had apparently gotten her father to send her a ticket to France. She was only fifteen at the time.

• • •

Malick's production deal with Paramount had ended in 1983 after the sudden death of Charles Bluhdorn. He supported himself by writing the occasional script. He did something for Louis Malle and also completed a rewrite of a Robert Dillon script called *Countryman* for producers Edward Lewis and Robert Cortes in 1984. "I couldn't communicate with him directly," recalls Cortes. "I would make a phone call to a certain number, leave a message, and then his brother would call me back." Once, Malick and Cortes actually met face-to-face at Universal executive Ned Tanen's home in Santa Monica Canyon. After the meeting, Cortes offered to give him a lift. "He was very cryptic about where to drop him off." Cortes continues. "I let him out at the corner of Wilshire and Seventh or somewhere. He waited for me to drive away, and then he just walked off."

Mike Medavoy, who then headed production at Orion Pictures and who had been Malick's agent, hired the director to write a script for *Great Balls of Fire!* Malick also did a rewrite of a script based on Walker Percy's novel *The Moviegoer*. In 1986, Rob Cohen, then head of Taft-Barish Productions, hired him to adapt Larry McMurtry's *The Desert Rose* for Barry Levinson to direct. "Malick was someone who was listening to a high whine in his head," recalls Cohen. "He was very tense and fragile, the least likely person to be a director. I once had to have a meeting with him in Westwood. He was getting up every five minutes and hiding behind pillars; he kept thinking he saw somebody he knew. He would call me, and I'd hear trucks rolling by on the highway, and I'd say, 'Where are you?' and he'd answer, 'I'm walking to Oklahoma!' 'What do you mean, you're walking to Oklahoma? From Texas?' 'Yeah, I'm looking at birds.' "

By the time Geisler reconnected with Malick in 1988, the producer was teamed up with another Texan, John Roberdeau, who had grown up in Austin. Roberdeau was also a Malick devotee, who had committed *Days of Heaven* to memory—every shot, every cut, every scrap of dialogue. Geisler and Roberdeau have a mixed reputation in the film and theater community. The are praised by many for their taste and generosity to artists, but disliked by others for their tireless self-promotion and record of running up bad debts. At the time they met Malick, they had produced several plays—including a Broadway production of Eugene O'Neill's five-hour drama, *Strange Interlude,* on Broadway with Glenda Jackson. But, after a decade in the business, they had completed only one movie, *Streamers* (in 1983). Robert Altman, the film's cantankerous director, had grown so frustrated with the pair's interference that the relationship completely broke down.

Geisler and Roberdeau approached Malick about writing and directing a picture based on D. M. Thomas's novel *The White Hotel,* a vividly erotic story of the Freudian analysis of a woman who dies in a concentration camp. In a characteristic display of largesse, they offered him $2 million, which they didn't yet have. Malick declined, but went on to concede that it might be time he went back to movies. Geisler recalls Malick's saying that if the two producers would be patient they could walk down that path together. Malick told them he would be willing to write an adaptation of Molière's *Tartuffe*—a classic farce—or James Jones's World War II saga *The Thin Red Line,* a sequel of sorts to *From Here to Eternity.* Geisler and Roberdeau sensibly chose the latter and paid Malick $250,000 to write a script.

Malick sent Geisler and Roberdeau a first draft in late May of 1989. The producers flew to Paris and met up with the director and his wife on the Pont Saint-Louis, a bridge which connects the precincts of Notre Dame to the Île Saint-Louis. In a gesture both thoughtful and seductive, they gave the Malicks a silver flask from Tiffany on which was inscribed a sergeant's chevron and one of their favorite lines from the Jones novel: "Billions of hard, bright stars shone with relentless glitter across the tropic night sky." They had dinner at the Brasserie de l'Île Saint-Louis, where Jones, who had died in 1977, and his wife, Gloria, had often lunched. The foursome walked up the Quai d'Orléans to No. 10, where Jones had lived, and Malick bowed before the former home of the master.

At Le Jardin des Plantes and other sites around Paris they settled in to discuss the script. Geisler had prepared four hundred notes, and he believes his seriousness impressed Malick. "Had we not delivered four hundred notes," Geisler maintains, "had we just said,

"Thanks for the screenplay, we'll be in touch later,' he would not have directed it. It was because we were in this dialogue that he did.

"The notion that we discussed endlessly," Geisler continues, "was that Malick's Guadalcanal would be a Paradise Lost, an Eden, raped by the green poison, as Terry used to call it, of war. Much of the violence was to be portrayed indirectly. A soldier is shot, but rather than showing a Spielbergian bloody face we see a tree explode, the shredded vegetation, and a gorgeous bird with a broken wing flying out of the tree."

Malick had agonized about every deviation from Jones's novel, no matter how trivial. He asked Gloria Jones's permission for the smallest changes. Eventually she told him, "Terry, you have my husband's voice, you're writing in his musical key; now what you must do is improvise. Play riffs on this."

Malick ultimately fashioned a remarkable script, infused with his own sensibility. But he had made some questionable choices. He retained several of Jones's more conventional situations, but dropped some interesting elements, including the suggestion of a homoerotic undertow among some of the characters. Later, he changed Stein, a Jewish captain, to Staros, an officer of Greek extraction, thereby gutting Jones's indictment of anti-Semitism in the military, which the novelist had observed close-up in his own company.

263

On the final night of the producers' visit, over dinner at the Café de Flore, in a dramatic appeal he had rehearsed ahead of time. Geisler beseeched Malick to direct the script himself, and assured him that he and his partner would wait forever if necessary. According to Geisler, Malick agreed.

But the director left open numerous doors through which he might make a hasty exit. Always cautious, he wasn't about to enter into any ironclad commitments. The producers realized that although they had hooked their fish, it was far from reeled in. "It was important that we find a way to remain in continual touch with Terry," Geisler says, candid about his efforts to cement the relationship. "The best way to do that was to commission him to develop another project." In late 1989, although Malick had never before written a play and was not much interested in the stage, he suggested adapting the story which had been the basis for the great

Kenji Mizoguchi film *Sansho the Bailiff* for the theater. Geisler and Roberdeau agreed to pay him $200,000, plus a $50,000 bonus, which Malick would collect the night the play opened on Broadway.

The producers plunged into the research, supplying Malick with anything and everything he needed. And often, expensively, going him one better. No script existed for the Mizoguchi film, so they had it transcribed and translated by both a Japanese linguist who spoke English and an American who spoke Japanese. (Debates over particularly enigmatic areas of the text were also incorporated.) The producers excavated tenth-century literature written in ancient Japanese—travel sketches and diaries. They taped Japanese children who were the same age as the children in the script, speaking Malick's lines, so he could hear what they sounded like.

The three men became what the producers considered to be close friends. Geisler corresponded with Emil Malick, sending him newspaper clippings on subjects of interest to him, and even two city guides to Washington, D.C., on the eve of a visit. When Roberdeau's brother was diagnosed with leukemia, Malick offered to donate his bone marrow. Even though the producers had other projects—they had enlisted the now deceased Dennis Potter to write *The White Hotel*—Malick was the focus. Claims Geisler, "We behaved like family toward each other. We liked each other, I thought, loved each other. He was the center and circumference of our lives."

Occasionally, the trio converged on Los Angeles. At the Beverly Hills Hotel, Malick asked them to request one of the first-floor rooms in the back, with the patios. Rather than use the valet, he parked on Crescent Drive, adjacent to the hotel, and instead of walking through the lobby, he crossed the grounds and entered from the rear, hopping over the little patio fence, rapping on the plate-glass door for admittance. Says Roberdeau, "It was as if he was Greta Garbo or something."

The producers' friends told them that they were crazy, that Malick would never finish a project. But, says Geisler, "I thought we were working with a guy who was one of the few true artists of the twentieth century. It wasn't an easy day's work, but it was a great day's work. Terry was the Holy Grail. He was thought to be unfindable, unapproachable, unconvincible. Others had failed; we would be successful. We realized how much that might mean to our careers."

Malick, still not entirely won over, had plenty of caveats. For a long time he would not allow the producers to keep a sample of his handwriting. They say original copies of documents bearing his penmanship were to be returned to him with no copies made. Handwritten notes were to be destroyed. It reminded Roberdeau of *Badlands,* in which Sheen's character would never sign his name the same way twice out of fear of forgery.

Geisler and Roberdeau practiced what they called "method producing," which consisted of elaborate (and expensive) trips, flying to San Francisco to see the Kodo Drummers, visiting an Asian collection at the Boston Museum of Fine Arts and then heading on to Grafton, Vermont, for a *Sansho the Bailiff* editing session while they ate cheese soup and watched the leaves turn. They booked Malick into the best hotels, reserved tables at the finest restaurants. Sometimes he took such first-class service for granted, but occasionally he balked, tried to plan his own trips, or rejected a car. They sent it anyway.

One day in the fall of 1990. Malick told the producers he had long been working on a script called *The English-Speaker,* based upon Dr. Josef Breuer's well-known nineteenth-century case study of Anna O., a hysteric. In Malick's silent world of secrets, this script was especially personal, private. He would allow no one but Geisler to read it. Of the project, the producer says, "It's as if he had ripped open his heart and bled his true feelings onto the page." It is indeed a remarkable script. *The Exorcist* as written by Dostoyevsky. So when Malick said. "Let's do this," Geisler and Roberdeau, drunk on his prose poetry, agreed, paying him $400,000.

Late in the summer of 1990. Malick had turned in the first draft of *Sansho the Bailiff.* The producers knew it wasn't quite there yet, but in early 1991 they sent it out to directors Peter Brook, Peter Stein, and Ingmar Bergman. Each turned it down. Undeterred, the producers conceived the ambitious notion of staging the play as a workshop and inviting the participation of the world's masters of set design, sound, lighting, and choreography. But they still needed a director.

In August 1992, Geisler and Roberdeau, along with the

Malicks—who by that time were estranged and living separately—met up at the music festival in Salzburg. They were impressed by the great Andrzej Wajda's staging of the Polish classic *Wesele* and were familiar with Wajda's celebrated trilogy—*A Generation, Kanal,* and *Ashes and Diamonds*—a masterpiece of world cinema. Wajda had never heard of Malick, but flew to New York in October to screen *Badlands* and *Days of Heaven* at the Tribeca Film Center. Afterward, at a nearby restaurant, he agreed to direct *Sansho the Bailiff.* The tables were covered with butcher paper, and Wajda drew a picture with crayons. He inscribed it, "For Terry from Andrzej Wajda." Geisler was so excited, he called Malick in Austin, saying: "Next stop, Warsaw!"

On a cold and wintry December evening of the same year, the Malicks and the producers converged on Wajda's family home in Warsaw. Faded photographs of ancestors and war heroes illuminated by flickering candles in sconces peered down at them from the green enameled walls as they shared a traditional dinner with Wajda and his wife, actress Krystyna Zachwatowicz, two enormous dogs, and various friends and relatives who dropped by.

Malick, who detests beets and fish with bones—or even the appearance of bones—seemed ill at ease as the guests hungrily attacked the three beet dishes (pickled and roasted beets, as well as borscht), four varieties of herring, along with kasha, duck, and ten or so other delicacies. The meal was washed down with generous quantities of Polish vodka, which Malick drank sparingly.

Wajda felt that the play required substantial revision. He expected Malick to roll up his shirtsleeves and do more, do better. Sitting by the roaring fire after the sumptuous meal, Wajda turned to Malick and said, "Terry, what you need to do to *Sansho the Bailiff* is make it more like Shakespeare."

Recalls Geisler, "That was the beginning of the end."

The workshop was budgeted at $600,000. As the first day approached, the producers' long-suffering backers abruptly pulled out. Still, the show went on. True to their word, Geisler and Roberdeau did manage to gather some remarkable international talents, including lighting designer Jennifer Tipton, sound designer Hans Peter Kuhn, and a collection of fine Asian-American actors.

But the six-week workshop, held at the Brooklyn Academy of Music (BAM) in November of 1993, was a bust.

The relationship between Malick and Wajda quickly deteriorated. A few days into the workshop, Michèle arrived from Paris to see her husband. To her, it seemed that Wajda was threatened by Malick's presence. Malick thought Wajda didn't understand his play; he was frustrated by how little the director was bringing to it. He was angered by what he regarded as Wajda's condescending attitude—"You, boy, go do your rewrites."

Wajda spoke English to Geisler and Roberdeau, but never a word to Malick, with whom he conversed through translators. He was annoyed that Malick had not done the work he wanted. Malick insisted on doing it his way, but he wasn't the director. Says Kuhn, "Terry didn't know anything about theater, and he was not interested in learning. He was very stubborn."

On the last day, just after Michèle returned to Paris, Malick asked the producers for a limo. Geisler and Roberdeau were puzzled; he had never asked for a car and chauffeur before. They were flabbergasted when they saw it was for Ecky Wallace, an Austin woman who was an old friend of Malick's from St. Stephen's. Later, she became Malick's girlfriend.

The workshop cost $800,000, alienated Malick, and left the producers devastated, although it was a disaster of their own making. The play just wasn't ready. Geisler and Roberdeau were besieged by angry creditors—BAM, caterers, travel agents, publicists, restaurants. The partners were dead broke. They sold their furniture to meet their payroll; Roberdeau sold CDs and books so they could eat. One creditor managed to have Geisler arrested. He was led from his town house, in handcuffs, marched down West Ninth Street in Manhattan's Greenwich Village, and thrown in jail overnight for grand larceny, a charge that was later dismissed. (In April 1996, Geisler and Roberdeau were evicted from the home they shared.)

Says Roberdeau, "It was ridiculous. We were sitting on all these assets that we had sunk our money, blood, and time into. It was time to put Terry on notice." In December, they began to press Terry about which of the two movie projects would go first, *The English-Speaker* or *The Thin Red Line*. Geisler, who was closer to

Malick, played the good cop, Roberdeau the bad. The latter angrily told the director, "Don't pretend you're not a participant in all of this." But, says Geisler, Malick blithely refused "to take any responsibility whatsoever. Our problems were our problems. He had forewarned us in the beginning that his timetable would be his timetable, and if we were still standing by the time that he got around to directing one or both of the movies, that would be great."

In January 1995, the producers sent Malick a note, begging him to allow them to approach Mike Medavoy, who was in the process of setting up his own company, Phoenix Pictures, to finance *The English-Speaker* and/or *The Thin Red Line*. They say Malick never answered. Geisler and Roberdeau borrowed money for tickets and flew to Los Angeles, arriving in a teeming rainstorm. Fallen trees blocked the narrow roads that thread the canyons of Beverly Hills. Later the two men came to feel that they had ignored a portent of biblical proportions. But Medavoy agreed to give them $100,000 to secure the project for his company: he said he would back *The Thin Red Line* with the other two men serving as producers.

But *Sansho the Bailiff* had badly damaged the relationship between Malick and the producers. Geisler and Roberdeau, terrified, made herculean efforts to mend fences. By the following year, Malick's wounds had apparently begun to heal, and the three men again professed affection for one another. Geisler and Roberdeau say that Malick asked them to hire him to adapt *A Tale of Two Cities* for the stage.

The producers spoke between themselves about how to keep the pressure on, how to steer Malick away from theater and toward starting *The Thin Red Line*. At the time, the feeling was that since the film's message was that war dehumanized the G.I.'s and made them anonymous, stars would not be used in the picture. The producers sent their two assistants on weekend trips to the Midwest to scout fresh faces, corn-fed boys at spelling bees and debating contests. It was expensive, but it was a way of moving Malick forward.

March of 1995 brought a reading of *The Thin Red Line* at Medavoy's home. The Malick magic worked its spell. The reading included Martin Sheen delivering the screen directions, Kevin Costner, Will Patton, Dermot Mulroney, Peter Berg, and Lukas Haas.

Malick was nervous. His face was flushed. He had prepared some remarks, but when he stood up his mind went blank. He was deeply embarrassed and looked as if he just wanted to survive to the end. Observes Roberdeau, "He was in his element, but he was painfully aware that everybody was looking at him as the master. This was a kind of coming-out." The fact that Malick turned up at all was a symbolic gesture that somehow made *The Thin Red Line* official. But there was still a long road ahead.

In June, a five-day workshop was scheduled, also at Medavoy's. A few weeks before it was due to begin, Malick said he couldn't sleep at night; he was worried that Geisler and Roberdeau might produce *Sansho the Bailiff before* he finished it, directed by someone else. They say he demanded that his producers relinquish all rights to the play to him. Geisler says, "Terry would have drawn a line in the sand, and *The Thin Red Line* wouldn't be happening today." By this time, they had invested nearly $1 million and a decade's effort in *The Thin Red Line*. They agreed to his terms.

Plans for the film workshop proceeded. One day Brad Pitt dropped by. Malick met Johnny Depp at the Book Soup Bistro, on Sunset. Recalls Geisler, "Depp basically said to Malick, 'Let's sign this napkin; you tell me where to show up, when, what to play.' After Depp and Pitt provided the affirmation Terry needed, it was easier to get him to meet with other actors." But there was a downside to stars; Geisler told the suddenly starstruck director, "You're going to compromise the movie." Finally Malick gave in. According to a source, Malick said, "The audience will know that Pitt's going to wake up after his death scene and collect his $1 million."

But word had gotten out that Costner, Pitt, and Depp were up for roles in *The Thin Red Line,* and a feeding frenzy began among male actors. Geisler and Roberdeau were even getting calls from actresses. "There are no actresses in it," Roberdeau told one agent. "There's only a photograph of a woman in one scene." Without missing a beat, the agent said, "She'll play that! She'll be the photograph."

Pre-production moved slowly, with Malick displaying his characteristic reluctance to make decisions. Says a source, "It was hard

for him to say something definite. He would couch [his ambiva-
lence] in a way that was very compelling on the surface, all about
being delicate, and he speaks so idiomatically that sometimes you
get caught up in the beauty of what he's saying, but fundamentally
it was hard to get him to commit to things." He met with scores of
actors, told each of them, "There is no one whom I admire more."

Around the beginning of 1996, Malick phoned Michèle in Paris
and told her he wanted a divorce. It did not come as a complete
surprise. There had been problems since her days in Austin. But
she claims when she had asked Malick if things had changed
between them, he had always said, "No, no, no."

Malick was inching toward production, but there were still unresolved issues. As soon as Medavoy got involved, Geisler says, a
turf war broke out. It was one that, without Malick's support,
Geisler and Roberdeau would inevitably lose. Medavoy says he
welcomed the participation of Geisler and Roberdeau. "I did
everything to keep them on," he says. "I took them out to lunch. I
said, 'Here's your chance to really learn how to make a movie.' "

But Geisler and Roberdeau had no experience with a project of
this scale. Medavoy hired his friend, veteran producer George
Stevens Jr., whom Malick had known and liked since the late '60s.
(Stevens had invested in *Badlands*.) He was to supervise the production, which would largely take place in Queensland, Australia,
and cost about $55 million.

Medavoy asked Geisler and Roberdeau to share their producers'
credit with Stevens. They refused.

In the fall of 1996, according to Geisler, Malick called him and
said that he was once again having trouble sleeping. Now he was
worried about *The English-Speaker*. He feared that, since his
exclusive five-year directing option had lapsed at the end of 1995,
the producers might turn it over to another director.

"I thought he wanted me to say a few words of love and reas-
surance," recalls Geisler. But he says Malick made it clear that he
would not proceed with *The Thin Red Line* unless the producers
extended his right to direct *The English-Speaker* in perpetuity. The
producers refused.

"Terry said that if we ultimately produced one of the three projects with him, we should feel ourselves lucky," Geisler remembers, summing up an exchange with Malick. "I said, 'You're scaring me now, because you're making me feel as if you have no intention ever of developing *Sansho* or directing *The English-Speaker,* which was not the spirit in which these other projects were commissioned.' "

Medavoy agreed with them, told Malick that if he felt so strongly about *The English-Speaker* he should buy the script back or enter into a partnership with the producers. But Malick was adamant, denied he had any ulterior motives, and held out a carrot. Again, according to Geisler, he said, "We'll clean our wound to the bone, proceed together on *The Thin Red Line* without doubt or suspicion. We will now be speaking pilot to pilot. I don't want to jump out and see that you're still on the plane. We'll be able to jump out of the plane together." Roberdeau broke in, saying, "I feel like I've already jumped out of the plane. I'm on the ground with my legs broken."

Geisler consoled himself with fantasies about the glorious day when *The Thin Red Line* would finally open, "A Terrence Malick picture, produced by Robert Geisler and John Roberdeau." He explains: "During those years of stress, selling furniture and books and CDs, I got through it because I said, 'Bring Malick back and, oh, what a day it will be. What a reward we'll have. We'll stand shoulder to shoulder, speak pilot to pilot.' "

Principal photography was to begin on June 23, 1997. Phoenix had a deal with Sony, which was slated to co-finance the picture. Geisler and Roberdeau learned from a story in *Variety* that Sony president John Galley had pulled his company out of the film. They say they faxed the article to Malick in Australia, where he was scouting locations. He flew to Los Angeles immediately and pressed Medavoy, who admitted he didn't have the financing. Geisler and Roberdeau claim that Malick was furious with his old friend, and asked them if, contractually, he could take the film away from Medavoy.

Medavoy responds, "I don't know if that's true or not, because Terry never mentioned it to me. I had told Terry that we ran the risk of not doing it at Sony, and since he was in Australia and unavailable, I waited until he got back to tell him that it wasn't going to be Sony, but that we would find another distributor."

• • •

In any event, Malick, Medavoy, and Stevens (*sans* Geisler and Roberdeau) were obliged to pitch the project, something Malick had hoped to avoid. Fox 2000 president Laura Ziskin agreed to pick up the film, but required the presence of some stars. They would play supporting roles while lower-wattage actors, such as Elias Koteas, Adrien Brody, and Jim Caviezel, took on the main parts. The last stone had been cleared from the path.

"In May of 1997, we were working our hearts out in New York, and I saw that people were beginning to move to Australia," says Geisler. "We called Phoenix. Under no circumstances were we to be in Australia, ever! I called Terry and said, 'What we just heard doesn't square with either our recent situation, in which you seemed to rely upon me, if not hourly, at least every other day, nor our relationship over the last ten or twenty years.' We just wanted the pleasure of seeing him say 'Action!' for the first time in twenty years, feeling we had earned that, and he would not be there were it not for John and me.

"Basically he said I should be grateful to him for directing this movie. It was not what he expected to direct, he didn't want to, he was doing it only for me. I said, 'Terry, this is going to sound melodramatic and biblical, but let me put it to you like this: I feel like Moses. I led this fucking movie through the desert, and now the fun starts, everybody else is walking into the promised land.' He said, 'Bobby, there is no one for whom I have more admiration than you. No one speaks the truth to me like you do. Bobby.' " Essentially, says Geisler, Malick blamed it on Medavoy.

Geisler continues. "To be really theatrical about it, this sums up my whole life with Terry Malick." He takes out a small manila envelope and turns it upside down, spilling a handful of brightly colored pills, like M&Ms, onto the table. He slowly counts out seventeen, some of which are vitamins. "Several years ago, I didn't take anything," he says. "My face has started falling off. High blood pressure, diabetes, I got fat, I drink too much. I'm never going to get over this. We were co-dependent. I don't like to think this about myself, but we were members of a cult." Adds Roberdeau, "We were the high priests of it. I'm the cardinal of Bobby's Malick cult."

• • •

Disputes between directors and producers are, as is well known, common in the film business. But what happened next was a little strange. Several journalists visited the set, among them Josh Young from *Entertainment Weekly*. Shortly thereafter, Young received a copy of a peculiar statement from the set on *The Thin Red Line* stationery, and a later letter, unsigned. The statement said, in part: "Bobby Geisler and John Roberdeau are imposters and confidence men who have no connection with Mr. Malick and who have had only a distant one in the past. Journalists should beware of letting these tricksters promote their own careers by using Mr. Malick's name . . ." The letter attacks them for crediting themselves "as the reason [Malick] has returned to filmmaking," and credits Ecky Wallace instead.

It seems extremely unlikely that Malick would have lent himself to so bizarre an exercise as this one. But regardless of who wrote the statement, it reflects the sentiments of the people around Malick. Says Medavoy, "The [producers] were really resourceful in getting to Terry and putting the impetus into it, but I don't think they convinced him to make the movie, maybe Ecky did. I don't know. But one thing is for sure: he came to it himself, and it wasn't about money, it was about passion."

Says Clayton Townsend, Oliver Stone's producer, who worked on pre-production, "Geisler and Roberdeau are two guys who live in their own world. They're very pretentious fellows and take great pride in their paper presentations. They just had a knack for putting on a lot of people along the way. I tried to stay clear of them."

Adds one source, "There are a lot of people Geisler and Roberdeau owed money to. The fact is, they might have had the police after them if this picture hadn't been set up. They are the great spenders of the Western world. They didn't have enough money to pay for the office help, but you ask them to go out and get you a list of actors and they Federal Express you a book full of pictures in a two hundred-dollar binder. The two guys are trying to get their careers started on Terry. They wore out their welcome."

Adds another source, "It wasn't that they were banned from the set. They hadn't been involved for a year prior to the shooting, except in their own minds. They're people Terry got involved with

PETER BISKIND

and wishes he hadn't. Terry said that not only did they not bring him back, their being around was discouraging him from coming back."

The source adds that Geisler and Roberdeau were working at cross-purposes with Phoenix. For example, he claims that the production was waiting for the delivery of uniforms, which never came. When the supplier was called, he said he had been fired by Roberdeau. (Geisler denies this.) Another source says that Geisler and Roberdeau were asked to give Adrien Brody, an actor they had recommended, a tape of *Il Posto*, a film that Malick wanted him to see. Instead they arranged a screening and dinner at the Royalton Hotel in New York for a dozen people. Malick was reportedly furious that they had "improved" on his instruction.

Adrien Brody plays Fife, a major character in the novel—Jones modeled him after himself. Now his scenes have been reduced, and the film, not unlike Oliver Stone's 1986 *Platoon,* turns on the conflict between idealism and cynicism as embodied in the clash between two characters—Welsh, who is played by Sean Penn, and Witt, who is played by Jim Caviezel. (Caviezel and Elias Koteas, who plays Staros, are the two actors whose performances are generating advance praise.)

Although people around Malick now say that it was, among other things. Geisler and Roberdeau's problems with creditors that estranged the director, their phone logs reveal that he was calling them frequently, often two or three times a day, as much as a year after the *New York Observer* went public with their financial woes, right up to the start of production.

The producers think Malick got rid of them because of their close relationship with Michèle. Says Geisler, "We and Michèle got divorced around the same time. We got the call and Michèle got the call. A chapter was closed and a chapter was opened." Geisler and Roberdeau are contractually allowed to thank four people in the credits. Michèle Malick was one of the people they selected. According to Geisler, when Terry heard about all of this, he threatened to take his name off the picture.

Concludes Geisler, "Terry's writing is obsessed with mercy and sacrifice and love and courage and comradeship, but that just doesn't square with who he is: utterly unmerciful. But great artists are not necessarily always nice people."

The fact is, we'll probably never know the entire truth about this relationship. But one thing is clear: Malick and the producers, who did manage to retain their screen credit, were made for each other. His genius sparked their ambition; their ambition cleared his path back to filmmaking. Geisler and Roberdeau ensnared Malick in a web of love that he may have come to experience as obligation, and he broke loose. They tried to seduce him, become the circumference of his life, but he seduced them and became the center of theirs. As playwright Charles Mee Jr., who wrote four drafts of *The White Hotel,* puts it, "When Bobby and John first encounter an artist, they are so appreciative, they are so generous, but there comes a time when they would like some consideration in return, and if they don't get it, they feel dissed. There comes a test of love—that most people fail."

The fact is, the director has returned and, despite his long absence, brought *The Thin Red Line* in on time and on budget. The much discussed result is a "meditation on men and war," as Laura Ziskin calls it, as far from *Saving Private Ryan,* the year's other big war movie, as you can get. "The technical virtuosity of *Saving Private Ryan* is stunning," she continues. "The artistic virtuosity of *The Thin Red Line* is equally stunning. There's a kind of hypnotic quality to Malick's movies, and this one is just mesmerizing."

DEEP FOCUS

PUNCHIN' JUDY

I had heard she was kind of a tough nut, but I dug her instantly. I think she's the greatest actress of her generation. I'm truly grateful to be working with her twice in a lifetime. We're the Astaire and Rogers of bizarre relationships." Peter Weller is splayed out on the floor of a Beverly Hills home, smoking a large cigar and riffing on the subject of Judy Davis. It's about 1 A.M., and he's taking a break from his second film with Davis, *The New Age*. He pauses, propels a cloud of smoke toward the ceiling, and says, "But if you don't have wings, she'll bury you."

Weller is right. Barring, perhaps, Meryl Streep, and allowing for the hyperbole that infects movie journalism, Judy Davis is indeed the greatest actress of her generation. She can do more with her mouth— she raises lip chewing and grimacing to a fine art— than most actors can do with their entire body. It's a pity she has been largely confined to marginal films, or marginal roles in weightier films, and now she is reaching an age—forty—when many actresses are forced to take up knitting. Her choices in projects have been less than fortunate. For reasons best known to herself, she has often worked with first- or second-time directors. Although she recently revealed a winning flair for comedy in *The Ref*, she once again played the role with which she has been most closely identified: the shrew.

Davis shines in *The New Age,* but the film itself is a mixed bag, best when it casts a cold look at contemporary upper-middle-class L.A. reality, worst when it becomes mired in New Age nonsense— "soul retrievers" and the like, which no one outside the 310 area code takes seriously. Her last film, *Dark Blood,* was never even finished, due to the death of River Phoenix, and she clashed bitterly with the director. All and all, hers has not been the meteoric journey many had predicted after her stunning debut in Gillian Armstrong's *My Brilliant Career* in 1979.

Davis probably brings some of this down on herself, and there are undoubtedly directors who run the other way when her name comes up. But an industry devoted to recycling '50s TV shows offers precious little in the way of material suitable for grown-ups, not to mention grown-up women with talent like hers. Davis should be working with Hoffman and De Niro and Pacino.

But the bad news is hardly news; so let's turn to the good news, which is Davis herself—outspoken, caustic, and wickedly funny. Wearing a charcoal gray pin-striped suit over a white T-shirt, she is sitting in Savoy, a small SoHo restaurant, tearing the wings off George Sluizer, *Dark Blood's* director. She looks askance at the bottle of China Soda the waiter delivers in lieu of the diet Coke she asked for, sighs, takes a couple of drags from her cigarette and crushes it in the ashtray.

"It's my fault, because when I first met George, he more or less told me what he was like as a director, and I only heard what I wanted to hear," she recalls. "He said that he believed in discipline, that film sets aren't democracies, and I'm saying, 'Oh, absolutely.'

"George was a bit scared of me. I thought he was foolish in his approach to actors. In my opinion he confused River about his character, constantly telling him how he should play it—angrier, or loonier, or whatever. I don't like having labels thrown at me by a director."

Davis expects her opinions to be taken seriously, expects to be heard. She and Sluizer came to blows right away, over rewrites of the script. "I tried to get out of the film, but I couldn't, after the [Kim] Basinger business," says Davis. "I think he felt that I was an incredible challenge to his control. Which I suppose I was. There are some directors who just want to be inside your head and in that way interpret their character through you, using you almost like a host. As an actor, I just felt I had no space. So I had to create it."

Davis makes quick, abrupt movements with her hands, which involuntarily fly up to the becoming tangle of dark hair that cascades off her head. She is well-known for her chalky, blood-sucked look, and indeed, she is pale—and small, with chiseled features, deep red lipstick, and the nervous manner of a trapped animal. She fingers her watch, lights another cigarette, stubs it out.

Sydney, Australia, where she has left her husband, actor Colin Friels, and her seven-year-old son, Jack, is presently ringed by forest fires. "It's very close to where we live," she says. "I spoke to Colin last s night. He said, 'It's perfectly safe; it's not going to come here, 'cause there are houses in the way.' I said, "What do you mean? Houses burn like trees burn!' " She pauses again, presumably contemplating the notion of flying back to be with her family. "To get burnt?" she asks rhetorically. Her eyes widen. "They can fly out!" She pauses. "I asked him to check if the insurance was paid up. It would be an act of God, wouldn't it? I'm really confused about this act-of-God business."

Davis stops. George Sluizer again pushes his way to the front of her mind. "He's an act of God," she says, with a wry grin. "He's an act of the devil."

Judy Davis was born in 1955 in Perth, a barren outpost of civilization on the western coast of Australia surrounded by ocean and desert. She grew up in a rather conventional and airless Catholic household, and space—to define herself, to become her own person—was in short supply. Young Judy was forbidden to see movies and was sent to a convent to be schooled by nuns. She was too smart and rebellious for this to have been a very happy experience. Like that of many lapsed Catholics, her constricted childhood seems to have left her with a lifelong inclination to tweak authority.

By the age of seventeen she would have done anything she could to flee Perth; she defied her mother's threats and joined a band, singing Simon & Garfunkel tunes as she made her way across the Far East. Beating a hasty retreat back to Australia, she ended up at the National Institute of Dramatic Art in Sydney, and landed her breakthrough role in *My Brilliant Career*.

The film tells the story of a nineteenth-century Australian woman who turns down a marriage proposal from a handsome and extremely eligible suitor (Sam Neill) in order to pursue her calling as a writer. The movie established Davis's MO with directors: She and Armstrong had a tug-of-war over her role. "I just didn't like the character I was playing—I didn't like the woman it was based on. She wrote these silly books about her early childhood in the bush that nobody was interested in. At the opening of the film in Sydney, I met her nephew. I said, 'What was she like?' He answered, 'She was a real bitch!' "

Davis apparently so frightened Neill that fifteen years later, when asked to talk about her, he would only read a prepared statement.

My Brilliant Career rode the twin waves of feminism and the New Australian Cinema to iternational success and established Davis as a talent to be reckoned with. On the publicity tour she displayed one of the endearing traits that distinguish her from most actors, who tend to be spectacularly cautious when speaking to the press: In an interview with Judy Stone in the *San Francisco Chronicle,* she trashed the movie. "I realized I couldn't lie to I.F. Stone's sister," Davis says. "She said, 'What do you really think of this film?' And with a flood of relief, I said I didn't like it. The producer, a woman, told a journalist in London that I was miserable during the filming and that all I needed was a good fuck! It may well have been true, but it is a strange thing coming from a woman who produced that film, and quite unnecessary to tell a journalist." Davis followed up *My Brilliant Career* with three Australian films, *Winter of Our Dreams, Hoodwink,* and *Heatwave,* and often collided with male directors. "I was perceived as antagonistic," she recalls, "strong-willed, difficult, a person who questioned too much. No guy was gonna make me believe I was antagonistic simply because I was asking questions about the job I was doing. It was driving me crazy."

In 1984, Davis got another big break, playing Adela Quested in David Lean's adaptation of *A Passage to India.* It is hard to imagine a more mismatched pair than the imperial Lean, in the autumn of his career, and the passionate young actress, bristling with intelligence and opinions—and questions, always questions. Needless to say, sparks flew, and Davis has dined out on Lean stories ever since.

"Any intellectual questioning made Lean highly nervous," she recalls. "You could actually see him twitch. Lean was a dummy at school, and he really had a phobia, a hang-up about his intelligence. When I worked with him, he was older and he didn't have the energy he needed. It was like cranking an old car, and he just couldn't do it. The film doesn't finally have any power.

"There was a touch of the bully about him—he'd take it out on the people who were weakest and most dependent. That meant [his wife] Sandy. She would come up and say, 'David, do you need anything?' If Lean got into a bad mood, which he did with regularity, he'd take it out on her. You could kind of judge what kind of mood he was in by his hand gestures toward her. If he was in a bad mood, he'd make a big hand gesture—she'd get out of his way. It was pretty disturbing to witness.

"Lean had been married to an Indian woman who played the sitar. Consequently, the sitar drove him crazy. Whenever a sitar was being played in a restaurant, he says"—Davis's voice, suddenly all proper and British, falls into a husky whisper—"'Shut that thing up.' One of his wives tried to knife him in bed, tried to put it through his throat. After seven months, I could relate to it. But there was something irresistible about him too."

The fireworks on the set by no means compromised her performance, and she was nominated for an Academy Award for Best Actress.

In 1987 she reteamed with Armstrong for *High Tide*, which many people regard as her best performance. She enjoyed the experience; it allowed her to write and improvise for the first time. Four years later she played French novelist George Sand in *Impromptu*, the movie debut of theater director James Lapine. "When we met," Lapine recalls, "she sat there for an hour, bad-mouthing every director she'd ever worked with." *Impromptu* called for Davis to play a passionate and sexually omnivorous woman. Once again she did a brilliant job; once again she complained about the movie. "She always complains about the writing," continues Lapine. "Judy's smart, and particularly when you do a historically based piece, she's gonna go and read everything she can about it, and she would have done it differently, no doubt."

Davis is very particular about her look, and Lapine claims "hair and makeup became this great, great issue. She likes a certain complexion—chalky. Our big problem was that she was playing opposite Chopin [Hugh Grant], who was supposed to look like a white, chalky sick person. So it would have been weird if she looked more pale than him.

"God knows, she gave us a lot of grief about certain scenes, like the big scene at the end of the movie when she and Chopin actually make love. Judy has a hard time saying things like 'I love you.' I said to her, 'Judy, do you tell your husband that you love him?' She said, half joking, 'No. Only my child and my dog.' She's a twisted human being." Lapine laughs. "She's not easy, and I'm sure a lot of people—in L.A., in particular—they want easy. It doesn't bother me. She delivers the goods, and that's really the bottom line."

After *Impromptu*, Davis plunged into *Naked Lunch*, a typically bent David Cronenberg film, where she worked with Peter Weller for the first time. "I hardly know her, and the second day, we gotta do this fucking scene, man. I gotta kiss her, plus we gotta be stoned, and all these other circumstances that *Naked Lunch* had laid on us—talking about cops, and being busted. But the thing is, she's really sexy and she charmed me. She's, like, this fabulous kisser, man. She's like a cushion of clouds. David and I are car freaks. I turned to him and said, 'Judy's like a Ferrari, man. You just crank it up, sit in it, and it just goes.' "

Davis played a small but vivid role in the Coen brothers' *Barton Fink*, and then stole Woody Allen's *Husbands and Wives* from an accomplished cast that included Liam Neeson, Mia Farrow, Juliette Lewis, and Sydney Pollack. "I had seen her in a few things," says Allen. "*My Brilliant Career, High Tide*. And I thought that she was one of the most exciting actresses in the world. She plays comedy, she plays drama, she projects intelligence, she's sexy. There's nothing that you could want that isn't there."

Lapine says Davis told him she enjoyed working with Allen—most likely because he left her alone: "That's what I think she wants. Ultimately, she'd like to show up, do what she does, and leave. I don't think she's interested in direction." The film earned her a second Oscar nomination.

The Ref, a Disney comedy with Kevin Spacey and Denis Leary, directed by Ted Demme, Jonathan's nephew, was an unlikely project

283

to attract Davis on the face of it, and the principals were surprised she agreed to do it. Most likely she was mainstreaming herself, although she has a genuine flair for comedy and liked the dark script, by Richard LaGravenese and Marie Weiss.

But *The Ref* got off to a wobbly start. Demme was virtually a first-time director, with a difficult star who was, to some extent, slumming. "There was kind of a snotty attitude going on," says a source from the production. "She said something in public that was embarrassing, because she was angry about other stuff. Ted is a regular guy, he's not a game player. At one point he said to her, 'Listen, we're all good people here. I don't want this bad feeling, so if you've got a problem—talk to me.' After that she was fine. You have to earn her trust and respect. She's like an abused child."

Another source close to the production says, "She's edgy, she tests the waters all the time. She tested it with Ted. She liked him, liked the movie. If she doesn't like the director, she could just kill you."

Davis almost killed George Sluizer, or he almost killed her, depending on who's talking. The plot of *Dark Blood* oddly resembles the plot of *The Ref* (and *The New Age* as well), a darker version of a comedy that was already fairly bleak: a married woman trapped in a triangle. If Davis's relationship with Sluizer was strained during preproduction, it snapped altogether when filming began in Torrey, Utah, by all accounts a difficult, even dangerous location. Everything was a struggle, from the nude scenes (predictably sensitive) to simple exteriors. Davis says she made it clear to the director that she needed to wear a hat to protect her skin, which is quite pale, if they shot in the desert. His reaction, as she remembers it: " 'Yes, yes, yes, yes.' " She was emphatic: " 'I just need that to be understood, so when we get out there you're not complaining about the fact that I'm wearing a hat, and if that's a problem you should say it.' 'Naw, naw, naw.' They scheduled this particular scene for mid-afternoon, when it was drenched in sun. It was maybe 9,000 feet. In the summer. So, okay, I can angle my chair to the sun so I'm protected."

Sluizer is Dutch. With her preternatural gift for accents, Davis mimics him with harsh, guttural growls and barks. " 'Naw, naw, tiss chair has *tiss* vay to be.' Then Ed Lachman, the DP, said, 'Don't worry about the sun; we're gonna scrim it, it's so harsh anyway.' So they build the biggest scrim I've ever seen in my life. As big as this room. The director started screaming and ranting and raving: 'Naw, naw. You are deestroyink my shot! Tees ees exactly vehr the cahmera hahf to go.' What the camera was going to do was come out the doorway past me, and there was this huge scrim in the way. If the guy just explained what he was doing, they wouldn't have gone to the trouble of making the scrim.

"So they took the scrim away, and I'm again left there in the sun. I went and got my hat. I said, 'I don't want to get cancer because of your film. I did let you know this, and I feel I shouldn't be in a position where I have to point it out to you in front of all these people.' He's bobbing up and down, and I said, 'Excuse me, George, would you mind not bobbing up and down, because it's very distracting.' He found that terribly cutting, to be told that he was a distraction. Which he was. He stormed off the set to write memos. He spent a lot of time writing memos."

"Judy is a very good actress," says Sluizer. "But she's not that easy to direct. Sometimes actors infringe on the movie. It's happened with Dustin Hoffman with some films, where he pulls the covers, everything to himself, and then other people might disappear behind the actor."

Sluizer seems to admire her despite himself. "There is a lot of energy, a kind of intensity that is fascinating. She's there. You just say 'camera,' and there's another person than the one you saw five seconds before." Would he use Davis again? "That would be quite difficult, because it has stressed me quite a lot," he says. "Obviously, when you've had problems, you're not going to be a fool—if I have a stomachache, I'm not going to take the worst foods. But once my stomach is better, I might take another of whatever it was that made me bad. I'm not saying it could never happen. I don't grudge."

"It's important to know what your strengths are," says Davis. "I absolutely believe in my intuition; I think that's a great asset to an actor. The weaknesses in my personality are impatience and sometimes intolerance. Which came out with this guy George. I was very quickly, utterly intolerant of him. I decided that he was dangerous, and kept away from him."

• • •

The New Age preceded *Dark Blood* and was a far happier set. It was written and directed by Michael Tolkin, and feels like a cross between *The Rapture,* Tolkin's directing debut, and *The Player,* which he wrote. "After *The Rapture,* I wanted to bring it back home," says Tolkin. "I felt there was enough going on in L.A. that had been avoided, ignored, or overlooked."

Explains Nick Wechsler, who produced *The Rapture,* "Michael and I have talked about doing a movie that would look at a certain element of L.A. society in the same way that Fellini looked at Italian society by doing *La Dolce Vita* in the '50s. When we were in Cannes, we spent every day talking about this movie, and we were hanging out with Peter Weller, so it was natural for us to shape the lead character around Peter's character—very charming, very smart, maybe follows his dick too much."

In *The New Age,* Weller plays an out-of-work agent who opens a clothing shop on Melrose with his wife and explores various New Age remedies. "Almost everybody I know is involved with some kind of religious quest," says Tolkin, "whether somebody does yoga, or somebody joins a synagogue, or goes to church, or meditates, or channels." Perhaps. But it's hard to generate much sympathy for an out-of-work agent whose crystal breaks. If the film is going to work, the characters' pain has got to cut through the sociology.

"Judy has been a hero of mine," Tolkin says. "She's the patron saint of modern emotions. One of the great things about her is that unlike most American actors she's not interested in playing characters that are likable. I have very uncomplicated feelings about her. She's the real thing; she's an artist. She pops. Judy Davis is a genius."

Like Sluizer, Weller is struck by Davis's "there-ness": "There are really charismatic and captivating people who stand in front of a camera and act their ass off, but it's like the difference between a great director and a great shooter," he says. "Some guys can shoot the shit out of a rnovie, but the story isn't present. And some actors, and maybe me too sometimes, can act the shit out of a scene, but the event isn't present—the feelings aren't there. She's always going for the guts of the scene, the reality of the thing. It's really a gift, man. She owns her own beauty somehow. It's the old Buddhist notion: Whatever you own becomes your own. The gift of living is being who you are and not aspiring to anybody else, and I think that's her magic." The irony, of course, is that Davis is also uncomfortable in her own skin—she's antsy, dissatisfied, and that's where the tension comes from, and her peculiar modern- or postmodernness. That, and her clarity (or coldness, depending on your opinion of it) and her lack of illusions.

Illusions, for example, about her *Dark Blood* costar River Phoenix. Although she cared for Phoenix, she refused to give herself up to the tears and lamentation that greeted his death. "The Monday after River died we all went on the set and we were asked to form a large circle," she recalls. "George gave his speech about River—it was true what he said, he was a lovely boy. And then Jonathan Pryce asked us to join hands and wish River's spirit a happy journey as it went across the . . . And I felt very uncomfortable with all that. I didn't want to hold hands, I don't believe in spirits passing. But I didn't have a choice, so I wished that I'd not gone to the studio. I don't like to be forced to be dishonest. I think it has to be remembered, in the midst of all this, that he was twenty-three and he made the choice. He thought he was immune, I think. There's something about stardom and the way it empowers people, the way people give these stars such power."

287

Judy Davis is a paradox: a brilliant actress with a not-so-brilliant career. A world-class talent who prefers, perhaps, to be a big fish in small movies. Sharply intelligent, yet shy and insecure, a wallflower at Hollywood parties. "To be perfectly honest, I don't know that she has her pick of projects," says Lapine. "She's not part of the circle. She doesn't live out there, play that game, and I don't think she would do a lot of crap. I wish Judy were more politic, because she's biting off her nose to spite her face. She's making herself into an art-house star. But on the other hand, maybe that's what she wants."

Peter Weller is standing amid his guests near the swimming pool behind the Beverly Hills home rented for *The New Age*. He is wearing a black shirt and an ugly tie covered with explosions of pink—perhaps flowers, perhaps nebulae—in any event, not a promising accessory for someone intending to open a hip clothing shop. Davis, fetching in a slinky black dress with spaghetti straps, chews her lip as she watches him flirt with an attractive blond. "Someone's knocking or something," says Tolkin, who's wearing an ankle-length overcoat in the mild April weather and looks like a character out of *Crime and Punishment*. "Can we cut?" says Davis. "I screwed up my lines." She says them again—perfectly, with a slightly different inflection, changing the meaning ever so subtly. Tolkin is pleased.

THE MAN WHO
MINTED STYLE

Orson Welles once said, "The two men who ruined the movies were Irving Thalberg and Charlie Feldman." Irving Thalberg, O.K.—the legendary MGM wunderkind had directors picking up his laundry during his reign as the studio's head of production in the 1920s and '30s. But Charlie Feldman?

Unless you're James Dean or Marilyn Monroe, dying prematurely is a bad career move in Hollywood. Feldman died at sixty-three in 1968, still in his prime, and today if you drop his name all you get is a blank dead-fish look. Except with people of a certain age, who remember him vividly as one of those bigger-than-life Hollywood characters verging on mythical, the man Louis B. Mayer, the industry's boss of bosses, tried to destroy and couldn't. As an agent, Feldman ruled the talent market for three decades, from the mid-'30s through the early '60s, representing three hundred or so of the biggest stars and directors in Hollywood, not only flameouts like Dean and Monroe, or dropouts like Greta Garbo, but lifers such as Marlene Dietrich, Claudette Colbert, Irene Dunne, John Wayne, William Holden, Gary Cooper, Kirk Douglas, Susan Hayward, Lana Turner, Rita Hayworth, Tyrone Power, and Lauren Bacall. When a mogul such as Twentieth Century Fox head Darryl Zanuck needed representation himself, he went to Feldman. Or when producer David O. Selznick wanted an agent for his wife, Jennifer Jones, he went to Feldman and begged him to represent her. Feldman's agency, Famous Artists, in its day was far and away the most powerful motion-picture agency in town. No surprise, then, that Feldman was a firm believer in the star system, once observing, "No one ever heard of Aly Khan until he married Rita Hayworth, and no one ever heard of Prince Rainier until he married Grace Kelly."

But Feldman's story is not just another stardusted exercise in nostalgia, for the simple reason that the changes he wrought in the business of moviemaking were so far-reaching that it is not an exaggeration to call him one of the principal architects of today's Hollywood. For better or for worse, he developed the concept of packaging, whereby an agent puts together the elements of a film— stars, director, writer—from his client list, ties them up with a bright-red ribbon, and sells the whole thing to some studio executive too lazy or dumb to develop projects himself. Feldman also broke the studio contract system, whereby actors were held in virtual servitude—albeit well-rewarded servitude—for seven-year terms, forced to take whatever piece of dreck they were assigned. Instead, Feldman made the majors pay his talent on a picture-by-picture basis; so when Tom Hanks and Tom Cruise receive their $25 million paychecks, they have Feldman to thank. And still he managed to play croquet every weekend with Zanuck (he was the only agent Zanuck would deal with personally) and be bosom buddies with Jack Warner and Sam Goldwyn.

Feldman was also a producer—not an agent first and then a producer, but for much of his career an agent and producer at the same time, because he was one of the first agents who managed to sweet-talk the Screen Actors Guild into waiving the conflict-of-interest rule that to this day prevents agents from also producing. Feldman made countless movies, from serious dramas such as *A Streetcar Named Desire* to mainstream comedy hits such as *The Seven Year Itch* and everything in between. He partnered with Howard Hawks, co-producing and packaging many of the director's most enduring films, including *Red River* and the great Bogart-Bacall pairings, *To Have and Have Not* and *The Big Sleep*.

He had a real genius for discovering talent—not only Montgomery Clift and Marlon Brando, but Jane Fonda and Woody Allen. In 1950, *Life* magazine called him a "one-man major."

So Welles was right to yoke Feldman with Thalberg. Welles was speaking as an auteur, of course, and in Feldman he recognized another, albeit of a different sort. By driving up star salaries and then stuffing these stars into packages the studios couldn't refuse, the agent was stacking the deck against directors, who in most cases were already little more than errand boys. The room wasn't big enough for Welles and Feldman, who produced one of Welles's lesser films, *Macbeth,* and supported the actor-director in his declining years by employing him to ornament his last, wildest production, 1967's *Casino Royale.*

"Charlie had all the qualities of a movie star," says David Picker, head of production at United Artists from 1969 to 1973. "He had the charm and the style." Off-camera, he defined "debonair" as much as Cary Grant defined it on; and with his first wife, actress Jean Howard, Feldman helped set the standard for Hollywood glamour during the glamorous '30s. He was movie-star handsome and wore a pencil-thin mustache that made him look like a Jewish Clark Gable. In fact, Loretta Young used to call him "Gabe." A prodigious womanizer, he was romantically involved with Garbo, Hayworth, Hedy Lamarr, Joan Fontaine, Olivia de Havilland, Ava Gardner, and many others. "Women loved him," says his widow, the former Clotilde Barot. "He was very kind, made a woman feel terrific. He liked actresses and models, and his taste in girls was very good. He was a big, big charmer, but you wanted to protect him."

Feldman was the last of the playboy producers, the men-about-town with the voracious appetite for life, the Bentleys in the garages, the French art on the walls, the starlets on the arm and in the bed. He bought handmade suits by the carload from an exclusive Beverly Hills tailor in only two colors, blue and gray, and owned three hundred ties from Sulka, all identical, dull blue and red stripes. (He had sets of identical clothes wherever he had a home, in New York, Los Angeles, London, Paris, and his friends always envied him for being able to travel without baggage.) He partied with Jack Kennedy when the future president was still a pisher, and had done business with his dad before that. As Samuel Goldwyn once put it, "He could charm you off your feet. When you left Charlie you're lucky if you still have your pants left."

By the end, though, Feldman's career had dipped into self-parody. As Richard Burton's agent, he was right in the middle of the *Cleopatra* catastrophe, and *Casino Royale* was a mess, too, with four credited directors and twelve screenwriters. Feldman came to represent, fairly or not, everything that was wrong with the industry in the '60s, everything that the New Hollywood directors of the following decade rebelled against: the decadence, the artificiality, the void at the heart of it all. But by then Feldman was gone. And even though he was taken, painfully, before his time, and even though his death tore a hole in the fabric of his circle, there was something appropriate about it. His era had ended.

Charles K. Feldman was one of those self-invented people Hollywood loves. All manner of fanciful tales swirl around his origins, shrouded in the mists of time. Feldman himself seemed to encourage the confusion. His birthplace has been variously given as London, New York, and Bayonne, New Jersey, and he sometimes said that his family name was Gould, although it was indisputably Gold. His father, Isaac, had been in the diamond business in London and possibly South Africa before he and his family immigrated to America and ended up for reasons unknown in Bayonne. Gold and his wife, Eva, had seven children, five boys and two girls. Feldman fell in the middle, the third-youngest. Most sources put his birth on April 26, 1905 or 1906, but Warren Beatty, who was a close friend, and the late production designer Richard Sylbert, also a friend, who once got a look at Feldman's passport, think he was born earlier, perhaps 1900 or 1901. Eva died of cancer in 1910, and Isaac followed three years later, a victim of the same disease.

Most of the children were adopted out to other families; at least one grew up in an institution. Lenette, Charlie's younger sister, was taken in by a family named Feldman in Bayonne and persuaded friends—bizarrely, another, unrelated Feldman family—to adopt Charlie. In a slightly different version of the story—as Jean Howard later wrote, perhaps apocryphally—the Gold children were taken to Samuel Feldman's furniture store. Feldman couldn't decide which child to adopt, so he told them to run the length of the showroom floor toward his outstretched arms; he would take the one who got there first, which, providentially for him, was young Charlie, despite the fact that he tripped over a pile of rugs and a chaise longue. Charlie was about seven, or perhaps as old as thirteen. According to Lenette's daughter Rhoda Krawitz, "My mother would walk along the street and see Charlie, but she was forbidden to say hello to him because she was supposed to be loyal to her adoptive family."

Charlie's Feldman family eventually moved their furniture business to Los Angeles, where it prospered. Charlie would work his way through the University of Southern California law school delivering mail. He set himself up in practice in 1928, occupying a cubbyhole in the Taft Building on the corner of Hollywood and Vine, then the Times Square of Hollywood, near the fabled Brown Derby, where he hung out with a claque of small-time agents who occasionally threw business his way. One of them threw him Edward G. Robinson, for whom Feldman negotiated a three-year, $1 million deal, of which he collected $5,000. "That's good pay for a lawyer," he later explained to an interviewer, doing the arithmetic. "But if I were that guy's agent, not merely his lawyer, I'd have been good for $100,000." At that moment the lightbulb went on: Feldman became an agent. His friends were horrified, and one of them admonished him, "Charlie, you sweated five years for that law degree. Now you want to give it up for a business where you don't even have to know how to read?" Undaunted, Feldman formed an agency in 1932 with Ad Schulberg, former wife of Paramount chief B. P. Schulberg. Their first clients were Claudette Colbert, Charles Boyer, and Dick and Joan Bennett.

It was the depths of the Depression, but you'd have never known it in Hollywood, where the Beverly Wilshire Hotel was holding regular tea dances from four to seven on weekends. One of the regulars was Jean Howard, then twenty-three. Formerly Ernestine Hill, Howard was a tall, willowy blonde who had modeled as a teenager and made it out to Hollywood from Longview, Texas, in the late '20s, becoming a Ziegfeld girl in time for the final filmed Follies in 1931. Howard was hard to miss, and Feldman, who was in attendance at the Beverly Wilshire one evening in

293

1933, was struck by Cupid's arrow. He subsequently plied her with candy and flowers, followed by a note, dated simply, with no eye for history, "1933." It read, "Dear Miss Howard—I saw you last night dancing at the Beverly Wilshire. Have something on my mind which I would like to discuss with you. Its (sic) so very very important. I will call you later. Say at six and I do hope you will see me. Incidentally you're lovely—Charlie Feldman." She asked someone who he was and was told he was an agent. In those days, agents were widely regarded as pond scum, so Howard imagined Feldman as a fast-talking, "unattractive little guy" and failed to reply. But the flowers and candy kept coming, and she started to think that he was, in her words, "some kind of nut."

Then one night a friend invited her to a party, where Howard sank into a sofa that gave her a view of the room. Suddenly, a man entered, and Howard thought, as she later put it, "That's the best looking man I have ever seen."

Feldman was of no more than medium height, but he was broad across the shoulders and immaculately attired, with a perpetual tan and a head of dark hair neatly combed in a wave to the left over a broad forehead. He had long curly lashes and eyes that were a surprising blue, and, of course, the dashing pencil-thin mustache. Howard turned to the man seated next to her, who happened to be Mervyn LeRoy, the director, and asked, "Who's that guy?" LeRoy answered, "Charlie Feldman." Feldman had spotted her too, and walked over. LeRoy introduced him: "Charlie, meet this beautiful girl, she's just out from New York. This is . . . Jean Howard." Feldman interrupted, "You're very rude, Miss Howard. You never answer my messages." Recalled Howard, many years later, "I apologized awkwardly. I was a nervous wreck, for in all my twenty-three years I had never felt the way I did when I first met Charlie. It was love at first sight."

There was only one problem. Louis B. Mayer, the all-powerful, very married head of MGM, was infatuated with Howard and was courting her energetically. She always denied they had had sex—not that she would have refused had he asked, she said later, but he never did. "He did nothing but talk all the time," she complained. She had begun seeing Feldman, but when she realized that, despite the candy and flowers, he was living with a hot

Mexican number named Raquel Torres, she became furious and accepted Mayer's invitation to rendezvous in Paris, where he was vacationing in the summer of 1934. No sooner had Howard gotten comfortable in her room at the George V hotel than Mayer summoned her to his suite. As she remembered it, "He was standing there with a lot of white papers, trembling and screaming, 'How could you do this to me?'" The papers—reports from the detective he had hired to follow her in Hollywood—detailed her meetings with Feldman. According to Howard, Mayer tried to throw himself from a fifth-floor balcony and broke the thumb of his P.R. wizard, Howard Strickland, in the ensuing tussle.

Hearing from Howard that Mayer was threatening to end his life because of their affair, Feldman was reputed to have exclaimed, "Good! Let's get married right away!" They did, more or less. The couple threw a wedding dinner at the Colony Restaurant in New York City on the night of August 24, and then got married at midnight in the Westchester town of Harrison.

295

Mayer subsequently refused to do business with Feldman, barred him and his clients from the MGM lot, and tried to blackball him at the other studios. But Feldman was close to Harry Cohn, the pugnacious head of Columbia Pictures. One day Cohn offered to help Feldman mend fences with Mayer. According to Howard, Cohn told Feldman, "Listen, you silly son of a bitch, you've got to say you're sorry you stole this lovely girl, and you've got to cry if you possibly can." (Mayer was a great sentimentalist.) Cohn and Feldman then drove the eight miles from the Columbia lot in Hollywood to Mayer's Culver City office in an open car in hopes that the breeze would make the agent's eyes tear. The story is picked up by Warren Beatty: "He and Mayer exchanged pleasantries, and then Charlie said, 'You're a son of a bitch,' and they got into a fistfight and ended up thrashing about on the floor of his office."

Despite his feud with Mayer, Feldman's agency managed to survive. The contract system, one of the pillars of the business, was a cozy arrangement not just for the studios but for the agents as well because it required of them little more than sitting behind their desks and watching their 10 percent roll in every year, like an annuity. But Feldman realized that his clients (and consequently he himself) could do much better charging by the picture. Irene

Dunne, for example, was making $1,500 per week, or $60,000 a year, at RKO. (The contract year consisted of forty weeks.) When her contract was up in 1935, Feldman refused to renew it. Instead, he demanded $150,000 a picture. Her first movie under this setup was Magnificent Obsession, directed by John Stahl, also a client. Claudette Colbert was getting $2,500 a week at Paramount. Feldman learned of a script at Columbia that had been turned down by several actresses—It Happened One Night. The studio was keen to fill the part, and when Colbert's contract at Paramount expired in 1934, Feldman demanded that Columbia pay her $150,000 for the picture—whose total budget was only $325,000—and got it.

Mayer's freeze-out of Feldman at MGM probably would have gone on indefinitely had it not been for the fact that in 1936 the studio's brightest star, Garbo, demanded that Charles Boyer play Napoleon to her Josephine in a picture called Conquest. Boyer had been a Feldman client from the beginning. According to the agent, by way of former United Artists executive David Chasman (who became friendly with Feldman in the '60s when Feldman produced What's New, Pussycat? for the company), Mayer summoned Thalberg to his office. Apparently still enraged by Jean Howard's perfidy, the little man was apoplectic. "I won't see him! I don't want that son of a bitch Feldman on the lot!" he bellowed.

"Louis, you don't have to meet with him," replied Thalberg, mildly. "I'll handle it." Feldman drove onto the MGM lot for the first time in years and made his way to Thalberg's office, where the great man kept him waiting for twenty minutes. "What are you getting for Boyer these days?" the head of production inquired once the amenities had been disposed of. Boyer was under contract to independent producer Walter Wanger, and Feldman replied, "His last deal with Wanger was $25,000 for ten weeks."

"This is an MGM picture! A lead opposite Garbo! You'll have to go a lot lower than that."

"Wait a minute. You asked me what I'm getting for Boyer, and that's what I'm getting, $25,000 for ten. But if you're asking what we want for this picture—it's $125,000 for eight weeks!"

"Louis was right!" yelled Thalberg. "Get off the lot!" Feldman left, but Garbo remained adamant, and Boyer got his money.

Feldman also included a clause that required the studio to compensate Boyer if the picture ran over, which it did. Boyer walked away with something close to 450,000 of Mayer's dollars, of which Feldman collected $45,000.

Feldman had put a lot of mileage between himself and his six biological siblings. As he confessed to a friend, "You know the feelings I have for any of my kin—which is nil." But they hadn't forgotten him, and often intruded with letters or cables imploring him to send money because they were sick or had been fired yet again, poignant reminders of the real lives in Depression-era America beyond the confines of Beverly Hills. Despite his distaste, he sent them money over the years, even put his brother Joe (whom he disliked intensely) on a monthly stipend, concealing the source of the income from him. He also sent his old clothes to his brothers.

During the war, Feldman rolled up his sleeves and plunged in. Among other duties, in 1942 he headed up the talent committee of the Hollywood Victory Caravan for Army and Navy Relief, which sent a dazzling array of stars on an unprecedented cross-country train tour. But Feldman kept his eye on his business. He was a bold and innovative strategist, and defying the contract system was only the beginning. He couldn't help noticing that the writers, directors, and producers he represented constantly needed work. Moreover, the careers of some of the actors who should have been working were in the doldrums. Marlene Dietrich seemed to be past her prime; John Wayne looked as if he'd never be able to climb out of shoot-'em-up programmers; ditto for Randolph Scott. Feldman realized that if he attached several of his clients to the same property he could sell them all at once. So sometime toward the end of the '30s, he started buying the rights to various short stories, novels, and plays.

"I didn't go into competition with the studios," he explained. "I just bought what they didn't want or had passed up. I would wrap a story up, then stick an important name on the label, usually the name of a star or a top director. The rest was easy. No producer in his right mind would turn down a deal like that." In 1942, for instance, Feldman put in motion the fourth remake of *The Spoilers,* a Klondike saga dating from the silent era. He hired a screenwriter, cast Dietrich, Scott, and Wayne, and, exploiting what remained of Dietrich's glamour, sold the whole ball of wax to

Universal. He collected 10 percent for each of the three leads, more for the screenplay. It worked like a charm, because everyone benefited. The clients got work, Feldman got his fees, and the studio got a ready-made movie.

When Feldman spotted a new face, he would put him or her under personal contract, paying a modest stipend. He nurtured their careers until he was able to sell their contracts to the studios, while retaining them as clients. He also quickly realized that, if he was going to buy properties, attach his clients, and sell the packages to the studios, he might as well take producing fees and credits as well. In 1939 the Screen Actors Guild granted him a waiver from its conflict-of-interest rule. In exchange, he agreed to relinquish his 10 percent cut from clients who appeared in pictures he produced. In 1942 he took the cast of *The Spoilers,* put them in a film with the unlikely title *Pittsburgh,* and produced it under the banner of Charles K. Feldman Group Productions. The picture disappeared without a trace, but as a business model it was brilliant.

On August 27, 1942, Feldman paid $18,000 for a sprawling Spanish-style home with whitewashed walls and a red tile roof at 2000 Coldwater Canyon. The house was decorated in signature chinois style by Billy Haines, a silent-film star turned must-have decorator for Hollywood gentry. He and Howard filled the house with the Regency and Chippendale furniture that were all the rage. The walls were painted a muted sea green, the rooms filled with unusual objéts—Oriental figures, pre-Columbian stone artifacts, tortoiseshell pedestals, and Chinese porcelain lamps—that Feldman had begun to collect in 1936 when Colbert asked him to pick up a Degas drawing for her during the course of his first trip to Europe. Feldman got the bug himself. He even tried his hand at painting.

When the war ended, Feldman began collecting in earnest. He bought nineteenth- and early-twentieth-century paintings—a Dufy, Vuillards, Bonnards. In the living room, over a fireplace that was framed by mirrored panels arranged like tiles, hung a Modigliani. He also had pieces by Renoir, Utrillo, Vlaminck, Rodin, and de Chirico, too many to hang. Feldman would even buy paintings sight unseen by the gross, like potatoes, the overflow canvases stacked in the furnace room, among them an Orozco and some Bernard

Buffets. One night he invited his dinner guests down to the cellar and casually gave away artworks as if they were party favors.

Feldman hated to go to the office. Casually dressed in a cardigan, he typically worked on the patio overlooking his pool, eating crackers dipped in honey, avoiding calls from his clients. When it couldn't be helped, he met with them at the house, soothed them in his quiet, reasonable voice, stroking egos, flattering, cajoling. He had a good sense of humor that not only made him fun to be around but also allowed him to defuse crises and get away with outrageous behavior. As often as not, he was the butt of his own stories. As David Chasman recalls Feldman's tales, "At gambling Charlie never won, in business Charlie never came out ahead, in romance Charlie never got laid." He loved to say that Marilyn Monroe, Rita Hayworth, and Lana Turner all fired him on the same day.

The agent was a firm believer in the principle that business is pleasure and vice versa, which meant that if he went to the office at all he didn't do so until the afternoon, when he might spend a couple of hours on the phone before meeting a friend for a drink, then dining at Romanoff's, and finally going off for a few hands of gin rummy. At one point in the '50s, when Twentieth Century Fox was in play, he and agent Irving "Swifty" Lazar contemplated making a run at it. Feldman asked Lazar, "What time do you get up?"

"Around 11:30, 12. What about you?"

"About the same." There was a pause, and then Feldman said, "I guess we should forget about Fox. Who's going to run it in the mornings?"

Feldman had met Howard Hawks through Hawks's brother Bill, an agent, and they became friendly. In 1940, Bill Hawks exited the agency business to become a producer, freeing his brother to become Feldman's client. Feldman immediately got him what a Hawks biographer calls "a ludicrous amount" to direct *Sergeant York* with Gary Cooper at Warner Bros., and then $100,000 from the Samuel Goldwyn Company for *Ball of Fire*, also with Cooper. In 1943, Feldman and Hawks went into business together as H-F Productions, with the notion of buying properties that they could convert into scripts and then sell to the studios. They produced *To Have and Have Not*, pairing Humphrey Bogart with Lauren Bacall.

It was her first film. Slim Keith, Hawks's wife, had noticed a model on the cover of *Harper's Bazaar* and brought the girl to her husband's attention. Hawks lit up and asked Feldman to bring her out from New York for a test. Betty Bacal (Feldman later gave her last name its second l) arrived at Union Station on April 6. The agent put her up at the Claremont Hotel in Westwood and took her out to dinner that night. He wanted to get her teeth fixed, but Hawks said no, preferring a natural look. According to composer Earl Robinson, a friend of Feldman's, "Charlie was sweet on Betty. He was trying to make her and she resisted him." Jean Howard flatly denied it, saying, oddly, "Betty, really, wasn't his type. She was a little too . . . Jewish. I don't like to say that, he didn't have a prejudice against them, but I know that he never had affairs with them."

For the second Bogart-Bacall pairing, Feldman and Hawks bought Raymond Chandler's novel *The Big Sleep* for $20,000, with an agreement that Warner Bros. would pay $55,000 for the literary rights and a screenplay. Feldman's creativity wasn't limited to dealmaking: when filming on *The Big Sleep* was completed, he persuaded Jack Warner to punch up the Bogart-Bacall relationship with three or four new scenes between the two conveying "the insolent and provocative nature" Bacall had exhibited in *To Have and Have Not.* They hired Philip Epstein, co-author of *Casablanca,* to write the film's double-entendre scenes, which would become famous.

Feldman's marriage to Jean Howard was not a happy one. He discouraged her from working, and although she picked up photography as a hobby, she was bored playing the Hollywood hostess. Worse, Feldman, who always had one eye cocked for the errant skirt, had cheated on her from the time he met her. (He once took Garbo out, and when they arrived back at her home, he put his foot in the door. According to his widow, Clotilde Barot, Garbo said something like "You can come in, but you're not going to like it." And he didn't.)

One evening, an epic fight took place after one of Charlie and Jean's famous parties. According to a 1991 *Vanity Fair* profile of Howard written by Ben Brantley, she had "danced twice that night with the same, good-looking man, and when the party was over, Charlie Feldman was, as usual, crazy jealous. When he started to hit her, in her bedroom, she reached for a gold cigarette box-the long kind . . . that could hold four packs—closed her eyes, and swung. When she opened her eyes, there was blood on her dress, blood on the walls, and her husband had fallen backwards—dead, she thought." He wasn't, and when he recovered, she told him, "Something awful will happen one day, Charlie. Either you'll kill me, or I'll kill you."

Neither did kill the other, but the marriage was dead. The couple slept in different bedrooms and separated several times as a result of his liaisons. Feldman continued to shower her with expensive gifts, but was rarely home. "Jean wanted to be married to a husband, not a bank account," said a friend. Howard got pregnant in the mid-'40s. According to her, Feldman's response was "We shouldn't have a child. I've just reached the point where I'm doing very well. We can afford to travel, we can do all these things." She lost it: "Listen, you son of a bitch, I'm going to have this baby, and you'll never see it." But Howard miscarried, and she later said this was the moment she decided to get a divorce, although in an interview with Howard Hawks's biographer Todd McCarthy she claimed the casus belli was Feldman's affair with a twenty-one-year-old starlet named Ella Raines, who had been passed on to Feldman by Hawks after the director's own ardor for her had cooled.

In any event, on December 3, 1946, the couple divorced in Las Vegas. Howard once said she "wanted to be the other woman in his life," and now she had her chance. As soon as they split up, they became closer, regaining some of their early intimacy. In the *Los Angeles Times*, an anonymous source referred to Feldman and Howard's arrangement as their "can't live with you, can't live without you postmarital relationship." Howard got the house in Coldwater Canyon, but Feldman kept the right to use it when she was away. The arrangement worked out well because both traveled extensively.

Although Feldman's tastes were catholic, he liked to think of himself as a quality producer. He shunned standard commercial fare, what he referred to as "groceries." In 1947 he purchased the rights to Tennessee Williams's play *The Glass Menagerie* for $150,000. Everyone in Hollywood believed that Williams was box-office poison, but Feldman then turned around and bought the playwright's *A Streetcar Named Desire* for $350,000.

Although it had been a huge hit on Broadway, it was widely regarded as unfilmable—the play's adultery, rape, and prostitution made it nearly impossible to put on the screen in the repressive climate of the early '50s. Undeterred, Feldman set it up with his pal Jack Warner, with Marlon Brando reprising the role of Stanley Kowalski and Elia Kazan directing, as he had on the stage.

Though Kazan, who had cultivated the image of a tough guy from the New York T-shirt school of filmmaking, didn't seem to much like Feldman, those feelings didn't stop Kazan from availing himself of the producer's hospitality when Kazan traveled to L.A. in 1951. He then scrutinized the mores of the Beverly Hills natives as if they had been Trobriand islanders. "In the next weeks, I had a fascinating time observing my producer and through him the men in this community," he would write in his extraordinary autobiography.

Charlie was . . . rather handsome in a soft, yielding way, his body suited to bed and armchair. He ran a successful agency, and this gave him prestige in the community and power over young actresses. Still he was full of complaints about his love life—if you can call it that. "Now it's Uncle Charlie," he griped, referring to the response young women were increasingly giving him. "I say, 'How about me?' and they laugh. There just aren't any real women anymore. High school girls!" He would spend long hours on the telephone, holding a little black book in his hand, trying number after number . . .

Often Charlie would have a date, and they were quite pretty girls, usually recent arrivals in the community. Charlie would ask them to come to his house in their own cars, so he wouldn't have to drive them home later, and they'd go out together to Romanoff's or Chasen's, always one or the other, and when they came back I had to assume they went into Charlie's bedroom. The next morning I'd say to my host at breakfast, "How was she, Charlie?" And his answer was invariably one word: "Nothing." He once had taken out Greta Garbo; he dropped this to me one day, and of course I asked him, "How was she, Charlie?" "Nothing," he said. "Nothing!" And he shrugged. I couldn't imagine what the hell he was used to, and I never heard him take any responsibility for his sexual partners' lack of ardor. It didn't occur to him that the fault might be his.

Kazan apparently didn't know then what we now know about Garbo, or perhaps he wouldn't have been so disdainful of Feldman's charms.

By the late '40s, Feldman's Famous Artists Corporation was the preeminent agency in motion pictures, rivaled only by William Morris and MCA, which were stronger in areas such as music and television. (MCA, led by Lew Wasserman and Jules Stein, would eventually buy Universal and be forced out of the agency business altogether.) Feldman, however, concentrated strictly on film, and as the decade turned he was still adding clients, including actors such as Richard Burton, Ava Gardner, Ida Lupino, Dana Andrews, Ingrid Bergman, James Mason, and Dick Powell. He also represented forty major directors, including Preston Sturges, George Stevens, Otto Preminger, Henry Hathaway, Frank Borzage, René Clair, John Stahl, Jean Negulesco, and Michael Curtiz. (Not that all his clients earned top dollar: he would represent Robert Evans when the future head of Paramount was a struggling actor.) "I'm all for stars getting big money," Feldman said. "When I first handled Gable he was getting a mere 3,000 dollars a week in pictures. I said to a bunch of studio executives: 'You'll see the day when stars will get a million dollars a film—and you'll be glad to pay it.' Well, they laughed. At that time 250,000 dollars a film was the highest money paid any star for a picture. I trebled that for John Wayne and Bill Holden. They were the first to get 750,000 dollars a film. Soon everybody wanted it. The funny thing is I only did it to see how far I could go. What do you think of that?"

He was still dreaming up new ways to cut deals. The producer David Brown, who was an executive at Fox in the 1950s and '60s, remembers when Feldman tried to negotiate an unusual contract for Wayne with the studio's president, Spyros Skouras: three pictures plus a percentage of the profits—a piece of the back end. Recalls Brown, "Spyros said it was the end of the industry, as he always did. And when he didn't give Charlie what he wanted, Charlie walked out of his office. Spyros then called him back and acquiesced. The point is, Charlie knew when to walk, but he also knew when not to walk." (The three pictures, *Barbarians at the Gate*, *North to Alaska*, and *Comancheros*, did not prove to be among Wayne's most memorable.)

Despite the big money he was getting for his clients, it was almost impossible for Feldman to keep all his stars happy all the time, and not all of them were. Kirk Douglas had been doing theater in New York when he was offered a small part in the film *The Strange Love of Martha Ivers* by the producer Hal Wallis. As Douglas recalls, "David Merrick walked me down to the station to take the train to La-La Land, and I said, 'David, I don't have an agent.' He said, 'Charlie Feldman is a son of a bitch, but it would be better if he were your son of a bitch.'" Douglas went to L.A. and did the movie—this was 1945. Famous Artists signed the actor, but he could never manage to meet Feldman himself, who one day kept him waiting all afternoon in the anteroom of his office. At the end of the day, Douglas was told that the agent was too busy to see him—come back tomorrow. He did, for four or five days running. When he finally did get an audience, and mentioned the wait, Feldman chewed him out: "Who the hell do you think you are? We're doing the best we can. When you become something, then you can complain."

Douglas went back to New York in disgust, then returned to Hollywood, did some films, moved his career along. But he still couldn't get Feldman to return his phone calls.

During this period, Douglas had run across two kids, Stanley Kramer and Carl Foreman, who were trying to produce an independent fight picture called *Champion*. Always a bit of a maverick, Douglas liked the script, liked the guys, liked the idea of working outside the system, and *Champion,* released in 1949, created a sensation. Suddenly Douglas's phone rang. It was Feldman. "You could've knocked me over," Douglas says. "'Hello, baby, how are you? You're having dinner with me Sunday night. We have a date with Jack Warner at his home. He wants to see the picture.' . . . I went around telling everybody, 'Boys, I'm in! My agent talks to me!'"

In the fall of 1959, Feldman was diagnosed with an enlarged prostate. Gary Cooper had been suffering from the same ailment, and the two men flew off to Switzerland together for treatment. Following surgery, Feldman for a time was saddled with a collection bag for his urine. One evening, as he later told David Chasman, he was invited to the Warner home for dinner and a movie. When the lights went up, Feldman to his horror realized that during the screening the bag had leaked and his urine had soiled Ann Warner's fine Louis XV fauteuil. As self-possessed as ever, he said his good-byes and left. A week or so later, he was in Warner's office when the phone rang. After listening for a moment, Warner exploded: "What?! . . . You're kidding! I'll be goddamned!"

"What was that all about, Jack?" Feldman asked after the executive had hung up.

"Remember that dinner last week? The next morning they found this stain on my antique chair. We sent it out to be cleaned. The upholsterer said they couldn't clean it until they knew what it is, so they had to send it to the lab. The lab just called. You know what it was? Urine! Piss! Somebody pissed on my Louis XV chair." Feldman looked at Warner for a second before replying, "Jack, why do you invite people like that?"

Angie Dickinson met Feldman later that year. He claimed to be interested in her as a client, but, she says, "I think he wanted to date me, because he asked me to come to his office, and you know where his office was." His office was, of course, his home. Trying to get her into bed, he jokingly alluded to his prostate operation and his supposed therapy for it. "I have to use this all the time," he told her, "this" being his penis. Dickinson went out with him, on and off, over the next three or four years.

But in the immediate wake of his operation Feldman had been warned by his doctors to take it easy, and so he left for the South of France to recuperate, accompanied by his steadiest companion at the time, the French actress and former model Capucine, who was then twenty-seven. Capucine had a finely chiseled face with high cheekbones, a long nose, and slightly flared nostrils that made her look like a high-strung, overbred filly. As a teenager she had become a top model for Dior and Givenchy. She then moved to New York in search of more money and an American accent. It was there that a scout for Feldman's agency spotted her in a restaurant and sent her out to L.A. for a screen test. Famous Artists put her under contract in 1957 for $150 a week. Feldman called her "Cappy" and became her lover and biggest fan. She was a wooden performer, but Feldman tried to put her in almost every movie he was producing, starting with 1962's *A Walk on the Wild Side*. The film was set in the 1930s, but he insisted on dressing her to the teeth in up-to-the-minute Paris couture while the rest of the cast wore period clothes. Her co-star Laurence Harvey didn't help matters by going public with his blistering attack on the young actress: "Kissing you is like kissing the side of a beer bottle."

Feldman then shoehorned Capucine into a Fox film, *The Lion,* starring his client and good friend William Holden. The actor's wife, Ardis, visited the set in Kenya; the couple fought bitterly, while noncombatants wondered if Capucine was the cause. After Ardis left Kenya in a huff, the two co-stars did indeed have an affair. Holden felt guilty for cuckolding Feldman, who subsequently broke off his romance with Capucine, though he would remain loyal to her and continue to put her in pictures. Says Dickinson, "I believe that Capucine fell for Bill, and that's what broke up her romance with Charlie. Otherwise he probably would have stayed with her." Holden apparently did not feel the same way about the actress. He is reputed to have said, nastily, "She's so marvelously ornamental—when her mouth is shut."

Feldman was in the habit of spending at least a month each year at the Hotel du Cap in the South of France. In the summer of 1963, when he was fifty-eight—or perhaps sixty-three—he met Clotilde Barot, the twenty-year-old daughter of a well-off but straitlaced Parisian couple. Barot, gorgeous and in the bloom of her youth, looked a little like Capucine. As with so many girls of her age and class, Barot had done time in a convent school—and hated every minute of it. When she got out she was fully prepared to make her way through the handsome young heirs to the great fortunes of Europe. (As Barot herself recalls, an ill-wisher once claimed she had "laid everything in Paris but the carpet.") One day at the Hotel du Cap, where she was visiting a friend, she swam out to a raft moored just off the hotel's Eden Roc restaurant—where two Rock Hudson-handsome, six-foot-five hunks were sunning themselves. She barely registered a third man, older and shorter, lying next to them. It was Feldman. "They introduced him, and from that time on he pursued me to death," she recalls. "He was like my father." She wasn't interested, and at the end of the summer returned to her family.

But Feldman wasn't one to take no for an answer. "He sent me a wire. Would I meet him in Venice? For some reason I said yes, and on the plane going there I was wondering the whole time, Why did I say yes?" At the hotel, she was afraid he was going to book them both into one suite, but, gentlemanly as always, he had reserved two. After she unpacked, he went to her room bearing gifts: a blackamoor figurine, a solid-gold evening bag, and a Piaget watch with a black face and adorned in diamonds, rubies, emeralds, whatever. She continues, "Somehow I didn't think I had to say thank you by letting him get into my pants. Finally, on the third or fourth day, he said he was tired and why didn't we take a nap together in my suite." For Feldman, once in Barot's bedroom, the rest was easy, with the exception of one small matter: "My God, of course he couldn't do it," she recalls, "and he used the excuse that he wanted me for so long he lost it. I thought to myself, Oh, yeah, right! I told him, 'Fifty-eight—what can you expect?' It was his favorite story: 'Guess what this girl told me the first time we made love.' After that, everything went normal."

Before Jean Howard returned from one of her trips, she would customarily call ahead to announce her intention to reoccupy 2000 Coldwater Canyon, saying, "Get the girls out of the house, Charlie, I'm coming home." After 1963, it was "the girl," and Howard did not take kindly to it. "Jean hated me, but I didn't care," says Barot. "Once, for Christmas, he sent her a check for $5,000, which would be about $15,000 today. She sent it back. We were in Saint-Moritz for Christmas, and he was laughing when he read me her letter. 'I'm sure this girl is costing you enough, so why don't you use it (on her).' Can you imagine? A bitchy thing."

Feldman wanted Warren Beatty as a client. The two had met in 1960 on a plane from L.A. to New York, where Beatty was going to star in *Splendor in the Grass,* and had immediately hit it off. As Clive Donner, who would direct *What's New, Pussycat?,* puts it, "They spoke the same language." Beatty often stayed at 2000 Coldwater Canyon when he was in L.A. Still, he never would become Feldman's client. "As nearly as I could tell," Beatty says, "he had no real interest in being an agent. But he was more fun than almost anybody I had met in Hollywood of the older guys. I liked his sense of humor about the movie business and the people in it, his objectivity, his lack of drive. I liked that he said he hadn't been to the office in ten, fifteen years."

By 1961, Feldman had indeed lost his taste for agenting, and

307

after watching the government break up MCA, he sold Famous Artists to the agent Ted Ashley. At the same time, his power as a producer was reaching its zenith, growing in direct proportion to the declining clout of the studio bosses. The 1960s were, in fact, a producers' decade, a time when men such as Feldman, Sam Spiegel, Walter Mirisch, and Marty Ransohoff moved into the vacuum left by the collapse of the majors and turned out a crop of bloated, if-it's-Tuesday-this-must-be-Belgium international productions— films where the country changes with the scene and the ads featured serried ranks of tiny, passport-size pictures of American and European stars; films such as *It's a Mad, Mad, Mad, Mad World* (1963), *The Longest Day* (1962), and *Paris Is Burning* (1966); films that, with a few exceptions, would nearly sink the studios by the end of the decade.

In the late '50s, Feldman had purchased *Lot's Wife* for Cary Grant. It was a Czech play by Ladislaus Bus-Fekete about a compulsive Don Juan, and Feldman hired Billy Wilder's writing partner I. A. L. Diamond to fashion a script. But Grant proved disinclined to do the film, and Feldman eventually settled on Beatty to play the lead. The actor had one stipulation: he knew that Feldman would find a part for Capucine if he could, and he wanted assurances that no Capucine-like character would find its way into the script. Feldman, who did not relish being told what to do, retorted, "Fuck you," or something to that effect, but eventually agreed, and work on the script proceeded.

Needless to say, *Lot's Wife* was not going to be the title of the movie, and Feldman was looking around for something more suitable. When Beatty was staying at Feldman's, the producer couldn't help but hear him on the phone giving his customary greeting to female callers, "What's new, pussycat?" Feldman exclaimed: "Title!"

He and Beatty were not happy with Diamond's script, which they didn't think was funny enough. They needed a good joke writer, and one night in 1964 they went to the Blue Angel, a club in New York's Greenwich Village, to catch a kid they had heard was funny, Woody Allen. Allen had no film experience, but they liked what they saw, or rather heard. Feldman offered Allen $30,000 to work on the script. Allen said, "I want forty." Feldman said, "Forget it."

Woody replied, "O.K. I'll take thirty if I can be in the movie." Feldman gave in. His one instruction to his new hire: "Write something where we can all go to Paris and chase girls."

Allen took Feldman at his word, but when the comic read the results—which he claimed had "a million great jokes"—to Feldman and Beatty, the honeymoon ended. According to Allen, Feldman hated his work, but by Beatty's account it was he who had the problem. As draft followed draft, the actor noticed that his part was growing smaller, while Allen's was growing larger. "In the original script, Woody's part might have appeared on six pages," Beatty recalls. "His first rewrite, the part went to twelve or fifteen pages, and it was funny. Then it went to twenty or thirty pages. By the time we got to what Woody thought was an acceptable rewrite, his part was almost half the script. Mine was almost as large but not quite as good."

And worse, from Beatty's point of view, as the project took on an increasingly French flavor, he could see Capucine coming over the brow of the hill. Indeed, Feldman had written Allen a memo urging him to strengthen the part of a French girl. When a gossip-column item subsequently appeared to the effect that the film would co-star Leslie Caron, to whom Beatty was then romantically linked, Feldman concluded that the actor, trying to force his hand, had planted it. After an angry confrontation, Beatty walked away from the production—bluffing, he thought. But by this point "they were only too happy to let me go," recalls the actor. Feldman and Beatty didn't speak for four years, until just before Feldman got sick.

Peter Sellers, then the biggest comedy star in the world, came on board, and Peter O'Toole, fresh from *Lawrence of Arabia* and *Beckett*, replaced Beatty. Allen watched Feldman operate, close-up, and was dumbstruck. The comic recalled, "He was a genius . . . I've seen him on the phone to Peter Sellers, on a second phone to United Artists, and on a third to the Italian government"—at one point the film was going to be shot in Rome—"saying, 'I can get Peter Sellers, maybe, to do this picture,' then picking up the phone to United Artists and telling them, 'I've got to have another $200,000 to get Peter Sellers,' and the Italian government saying, 'You can shoot the picture, but you have to have this certain deal,' and then Sellers saying, 'I won't work in Italy,' and it went on and on."

309

Ultimately, *What's New, Pussycat?* was shot in Paris. Feldman stayed in a luxurious suite at the Hotel Plaza Athénée for six months. "It was a very glamorous life," recalls Barot. "I invited ten girlfriends to lunch at the Plaza Athénée, charged everything to the hotel. Kinda fun." (It's no wonder there are never any net profits in Hollywood!) Recalls David Chasman, whose company, U.A., was producing the film, "He would load everything onto the expenses of a picture. [U.A. head] Arthur Krim once objected to his unconscionable expenses. I listened to a conversation between the two of them where Charlie was describing his spartan lifestyle, claiming all he had was a raw egg for breakfast!"

The film grew from a small comedy to a $4 million extravaganza, packed with a Who's Who of '60s stars and stars-in-training: in addition to O'Toole and Sellers, it featured Ursula Andress, still dripping seawater from *Dr. No*, Romy Schneider, Paula Prentiss, and, yes, Capucine, who needed a hit of vodka before she could go on. Even Richard Burton did a cameo. Allen was furious with Feldman for ruining his material and giving his best lines to Sellers and O'Toole. "One night at rushes I told Feldman to fuck off," Allen recalled. "My outburst slid right off him. Probably he'd been cursed out so often that it was not a bothersome moment to him."

What's New, Pussycat? opened in June 1965. It grossed $17 million, at that time a record for a comedy. The success of the film, chaotically produced from a script that was in constant flux, packed with stars who pretty much did what they wanted, seemed to legitimize the worst excesses of the mid-'60s' overproduced blockbusters.

Feldman moved on to *The Group*, Candace Bergen's first movie and a hit with critics that did fairly well at the box office. (His office was full of the books he had bought to drive the Mary McCarthy novel up the best-seller list.)

But Feldman wasn't so lucky with *Casino Royale*. He had acquired the rights to the first James Bond novel in 1954, when Ian Fleming was a nobody. The property sat undisturbed until the early '60s, when the series produced by Cubby Broccoli and Harry Saltzman, based on subsequent Fleming novels, began to mint money. Still holding the rights to *Casino Royale*, Feldman decided to shoot it as a parody, but the joke turned out to be on him. He packed the film with some fifteen high-profile actors—friends, ex-clients, everyone who owed him a favor or hoped to collect a favor from him in the future, including Sellers, Welles, Holden, Boyer, Andress, David Niven, Jacqueline Bisset, Frank Sinatra, Sophia Loren, Peter Ustinov, and Sara Miles. There were at least twelve screenwriters, four of them credited (Ian Fleming, Wolf Mankowitz, John Law, and Michael Sayers) and eight uncredited (Welles, Sellers, Allen, Val Guest, Terry Southern, Ben Hecht, Billy Wilder, and Joseph Heller). "We were not supposed to know the other one was working on the picture!" Welles once said. But Feldman had put them up on different floors of the same hotel, apparently without anticipating that they might stumble across one another. Unbeknownst to the producer, the screenwriters had lunch together every day and discussed the script, undoubtedly charging the meals to Feldman. There were five credited directors: Guest, Ken Hughes, Joseph McGrath, Robert Parrish, and John Huston. For a crate of champagne, O'Toole also agreed to appear in a scene for thirty seconds. There were even four James Bonds. Recalls Andress, who left before her filming was finished, "It was completely crazy, crazy, crazy. I didn't want to go on being on the film, because it went on and on and the fighting went on and on and on, so I quit and went with Jean-Paul Belmondo to Tahiti. Charlie was very upset with me. He said, 'You'll never work in America again.'" As Richard Sylbert summed it up, Feldman "turned this one property he owned into a lunatic asylum and supported London for a year."

Casino Royale opened in April 1967. Sylbert saw it with Billy Wilder. "Wilder said to me, 'It's not a picture you dislike, it's a picture you loathe!'" Adds Barot, "When the reviews were bad, Charlie was devastated." It turned out to be the last film he would produce.

The following Christmas, Feldman and Barot went to Acapulco. He was very careful with the food and water, but he got sick anyway. The couple returned to New York, where he was diagnosed with diabetes, put on a diet, and told there was, in Barot's words, "nothing to worry about." But he started to complain of backaches. On the flight from New York to L.A., Barot mentioned that the whites of his eyes had turned yellow. He replied, "It'd better not be hepatitis, because I've got work to do." He went for tests, and his doctor asked Barot to come in for a hepatitis shot. When she arrived, she recalls, "he told me, 'You don't need any shot. He's got a tumor at the head of the pancreas.'"

Before he went into the hospital for exploratory surgery, he told the doctors that, whatever they discovered, he wanted the truth. Pancreatic cancer is usually fatal, and the truth was that it had spread to his lymph nodes. Recalls Barot, "When I went to see him in intensive care, the first thing he said was 'Is this the ball game?' I said, 'No, it's not.' He said, 'If I've got cancer, I marry you.'" Reflects Kirk Douglas's wife, Ann, "He had no intention of marrying anybody—in his own mind he was married to Jean. But when he knew he was going to die he wanted to do something for Clotilde, and he married her, which was fantastic." Even so, Feldman joked about his impending wedding: "With my luck, I'll get better."

Feldman checked into the University of California Hospital for Abdominal Surgery in late April 1968. In unbearable pain, he begged his lawyer, "Give me a gun, I'm not going to go through this." He never used the c-word, referring to the illness as "this thing I've got." Jean Howard was eager to be at his bedside, but Barot confined her access to the early morning.

Feldman was released from the hospital on Thursday, May 11. Three days later, on Sunday, May 14, he married Barot among a profusion of orchids on the grounds of 2000 Coldwater Canyon. His tan had been replaced by the pallor of the sickroom, and Beatty gave him some tinting cream to put on his face. Barot got a shot of vitamin B12 and put on a short white dress from Galanos. Forty guests attended, a gathering of Hollywood royalty including Sam Goldwyn and his wife, the Billy Wilders, the Danny Kayes, the Irving Lazars, Richard Zanuck with Linda Harrison, Shirley MacLaine, Beatty and Julie Christie, Robert Evans, David Brown, Ray Stark, Angie Dickinson, Frank Sinatra, and Mike Romanoff. The food, including nine pounds of caviar, was catered by the Bistro for $1,953.85. The joy of the occasion was shadowed by Feldman's imminent death, which everyone was aware of. Most of the guests wore sunglasses, and when the judge admonished the bride and groom to "love, honor, and obey until death do you part," the shades served their purpose, concealing tears. "It really broke my heart that he married someone else," said Jean Howard later. "And under those circumstances. I had to step out of the way, and I did."

After his hospital stay in April, Feldman seemed better and resumed a limited schedule. He told Barot, "Oh, my God, now we're married and we can't have sex." She reassured him that his illness was temporary. Ray Stark, who early in his career had worked for Feldman, was almost always at the house, gossiping with him about the business, keeping him engaged. Beatty also went every day. "He would stay with me until four o'clock in the morning," Barot recalls. "When Charlie started to throw up blood, Warren was there." Adds Ann Douglas, "At the end, Charlie had nurses around the clock. He didn't want them to do anything to his body, just Clotilde. She did everything, things I can't imagine I could do. And did them with really loving care. We all had a lot of respect for her for that." One day Feldman started to hemorrhage, which meant that his liver was going. On Saturday, May 25, the nurse awakened Barot in the middle of the night, told her the end was near. Feldman's breathing was rapid and shallow. He died at 4:30 A.M. Barot ran to the bedroom where her mother was sleeping in the same bed as Grace Dobish, Feldman's secretary of forty years. Barot screamed, "He's dead, he's dead!" She opened his closet and sank to the floor among his clothes and cried.

313

Feldman requested that there be no service. He was buried in the Feldman-family plot at Hollywood Memorial Park Cemetery. He had risen like a rocket in the Hollywood firmament, successfully leaving Charlie Gold and Bayonne far behind him, but he could not elude the disease that had killed his biological parents.

Feldman had given a lot of thought to his will, even paid the gift taxes on each bequest. He distributed his automobiles and art collection to his friends with care. Beatty got a Degas bronze, Shirley MacLaine a Rouault, Arthur Krim a Renoir, Holden, who was into things African, a group of primitive masks. He left $75,000 to Capucine, but nothing to his biological family, who blamed Clotilde.

The animosity between Howard and Barot survived him. According to Barot, "When he died, I got this telegram from her saying that I could stay [in the house] as long as I needed, only to hear ten days later that I had to get out of there, and not to take any silver!"

Capucine called Barot from France. She said, "Please, can I come and see the house again?" She walked through it rubbing a rosary "like she was the widow," recalls Barot. On March 17, 1990, depressed and alone save for her three cats, Capucine, who believed that in a prior life she had been a French Crusader, jumped to her death from the eighth-floor balcony of her apartment building in Lausanne, Switzerland. She was fifty-seven.

Jean Howard died on March 21, 2000, at the age of eighty-nine.

Beatty had been a very young man when he met Feldman, then near sixty, and he was not given to intimations of mortality. But from him "I learned," says the actor, "that life is short, that movies are written on water, that the quality of your own life is the ultimate reality, that the important thing is to enjoy life rather than stack up wealth and fame." Adds David Brown, "Charlie was a voluptuary. He loved good food, beautiful women, the South of France. I never thought he was interested in empire building. He would never have created an MCA or a William Morris, nor could he have worked for them. He was an icon and iconoclast both at the same time."

Among the projects that were pending when Feldman died was Woody Allen's first film, *Take the Money and Run,* and it is perhaps appropriate to let him have the last word. Charlie "was crap to work for," Allen told his biographer Eric Lax in 1991. "He was a big-time charming con man and I never trusted him on anything for a second. He was just an out-and-out, hundred-times-over proven liar to me. I worked with him knowing that. Yet I have enormous affection for him. When you see those other big-time producers, they were so cheesy and drippy. Charlie was charming and funny. He would go over to the baccarat table and lose a hundred thousand dollars the way you'd lose your Zippo lighter. I wasn't happy about *Pussycat.* It was clearly a star vehicle . . . I wish he were alive, though; not just because I wish he were alive, but I'd love him to see I was able to get into my own films. He started me and I think he would like them."

WHEN SUE WAS QUEEN

Sue Mengers is dead!"

The voice on the phone is deep, sandpaper-rough, too many cigarettes, too many deals. It is immediately recognizable, if you've heard it even once, as the voice of Sue Mengers, very much alive but not feeling all that well, in a worse humor even than usual. This is how it's been since 1996, when her husband of twenty-three years, Jean-Claude Tramont, died of cancer and she entered a tunnel that led to radiation therapy for cancer of her own on top of quadruple-bypass surgery and then her mother's death—a tunnel from which she has yet to emerge. She's definitely not up to talking, certainly not about herself in the 1970s, when she was famous throughout the Western world as the first "super-agent," the agent who could pick up the phone and reach anyone, who could make things happen, and a woman to boot, and funny, very funny. *That's* the Sue Mengers who's dead, ancient history. Why dredge up those stories people have heard a thousand times? And the other Sue Mengers, the one rattling around the house in Beverly Hills, who's interested in her? She rarely goes out, puts off would-be visitors with excuses, lies around reading novels and watching television, rarely even bothering to dress. She was going to write her memoirs, but discovered that calling up the past depressed her even more than she was already. "Memory lane is O.K. if you're currently happy," she mutters. "If you're not, it's a reminder of things that are never going to be again. I'm not feeling good about myself. You got me on a bad day."

"It's always a bad day."

"I'm bored with myself, I'm too fat, I'm going to lose some weight, call me back then."

The "late" Sue Mengers was the anti-Mike Ovitz. Or, rather, Ovitz—who followed in her diminutive footsteps in the '80s, when most of the drugs were flushed and the business finally became a business—was the anti-Mengers. Blonde, zaftig, and abrasive, always a great quote, she was a magnet for the media, a star in her own right, as famous as some of her clients, which eventually became a problem. There was nothing buttoned-down about Mengers. What you saw was what you got. She kvetched, she kvelled, she wheedled, flirted, and threatened like no one else, and she usually got her way. In the prime of her career, a span which lasted a good ten years before her world crashed around her, she represented nearly everybody who was anybody. As her friend David Geflen puts it, "She had the greatest client list of any agent in Hollywood." Her stable included most of the top-of-the-line actresses of the era, first and foremost among them Barbra Streisand in her glory days, when her voice could make strong men weep; but also Ali MacGraw in hers, before Steve McQueen put her in front of a stove; Cher; Cybill Shepherd; Candice Bergen; Faye Dunaway; and Dyan Cannon, as well as a handful of important male stars such as Ryan O'Neal, Burt Reynolds, Gene Hackman. Tony Perkins, Michael Caine, and Nick Nolte. She also represented many of the blue-chip *auteurs* of the director's decade, men such as Arthur Penn, Peter Bogdanovich, Mike Nichols, Brian De Palma, Sidney Lumet, and Jonathan Demme. "You couldn't do a movie without Sue," says John Galley, who was a top Warner executive throughout the '70s and today heads Sony Pictures Entertainment. "When you'd have a problem, you'd go to her, and she would make it go away. She was the Man."

"The Man." Mengers was the first woman to breach the boys' club that ran the town. "They can talk about Dawn Steel—whatever." says Toni Howard, now an agent at International Creative Management and once a colleague of Mengers's, "but there is only

one woman that broke the ground for women, and that was Sue."
The industry's powerful male executives treated her like an equal.
She counted among her friends Robert Evans when he headed production at Paramount, Barry Diller when he later ran the same studio, and Galley, who went so far as to take Mengers along on his
honeymoon in 1973. She was famous for her parties, which were
de rigueur for anyone who was happening or hoped to happen.
They were such select, star-studded affairs that Bogdanovich once
had to drag Cybill Shepherd by the arm up Mengers's driveway
because she was afraid to go in. At one such event, Johnny Carson
is reputed to have griped, "God, there are too many stars here, not
enough sycophants!"

Larger than life, outrageous, and gifted—some would say
cursed—with the tongue of an asp, she became a legend in her own
time. According to a chapter about Mengers in the late Paul
Rosenfield's book *The Club Rules,* when Sharon Tate was murdered
by the Manson family in 1969, Mengers reassured Streisand, "Don't
worry, honey, stars aren't being murdered. Only featured players."
She once said, "I was so driven I would have signed Martin
Bormann." When Sidney Lumet was a hot director she called him at
midnight to pitch a client. Lumet told her, "If you're this pushy, I
want you to be *my* agent." She was the model for Dyan Cannon's
impersonation of a loudmouthed agent in the 1973 film *The Last of
Sheila,* a Hollywood whodunit written by Stephen Sondheim and
Tony Perkins. Her friends called her a female Billy Wilder.

Naturaly, the most acerbic commentator on the Mengers legend
is Mengers herself. "Mostly these stories are made up," she complains. "One story David Geffen loves to tell is about when I was
a receptionist at the William Morris office and an ape act was
brought in and put in the waiting room with me." Geffen does
indeed like this story, and, as told to me, it goes like this: The act,
famous in its day, was the Marquis Chimps. Their trainer had
come to the office with one of his apes to meet with his agent,
Harry Kalcheim, who also represented Elvis Presley. In Geffen's
telling, "The trainer went to the bathroom, left the monkey, and as
he came out he heard Sue saying to the chimp, 'Ooh, little monkey,
want to fuck Baby Sue?' He grabbed the chimp, ran into
Kalcheim's office, yelling, 'Your receptionist just tried to fuck my

317

monkey!,' and tried to get him to fire her." Thinking about it, Mengers rolls her eyes and exclaims, "Can you imagine?"

The good times, inevitably, came to an end. Bergen walked in the late '70s, so did MacGraw, and in 1981, Streisand left too. After that it was a hemorrhage, and Mengers never recovered. It was Ovitz time. His Creative Artists Associates, with its corporate-lockstep style, would gain a stranglehold on the industry. While Mengers had created a family, he built an empire.

Why Mengers fell from grace when other, lesser agents survived seismic changes in the business and are still working remains something of a mystery. What happened between Mengers and Streisand may never be fully known. Most of her old clients don't call anymore; the only people she seems to see or talk to regularly are Geffen and Fran Lebowitz. She keeps up with the trades and watches the Oscars on television. The small group of intimates who watch with her has gradually diminished. Last year she watched alone.

Chris Mankiewicz, a former studio executive at United Artists and Columbia and a scion of the famously talented family of writers and directors—he is the son of Joe (*All About Eve*) and the nephew of Herman (*Citizen Kane*)—puts it this way: "I grew up with agents and movie stars, and none of them had the kind of charisma she had. When she walked into a room or when she sat down to talk to you, she was just the best. What happened to her, and why she didn't go on forever, is a story."

Mengers's house, modest by Hollywood standards, is Beverly Hills Georgian, or maybe it's architect John Woolf's L.A. version of Greek Revival—architectural styles are notoriously fungible in Southern California. The house was built in the 1950s in a mini-monumental style that makes it resemble a dressed-up mausoleum. Mengers is a cozy girl, yet her house is anything but. She seems like a stranger among the scattering of Biedermeier pieces. The tall windows at the back of the living room look out on an oval pool she never uses.

Although it is two o'clock in the afternoon, Mengers looks as if she's just gotten out of bed. She's dressed in a loose-fitting, comfortable, otherwise nondescript garment that could be any-thing from one of the muumuus she favored in the '70s to a night-gown. She lights a cigarette and solicitously offers me a tuna-fish sandwich, then says, "Do you want to come into my bedroom, big boy? I took out some pictures." She shows me photos of her late husband, adding, sourly, "I guess I must have been happy once." Then it's into the den to watch a tape of a memorable *60 Minutes* profile of her done in 1975. I'm on the Mengers museum tour. Before she hits the play button, and just as the features of Gloria Swanson in *Sunset Boulevard* are beginning to swim before my eyes, she says, with a noise more like a bark than a laugh, "I feel like I've become Norma Desmond, showing my old pictures." This is very Sue Mengers: in the business or not, healthy or ill, she's always there a beat before you, dead on target.

And then, after a hiccup of video, her image is on the television screen, perky and blonde, with the familiar round face, upturned nose, and signature oversize glasses, twenty-five years younger and somewhat thinner, charming Mike Wallace and explaining how it was that this kid from the Bronx became the Queen of Hollywood. "I was a little *pisher*, a little nothing making $135 a week as a sec-retary for the William Morris Agency in New York," she purrs on the tape. "Well, I looked around and I admired the Morris office and their executives, and I thought: Gee, what they do isn't that hard, you know. And I like the way they live, and I like those expense accounts, and I like the cars. . . . And I suddenly thought: That beats typing."

It did beat typing, and Mengers made it sound easy, but that was just part of the legend she was weaving around herself. The truth is: It was hard. It cost her.

Sue Mengers was born in Hamburg, Germany, at some point in the 1930s. (She won't say just when.) Both her parents had been well-off. "They never really had to work," she recalls. "They lived the middle-class life." Mengers describes her father as a "spoiled play-boy." Like the parents of others who made careers in Hollywood—Bogdanovich and Nichols come to mind—hers fled the Nazis. The family's fortunes reversed, her mother wanted to go to Palestine with her relatives, but "not my father." she continues. "He wanted to go to America, gold in the streets. So they came here, without knowing a word of the language. It was very tough for people who weren't used to toughness. It was too tough for my father. He was a door-to-door salesman."

Mengers's family left Europe in 1938 and joined a small enclave of struggling refugees in Utica, New York. Her mother was distant and proper, rarely affectionate. "She was a very domineering woman," Mengers recalls. "He was a lot more fun than she was." But when Sue was in early adolescence, her father killed himself. "He ran into some money problems, and he was reduced to going to friends, none of whom were wealthy. And rather than face my mother and say, 'I don't have that hundred dollars,' or whatever, he went to New York, checked into a Times Square hotel, and the rest is foggy to me. I think it was pills. I don't think he shot himself. He never left a note. Or if he did, I never got it. It must have been such a shock that I blocked it all out. Except I'm getting angrier at him as I grow older. I told Dustin Hoffman that when I went to see him in *Death of a Salesman* I had every intention of going backstage, but I was so upset by it that I couldn't. My father *was* Willy Loman." She pauses. Then: "God, I hate to talk about myself. How do you like the tuna fish?"

According to the Rosenfield book, Mengers moved with her mother, by now a bookkeeper, to the Bronx. In 1955, she answered an ad for a receptionist at MCA, the powerhouse talent agency run by Jules Stein and Lew Wasserman (which later bought Universal and divested its agenting business). Mengers worked at MCA for a couple of years, until she was unceremoniously given the boot for failing to summon an agent from the men's room to take a call from Tyrone Power. From there she went to the smaller Baum-Newborn agency. Again she was frequently in trouble. Her boss, Marty Baum, "had a roaring temper and Sue was a total fuckup," according to Tom Korman, then a young agent, now a manager. An indifferent typist, she was not cut out to be a secretary, and Baum, Korman told Paul Rosenfield, "must have fired her fifty times. One day an actress, who was our client, was supposed to audition for *The World of Suzie Wong,* and nobody could find her. Sue, only Sue, knew she was having an affair with a married musician. Sue was in sheer panic from Marty Baum screaming at her every three minutes. . . . Finally she called the musician at home, and a woman answered. Sue said, 'You old sneak! I found you.' Well, of course, it was the musician's wife. And Marty Baum fired Sue once again."

Her next job was as secretary to Charlie Baker, head of the theater department at the William Morris Agency. One of his clients was Gore Vidal, who had a hit on Broadway called *Visit to a Small Planet*. Vidal, who became a good friend of Mengers's and eventually a client, remembers her from those days: "She had an outer office, he had an inner office. She was very flirtatious. One day I popped in to see Charlie, and suddenly I said, 'Oh, I've got to go,' and opened the door to his office, nearly putting her eye out as she was down peeping through the keyhole, or with her ear to the keyhole—I never could get her to admit which it was. In due course, she left the Morris office and went to work for another agent."

The other agent was Korman, who had left Baum-Newborn in 1963 to start his own agency, Tom Korman Associates. That same year he wooed Mengers from Morris by offering her her first job as an agent. Korman's shop started out with only three clients: the fading movie star Joan Bennett; Claudia McNeil, who had appeared in *A Raisin in the Sun;* and the writer-actress Lillian Roth, whose memoir *I'll Cry Tomorrow* had been adapted into a hit movie in 1955. But Korman Associates quickly became known as the Jolly Robbers, for the boldness with which it purloined clients, or, alternatively, the Relative Wrong agency, as in dancer-actress Marge Champion instead of Gower, actress Jocelyn Brando instead of Marlon.

Vidal continues the story: "I believe she took Charlie Baker's Rolodex. She had everybody's phone number, and as she had been listening to everything that was going on, she was perhaps the most knowledgeable agent in the business." She wooed people such as Tom Ewell, who was then a big Broadway star, with *The Seven Year Itch* and a lot of other plays to his credit. In those days, actors would come in early, before their matinees, and have lunch at Sardi's, where Mengers would troll for clients. One afternoon, Mengers stopped by Ewell's table, dropped her business card in his water glass, and said, "Hi. I'm Sue Mengers, I met you with Charlie Baker, I'm now on my own, I just want to be frank with you—I'd love you to be our client." According to Vidal, "Ewell said, 'What can you do for me that [my agent] Abe Lastfogel can't do?' She said, 'Fuck David Merrick!' With that, a star was born. She got him, too."

At the time, Merrick, the powerful producer of such Broadway hits as *Gypsy* and *Hello, Dolly!,* and the film director Otto Preminger (*Laura, Anatomy of a Murder, Exodus*) were "the two most formidable, frightening names to agents," according to Mengers. "But Merrick would take my calls because he knew I would be either amusing or I'd give him a free idea. When *Hello, Dolly!* opened, I called David and gave him a list of replacements, from Ginger Rogers on down, and in fact I tried to get Ginger Rogers to let me negotiate it for her. I thought I would faint on the way up to her suite in the elevator. And there she was, sitting behind a tray, sipping coffee, and she never even offered me a cup. She made me feel—ugh."

In 1967, Preminger was directing *Hurry Sundown,* and Mengers was trying to sell him on one of her male clients. Preminger was a liberal, famous for openly employing blacklisted writer Dalton Trumbo on *Exodus*. As she recalls, "He said to me, 'Miss Mengers, your client is a fairy!' Of course he was, but I said, 'Oh, Mr. Preminger, that's not true—I've been to bed with him.' I would go that far, yes. I wish I could say he gave the guy the part, but he didn't. He may have broken the blacklist, but gay was verboten in movies."

One of Mengers's clients was Constance Bennett, Joan's sister and a fading star in her own right. Mengers knocked herself out to get Bennett into her "comeback" film: *Madame X* (the umpteenth remake of a 1908 French melodrama), which starred Lana Turner and Ricardo Montalban and was produced by Ross Hunter. Instead of being grateful, Bennett complained about her billing below Turner, demanding that her name be set off by a box on the ads and posters. It wasn't. Bennett, who had gotten a hefty salary, refused to pay her commission to the agency. Then, just before the movie came out, she died. Mengers sent Hunter a telegram that said, CONSTANCE FINALLY GOT HER BOX!

Mengers was shameless hustling clients. One of her favorite

lines was "Get rid of that asshole your agent." She explains, "What should I have said? 'Your agent's wonderful, stay with him'? I was at times very bombastic, because I thought it was the only way I could get people to listen to me." She had two signature phrases. When she heard something that she thought was off the mark, which was often, she snorted, "HellOHH?!," as if it were the dumbest thing imaginable. Then she'd say, "I loooaathe —" and fill in the name of the movie star.

It was in 1962, while she was still a William Morris secretary, that she met a woman who would become key to her career: Barbra Streisand, then a relative unknown playing New York City nightclubs. A year later, when Mengers went into business with Korman, she began to see more of Streisand through the singer's husband, Elliott Gould, who was a client, and through Martin Bregman, Streisand's business manager, who also handled Korman's insurance. For Streisand and Mengers it was something close to love at first sight. The two had much in common, both bright, angry, ambitious Jewish girls from the outer boroughs, with fathers who had died young. The agent Abe Newborn had famously said of Streisand, "She'll never be a star unless she gets her nose fixed." But in 1964 Streisand became a nationally known figure, starring on Broadway in *Funny Girl*—despite her nose—and Mengers began to dream about signing her as a client. Though brazen with everyone else, she treated Streisand with kid gloves. According to Korman, "She was afraid to upset Barbra." Mengers would instruct her boss, "Now, don't open your mouth until [she] talks to you." Which may be the only recorded instance of Mengers counseling circumspection.

Streisand was represented by Freddie Fields and David Begelman, the co-heads of a scrappy, up-and-coming agency called Creative Management Associates, which later became one of the most powerful in the business. According to Korman, Streisand pressured Begelman and Fields to bring in Mengers to service her. Success has many fathers, however. Both Gould and Bregman say they themselves called CMA and suggested the agency hire Mengers. Fields himself doesn't remember the circumstances.

Mengers has her own, needless to say more colorful, version.

323

Gore Vidal had introduced her to two friends of his she was dying to sign: Paul Newman and Joanne Woodward, both of whom were represented by CMA's John Foreman. Newman was a huge movie star, Woodward a couple of rungs lower on the ladder, but the couple's hearts, if not their pocketbooks, belonged to Broadway. Right away Mengers recognized how she could appeal to their vanity and make trouble for their agent. "I was zetzing them all the time in my fantasy, thinking I'd get them as clients. 'Oh, Paul, you should do Strindberg. Call up Tennessee, have him write a play.' That's half of what agents do to get new clients, is to make them unhappy with their current representation. So John Foreman had to spend his time explaining to Paul and Joanne why he can't call Arthur Miller and have him write a play. Finally, John went to Freddie Fields and said, 'Will you hire that broad, what's her name, that little agent, Sue Mengers. She's driving me crazy—she keeps telling Paul and Joanne they should do theater.' " However it happened, around 1966 Mengers ended up at CMA, where she would begin her ten-year reign.

CMA was considerably less tightly wrapped than the Morris agency, its main competitor, and would come to represent most of the big stars of the 1960s and early '70s. Geffen worked there as a young agent. So did Mike Medavoy, who went on to become an executive at United Artists and Orion, then head of Tri-Star, and most recently chairman of Phoenix Pictures; Alan Ladd Jr., who later ran Twentieth Century Fox, where he gave *Star Wars* a green light; and Guy McElwaine, who headed Columbia Pictures in the 1980s. Jeff Berg, now chairman of ICM, was a trainee.

"With Freddie Fields you got the straight story," says Korman, "you always knew where you stood. David Begelman was hail-fellow-well-met, then he'd turn around and bury you." Begelman later became notorious for embezzling money when he headed Columbia Pictures in the mid-'70s, and eventually he committed suicide, but in those days he was riding high, known for his golden tongue and imperial habits, rich even by Hollywood standards. (He had the detailing on his Rolls polished with a toothbrush, and in later years he was reputed to have had one of the first penile implants in Beverly Hills, of which he was immoderately proud.)

Begelman knew movies and had charisma to burn. In CMA's London office he'd hold forth from behind his desk to the likes of Richard Burton, Richard Harris, Stanley Baker, Michael Caine, Roger Moore, all sitting on the floor at his feet, spellbound.

There was no better place for Mengers to learn the business than CMA. "David put a lot of time and effort into her and so did I," says Fields. "We did everything to support her and made her an important woman in the movie business. With great pride, by the way." Mengers started in the agency's New York theater department, then moved out to Hollywood in late 1968. "I loved it," she remembers. "I saw Fred Astaire walking in Beverly Hills my second day. People you just dreamed about—Lana Turner, Rita Hayworth, Glenn Ford. I was in heaven." It was a great time to be there: the giants of the studio era were still walking and talking, while a new golden age, the 1970s, was in its infancy. Right away, she was a hit. "Talent responds to enthusiasm, and I was genuinely enthusiastic about these people," she says. "They could sense that." Her secret weapon was her relationship with Streisand, who by that time not only was a huge recording and Broadway star but had also hit it big in Hollywood with the 1968 movie version of *Funny Girl,* for which she won an Oscar. "I loved her," Mengers says. "She was like family. Barbra schlepped me around when she was invited someplace, so I was given a golden opportunity to meet people, which is half the battle. You can't sign them till you meet them."

Mengers signed a young Peter Bogdanovich after seeing his debut feature, *Targets,* a zero-budget thriller he directed for Roger Corman in 1968. But her first real coup at CMA was landing Ryan O'Neal, then best known for his role as Rodney Harrington on TV's *Peyton Place,* just before the release of a picture he did for Robert Evans at Paramount called *Love Story.* Evans persuaded his new flame, Ali MacGraw, to leave her agent and sign with Mengers, too. Thus, when *Love Story* became the year's biggest hit upon its release in 1970, she found herself repping two of the hottest stars in Hollywood. That same year, Mengers shoehorned Gene Hackman into William Friedkin's *The French Connection.* Recalls Richard Zanuck, who was then president of Twentieth Century Fox, which financed the movie, "I didn't think Gene was totally right for the part. I was hoping to land a bigger star, because at that time he was a secondary player, and Billy [Friedkin] felt the same way. Sue singlehandedly got him this job. She would call me three times a day, she was a relentless bird dog on this issue. I'd never been campaigned in my entire career like she campaigned for that role. She beat up on us, and we just couldn't take it anymore, so we did it. And how right she was. The picture won an Academy Award"— as did Hackman—"and he became a huge star. Gene should have a shrine [to her] in his house that he kneels before."

Bogdanovich's second feature, *The Last Picture Show*, an elegiac deconstruction of small-town life in Texas, opened in 1971 to wild critical acclaim and strong box office, which put him among the pack of Young Turk directors then challenging the Hollywood establishment. Mengers signed his girlfriend, Cybill Shepherd, a stunning former model who had made a splash in the film. Recalls Shepherd, "When our relationship began, Sue would talk to me very slowly, as if my brain was blond. She might have told me, 'Don't talk too much in an interview.' "

Mengers had finessed an early screening of *The Last Picture Show* for Streisand, who was anxious to do something serious, something "significant." She loved it, and immediately signed on for the director's as-yet-to-be-determined next feature, to be produced at Warner under Galley, which she imagined would be something in the same vein. To Streisand's dismay, Bogdanovich developed a script for a screwball comedy, an homage to films such as Howard Hawks's *Bringing Up Baby*. The actress had one foot out the door, but Mengers and Bogdanovich talked her into staying with the project, which was eventually titled *What's Up, Doc?* when it was released in 1972. "Barbra and I saw it together at the first screening, and we both thought it was a disaster," recalls Mengers. "Her manager, Marty Ehrlichman, hissed at me after the screening, 'Are you satisfied? You've ruined her career.' I flew to Klosters for Christmas. I remember Calley calling me there, saying. 'It's a smash.' " Indeed, it was—Bogdanovich's second consecutive triumph. Not that that caused Mengers to alter her opinion: "I still don't think it's so funny."

After *What's Up, Doc?*, which co-starred Mengers's client Ryan

O'Neal, the agent was white-hot. As Richard Benjamin, another client, remembers, "You wanted to be with her, because she seemed to be at the center of everything." She went from score to score. Nineteen seventy-three's *Paper Moon* was Bogdanovich's third hit in a row; it also starred O'Neal, as well as his daughter, Tatum, another Mengers client (who won an Oscar for the part). Mengers secured the title role in the 1974 version of *The Great Gatsby* for Robert Redford over Jack Nicholson by convincing Evans, who was looking for a male lead to pair with MacGraw, then slated to play Daisy, that casting two brown-haired stars would make for a boring film. (Mia Farrow would eventually be Redford's co-star; leaving Evans with two blondes.) Mengers got Faye Dunaway the role of Evelyn Mulwray in Roman Polanski's *Chinatown* by telling Evans, who preferred Jane Fonda, that Dunaway was about to take an Arthur Penn film—a lie. As Mengers recalls, "Of course we got Evans's offer for Dunaway, and at the end of the conversation I said, 'Bobbee, there is no Arthur Penn picture.' And he said, 'You cunt!' "

Mengers thought it would be good for Paula Prentiss if she worked with Alan Pakula—who had had a big hit with *Klute*—and insisted she woo the director for a part in *The Parallax View,* the 1974 political thriller starring Warren Beatty. Recalls Prentiss, "Sue said, 'Hon-eee, go to lunch with him and wear very, very tight pants,' which I did. She said it was the way they do it at MGM, which is that they sew them to your underwear."

Mengers's efforts made Michael Caine a household name. In the '60s he was known for English films like *The Ipcress File* and *Alfie;* in the '70s he began to appear in Hollywood fare like Neil Simon's *California Suite.* "She was trying to get me accepted in America as being a Brit," he remembers. "Now I am kind of accepted as an American who talks funny, and that's based on Sue. Just smashing through. She was a bulldog with charm."

In 1975 she got a then astronomical $1 million for Gene Hackman to do the ill-fated *Lucky Lady* opposite Liza Minnelli and Burt Reynolds. That same year she rescued Cybill Shepherd's career after the disastrous opening of Bogdanovich's musical, *At Long Last Love,* in which Shepherd, Reynolds, and Madeline Kahn warbled Cole Porter tunes. (At the time, Gene Shalit said,

"Cybill Shepherd cannot walk or talk, much less sing.") Mengers got her a part in Martin Scorsese's *Taxi Driver*. "At that time, she had icicles forming on her body," explains Mengers. "She needed to work with a director of that cachet."

Mengers had clawed her way up in the pre-feminist era, and she had no qualms about playing the gender card. One minute she would be batting her eyelashes and burbling baby talk, and in the next breath she would say something like "Fuck yourself, you little kike!" She could kill you in a negotiation, and then scold you for not opening the car door for her. She herself never thought her gender created problems for her. But younger women whom she nurtured professionally disagreed. Toni Howard, the ICM agent who represents Samuel L. Jackson and Christina Ricci, was Freddie Fields's secretary when Mengers first arrived in L.A. She recalls, "It was like Little Sue and 'the guys.' The guys tried to hold her back, not particularly Freddie. Somebody would sign some kind of ordinary person, and *everybody* would go, 'Oh, how fabulous!' And Sue would sign Ali MacGraw and Ryan O'Neal, and she didn't get the kind of attention somebody else would have gotten."

As cutting as Mengers could be to others, she often made herself the butt of her own jokes. If she wasn't getting enough sex, she'd complain, "Sue's cooze is cold." Recalls manager Michael Black, who worked with her at CMA and ICM, its successor, "She would be the first to make fun of her size, make fun of the fact that here is this Jew—she would refer to herself as 'this Jew'—sitting down at lunch with, say, Jacqueline Kennedy." Black regarded such extravagant displays of self-immolation as a business strategy. "If someone were likely to dish her, it undercut them if she said it about herself first," he continues. "And for someone who was intimidated by her, it relaxed them, made it easy to bond with them, get information."

She was so entertaining that Bob Sherman, the agent whose office was next to hers at CMA, used to put a water glass to the wall to eavesdrop on her conversations. He discovered that her usefulness to her clients far exceeded career advice. One day he overheard her tell someone, "You don't have to come *every* time." Says Dick

Shepherd, one of the original CMA partners and Mengers's titular boss there, "She marched to her own drummer. She'd do what her instincts told her to do, and if it was done wrong, she would expect somebody to bail her out. I always said to her, 'Your instincts are perfect, but your execution sucks.' " The problem was that Mengers ignored the nuts and bolts of agenting. She would nail down a great salary, but leave the fine points of negotiating, the minutiae of the contract, to others.

Nor was she much of a team player. There was a staff meeting every Wednesday morning at CMA, which Shepherd chaired. Mengers was always late and "obstreperous," he recalls. One Tuesday night he ran into her at a black-tie function on the Warner lot. In front of a group of people, he instructed her, "Just do me a favor—try to get to the meeting on time tomorrow, nine o'clock." The next morning, forty or so people, including several clients, were gathered in the conference room when Mengers arrived, promptly at nine, still wearing her gown and wrap from the previous night. Trying mightily to maintain his dignity, Shepherd was damned if he was going to laugh. But she dropped into the seat next to him, looked down into his lap, and said in a voice loud enough for the whole room to hear, "Dick, your fly's open."

Mengers may have been a diva, but, adds Shepherd, "she made a huge difference. A lot of the people whom we represented became clients or stayed with the agency because Sue was fun to be around. She held on to certain people that I don't think Freddie [Fields] could have kept, like Barbra. No matter how sloppy she was in her agentry work, at the end of the day, she could make things happen. I never knew anyone quite like her."

Mengers was so quotable that people dined out on delicious Sue-isms. Stevie Phillips, one of the few other female agents at CMA and a rival, was the opposite of Mengers in every respect: prim, proper and reserved. One afternoon at someone's home—the particulars have been lost to time—Mengers was chugging along in the pool, swimming stark naked, when out of nowhere, the story goes, appeared the Greek actress Melina Mercouri, famous for her hit 1960 film, *Never on Sunday,* and her husband, blacklisted director Jules Dassin (*Naked City*). Even Mengers was embarrassed, but she stepped out of the pool with aplomb, shook off the water with a toss of her blond mane, and without missing a beat said, "Hi! I'm Stevie Phillips!"

As Vidal remembers her in those years, "she was a bit lax in the flattery department, which was interesting because that's where agents usually shine. So she was something of a relief from those agents who were always telling their clients, 'You're the greatest, baby, you're the greatest.' She would be saying, 'Take it. You may never get another offer.' Joan Collins was turning middle-aged, with children, a broken marriage, going through a bad patch. Sue said to Joan, 'Give it up. You've got enough money to live on, you've got children to raise, just settle down, forget the business.' With that, Joan left Sue and got *Dynasty,* I think just to show her up."

Mengers was her own best press agent. She couldn't resist sharing a good story. As she recalls, "A couple of days before New Year's Eve 1973, Bob Evans called me and said, 'You cannot tell anybody, this is top-secret, but Kissinger is coming here for New Year's Eve and you have to bring Candy [Bergen].' I said, 'I can't get Candy to go out with Kissinger.' 'You gotta do it, you gotta do it, he wants to see Candy.' So I called Candy. I said, 'Candy, look, it's history. The secretary of state . . . we'll be with you, nothing's gonna happen.' So we prevailed upon Candice, and Bob kept saying, 'You cannot tell anybody, this is top-secret.' Well, I wasn't *not* going to tell people that I had New Year's Eve with Henry Kissinger, *intime* dinner, six people, so I called Joyce Haber, the gossip columnist at the L.A. *Times*. 'Joyce, I just want you to know on New Year's Eve . . .'" Little did I know that Kissinger had told his fiancée, Nancy, that he was going to Hanoi or someplace, and that it was only when it was in the paper that she found out he was spending New Year's Eve with Candice Bergen at Bob Evans's house. That is when Nancy said to Henry, 'Marriage, or bye-bye.' So Henry called Bob, said, 'Bob, I want to thank you for helping me get married.' "

Mengers's own parties were all business. "I ran those parties like—if my mother had been outside in the rain, she wouldn't have been able to get in," she continues. At one dinner she put Ann-Margret together with Mike Nichols, who then cast her in *Carnal Knowledge*. She introduced Burt Reynolds to Alan Pakula, who cast him in *Starting Over,* a hit 1979 romantic comedy, opposite Bergen and Jill Clayburgh. Paul Schrader met Lauren Hutton and used her to play one of Richard Gere's clients in the 1980 film *American Gigolo.* Michael Black remembers taking Hutton to that particular party. "When I picked her up at the Chateau Marmont, she was wearing a long, white gauze skirt, and no underwear. I gave her my drawers and I said, 'Darling, it's one thing to walk into Sue's party and try to get this role in *American Gigolo* and look fabulous and sexy. It's another thing to give a floor show with your beaver.' "

But all work and no play makes even movie stars dull boys and girls, and, after all, it was the '70s. "The big thing was grass," Mengers remembers. "It was like a ceremony. People sat on the floor, you'd smoke a joint. Darling Annette Funicello was there one night. I thought, How great, if I can turn her on, and I handed her the joint, and she looked at me, and she laughed and said. 'Not a chance.' I turned Billy Wilder on once. He had a Thanksgiving dinner at his house/apartment. I sat between him and George Burns, and I lit a joint. Billy was always against all that stuff. He took one or two tentative puffs. And now, when I see him, I talk to him as if he were Tim Leary."

The only cloud on Mengers's horizon in the mid-'70s was Jon Peters, the hairdresser who became Streisand's boyfriend in 1973. Streisand was a difficult client even on a good day. "Barbra was demanding, and it was impossible to get her to read scripts," says Mengers. "She was one major star whom you had to force into committing to a movie. The wonderful thing about her was you could say anything to her—'I don't like the way you look in this movie'—and she would listen. She wouldn't do what you wanted all the time—she was offered *Cabaret,* and I begged her to do it—but she didn't get annoyed. She only wanted the truth."

But by 1974, Peters became Streisand's de facto manager and agent (and eventually producer, beginning with the 1976 remake of *A Star Is Born*). Streisand had passed up parts in *Klute* and *Cabaret*—for which Jane Fonda and Liza Minnelli, respectively, had won Oscars—in favor of roles in pictures such as the 1972 dud *Up the Sandbox*. Peters, a full-service Svengali, took advantage of this to persuade Streisand that she wasn't receiving good enough advice. As Mengers remembers it, "I was very possessive of Barbra, and I felt Jon had a lot of self-interest [in the relationship], because he wanted to establish himself, so there were a lot of bloody battles, and Barbra let us fight them out." It didn't help that Streisand had set her heart on adapting an Isaac Bashevis Singer short story called "Yentl," which she wanted to star in—playing a boy, yet—and direct. Mengers was less than enthusiastic, not to say openly discouraging, as only she could be. "I thought of her, not as disorganized, but I was always concerned about her attention span, and [*Yentl*] was a hard, hard period picture. I never thought it would get off the ground, and it didn't, until she announced she was doing it as a musical, and you figure when that throat opens, you're home free. The minute I heard the word 'musical,' I thought, Oh, great, that's money in the bank. And I did love the picture," which was eventually made in 1983. But in the late '70s it had been an issue between them.

332

In the summer of 1970, Mengers had met Jean-Claude Tramont at a dinner party at the home of Henry Ford's daughter Charlotte. Tramont was a screenwriter (*Ash Wednesday*, the 1973 film in which Elizabeth Taylor gets a face-lift) and director of Belgian extraction. He was a striking man—"this tall, elegant borzoi or Russian-wolfhound-looking kind of guy, immaculately turned out," in the words of Chris Mankiewicz, who knew Tramont well and spent a lot of time with the couple.

"I was not at all interested in him," Mengers recalls. "Too good-looking. I've never liked handsome men. My attitude was: Gotta be something wrong with them. And it wasn't hard, because they didn't come calling, ya know? I think Jean-Claude was intrigued that this short, fat Jewess didn't pay attention to him.

"About a week after the dinner, he called, and I didn't recognize the name. It was the only time in my entire life that a man pursued me. And I was no chicken. I was gettin' way up there in my thirties. He's the first man who ever—not wanted me, because I had my share—who wanted *me*. He came over for a drink, and that was it." This was in June. By September they were living together.

Mengers used to tell a story about the early days of their relationship: When Tramont spent the night with her, in the morning he would complain about her snoring. She replied, "I don't snore."

"You do snore."

"I don't snore." He put a tape recorder under her bed, and, lo, when he played back the tape, the sounds of Mengers's honking filled the room. She thought, "Oh God, and he still loves me—I have to marry him! There's nobody else who would put up with that snoring."

A few months after they met, Tramont proposed to her during a flight from New York to L.A. He pretended to be drunk, said, "Why don't we get married?" She replied, "Don't be ridiculous!" That's where the matter stood until a few years later, when Galley invited them to accompany him to Greece on his honeymoon. One night, before the trip, when Mengers and Tramont were in the middle of a fight, she said to him heatedly, "If you think I'm gonna go on John Galley's boat on *his* honeymoon and not be married, you're crazy."

So in May 1973 the couple wed at Ventana, a Big Sur resort popular among the hipper elements of Hollywood. Gene Hackman was shooting a film up there, and Mengers, who was always working, even on the day of her nuptials, felt she might as well be near him in case he needed anything. The bride and groom had planned to fly up to Big Sur for an anonymous service by themselves, "like two orphans, two sad souls," as Mengers recalls. "We arrived at the airport, and suddenly Streisand showed up, a total surprise, with her then beau." This was a few months before she took up with Peters. "She became my maid of honor," Mengers continues, "and this strange guy that Jean-Claude had never met was his best man. But the whole ceremony was about Streisand. The justice of the peace, who looked exactly like Spencer Tracy, kept staring at Barbra, and the music they played was 'People.' And that night, our wedding night, Streisand and her beau joined us for dinner. She looked more like a bride than I did, and when they brought out the wedding cake, they put it in front of her! I could feel Jean-Claude's anger building. My poor husband, what he went through. But Barbra gave us the most unique wedding present. She taped German lieder for me, love songs, and, on the other side, French songs for Jean-Claude. That was so unbelievable, such a lovely, personal gift."

Once married, Mengers and Tramont did indeed accompany Galley to Greece, though he insists that the trip was actually Sue's honeymoon. In any event, Galley had recently married a Czechoslovakian former actress, and as Mengers recalls, "Olinka would get up every morning looking like Miss Czechoslovakia, the most gorgeous girl in a little bikini, and I was like Jeannie Berlin in *The Heartbreak Kid* [the 1972 Elaine May film in which newlywed Charles Grodin dumps Berlin on their honeymoon for Cybill Shepherd]. I'd come out wrapped in a towel, and my husband would look at Olinka, and then he'd look at me, just like Chuck Grodin. Olinka would jump off the boat and swim, and I'd still be huddled there."

("She's forgetting a big part of it," Calley says when I relay Mengers's account to him. "It was like word had gotten from island to island that Sue was coming, because when we pulled into port, there would be, like, fifty Mustache Petes waiting for a shot at her. She was a bit heavy, but Greek guys like their women slightly heavy, and she would put on her transparent schmatte and walk along the beach and have a line of guys following her, apparently playing with their worry beads but actually playing pocket pool, trying to get behind her so they could look through this garment into the sun, see her outline as she jiggled along in her high-heeled shoes.")

Mengers and Tramont were an unlikely match, a union of opposites if ever there was one. "Jean-Claude was this kind of aristocratic, very sophisticated, incredibly witty, incredibly cultivated person." says Chris Mankiewicz. "He was embarrassed by shows of emotion and affected considerable dislike for the vulgarity of Hollywood. He loved to talk about world affairs, which never interested her at all. He just loved Hollywood movie stars and loved all the gossip. He was this Catholic aristocrat and she was like the maid, almost, in terms of how she looked. She would like to hang around in her bathrobe, the quintessential Jewish hausfrau. What they had in common was this extraordinary sense of humor."

"My husband was a very witty guy." says Mengers, offering the ultimate compliment: "He made me sound dumb." Tramont gave vent to one of his more notorious lines while he was watching the Academy Awards on TV. Noticing that yet another Holocaust documentary had won an Oscar, he said, "There's no business like *Shoah* business!" On another occasion, a party for Sue's mother's eighty-fifth birthday, he surveyed the guests, her mother's friends, all women of advanced years, eighty-five, ninety, with their walkers, all Holocaust survivors, and exclaimed, "Schindler's B-list!" Adds Mengers, "He had me believing for a while he was half Jewish, until I found out he was full of it. But he had that kind of angry Jewish humor. He was anti-everything. It was because he wasn't being paid enough attention, because in this town you walk into a room, you're immediately judged by your accomplishments. So he became a provocateur to get attention." Eclipsed by her notoriety, he suffered from being Mr. Sue Mengers.

"Nick and Nora Charles were nothing compared to Sue and Jean-Claude," says Mankiewicz. "On a good night it was like watching two of the greatest swordsmen of France thrusting at each other with rapiers, because they were both incredibly quick, witty, and funny. [On a bad night] he was, at times, cruel to her. Sue likes to cuddle. She gets to be like a little girl at home, and she loved Jean-Claude, and she loved to snuggle up to him—she called him Moojie. And he'd say, 'Sue, stop it! Stop it!' and they'd yell and scream. He would say, 'You kike!' There were times when she was hurt by him, and she would either start crying or she would just leave. And be really pissed off."

Most of their friends were her friends, and some of her friends, the ones who loved her, didn't like the way he spoke to her. He'd say, "You're a lazy cunt," and she'd say, "Yeah, I am." But others understood that this was part of their dialogue, just the way they were together. Mankiewicz: "Once Jean-Claude and I wanted Sue, whose idea of exercise is to get out of bed and call her housekeeper to bring her some Häagen-Dazs, to work out more, so he and I set off to get a treadmill for her at a sporting-goods store. The man came over, asked. 'Are you looking for anything in particular?' And Jean-Claude looked at him and said, 'Well, yes, have you got one of these Isadora

Duncan models?' I just started screaming with laughter, because the whole image was of Sue's scarf getting caught in the treadmill. It was like, how many ways can you murder your wife?

"There were a lot of women in this town who would have thrown themselves at Jean-Claude's feet if he ever left Sue. And people kept thinking, Why does he stay with her? She hasn't done much for his career. But I don't think it was ever the case that he really wanted that. This was not a marriage of convenience from his point of view. He really loved Sue, really adored her."

During an interview with Mengers in 1987, Paul Rosenfield remarked on the fact that Mengers had represented several couples—Ryan O'Neal and Farrah Fawcett, Bogdanovich and Shepherd, Prentiss and Benjamin, Jacqueline Bisset and Michael Sarrazin—and wondered whether she had been using her work to look for a family. "Don't forget," she responded, "I had no brothers or sisters, no cousins, for a long time no boyfriend, no husband. *This* was family." In Tramont, despite his caustic wit, she finally found the warmth she had lacked growing up. "He was willing to become my daddy," she says. "He was willing to take care of me. It wasn't his looks, it was the compassion that he had."

On January 27, 1979, Tramont got a collect call from Mengers's mother—" 'Collect call' were the only English words she learned," says Sue—informing him that his wife's L.A.-to-New York flight had been hijacked. A woman who claimed she was wired with nitroglycerin was holding the plane hostage on the ground at J.F.K. According to Joe Armstrong, who was also on the plane—he was then the editor in chief and publisher of *New York* and *New West* magazines and is now vice president of Talk Media—the passengers were terrified. "People were on their knees praying, you saw people with their hands in their faces in fetal positions on the floor. We thought a big ball of fire could come roaring down that aisle. Except Sue. She kept saying, 'I'm keeping Candy waiting at Elaine's.' The rest of us are thinking, 'We're gonna die any minute!' "

The hijacker wanted Charlton Heston to read a largely incoherent statement on television. When Mengers heard this, she was flabbergasted. Recalls Armstrong, "Sue said, 'Charlton Heston!??'—like he's a B actor—'I can get *Barbra Streisand*!' " Adds Mengers,

"But she wanted fucking Charlton Heston, no substitutes. With my luck Streisand would have said no anyway. 'Blow her up!'

"Meanwhile," Mengers continues, "Jean-Claude didn't feel like talking to my mother, so she screamed at the operator, 'She's been hijacked!' So then Jean-Claude had a dilemma. Should he fly in? If it was gonna explode, I was already dead, so who did he call for advice? Bob Evans [the marriage expert]! Bob said, 'What if she doesn't die? You gotta keep your marriage going, you better go.' So, begrudgingly, he got on a plane, figuring he'd either bring me home or my ashes."

After five, six, seven hours, in Mengers's words, "I realized. This could be serious. I'm gonna fuckin' die here, and I thought. I'm not going to go without being stoned. So I lit up a joint. Theodore Bikel, who was on the plane, took his guitar and started striding up and down, singing, 'Hava Nagila, hava Nagila' . . . There is nothing worse than Theodore Bikel. Nothing. And so I was thinking, I'm gonna die listening to Theodore Bikel, and he wouldn't fuckin' sit down and shut up. Like he's consoling us with these songs." Finally, after eight hours on the ground, an F.B.I, agent was able to overpower the hijacker and disarm her; the bomb turned out to be a phony. As the passengers disembarked, Armstrong noticed eighty-odd stretchers, with bottles of plasma, waiting in a hangar while ambulances stood outside. Mengers went off to Elaine's with some of her fellow abductees, "having the best time." she adds, "and when I got to the hotel at two in the morning, there was Jean-Claude, livid."

Mengers had a great run at CMA under Begelman and Fields. But by the mid-'70s, agents were leaving the business in droves, becoming studio executives and producers. "A lot of those guys just looked down the road and said, 'It's not how I want to grow old.'" Mengers explains. "Being an agent is like being in the gulag. A lot of them didn't want to spend their lives being beat up, which is what you are most of the time. I never thought of being an agent as a stepping-stone. It was the ultimate, a calling from God. I was written about so much, and made such a fuss over, I really began to believe I knew everything, and that if I ever left the business, it would collapse. I thought I was the most important person in the entire industry. It never occurred to me that the clients I really cared for could leave me. Or that they'd get old. I was totally an idiot." Begelman left to go to Columbia Pictures in 1973. Mengers, too, got offers to go to the studios. She adds, "But Freddie Fields threatened them. I may have wanted to, but I couldn't." ("I wasn't in a position to threaten any studio," counters Fields. "It was not like today. You didn't go in and say, 'You're not going to get so-and-so.' ")

In 1975, Marvin Josephson's International Famous Agency bought CMA. The new mega-agency became ICM. Fields soon left for a producing deal at Paramount. At the same time, five obscure agents led by Michael Ovitz left William Morris to form CAA. With all the fire and smoke surrounding the ICM deal, no one really noticed, but an era had ended. The agency business would become considerably more regimented. Armani would replace muumuus.

Mengers had enjoyed a love-hate relationship with Begelman and Fields. "They were wonderful to me," she says, "but why not? They had a genius agent working for them for scale. I was like a little puppy, I was so thrilled to be doing what I was doing. They screwed me pretty good when it came to money. There were a lot of promises, I never had stock, I was always told, 'Don't worry about it. If we ever sell the company, we'll take care of you.' Of course, they didn't, and those were my good years, so I have no love lost. If I never see Freddie again, it'll be too soon."

Says Geffen, "She really had no clue. She so completely trusted them. They always said they were going to take care of her, and they didn't. By the time they sold the agency, she had virtually no money. On some level, Sue was her own worst agent." "Sue has always been bitter about [the sale]," says Fields, "but she was unrealistic. I didn't get rich, David didn't get rich, no one got rich. The company didn't sell for that much." He adds: "Sue was treated equally with her peers."

By the late '70s, several of Mengers's oldest and biggest clients were in the grip of career crises that she was powerless to ameliorate. First there was MacGraw, still in thrall to McQueen. "As Jon and I fought over Barbra, Steve and I fought over Ali," she recalls. "They only had one telephone line in the house. I would say to my secretary, 'Get Ali MacGraw,' and the line would be busy for hours. And then, finally, the phone would ring and Steve would pick up, and my secretary would say, 'Miss Mengers calling Ali MacGraw.' He'd say, 'If she wants to talk to Ali, let her dial the phone herself!' And hung up." Eventually, MacGraw left her.

She and Bogdanovich also parted company. Bergen left after 1979's *Starting Over,* which was a hit. "She was annoyed with me because she wanted the Jill Clayburgh part, I was too negative, I was this, I was that, I was pissed," Mengers remembers. "A star is the star. They don't want their agent to be a star. And they're right. I wouldn't want to read about my lawyer and his life. But on the other hand, when you've been an unknown all your life, it's very flattering to have people call you up. It was wonderful to talk about myself. But I don't think it helped." Says Michael Black. "Historically, when Sue lost a star, she would re-sign someone two weeks later that was just as big. All of a sudden she had departures and she wasn't re-signing bigger stars to take their place."

The way Mengers treated Cybill Shepherd says a lot about her complacency in this period, not to mention her bluntness. Despite the plum role in *Taxi Driver,* Shepherd at the end of the decade had returned to Memphis (where she grew up), married a local man, and had a baby, effectively leaving the business. Then she tried to get her career back. "I couldn't get a job in TV or movies," she recalls. "The only jobs I had were singing in small jazz clubs and doing regional theater, and I was kind of desperate. So I called Sue, and I said, 'Well, Sue, would you represent me again?' She said, 'Cybill, you've been gone so long you might as well be dead.'" (When Shepherd hit it big with *Moonlighting* a few years later, Mengers approached her, but Shepherd turned her down. "I have tremendous affection for Sue Mengers," Shepherd says, "but I was already represented by someone I was very satisfied with, and I wasn't going to leave.")

Still, there was Streisand. As Black puts it. "Sue never considered Barbra a client, she considered her a sister. Even though others would come and go, she and Barbra would always be in business together." Then, in 1981, Mengers finally secured a feature for Tramont to direct, a Universal picture called *All Night Long,* an offbeat comedy about an unhappy drugstore manager with Gene Hackman in the lead, opposite Lisa Eichhorn, a promising actress who had appeared in *Yanks* and *Cutter's Way*. But several weeks into production, Eichhorn was gone, and Streisand took her place as the neglected housewife and aspiring singer with whom Hackman's character has an affair.

Tongues wagged. To Mengers's enemies, the people whose calls she never took, the people she steamrollered, the people she wounded with her tongue, the people who were just plain envious of her power, it looked as if she had strong-armed Streisand into saving Tramont's picture. People said Mengers had finally lost it. Indeed, prodding your biggest client and best friend to prop up your husband's movie could have been dangerous, even suicidal, if that is what happened. Her friends warned her that it smelled bad, but she looked at them as if they were crazy—for someone who was such a savvy agent, Mengers could be unbelievably naïve, especially where relationships were concerned. She loved Tramont, she loved Streisand, and that was enough.

According to the film's screenwriter, W. D. Richter, Hackman from the start had had his heart set on Streisand, who read the script and turned it down. Hackman was inconsolable, and made Eichhorn, Tramont, and everybody else miserable. Then Streisand changed her mind. As one source who is familiar with the players observes, "Barbra did it not for Sue, because Barbra would not do something for somebody else in a million years. She did it because she wanted to do it." Mengers negotiated a very rich deal for her: $5 million, plus 10 percent of the gross, for five weeks' work—a stunning amount at the time. Richter says that Streisand was so pleased with her compensation that she figured out how much she was getting by the hour. Also, according to Richter, she seemed quite content, required no script changes, and got along well with Tramont.

But after the production wrapped, Streisand fired Mengers, who has always denied that the movie's eventual failure had anything to do with the breach—for one thing, the call from Streisand came before the movie opened. Instead, Mengers detected the hidden hand of Jon Peters. "*All Night Long* caused a lot of strain between Barbra and Jon," she says. "Because it was the first thing Barbra had done where Jon wasn't involved. He liked to get producer credit—and this one announced to the industry: She's a free agent. Producers didn't feel, 'Omigod, if I bring that script to Streisand, I'll have to bring in Jon Peters.' I think it was wearing her down, living with a man who hated her agent and closest friend. So ultimately she made the choice. You know?" Streisand and Peters both declined to comment for this article.

"When Barbra called to tell me that she was leaving, I was livid," Mengers says, "because I felt I had been an impeccable agent for her. And she then said, 'But we can still be friends!' My reaction was anger: 'Of course we can't be friends. You've rejected what I do, you've announced to the world I'm not good enough.' And her reaction was: 'Oh my God, she only cares about me if I'm her client.' She couldn't understand, and it hurt her for a long time. I don't think we talked for over three years. For me it was not just, 'Oh, well, I've lost a client,' which would upset me under any circumstances. But Barbra was and is very special to me. She was the jewel in the crown. Not only did I love her, I was proud to be representing her. While I was working with her it was the joy of my life, even though she never expresses gratitude or even acknowledgment of anything you may achieve. It's such a thin line an agent walks between friendship and a work relationship. You can never forget, no matter how close you are to a client, you're the employee." But in those days this was a reality Mengers didn't want to acknowledge.

341

In any event, by the time *All Night Long* opened, Mengers and Streisand were not speaking. Tramont's picture is a winning, underappreciated gem, but it is a small film, European in sensibility, character-driven rather than tightly plotted. It might have done well in the early '70s, but by 1981 it was too late for films like that. It flopped, unable to compete with movies such as *Raiders of the Lost Ark*. Two years later, Hackman left Mengers, too.

Mengers had always had difficulty controlling her anger. After she lost Streisand, her foot came off the brake. When clients were having difficulty finding work, she blamed them. She'd tell them to lose weight, do fewer pictures. As Geffen puts it, "Sue was famous for her 'Let's-face-it conversations.' And a lot of people don't want to face it. Sue felt she was being honest, and without intending it, she became insensitive. It was because she was so hurt herself." As Mengers once put it, "Looking over my career, I see negativity as probably my major fault." She became increasingly bitter. "None of the actors who received Oscars because of what I did ever wanted to acknowledge that I helped them get a gig," she says. "Never. Never."

In 1986, Mengers ankled ICM, as the trades would put it. "It wasn't burnout, it was blackout," she explains. "When Streisand left, I already wanted to stop working. I knew it was over. I just knew that my marriage needed more time, it was going south, and I was dispirited. I had lost more clients than I wanted to, ever, and watched other people lose theirs. Anyone else, a normal person, would have said. 'Well, Barbra left, too bad, on to the next.' I really let it affect me. And then Hackman—I didn't want that pain. I felt I was too good."

After she finally left ICM, Mengers spent the next two years getting to know her husband, enjoying the extended honeymoon she had always been too work-obsessed to have. The couple split their time between Beverly Hills and their apartment in Paris. They were good years. She had even patched things up with Streisand.

But in the end Mengers couldn't stay away from the business, and in 1988 she succumbed to the blandishments of the Morris agency, whose once potent movie division was in trouble, having been surpassed by its more forward-thinking competitors at CAA and ICM. (The famous line was "I don't have an agent; I'm with the Morris office.") Morris was the worst place she could have chosen. Hidebound, clubby, and paternalistic, it was a bastion of the golf-and-cigar culture of old Hollywood. The board members were the kind of men who put their initials on their license plates and called the female agents "girls." "I went back because I wanted the money," Mengers explains, "and I thought, maybe I was too hasty. I'm still a young woman. But I knew I had made a mistake from the first day. You can't go home again."

While she was there she served as mentor to a group of women agents who today are among the most powerful in the business, including Toni Howard; Elaine Goldsmith-Thomas, who represents Julia Roberts, Susan Sarandon, and Tim Robbins; Risa

Shapiro, who represents Rosie O'Donnell and David Duchovny; and Boatie Boatwright, who represents Norman Jewison and Joanne Woodward. Says Goldsmith-Thomas, "I learned a lot from her, because she'd always preface everything by saying, 'Don't make the same mistakes I did. I used to beat them up, I used to talk like the guys, and they hated me for it.' "

But Mengers continued to cling to old habits. For instance, she had come to prefer established stars to young talent. As Goldsmith-Thomas recalls, "When she first came in, she looked at my client list and went, 'Who's this Julia Roberts?' I said, 'Oh, she's great. She's got the lead in this movie, *Steel Magnolias,* with Sally Field, Shirley MacLaine, Daryl Hannah, Olympia Dukakis.' And she said, 'HellOHH! Do you notice a pattern? They're all well known, she's not. She's an unknown—drop her!' When I said, 'This guy Tim Robbins, whom I'm working with, is great—he wants to be a filmmaker—' 'HellOHH! Please, actors can't direct!' She now writes him notes, 'Dear Kurosawa . . .' "

Nevertheless, Goldsmith-Thomas insists, "Sue was incredibly helpful." One day, the younger agent recalls, she and Julia Roberts were at the office discussing her next film, *Pretty Woman,* with the actress insisting she wouldn't do any nude scenes. As Goldsmith-Thomas remembers it, "She had no advance warning about Sue, was not prepared for her. Suddenly Sue came in and said, 'Hello. Sue Mengers, no need to stand!' And without taking a breath, she said, 'Let me give you a little hint. This is a movie about a hooker.' Julia said, 'What do I say to my mom?' 'Tell her you're working for Disney, she'll be fine.' Julia just went, 'Uhh,' and Sue looked at her and said, 'What do you have to hide? If I had your body I'd be walking down Wilshire Boulevard [naked].' "

As entertaining as ever, Mengers was nevertheless unable to rebuild her old power base. She had expected that her former clients would flock back to her—as the Morris office had hoped when it hired her—but they didn't. "That was shocking to me," she says. "People like Sidney Lumet, we'd had such a wonderful relationship, and Nolte, and Demme, the whole list of them." Though the breach with Streisand had been repaired, she was another who stayed away. According to Chris Mankiewicz, even in this period, "Sue and Barbra talked all the time. . . . Barbra couldn't wait to ask Sue

343

about everything, including getting a date. Jean-Claude, who called Barbra the 'Jewish camel,' was deeply unhappy that she did not go back to be with Sue, given the fact that Sue really needed a couple of names to shore up her position at William Morris."

Even a maverick agent like Mengers is more effective as part of a team, and Morris didn't have the depth that either CMA or ICM had had. "The system that she went into at Morris was not supportive," says Fields, contrasting the agency to what he says was a more collaborative ethos at CMA. "That's what she missed. She lost touch with who was out there." At the same time, with a blizzard of new ancillary markets such as home video and cable, the business had changed dramatically. Says producer Gary Woods, who was an agent at the Morris office at the time, "When Sue was in her prime, the deals were less sophisticated. Like the other big agents, she would ask for as much money as she could get up front, and didn't really get into back-end deals. When she returned, she walked into a different business." Says Mengers, "I had lost it. I could not find that old excitement. I knew too much, having seen how callously people leave the agent that started them. So it's harder to give them that dedication, because you're steeling yourself against being hurt." Mengers finally resigned in 1991. Says Goldsmith-Thomas, "When Sue left, it felt like the halls were empty, like the creativity got sucked out. I felt I had lost a wealth of information."

Mengers hasn't worked since.

There's a parlor game to be played with the names of people who were too smart for Hollywood and suffered for it. But that's not quite accurate. There are a lot of smart people in Hollywood, most of whom do quite well; it's more the loose cannons who lose out, the people who don't have the stomach for the bullshit, who can't or won't keep their mouths shut, who aren't politic or careful. Mankiewicz is certainly on this list, and so are people like Vanessa Redgrave, Sean Penn, Alec Baldwin, Alex Cox. Mengers and Tramont as well.

"This is a business that is ruled by fear and insecurity," says Mankiewicz. "So I admire courage and guts and honesty almost more than anything else. Sue and Jean-Claude were both fearless, and in the end it probably cost them both their careers. She didn't make it because she knew somebody or she was related to somebody or because she got a break or blackmailed somebody or fucked somebody. She made it because she was simply fucking brilliant, and terrific at what she did. She earned every penny she got in this business. She was the last of the great gunfighters, the people who could walk into a town and make deals happen. At the end of the day, that's not a bad epitaph."

Five years after Mengers left William Morris, in the fall of 1996, Tramont called Mankiewicz from Paris. Following an exchange of pleasantries, Jean-Claude confessed, "I'm not well, I'm having trouble walking up the stairs, I have this thing on my spine." It was a tumor. Tramont and Mengers returned to Los Angeles, where he was treated with radiation. Mankiewicz went out of town for Christmas, and just before he left he spoke to Tramont in the hospital. Jean-Claude said, "I'm coming home in a day or two. When I get a little bit better, I'll see you, and we'll talk." Mankiewicz recalls, "Five days later I came back, and he had died. I was just devastated. He was the closest friend I had in the world." The funeral was small and private, a requiem Mass at a Catholic church in L.A. Among the attendees were Mankiewicz; Bergen; Sidney Poitier and his wife, Joanna Shimkus; Marcia Diamond, Neil Diamond's ex-wife; and, of course, Sue.

"Without him, nothing really interests me," says Mengers, three years later. "I don't like to shop, I don't like to go out. Maybe it's a stage, maybe I'm still in mourning. Sometimes when I get depressed I think, Maybe I should have had a kid. But I remember panicking at the thought of having to give up any of my time. The baby to me seemed extra. But if I had it to do all over again, with hindsight, I would have worried less about the clients and more about a baby."

Says Boatie Boatwright, the agent and a lifelong friend of Mengers's, "We finally gave up thinking that she's going to get up one morning like the rest of us and try to live a normal life. Thank God for Geffen. At least he gets her out of the house."

So many relationships in Hollywood revolve around who you are in the business—can you help me?—that when people leave, no matter how powerful they are or have been, they cease to exist. There's a well-known story about John Galley at a party right after his exit from Warner. An actress went up to him and asked, "Are you John Galley?" Galley replied, "I was." Pointing to his successor, who was standing nearby, he added, "That's the man you want."

It is testimony to Mengers that it didn't happen to her. Even clients who had dropped her were supportive and compassionate. She says, "When my husband died, I was astounded at the letters I got from people I perceived weren't that fond of me. I've [even] had a sort of rapprochement with Jon Peters. It's only taken twenty years."

On occasion, she's almost cheerful. "I found myself very comforted by just being here quietly," she continues. "It's wonderful not to have to wake up with an alarm, just when I feel like it. My todays are what I want them to be, quiet, divided between reading, watching TV, and sleeping. And I love it. Everyone said, 'Oh, you'll miss working.' Never. When I hear the anxiety in the voices of the people that *are* working, and I'm lying in bed reading the *National Enquirer*—joke—I think to myself, How was I able to do it?"

But for all her protestations to the contrary, the business is too deep in her bones for her to shrug it off entirely. She can't help playing virtual agent in her mind: "I like this Vince Vaughn. Julia Roberts. She's of an age now where she can really do some interesting things. Cameron Diaz is enchanting. Parker Posey. She's a great comedienne. Very versatile. Christina Ricci. I love her. She's hot. I kind of like Drew Barrymore. In certain scenes she can look ravishing, and then she doesn't. I also love Michelle Pfeiffer. Janeane Garofalo, love her."

Directors?

"Paul Thomas Anderson. I loved *Boogie Nights*."

Tarantino?

"I loved *Pulp Fiction*. Because Tarantino had the imagination to bring back Travolta, Who would pick Travolta to play a punk killer? He was out of the business. I tried to sign him every minute I was an agent. He's one of the ones that got away. I think the reason I didn't get him is he once saw me smoking marijuana at a party, and I saw his face, and I thought, Uh-oh."

Mengers pauses, her face breaking into a mischievous grin. "If Tom Cruise, Tom Hanks, and ten or twenty people of my choosing said, 'Sue, we're signing lifetime contracts with you that stipulate that we cannot fire you until you die, but you can fire us'—*then* I would be an agent again."

GOOD NIGHT, DARK PRINCE

Like all of Don Simpson's movies, _Top Gun_ was Party Central. There was a wrap party every Friday, as director Tony Scott put it. The third one began as an elegant affair at a Navy officers club, but it soon degenerated into a free-for-all by the pool. Kelly McGillis stripped off her clothes and jumped in. The actors and the pilots decided to throw Simpson and Jerry Bruckheimer, his longtime partner, in after her. Bruckheimer, of course, was smart enough to pull off his expensive cowboy boots, go limp, and let them have their way with him. Simpson, on the other hand, put up a terrific fight. He grabbed on to a metal stanchion by the pool and just would not let go. He resisted so fiercely that it wasn't fun anymore, and the actors finally gave up. The pilots, though, were not going to let some Hollywood producer get the better of them, so they broke his grip— it took five of them—and threw him into the pool, where he sank to the bottom. Don Simpson could not swim.

It was October of last year, midnight in the house on Stone Canyon Road, and Simpson was seated behind the desk in his study. He had just returned to town, after an abrupt disappearing act following the death of his friend Dr. Stephen Ammerman, who had seemingly OD'd in his pool house. He called it, with apparent amusement, his "flight from justice," and kept referring to Ammerman's death as a "suicide."

Simpson was always going up and down in weight, constantly checking into clinics for a tune-up, a nip here, a tuck there, so he looked different every time I saw him; he was an essence in search of an appearance. That night his weight was up, dramatically. His neck had disappeared into an aureole of fat that obscured the planes of his face. His hair, which looked unwashed and greasy, was long and pulled back into a ponytail. He was wearing a black T-shirt with the sleeves cut off. His arms were beefy, like sausages, and he was toying with a letter opener shaped like a dagger. It was not the way I wanted to remember him.

Simpson had a lot to be unhappy about. His partnership with Bruckheimer was coming to an end. Ammerman's death had been the last straw, and Bruckheimer finally seemed ready to go on without him. "I think Jerry was convinced that this was the only way he could shock Don into losing fifty pounds, get him to stop drinking like a fish and stop coking and stop whoring," speculates Simpson's old friend producer-director Rob Cohen. "He was saying, 'I'm not going to be dragged down by you and your scandals and your lawsuits and all this crap.' But it didn't work."

Simpson had also been unhappy at Disney. He was used to producing the big event movies of the '80s, while Disney was in the vanguard of the penurious '90s, when executives, not producers, called the shots. Simpson complained that studio chairman Jeffrey Katzenberg's notorious tightfistedness had prevented him from bidding competitively on the high-profile projects he wanted, such as *Presumed Innocent, Disclosure,* and *Apollo 13.* "Jeff is not creative at all," he once complained to me. "He is a businessman. He's about commerce, and product, and shelf life, and crap like that, which is why Disney made the worst movies in the world."

Still, Simpson and Katzenberg were close friends. Katzenberg, by now running DreamWorks SKG, was said to have fruitlessly tried to get Simpson into rehab, and recently had offered to oversee his financial affairs, telling him to take time off to get himself together. Simpson refused, and fretted about his career: "I always thought that I would end up acting and directing some day," he told me. "I didn't want to produce. I still don't want to produce."

Simpson was prone to black depressions, and this one, dating from Ammerman's death in August, was one of the blackest. He wouldn't leave his house. He was a vain man. As DreamWorks cofounder David Geffen put it, "He wouldn't go out unless he could get into a pair of size-twenty-eight Levis." Cohen invited Simpson on one of the celebrated rafting trips that Simpson had been part of since the early '80s, along with Katzenberg, MCA vice-chairman Tom Pollock, UTA head Jim Berkus, and ICM president Jim Wiatt, among others, but Simpson refused, telling Cohen that his old friends were out to get him. Then there was *You'll Never Make Love in This Town Again,* the book by four pseudonymous hookers, one of whom, "Tiffany," had some exceedingly distasteful tales to tell about Simpson's nocturnal habits.

The day before his death, Simpson had been talking to his agent and his lawyer, Wiatt and Jake Bloom respectively, about setting up a new company at Universal. Simpson wanted Universal production head Casey Silver to be part of it. The Friday that Simpson died, Wiatt and Bloom were on the phone to Silver. *Did you call Don yet? We've got to get this done.* Silver had been putting off the call. "I wanted to make sure I was ready to dance," he says. He finally phoned him around four o'clock in the afternoon, and never got a call back. Simpson was already dead, had passed away the night of January 19, at the age of fifty-two, on the toilet, reading a new biography of Oliver Stone.

None of Simpson's friends were enormously surprised by his death. "He succeeded at everything he ever tried to do," says Cohen, "and he'd been trying to do this for a long time." Simpson had once appeared in a documentary made by James Toback, called *The Big Bang,* in which he'd stared straight into the camera and said, "I hope that death, when it comes, just strikes me down suddenly, in the night, without warning." Simpson got his wish.

The first published reports said Simpson died of natural causes; nobody who knew him believed a word of it. He was an unrepentant user and bad boy. "The reason I did drugs is because they were fun," he told me, unaccountably dropping into the past tense. "I had a great time and I'm glad I did it." He'd gone beyond recreational drugs into "smart" drugs and growth hormones, on which he considered himself an expert. He was a patron, in both senses of the word, to the late Madame Alex; he was into kinky sex, B&D, S&M.

The Don Simpson story was a classic Hollywood morality tale: a wild life chastised by an early death. It is a story of the glittering '80s, when Simpson and Bruckheimer made four smash hits— *Flashdance, Top Gun,* and the first two *Beverly Hills Cop* films— and in the process redefined (not, it should be said, in a particularly good way) the Hollywood movie of that decade, refashioning it into a loud, tactile, MTV-like "experience." This is a story Simpson might have liked, a rags-to-riches tale of a kid from Alaska who became top gun in Hollywood—if he could have jettisoned the morality angle and tied up the story before the unhappy ending, because he knew audiences didn't like unhappy endings.

But the real story is more interesting. Simpson was something other than the producer of *Top Gun,* other than an alchemist of empty sound and fury. He was a man divided against himself, a tormented soul, a vessel of brilliance and self-hatred, adrift in a sea of fleshly delights, a hostage to pain and humiliation, a man who defeated every effort to understand or humanize him. "Don was a guy who spoke very, very highly about a man he really loathed. Which was himself," says Cohen.

Why the torrent of grief in the wake of Simpson's death? "He was always so fearless in his recklessness, so unabashed in his hungers, and so fierce in his depressions," says one Hollywood denizen. "He had courage, and you don't like to see courage go down." As his friend producer Dawn Steel put it, "He died of spiritual suicide."

One week after his death, his friends gathered at his home to warm one another and discover whatever meaning was to be had in his death. Among those present was actress Susan Lentini, who had gone out with Simpson on and off for ten years—longer than any other woman. She hadn't seen him for five years, had never even set foot inside the Stone Canyon house. She was surprised to find so many pictures of herself. Had he felt more for her than he'd ever been capable of expressing? She wandered into the bathroom, rummaged around in the drawers. She found a box of Tampax, and on top of that a cosmetic bag. The bag brought it all back: the other women, the distance, his emotional unavailability. No, she decided, the pictures were part of the act; he had put them there to appear normal. She started to cry.

"I, Donald C. Simpson, being of sound mind and sickly body, do hereby bequeath to all underclassmen my ability to 'walk on the wild side' while still maintaining a reputation that's 'above reproach.' "—Last Will and Testament, *The Eagle's Cry*, West Anchorage High School, 1962.

The first son of Russ and June Simpson, Don Simpson was born in Seattle in 1943 and raised in Anchorage, the godforsaken gateway to the natural splendors of Alaska. The family lived on a dead-end street in Spenard, a seedy, blue-collar enclave of boxy, single-story shacks separated by garbage-strewn vacant lots that would in later years give way to topless bars and massage parlors. Spenard is best known for the "Spenard divorce," in which husband shoots wife or vice versa. "So many of our parents seem to think that family life is supposed to be as it was represented on television in the '50s," Simpson told me. "And in fact it was quite the opposite. I'm a twisted sister, as a function of all that stuff. I didn't know anybody who didn't have a bad dad. How did it affect me? I cannot stand anybody telling me what to do."

In later life, Simpson simply cut his parents off. Screenwriter Robert Ward once had a meeting with him about a script. "I was a total stranger, and he went into a tirade about his father," recalls Ward. "He said, 'My father whined and bitched about his life, but you know why he didn't do anything? Because he was a fuckin' loser. You either win or you don't win, and everything else is bullshit.' "

When his parents phoned his office, he refused to take their calls. They would come out to L.A. about once a year, drop by the lot in the morning, and leave before he came in, around one o'clock. Says one assistant, "It was almost as if it was an understanding of some sort. He would avoid them at any cost." But he made sure they got expensive gifts—a tractor, a new car—on the appropriate occasions.

According to Simpson's boyhood chums, Russ Simpson was a splendid, selfless man who never forced Don to go to church, and if anything spoiled him. "Don loved to blow smoke to the newspapers," says his classmate Ken Hinchey. "To him a résumé was a lie sheet."

Then there's Heidi Fleiss's Fat-Boy Theory. Fleiss says she knew him well. "He told me he was obese, and I think probably in school, girls would go, 'Oooh, it's Don,' and make fun of him," she says. "When he came to Hollywood, he lost weight, got cosmetic surgery, became a millionaire, and the girls went, 'Oh, it's Don, the babe.' Inside, he still remembered girls abusing him. But I'm not a doctor, I'm just a criminal."

Simpson started acting in high school. In the brutally cold Anchorage winters movies were a window on another world, and Simpson was ambitious. Says Carl Brady, Jr., a high school classmate, "I once asked him what he was going to do with his life. He said, 'I'm going to Hollywood to be a movie star.'"

Simpson went off to the University of Oregon and eventually made his way to Hollywood. It was the late '60s, and he got a job at Warner Bros. "I was their in-house hippie marketing person," he said. While he was at Warner's, he worked on *Mean Streets* and *A Clockwork Orange*. He ran into producer Julia Phillips, an encounter she immortalized in her book *You'll Never Eat Lunch in This Town Again,* in which she says he diverted her with oral sex while they were in New York on business.

Said Simpson, "It's true I did have to give head to Julia 'I am a genius' Phillips. But she blackmailed me. We were in a hotel elevator. I got out, and she jumped on me. She said, 'You're gonna come to my room and fuck me.' I said, 'No, I'm not. (A) I don't want to fuck you. (B) You're married to a man I really like, Michael Phillips.' I said, 'I don't do that.' Homey don't play that. I went to my room and she called me. Called me, called me, called me. She said, 'Don, put simply, you gotta come up and fuck me.' This was what she left out of her book: 'If you don't fuck me, I will get you fired.' She had the power at the time. Counter to now, where she has no power and no ability. She called back three times. Finally I thought, I'll have to go talk to her. I went upstairs. She was smoking a huge joint. I saw my opportunity. I figured, Maybe if I can get high with her, it'll take her mind off it. So I did a couple of hits. Boom. She said, 'Simpson, I want you to know my body isn't as good as you think it is.' My mind, like a neon sign, said, I always thought you had the worst body in L.A. You mean even you're admitting it's worse than *that*? So she got stoned, and I managed to go down on her rather than fuck her, much to my credit, and got her off. True story. Yes, I gave my body for my career. And I'm proud to have done it. Thank you, Anita Hill."

Says Phillips, laughing, "It's not true. I would never have fired anyone over sexual favors. I don't care enough about sex. If I can be remembered as the one woman who sexually abused Don Simpson, the worst sexual abuser in the world, I would consider that a badge of honor."

Simpson left Warner's, turned down a $50,000-a-year offer from Stanley Kubrick, and went on unemployment. He moved in with Bruckheimer, whom he had met at a screening of *The Harder They Come* through Bruckheimer's then wife, Bonnie. It was a party house, and even then Simpson was known for his world-class collection of pornography. But he was serious about movies. "Contrary to popular opinion, I wasn't out getting high," said Simpson. "I lived with Truffaut and Hitchcock. I had this big bed, and there'd be books stacked all over the floor. Bruckheimer used to joke that he only knew I was going to get laid when there would be a path through my books."

Simpson met director Paul Bartel at Schwabs drugstore, where he hung out. The two of them decided to collaborate on a script titled *Cannonball*. "Within forty-eight hours of pitching, I had $6,250 in my jeans!" recalled Simpson. "I thought, This is it, I'm a star." Barrel was off to the Edinburgh International Film Festival with his film, and Simpson came too. They shared a hotel room. "My one real regret was that I didn't have sex with him when I had the opportunity," says Bartel. "Don told me he had had homosexual experiences in jail when he was sixteen or so. He and a friend had stolen a giant spool of copper cable from the telephone company, melted it down to sell it, and got caught. My impression of him was that although he was basically heterosexual he was open to all kinds of sexual experiences."

Eventually, they ended up at the Deauville Film Festival. The hotel was full of film people. One night there was a knock on the door. Said Simpson, "It was Melanie Griffith, totally *nude*. She was only nineteen then—her body, you could bounce quarters off it. So I went to her room and partied till the sun came up. I mean, thank you, God."

Through producer Steve Tisch, a longtime friend, Simpson got an interview with Dick Sylbert, who was then head of production at Paramount. Sylbert hired him on the spot. Said Simpson, "All of a sudden I was a studio guy. And in two years I had his job."

When Simpson hired Katzenberg as his assistant, the so-called Dream Team that would put Paramount over the top in the late '70s and early '80s was in place. But they did more than turn Paramount around. They changed the way Hollywood worked. If directors had reigned in the '70s, studio executives and producers dominated the '80s and '90s. "Don redesigned the way studios related to the material they produced," says Craig Baumgarten, who was also an executive at Paramount. "Studios took charge of their movies."

"Don was the best at recognizing a movie moment when he saw it," says Larry Mark, at that time a junior executive. "He knew when a movie needed one, he knew how to get to one. And if you know his movies, you know that he delivered."

And then there were the script notes. Sometimes they were longer than the scripts themselves. Says Katzenberg, who refined the practice when he later went to Disney, "When Don was writing them, they were gold. He really was laser sharp, without peer when it came to his skill working with material and being able to pinpoint the things that made a script work."

But for many writers, Simpson's practice inaugurated an era of decline, when executives would convince themselves that they knew best. He once told a writer, "I use a lot of writers. People think that's bullshit, but I figure I owe a project, if it's gonna be any good, ten or eleven writers."

At Paramount, Simpson was in a pressure cooker, especially during the writers strike of '81, when the studio rushed seven movies into production. "The scripts were ridiculous," says Steel, "and Don took the hit for a lot of them." One night, Simpson's boss, Michael Eisner, Simpson, and a handful of executives attended a preview of one of their new releases, *Grease 2,* at the Cinerama Dome. According to a source, "Michael was looking at this movie, thinking, Oh my God, it's a mess. And turning to Don he said, 'I can't believe you didn't make the changes that I told you to make.' Don was so burnt out that he fucked up." Of course, the movie also lacked John Travolta and Olivia Newton-John. But, continues the source, "for Michael, I think, that was the the final straw, 'cause then it was announced that Don was leaving. Don was in a state of shock. Because I don't think that he ever expected to be fired."

Whether he went willingly or was pushed, Simpson was stricken with a severe case of executive withdrawal. Instead of three hundred phone calls a day, there were ten. "Don went into a very deep depression at that point," recalls Steel, who was the executive on *Flashdance*. "I had numerous story meetings with him and Joe Ezsterhas on the call box, cause I couldn't get him to come out of his house. So even then it was a pattern for Don to hide."

The Friday night the movie opened, Simpson, Bruckheimer, and Steel were pacing in the back of a theater in Westwood. They looked through the doors and saw teenage girls dancing in the aisles. "We knew then," says Steel, "Don and Jerry were on their way."

Indeed. *Flashdance*, which cost about $10 million, grossed a reported $175 million worldwide, and Simpson and Bruckheimer went on to *Beverly Hills Cop*, which Simpson transformed from a Sylvester Stallone vehicle into a huge Eddie Murphy hit. *Top Gun*, based on a magazine piece but otherwise their own contrivance, was another giant hit. Simpson and Bruckheimer regarded themselves as "auteur" producers. Oddly enough, for someone who was so good on scripts, none of these films had much of a story. (One report has nineteen drafts of *Top Gun*, thirty-seven of *Cop*.) They were star vehicles comprising a series of movie moments set to music. Simpson and Bruckheimer appreciated stars; they fought Paramount to get Tom Cruise the salary he wanted, and they presented stars in the way that the audiences of the '80s wanted to see them. *Cop* is little more than a playground for Murphy's improvisation.

As he became more successful, Simpson became hell to work for. According to one estimate, he ran through twenty or thirty assistants in a three-year period. He was abusive in an extremely articulate and demeaning way, which was worse than merely calling someone a "dumb motherfucker," which he did anyway. Nevertheless he gave large bonuses and expensive gifts: several hundred-dollar Chanel bags, VCRs, jewelry from Tiffany, sometimes bonuses in four figures.

Simpson was a control freak, and the first thing the assistants had to learn was that his personal needs were paramount. The assistants were on call twenty-four hours a day, seven days a week. He would stay at the Regency in New York, and if he wanted a bagel in the middle of the night, he would wake up an assistant in L.A. and have *her* call room service. If it took too long, he would-n't answer the door. When he was dieting, it had to be a whole-wheat bagel, toasted, with French's mustard, and if the bagel was-n't prepared correctly, he would throw it on the floor.

Then there was the incident with the clouds. There were too many of them, and his plane couldn't land. He called his office and read the riot act to the person who booked the flight. Once, when there was an opening in Hong Kong, an assistant arranged for him to go to a gym there, and there weren't any towels. He called the assistant in L.A. and screamed, "How come you didn't know that they didn't provide towels in Hong Kong?"

Once, at the Regency hotel, the bellboy delivered one of his precious black Levi's 501 jeans to his room, pressed and starched. In a *Mommie Dearest* moment, he went berserk, had the whole housekeeping staff trembling with fear as he screamed, "I asked for fluff and fold. How dare you! *Fluff and fold!*"

Simpson's relationship with Bruckheimer became increasingly fractious. "I heard Don use the most vile choice of words, in the most nasty and disgusting way to destroy everybody," recalls Tisch, and Bruckheimer was no exception. In most ways, Bruckheimer was the antithesis of Simpson: quiet, detail oriented, the follow-through guy. Simpson spoke to Bruckheimer like a man embarrassed by sentiment, who would cloak his feelings in abuse. To outsiders it was sometimes shocking. He made fun of Bruckheimer's reticence in front of journalists, saying things like "Now let's hear what Jerry has to say" or "That motherfucker would be lost without me. All he knows how to do is make up budgets." For the most part, Bruckheimer just rolled his eyes and shrugged him off. But they were a great team. Without Bruckheimer, Simpson at best would have been just another smart guy with a lot of ideas; at worst he would have spun out of orbit.

Simpson worked hard and played hard. He only had two long-term relationships in his life, one with film editor Priscilla Nedd in

357

the late '70s, and the other with Susan Lentini. For her it was like being an arm piece. They would go to premieres, dinner parties, take trips to Aspen. Mostly, she felt, he ignored her. He would be physically present but emotionally gone, watching TV, stuffing himself with pizzas, reading scripts or books. He was the kind of man who thought that money would make things right. He would say things like, "Here's my credit card, that means I love you, doesn't it?" One Christmas in Aspen, after not seeing her for weeks, he gave her diamond earrings and then ignored her the whole evening. She yelled, "You can't buy my love!" and threw the earrings through the window out into the snow. (Later she retrieved them.)

He would rarely sleep with friends or colleagues. He preferred to hit on AMWs (actress-model-whatevers) who would do it for a few lines of blow and a bottle of Cristal, or do a casting-couch number. B-movie actress Jewel Shepard once read for one of his movies while Simpson was lounging on a sofa. She says the dialogue went like this:

Simpson: "Okay, do you want to do some coke, or would you like to fuck me?"

Jewel: "Excuse me?"

Simpson: "What part of it did you not understand?"

Adds Shepard: "He took me into the bathroom and showed me a jar full of coke and said, 'We could either discuss this nicely and you could probably get a part, or you could go through the charade of reading for it.'"

But for the most part, Simpson preferred to pay for it; it was a deal he understood. He chased girls around in his underwear carrying an Uzi. And, of course, there was the S&M, for which he was so notorious that Fleiss says she would never send her girls to him.

The chaos of his personal life invaded the brittle structure of the office. One employee had to get hookers on the phone. "He would say, 'Get so-and-so.' He never knew their names. I had a file that said, GIRLS. I'd filed them by hair color—brunette, or blond with good legs."

Simpson occasionally got into trouble. One time, the word around the office was that he either hit on or beat up a girl who was seeing a made guy in Las Vegas. The guy put a contract out on him, the story went, and Simpson had to pay him off. "I had to get

$10,000 in cash in an envelope, and give it to some guy at a movie premiere," says a staffer.

Simpson made videos of the things that happened behind the doors of his bedroom. One was called *Bonnie Beats Mary* or *Mary Beats Bonnie*. An assistant, who found the tape lying around the office and popped it in the VCR, describes it: "It was just a girl tied up, S&M style, and the other girl is beating her, and she's screaming, 'Beat me, mistress, beat me.' And in the background, you could hear, 'Every day's a savings day at Thrifty's' from the TV or radio." At the end, "Bonnie" pees on "Mary," or the other way around. Simpson apparently failed to elicit very good performances from his actors. The assistant says that, awkward as the girls were, the tape had a disturbing effect. "You couldn't tell if 'Mary' was really hurting," the staffer continues. "I didn't know if she was getting something out of it, and entertaining him, or if he was making them do it."

The drinking and the drugs spilled over as well. In the office, around four in the afternoon, he would start in on twenty-five-year-old scotch, the Macallan, and by the end of the day he'd be loaded. One of his PAs would drive him home. Simpson was more discreet about his drug use. He never did cocaine in front of the assistants, but there were leftover lines on his hand mirror in the executive bathroom, which only he used. Simpson suffered from the paranoia that went with the drugs and booze. He was convinced that "the cleaning help of the Negro persuasion" were stealing his scotch, and he wanted to hire the Paramount security guards to protect it.

Simpson moved into a larger suite of offices in between *Top Gun* and *Beverly Hills Cop II*. He and Bruckheimer shared one vast desk—like an aircraft carrier—one seated across from the other. He used to party in the office with friends. Sometimes the staff would leave the office late, and Simpson and his friends would still be there, boozing it up. One morning, a staffer came in and discovered that Simpson had carved a gash in his huge, mahogany landing strip of a desk, presumably while cutting cocaine. He insisted that the staffer get it fixed. Because it was built into the wall, the staffer had the man who had built the desk come in over the weekend, sand it down, and relacquer it. When Simpson came in Monday morning, he started screaming, "I can't breathe!" because of the smell. So after Simpson and Bruckheimer left, two staffers took a hammer and broke all the casement windows, and were able to get cross-ventilation through the office.

On the heels of the success of *Cop II,* the boys announced an unprecedented deal with Paramount that essentially gave them a blank check to make five movies of their own devising, with no supervision. Chest-thumping ads in the trades touted the "Visionary Alliance."

Days of Thunder, the first and only fruit of the visionary alliance, started production in January 1990. It starred Tom Cruise and boasted a Robert Towne script. Simpson is reputed to have given Towne seventy-eight pages of script notes, but the length of his notes was not the only extravagance on a six-month production that became famous for extravagance.

The boys threw two huge parties for the cast and the two-hundred-odd-person crew at a hot club in town, the Coliseum. From the ceiling hung life-size black-and-white pictures of the actors in char-acter, including Simpson, who played one of the drivers. Invitations were printed saying it was Simpson, Bruckheimer, and Cruise's party. Simpson sent the PAs down into the Keys to get girls from a chain of strip joints, and flew them in.

While he was in Daytona, he had staffers get Norma Kamali dresses for the girls he was going out with. They literally had them gift-wrapped in the closet and marked by size—small, medium, or large.

Thunder didn't do badly ($170 million, worldwide), but it didn't perform up to Simpson-Bruckheimer expectations. Not that the boys suffered; they were in line for a big chunk of the gross before the studio started to recoup its share of the profits. Paramount was rumored to have asked for $9 million back. As Tom Pollock puts it, "When you ask for money back, that usually means they want you to leave." Simpson insisted he left of his own accord.

While he landed on his feet at Disney, Simpson was never com-fortable there. More and more he just withdrew, stayed home. "The only time I ever ran into him he looked like hell," recalls Bonnie Bruckheimer. "Catatonic. I just saw it in his eyes, in the way he looked, and it made me sad. Because of all that talent and all that success and all those smarts and all that money, and not a minute's happiness. And to see an end like that to a guy at fifty-two years old is terribly tragic."

Simpson's legacy is ambiguous and paradoxical. Despite his efforts to control "product" as a production head, as a producer he strengthened the hand of the talent agencies. He bequeathed us two huge stars, Cruise and Murphy, and if he gave us Katzenberg's Disney, he also made the world safe for Joel Silver at the Warner's of the '90s.

He was an inspired practitioner of a certain kind of commercial moviemaking, but borrowing the term *auteur* from the great directors of the '70s—whom Simpson, as much as anyone, admired—was ludicrous. Simpson understood that he had never fulfilled himself artistically. As Steel puts it, "He had a lot of aspirations artistically that he never satisfied. I think that's where his emptiness came from—Don wanted to be famous, and he also wanted to be respected. But fame and respect are not the same thing, and a lot of people out here get them mixed up."

Brilliant as he was, Simpson was too hooked on fame to take the risks, and lived in a place too distant from himself to make the great movie. As Tony Scott put it, "*Crimson Tide* was a departure from Don's popcorn phase. It was character driven. Jerry always wanted to do more serious pieces, but Don was reluctant. He wanted to direct, but he was scared he'd fall down."

Simpson defeated everyone's attempts to sentimentalize him. He was not like Warren Beatty or Jack Nicholson, the famous bad boys who eventually settled down. When Wiatt is asked if Simpson had ever expressed interest in having kids, he responds sadly, "No. I don't think that interested Don at all."

In the year before he died, he had apparently begun to turn things around. After the Ammerman episode, he visited the Menninger Clinic, and for the first time was seeing a therapist in L.A. every day whom he felt was helping him. He was even turning his career around again, with three straight hits, *Bad Boys, Crimson Tide,* and *Dangerous Minds.* When he plummeted to the bottom of the premiere Power List, he would joke about it. In 1992, he mused, "The truth of the matter is, this year we were so low on the list, I said to Jerry, 'Our profile has shrunk so much that we're not a big enough target to shoot at anymore.' He said, 'Is that good?' I said, 'Yeah. We used to be elephants stomping through the grass, now we're little mice.' He said, 'Are we going to be elephants again?' I said, 'Well, Jerry, I don't know about you, but I'm not going to be an elephant again, I'm going to be a tiger.' "

But the demons were too strong. "The last time I saw him was in the fall," recalls Steel. "He was coming out of an elevator in the Turner building. He was like a magnet, and I was drawn to him, like *vroom!* I ran up to him, put my arms around him, and started to kiss him all over his face. I was so happy to see him. He held me close and whispered in my ear, 'I am so depressed. I don't know what to do.' "